The Game of the World

The Game of the World

Kostas Axelos

Translated by Justin Clemens and Hellmut Monz

EDINBURGH
University Press

Edinburgh University Press is one of the leading university presses in the UK. We publish academic books and journals in our selected subject areas across the humanities and social sciences, combining cutting-edge scholarship with high editorial and production values to produce academic works of lasting importance. For more information visit our website: edinburghuniversitypress.com

Edinburgh University Press Ltd
The Tun – Holyrood Road
12(2f) Jackson's Entry
Edinburgh EH8 8PJ

Typeset in 10.5/13 GoudyStd by
Cheshire Typesetting Ltd, Cuddington, Cheshire,
and printed and bound in Great Britain

A CIP record for this book is available from the British Library

ISBN 978 1 4744 4906 9 (hardback)
ISBN 978 1 4744 4908 3 (webready PDF)
ISBN 978 1 4744 4909 0 (epub)

Published with the support of the University of Edinburgh Scholarly Publishing Initiatives Fund.

Contents

Translators' Introduction

Justin Clemens and Hellmut Monz

With the present publication, Kostas Axelos's masterpiece *The Game of the World* is finally – belatedly – available in English translation, over fifty years since its first appearance in France in 1969.[1]

This belatedness is at once understandable and puzzling.

It is understandable, at least in the usual ways in which the market understands what is understandable. The book is gargantuan, a grand tome of scholarship, intelligence and vision; it is extraordinarily ambitious in its conceptual and linguistic scope; it presents many difficulties for interpretation and translation, even for cognoscenti of late twentieth-century French language philosophy. Its commercial potential is not necessarily perspicuous.

Yet this delay is also puzzling. After all, hasn't anglophone literary theory and philosophy – which has put figures such as Henri Lefebvre, Jacques Derrida and Gilles Deleuze onto university reading lists around the globe, and even at times permitted such terms as 'deconstruction' into mainstream political and journalistic discourse – been entirely transformed by post-World War II 'French Thought', its contexts, its conditions, its terms of reference and ambitions? Moreover, do not the very same luminaries expressly name Axelos as a critical figure in this context? For Lefebvre, Axelos is 'the first or one of the first of a species that supersedes the derisory human' and 'extends philosophy through Heidegger, but does so by turning his back on

---

[1] Kostas Axelos, *Le jeu du monde* (Paris: Éditions de Minuit, 1969). Republished as: Kostas Axelos, *Le jeu du monde* (Paris: Éditions Les Belles Lettres, «Encre marine», 2018).

him'.[2] Derrida, too, credits Axelos's theses regarding the play of the world.[3] For his part, Deleuze not just acknowledges Axelos[4] but recognises in him the 'salvation of philosophy', proclaiming that 'Axelos is to Heidegger what a kind of Zen is to the Buddha'.[5] Examples could be multiplied.

As these encomia also attest, a crucial part of Axelos's achievement has been his development of a unique and radical thinking of the notion/s of the 'game' and of 'play'. Play is not only central to Axelos's work, but one of his major contributions has been to show how pivotal it is to the history of philosophy, extending from Presocratic to contemporary thought. Indeed, Axelos maintained this standpoint throughout his life. As he states in an interview from 2004:

> The *world* deploys itself as a *game*. That means that it refuses any sense, any rule that is exterior to itself. The play *of* the world itself is different from all the particular games that are played *in* the world. Almost two-and-a-half thousand years after Heraclitus, [Friedrich] Nietzsche, [Martin] Heidegger, [Eugen] Fink and I have insisted on this approach to the world as game.[6]

With the world as game, Axelos is alluding to an influential statement by the ancient Greek thinker Heraclitus: 'Time is a child playing a game; the child's kingdom.'[7] Saying that Heraclitus plays a key role for Axelos would

[2] Henri Lefebvre, 'The World According to Kostas Axelos', in *State, Space, World: Selected Essays*, ed. Neil Brenner and Stuart Elden, trans. Gerald Moore, Neil Brenner and Stuart Elden (Minneapolis: University of Minnesota Press, 2009), 259–89: 259, 262.

[3] Jacques Derrida, *Of Grammatology*, trans. Gayatri Chakravorty Spivak (Baltimore: Johns Hopkins University Press, 1976), 326, n. 14.

[4] See for Deleuze commenting on Axelos: Gilles Deleuze, 'En Créant la Pataphysique Jarry a ouvert la Voie a la Phénoménologie', in Gilles Deleuze, *L'Île Déserte: Textes et Entretiens 1953–1974*, ed. David Lapoujade (Paris: Éditions de Minuit, 2002), 105–8; translated as 'How Jarry's Pataphysics Opened the Way to Phenomenology', in Gilles Deleuze, *Desert Islands and Other Texts: 1953–1974*, ed. David Lapoujade, trans. Michael Taormina (Los Angeles: Semiotext(e), 2004), 74–6; and Gilles Deleuze, 'Faille et Feux Locaux', in Deleuze, *L'Île Déserte*, 217–25; translated as 'The Fissure of Axaagoras and the Local Fires of Heraclitus', in Deleuze, *Desert Islands*, 156–61.

[5] Deleuze, *L'Île Déserte*, 225.

[6] Kostas Axelos and Stuart Elden, 'Interview: *Mondialisation* without the World', *Radical Philosophy*, no. 130 (March/April 2005), 25–8: 28; italics original in the interview transcription.

[7] Heraclitus' fragment 52 as catalogued by Hermann Diels: Heraclitus, 'B: Fragmente', in *Die Fragmente der Vorsokratiker: griechisch und deutsch*, ed. Hermann Diels

therefore be an understatement.[8] Moreover, Axelos is part of a heterodox tradition for which the Heraclitean pronouncement proves determining, and his work self-consciously draws on as well as extends this tradition in a number of ways. For example, as part of his book series *Arguments*, it was Axelos himself who published the French translation of *Spiel als Weltsymbol*,[9] the first lengthy study of the world as play by the German phenomenologist Eugen Fink, in 1966, only six years after its original release.[10] Echoing the anglophone delay of Axelos's masterpiece on play, Fink's book had to wait fifty years to be translated into English as *Play as Symbol of the World*.[11] Axelos, who was himself a key contributor to the development of many of the key trends of what is often denominated 'post-structuralism' in the anglophone world, has somehow slipped the net of this global academic enthusiasm – the fish that got away.

The Gap in Play Scholarship

Although well known and highly regarded by French thinkers, and presenting the most voluminous[12] and in-depth treatment of the world-in-and-as-and-through-play of all the French, German and English thinkers, Axelos's work has to date been almost entirely ignored by the vast English scholarship.[13]

(Berlin: Weidmännische Buchhandlung, 1903), 66–84. Günter Wohlfart dedicates a whole book to this one sentence and its significance for Nietzsche: Günter Wohlfart, *Also sprach Herakleitos: Heraklits Fragment B 52 und Nietzsches Heraklit-Rezeption* (Freiburg: Alber, 1991).

[8] In his study on Heraclitus, Axelos traces him through the history of Western and Eastern thought to pose the dichotomy as a Western construct: Kostas Axelos, *Héraclite et la philosophie: La Première Saisie de l'Être en Devenir de la Totalité* [*Heraclitus and Philosophy: The First Grasp of Being in Becoming of the Totality*] (Paris: Éditions de Minuit, 1962).

[9] Eugen Fink, *Spiel als Weltsymbol* (Stuttgart: Kohlhammer, 1960).

[10] Eugen Fink, *Le Jeu comme Symbole du Monde*, ed. Kostas Axelos, trans. Hans Hildenbrand and Alex Lindenberg (Paris: Éditions de Minuit, 1966).

[11] Eugen Fink, *Play as Symbol of the World: And Other Writings*, trans. Ian A. Moore and Christopher Turner (Bloomington: Indiana University Press, 2016).

[12] Axelos's French work on play unfolds on about twice as many pages as Fink's German work on play.

[13] Only two influential major studies on play briefly address Axelos's play. One mentions Axelos in a note: Mihai I. Spariosu, *Dionysus Reborn: Play and the Aesthetic Dimension in Modern Philosophical and Scientific Discourse* (Ithaca: Cornell University Press, 1989), 127, n. 77. Likewise, the second mentioning keeps Axelos mostly in notes: Brian Edwards, *Theories of Play and Postmodern Fiction* (New York: Garland

Yet – despite this patent absence – Axelos nonetheless exerts an occult influence on a range of play scholars. For example, about a decade after the first publication of *Le jeu du monde*, James S. Hans published a book that echoes Axelos's title: *The Play of the World*.[14] Although Hans traces theses regarding play in Deleuze, Derrida, Hans-Georg Gadamer (a colleague of Fink and Heidegger) and, indirectly, in Heidegger to Nietzsche,[15] he seems unaware of its Heraclitean lineage and the kinship of his work with that of Axelos. Despite this lack of any direct nomination of Axelos, Hans cites such collections as *Game, Play, Literature*, which of course include Axelos's contributions.[16] Even Mihai Spariosu, who traces the concept of play in most of the aforementioned authorities – including Nietzsche, Fink and

Publishing, 1998). While Edwards places Axelos correctly among Ehrmann, Fink and Hans (ibid. 21; 34, n. 23), he errantly argues that Axelos does not separate 'game and play' and is 'similar in approach to' the dramatist of German idealism Friedrich Schiller (ibid. 32, n. 8). The sameness between 'game' and 'play' is meaningless due to Edwards referencing two English translations of two texts by Axelos (ibid. 277) originally written in French, a language like German that has for both 'game' and 'play' one word: *jeu* (and respectively *Spiel*). Presenting Axelos's play within the German idealism of Schiller, who derives his concept of play as a synthesis of opposing drives from synthesising Kantian play and Fichtean drives (see Friedrich Schiller, 'Briefe über die ästhetische Erziehung des Menschen', in *Lektionen 1: Dramaturgie*, ed. Bernd Stegemann (Berlin: Theater der Zeit, 2009), 270–3), misses that it is precisely the project of Axelos's play to overcome such – idealist as well as materialist – dialectics.

[14] James S. Hans, *The Play of the World* (Amherst: University of Massachusetts Press, 1981).

[15] See for a study that identifies play as a key Nietzschean contribution: Eugen Fink, *Nietzsche's Philosophy*, trans. Goetz Richter (London: Continuum, 2003), 171. As an example of Nietzsche's playful influence, note the aphorisms throughout the following seminal meta-study on play: Brian Sutton-Smith, *The Ambiguity of Play* (Cambridge, MA: Harvard University Press, 2001).

[16] Hans, *The Play of the World*, 201, n. 1. See one English essay taken from a book by Axelos appearing in a work edited by Ehrmann and another one in his remembrance: Kostas Axelos, 'Planetary Interlude', in *Game, Play, Literature*, ed. Jacques Ehrmann, trans. Sally Hess (Yale French Studies 41, 1968), 6–18; and Kostas Axelos, 'The Set's Game-Play of Sets', in *In Memory of Jacques Ehrmann: Inside Play Outside Game*, ed. Michel Beaujour, trans. Beverly Livingston (Yale French Studies 58, 1979), 95–101. Hans (*The Play of the World*, 76) asks what happens when 'we say our book on play is nothing more than an attempt to imitate Gadamer, Derrida, Deleuze and Guattari, Nietzsche, and so on, as far as we are aware of our imitative lineage'. Considering the silence regarding Heraclitus and Axelos in the light of Hans's title, his awareness of the French thinkers of play, Fink's and Ehrmann's book on play, and their lineages, must we conclude that Hans's book on play unconsciously imitates Axelos's book on play obscured in the ambiguity of an and-so-on?

Heidegger in their consideration of Heraclitus – only acknowledges the existence of Axelos's contribution in a note.[17] Axelos's book on the play of the world, a notion that lies at the heart of Spariosu's own approach, eludes him. It is rare to find English scholarship locating Axelos in the proximity of play philosophy, as briefly done by Ian Moore and Christopher Turner in the introduction of their 2016 *Play as Symbol of the World* translation.[18]

Axelos's treatment by English play scholarship cannot therefore be *simply* due to ignorance, absence or irrelevance. Perhaps, then, its insistent obscurity is in part because – as the reader of this work will very rapidly acknowledge – Axelos's work moves 'diagonally' to the best determined aspects of this situation.[19] As part of the Greek resistance during World War II, Axelos had to flee his homeland due to having been sentenced to death by the emerging rightist government.[20] Fleeing in 1945 on the *Mataroa*, with other left-wing intellectuals such as Cornelius Castoriadis, Axelos, who was also fluent in German and French, arrived in France. He then undertook research at the Sorbonne, as well as at the Centre National de la Recherche Scientifique and at the École Pratique des Hautes Études.

Despite his own training and teaching in the prestigious research centres of Paris, Axelos himself admits that he was not very academic; or, at least, that it was not the academic milieu and training that provided the key impetus for or aims of his interests. He was an important contributor to the post-World War II intellectual milieu in France – which is now almost universally acknowledged as one of the great epochs in recent philosophical

---

[17] Spariosu, *Dionysus Reborn*, 127, n. 77.

[18] Ian A. Moore and Christopher Turner, 'Translator's Introduction', in Fink, *Play as Symbol of the World*, 1–14.

[19] The scholar who has done the most to establish Axelos and his import for English language discussions is unquestionably Stuart Elden, by way of a sequence of interviews, articles, discussions and introductions, including: 'Introducing Kostas Axelos and "The World"', *Environment and Planning: D Society and Space*, vol. 24 (October 2006), 639–42; Axelos and Elden, 'Interview: *Mondialisation* without the World'. For Elden's own bibliography of Axelos in English, see his website: <https://progressive geographies.com/resources/kostas-axelos-in-english-a-bibliography-with-links/> (last accessed 5 September 2022).

[20] More biographical information on Axelos can be found in the introductions of the two existing English translations of Axelos's work: Ronald Brunzina, 'Translator's Introduction', in Kostas Axelos, *Alienation, Praxis, and Technē in the Thought of Karl Marx* (Austin: University of Texas Press, 1976), ix–xxxi; and Stuart Elden, 'Introduction: Kostas Axelos – A Left-Heideggerian or a Heideggerian-Marxist', in Kostas Axelos, *Introduction to a Future Way of Thought: On Marx and Heidegger* (Lüneburg: Meson Press, 2015), 9–29.

thinking – where he became familiar with such figures as Roland Barthes, Georges Bataille, Jean Beaufret, Gilles Deleuze, Jacques Lacan and many others. He was one of the editors of the important journal *Arguments*, which, following its closure, he then parleyed into a famous and influential series for Les Éditions de Minuit. He continued to write and publish extensively up until his death in 2010.

Yet it is above all for his work on games and play that Axelos's intervention must be counted. On this point, Deleuze is clear: 'From the outset of his œuvre, Axelos has taken this concept of play to the highest point.'[21] Against this, many influential works on play seem content to approach play through fragmenting it into games and rules in the world,[22] dissociating play from reality,[23] or disjoining 'free' from 'regulated' play.[24] But fragmentation and separation only bear upon a total partiality of a partial totality, and miss the play of the world that is not simply one moment, instance, act or modality of play among many, with rules imposed from an outside. It is Axelos's contribution to pronounce the play of plays that binds fragmentation and separation through deploying itself in the world precisely as heterogeneous kinds of games and various modalities of play. Perhaps the most important point to emphasise here is that 'the game of the world', as ungrounded totality of all that takes place, is not one game or play among others, but is productive of all such differences without ever being reducible to any one of them. In being so, the latter – regional games, varying rules, this or that activity of play – are nonetheless paradoxically articulated by the game of the world in a non-reductive fashion. We shall say more about this extraordinary conception below.

Moreover, while the theme of play reappears throughout Axelos's multilingual body of work, it is this magnum opus, *Le jeu du monde*, that fully engages the 'theme' on all registers. The book thus plays the key role in his

---

[21] Deleuze, *L'Île Déserte*, 224.

[22] Katie Salen and Eric Zimmerman, *Rules of Play: Game Design Fundamentals* (Cambridge, MA: MIT Press, 2004).

[23] Johan Huizinga, *A Study of the Play Element in Culture* (Boston: Beacon Press, 1955). See for a discussion of Huizinga separating play from reality: Jacques Ehrmann, 'Homo Ludens Revisited', in *Game, Play, Literature*, 31–57.

[24] Roger Caillois, *Man, Play and Games*, trans. Meyer Barash (Urbana and Chicago: University of Illinois Press, 1961). See for a critique of Caillois's reductionist separating of play into categories (agonistic competition, aleatory chance, mimetic simulations, and whirling vertigo) and dimensions (the free play of paidia opposing the regulated play of ludus): Martin Esslin, 'Brecht and the Scientific Spirit of Playfulness', in *Cultura Ludens, vol. 2, Auctor Ludens: Essays on Play in Literature*, ed. Gerald Guinness and Andrew Hurley (Philadelphia: John Benjamins Publishing, 1986), 25–37.

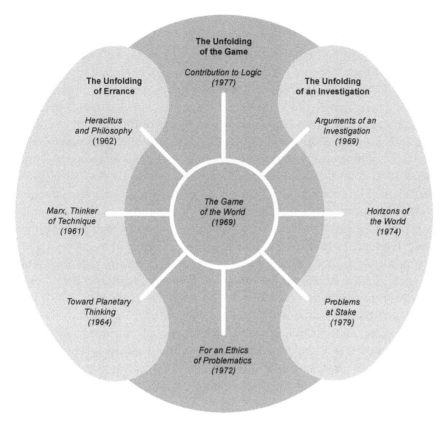

**The Unfolding
of the Game**

*Contribution to Logic
(1977)*

**The Unfolding
of Errance**

*Heraclitus
and Philosophy
(1962)*

**The Unfolding
of an Investigation**

*Arguments of an
Investigation
(1969)*

*The Game
of the World
(1969)*

*Marx, Thinker
of Technique
(1961)*

*Horizons of
the World
(1974)*

*Toward Planetary
Thinking
(1964)*

*Problems
at Stake
(1979)*

*For an Ethics
of Problematics
(1972)*

Fig. I.1 Axelos's *Le jeu du monde* at the centre of his trilogy of trilogies.

oeuvre, indeed occupying the centre of his work, of which the main body forms three trilogies. Each trilogy names a specific unfolding, *déploiement*, which together position *Le jeu du monde* as the second volume of the second trilogy and thus as the fulcrum of Axelos's key writings (see Fig. I.1).

As should already be evident, Axelos's work intervenes into a very complex and crucial twentieth-century intellectual situation in which the question of games and play came to occupy the very centre of thinking, if according to quite heterogeneous – even antagonistic – projects and references. Here, we will indicate five key tendencies: the phenomenological, the sociological, the psychoanalytic, the analytical-ethical and the cybernetic. This quintuple is self-evidently neither extensive nor exhaustive, but it can perhaps serve to outline some of the most important features of a complex general context that bears upon Axelos's own specific contribution to the thinking of the nature of games and play.

Phenomenological Aspects

Perhaps the first and most decisive reference for Axelos himself is that of phenomenology, above all the work of Martin Heidegger and his disciples, notably Eugen Fink. In this, Axelos is also a part of the French radicalisa-tion of phenomenology in thinkers such as Emmanuel Levinas, Maurice Blanchot, Derrida and others. Simply put, this tradition attempts to think the internal dispersion *and* consistency of the concepts and practices of play as simultaneously utterly historical and essentially ontological – and which therefore entails thinking play as ahistorical and non-ontological too. Heidegger, for example, in the course of his own notorious reconstruc-tion of the historicity of the forgetting of (the meaning, and then the truth of) being, engages with Presocratic thinkers, above all Heraclitus, for whom 'play' is a fundamental cosmic modality, while offering, in his own vocabu-lary, a way of thinking games and play which attempts to evade the meta-physical closure. At various key places in his writing, Heidegger poses being and play in proximity. For example, he contemplates a play that 'plays because it plays',[25] without rhyme or reason, without foundation, thereby constructing 'being-in-the-world as archaic play of transcendence'.[26] For Heidegger, this is a kind of attestation that 'the whatness of being is the Game itself'.[27] Or, as he further phrases it in an important post-World War II essay, which speaks of the interrelation of 'earth and sky, divinities and mortals':

---

[25] Martin Heidegger, *Gesamtausgabe Band 10: Der Satz vom Grund*, ed. Petra Jaeger (Frankfurt am Main: Vittorio Klostermann, 1997), 169.

[26] Martin Heidegger, *Gesamtausgabe Band 27: Einleitung in die Philosophie*, ed. Otto Saame and Ina Saame-Speidel (Frankfurt am Main: Vittorio Klostermann, 1996), 311. See also on Heidegger's play: Martina Roesner, *Metaphysica Ludens: Das Spiel als phänom-enologische Grundfigur im Denken Martin Heideggers* [*Ludic Metaphysics: The Game as Phenomenological Groundfigure in the Thought of Martin Heidegger*] (Dordrecht: Kluwer Academic Publishers, 2003).

[27] Martin Heidegger, *Gesamtausgabe Band 11: Identität und Differenz*, ed. Friedrich-Wilhelm von Hermann (Frankfurt am Main: Vittoria Klostermann, 2006), 72. This alluding to play eludes the English translation: Martin Heidegger, *Identity and Difference*, trans. Joan Stambaugh (New York: Harper & Row, 1969), 66. See for the importance of Heraclitus for Heideggerean thought in the ceaseless alluding to fire and play, *Feuer und Spiel*, in Heidegger's study of Heraclitus: Martin Heidegger, *Gesamtausgabe Band 55: Heraklit: Der Anfang des abendländischen Denkens; Logik. Heraklits Lehre vom Logos* [*Heraclitus: The Origin of Occidental Thought; Logic. Heraclitus' Teaching of Logos*], ed. Manfred S. Frings (Frankfurt am Main: Vittoria Klostermann, 1994).

The gathered presence of the mirror-play of the world, joining in this way, is the ringing. In the ringing of the mirror-playing ring, the four nestle into their unifying presence, in which each one retains its own nature . . . Out of the ringing mirror-play the thinging of the thing takes place.[28]

Such philologico-poetic reconstructions at once seek to locate the thinker in a situation of thinking beyond the closures of metaphysics, amongst the presencing or eventing of being, affirming the primacy of language as unveiling in, through and against the historicity of this very language.

'Play' in such accounts therefore tends towards naming something so fundamental it cannot any longer be considered a region of existence, but indicates the difficulty and destiny of thinking the event of being itself. Time itself needs to be considered, à la the Heraclitean image, like a child playing chess. In taking up and further radicalising this phenomenological sequence, Axelos thinks the game and play as 'modelling' the becoming of being and beings themselves. We will return to this quasi-ontological claim below, as its consequences are self-evidently extraordinary. For the moment, however, let us simply underline the centrality for Axelos of the motif of an existential ur-game which plays and is played in and as the fragmentation of every inherited anthropological project.

Sociological Aspects

A second determining reference is sociological. Here, for Axelos, the Marxist intervention is crucial:

Perhaps the world game also revealed itself to Marx as a game: after the resolution of the alienation of labor, and even after communism has been overcome, couldn't the history of humanity – and not only this – manifest itself as a game, a game in which the inviolable essence of alienation would also play a role?[29]

One can see not only Axelos's unique attempt to articulate the irreducibly antagonistic projects of Marx and Heidegger on the terrain of game

---

[28] Martin Heidegger, *Poetry, Language, Thought*, trans. and intro. A. Hofstadter (New York: Harper & Row, 1971), 180.
[29] Axelos, *Introduction*, 82.

and play, but, in doing so, to enable the possibility of another relation to transforming the world that is not simply under the technical, nihilistic or metaphysical domination of teleology, of supersession, of the necessity for destruction. Part of the 'task' then – a word that is itself clearly insufficient here insofar as it retains connotations of seriousness, labour and commitment that have usually been arrayed against the alleged levity of play – therefore comes to be a question of how we can and must *play* with the inexpungible residues of (our own) oppressiveness and oppression.

We should also mention the sequence of important twentieth-century historical and sociological studies of the centrality of play in human affairs, often non- or anti-Marxist, such as those of Johan Huizinga, Nobert Elias or Roger Caillois. For such scholars, civilisation is incomprehensible without an attention to its sport and leisure activities, which integrally bear on religion, law, economics, politics, warfare, technology and so on. Huizinga's important text *Homo Ludens*, for example, seeks to establish play as an essential anthropological activity separated from purposive economic activity, to the extent that all culture is born from and is sustained by play, inducing players' intense absorption in unproductive and separative games.[30] Cultures are inevitably caught up with games of every kind, and yet cultures are also differentiated precisely by the different sorts of games they play in different circumstances and with different ends.

For his part, Caillois both criticises and extends Huizinga's researches, in showing that, while play is not necessarily productive, it is not always entirely uneconomic in that it often prioritises the exchange of property – even if often to the point of destruction and ruination. Games themselves do not always have established rules (child's play with dolls, for instance), and often have a relation to the *as if* of fiction-making. Caillois accordingly develops a taxonomy of four different *kinds* of games, which he names *agôn*, *alea*, *mimicry* and *ilinx*:

> All four indeed belong to the domain of play. One plays football, billiards, or chess (*agôn*); roulette or a lottery (*alea*); pirate, Nero, or Hamlet (*mimicry*); or one produces in oneself, by a rapid whirling or falling movement, a state of dizziness and disorder (*ilinx*).[31]

---

[30] Johan Huizinga, *Homo Ludens: A Study of the Play-Element in Culture* (London: Routledge, 1949).
[31] Caillois, *Man, Play and Games*, 12.

This quadrature of 'competition, chance, simulation or vertigo' moreover does not cover the entire universe of play, which indicates the becoming-rule of chaos in human existence, indexing the powers of *paidia*, a drive for freedom, on the one hand, and *ludus*, an enjoyment of difficulty, on the other. Here, Caillois's divisions start to index the integration of sociology with psychology, another division and relation of importance to Axelos.

Psychoanalytical Aspects

This leads us to another determining reference, that of psychoanalysis, which, in its attentiveness to libidinal development, identifies several roles for play in the constitution and support of psychic and political life. Although Axelos often evinces suspicion towards the work of Sigmund Freud and his inheritors, even at times almost condemning what he sees as a kind of crudeness in their vision, psychoanalysis remains self-confessedly crucial to him insofar as it offers a developmental account of the becoming-human that simultaneously integrates play and libidinal drives on a terrain that is constitutionally unconscious and therefore extra-volitional. One does not simply choose to play or not to play; the questions of pleasure, desire and drive are always in play with those of suffering and trauma; one is never not being-played.

Perhaps the most famous of Freud's examples of a child playing is found in *Beyond the Pleasure Principle* (1920):

> This good little boy, however, had an occasional disturbing habit of taking any small objects he could get hold of and throwing them away from him into a corner, under the bed, and so on, so that hunting for his toys and picking them up was often quite a business. As he did this he gave vent to a loud, long-drawn-out 'o-o-o-o', accompanied by an expression of interest and satisfaction. His mother and the writer of the present account were agreed in thinking that this was not a mere interjection but represented the German word '*fort*' ['gone']. I eventually realized that it was a game and that the only use he made of any of his toys was to play 'gone' with them. One day I made an observation which confirmed my view. The child had a wooden reel with a piece of string tied round it. It never occurred to him to pull it along the floor behind him, for instance, and play at its being a carriage. What he did was to hold the reel by the string and very skilfully throw it over the edge of his curtained cot, so that it disappeared into it, at the same time uttering his expressive 'o-o-o-o'. He then pulled the reel out of the cot again and

hailed its reappearance with a joyful '*da*' ['there']. This, then, was the complete game – disappearance and return.[32]

Freud himself gives a number of possible interpretations of this game, of which we will only mention a few. By turning a passive experience into the activity of a game, the child essays to master the trauma of his mother's absence by staging her going-and-return in another way, at once effecting an instinctual renunciation and issuing a defiant revenge on the mother. Freud notes that such a libidinal invention, in which repetition is essentially deployed as a binding of trauma, is not necessarily mimetic (in the sense of re-enacting another real situation); moreover, it does not in itself enable any '*evidence of the operation of tendencies beyond the pleasure principle*'.[33] It does, however, provide a yield of pleasure even if what it repeats is founded in unpleasure. Moreover, as Jacques Lacan will later emphasise, this game also evinces the fundamental differential function of language as such: the division itself (between *fort* and *da* – 'there' and 'here') is what comes to be repeated and expressed in other signifiers, other circumstances, as the vicissitudes of desire.[34] In this frame, the role of play is paramount not only as psychopathology but as political foundation.

The 'compulsion to repeat' discernible in such games is to be distinguished from the organic implications of the trauma-dreams of shell-shocked war veterans, whose own compulsive repetitions – insofar as they exhibit no aggregative aspects, or whose repetitions rather perhaps express the continued *failure* to bind trauma – suggest another, more secretive operation altogether, that of the death drive. Freud famously articulates this speculation as 'an urge inherent in organic life to restore an earlier state of things'.[35] This would mean, in other words, that there are at least two kinds of 'compulsive' repetitions at work in the organism – erotic binding *and* mortifying undoing – which can hardly be told apart. One sort of repetition would be inherently tied to the erotic world of play; the other, if it does indeed exist, would be play's graveyard, its extinction.

In any case, the inventions of children at play become one of the key sites of development for psychoanalysis, not merely as a form of instinctual

---

[32] Sigmund Freud, *Beyond the Pleasure Principle*, in *The Standard Edition of the Complete Psychological Works of Sigmund Freud*, vol. 18 (London: Hogarth Press and Institute of Psycho-Analysis, 1950), 14.

[33] Freud, *Beyond the Pleasure Principle*, 17.

[34] See inter alia Jacques Lacan, *Écrits*, trans. B. Fink with H. Fink and R. Grigg (New York: Norton, 2006), 262.

[35] Freud, *Beyond the Pleasure Principle*, 36.

renunciation-in-invention as the motor of ontogenesis, but also as a primary means of creating imaginative-real zones to enable psychic and physical transitions from one stage or position to another. In this regard, the work of the object relations theorists has been extremely influential, perhaps above all that of D. W. Winnicott.[36] In a famous essay, Winnicott notes the gap between the neonate's typical use of a part of their own body to simulate maternal satisfaction (e.g. thumb-sucking) and the transition – a key term here – to playing with dolls or with another external object of some kind.[37] For Winnicott, what is of interest is the development of an intermediate psychic zone 'between the subjective and that which is objectively perceived'.[38] The transitional object is accordingly '*the original not-me possession*', and, as such, it is not only critical in enabling for the child variations in affect-regulation (protection, soothing, reassurance and so on) but, in being part of psychological development in shifting from pure fantasy to real movement, conditions a simultaneously liminal and integrative relationship to the external world, with ongoing consequences into adulthood.

Psychoanalysis establishes play as an essential part of development, which serves a number of related functions, including moving from passive to active, from fantasy-dominance to reality-testing, from the primacy of disordered wishes to the renunciation of instinct. Yet it also therefore tends to see play and games as not only founding the possibility of civilisation more generally, but of sustaining and shifting culture as well. Hence Freud will speak of the sustenance of infantile fantasies of omnipotence in the realm of art, of its links to rituals, magic and sacrifice, and to festival – and it is this role of play in enabling (and undermining) such articulations that is determining for Axelos too.

Analytical-Ethical Aspects

We also find yet another crucial reliance on play and games in the work of ordinary language philosophy, especially as delivered in the later work of its key progenitor, Ludwig Wittgenstein. As Wittgenstein very famously professes, we are now in the realm, not of being and beings, of sociological

---

[36] The groundbreaking work of Melanie Klein, prime progenitor of object relations, on child analysis and play remains central here.

[37] D. W. Winnicott, 'Transitional Objects and Transitional Phenomena – A Study of the First Not-Me Possession', *The International Journal of Psychoanalysis*, no. 34 (1953), 89–97. He would later follow up this work with a sequence of works, including *Playing and Reality*.

[38] Winnicott, 'Transitional Objects', 90.

facts and psychic realities, of confused actions able to be recomposed as logical descriptions, and so forth, but of many different kinds of games and many different ways of playing them. As he puts it very early in *Philosophical Investigations*:

> this multiplicity is not something fixed, given once for all; but new types of language, new language-games, as we may say, come into existence, and others become obsolete and get forgotten . . . Here the term 'language-*game*' is meant to bring into prominence the fact that the speaking of language is part of an activity, or of a form of life.[39]

'Language' is not a single or simple thing, but a sprawling and shifting complex, linked to certain sets of activities, situations and ambitions. Moreover, it is not just that 'games' provide the key metaphor – if that is indeed what it is – to help Wittgenstein investigate the multifarious peculiarities of language-use. Certain games, or certain kinds of games, also provide him with a method or, rather, a variety of means for approaching the varieties of linguistic experience.

As even the most cursory acquaintance with *Philosophical Investigations* reveals – and which constitutes one of the most evident ruptures with his own earlier work – Wittgenstein is constantly asking his reader to 'imagine a language for which' or asserting that 'it is *like* looking at . . .', which inter alia suggests that philosophy itself has to be expressly played as a kind of game of experimental make-believe if it is to evade the metaphysical traps that it is ceaselessly and secretively setting for itself. For Wittgenstein, then, the very nomination 'language games' serves to indicate the differences and multiplicities of ways in which so-called 'language' is part of different and multiple forms-of-life; that there are indeed only such 'games', that is, that 'language' as a whole or a reality does not exist except as a confused abstraction; that there is an important distinction between *games* and *rules*, such that many games do indeed have rules but those rules never entirely exhaust or define the playing of such games, and rules themselves are often ambiguous or multiple, suggestive or indicative rather than determining; that it is their *use*, at once linguistic and embodied, that is of most interest; that there is no ultimate game which subsumes, surveys or models all other games; that games do not require any particularly deep foundation to be sustained; and so on.

---

[39] Ludwig Wittgenstein, *Philosophical Investigations*, trans. G. E. M. Anscombe (Oxford: Basil Blackwell, 1958), 11, n. 23.

Cybernetic Aspects

But perhaps the most fraught and determining context is one which is at once global, actual and linked to a bundle of technological and intellectual projects that were given their most determining configuration in and by World War II: game theory. As we enter the third decade of the twenty-first century, this 'project', having enhanced and then merged with cybernetics and associated developments, served to found the success of what is today too-easily called 'neoliberalism': the planet has been globalised in real time by such developments as the World Wide Web, and there is nobody whose life is not directly and immediately affected by the products of Silicon Valley and its epigones. From mineral extraction, material transportation, industrial assembly, retail, advertising, product design, logistical planning, financing and beyond, all anthropological activity on the planet is now coordinated and organised according to the exigencies of computational technology – and one of the primary ways in which this technology has so successfully globalised itself while globalising the planet is precisely through the absolute centrality of games in its theory and practice.

Indeed, one text that is widely considered to have given this formation its decisive impetus bears the word in its title: John von Neumann and Oskar Morgenstern's *Theory of Games and Economic Behavior* (1944).[40] In 'Chapter II: General Formal Description of Games of Strategy', the authors make a number of fundamental distinctions:

> First, one must distinguish between the abstract concept of a *game*, and the individual *plays* of that game. The *game* is simply the totality of the rules which describe it. Every particular instance at which the game is played – in a particular way – from beginning to end, is a *play*. Second, the corresponding distinction should be made for the moves, which are the component elements of the game . . . The specific alternative chosen in a concrete instance – i.e. in a concrete *play* – is the *choice*. Thus the moves are related to the choices in the same way as the game is to the play. The game consists of a sequence of moves, and the play of a sequence of choices. Finally, the *rules* of the game should not be confused with the *strategies* of the players.[41]

[40] John von Neumann and Oskar Morgenstern, *Theory of Games and Economic Behavior: 60th Anniversary Commemorative Edition* (Princeton: Princeton University Press, 2004).

[41] Neumann and Morgenstern, *Theory of Games*, 49.

These distinctions – between game and play, move and choice, rule and strategy – are mathematised and technicised in such a way as to determine and evaluate potential strategies and maximise rational outcomes. Moreover, this is done precisely in order to render a hitherto-unexpected diversity of human activities susceptible to fundamental rationalisation: economics most obviously in the first instance, but also, quite immediately, the game of war.

Indeed, given the context of total war in which it was forged, in its expansion and integration of previously relatively autonomous divisions of the life-world, game theory perhaps almost inevitably entailed their concomitant *militarisation* too. Such a militarisation, crucially, did not simply revive older or received notions of the status of the enemy – that of a subhuman aggressor or anonymous victim, nationalist or racist, for example – but rather, as Peter Galison has put it, as 'a mechanized Enemy Other, generated in the laboratory-based science wars of MIT and a myriad of universities around the United States and Britain, not to speak of the tens of laboratories in the countries of the Axis'.[42] What is crucial here is that in its implementation in economics, finance, human resource management and so on, every ludic interaction thereafter becomes de facto a face-off with an enemy who knows the game at least as well as you do and whose basic strategy must *a priori* be considered to be the seeking of their own maximal outcomes. In other words, the Other must now be practically considered an automated inhuman rationator who will play the game in the most implacable way. One immediately sees how and why such thinkers as Heidegger in his post-World War II work took cybernetics to be an absolute enemy of his own project of thinking, naming and shaming it as one contemporaneously dominant expression of the essence of technology as *Gestell* ('enframing' in the standard English translation), and whose own roots are sunk deep – if in a complex and overdetermined fashion – into the metaphysical tradition.

We now have a general context for games and play from which Axelos's work emerges and into which it is intervening. This context is simultaneously: *ontological*, in that it gathers and expresses something about the emergence, transformation and orders of existence across vast temporal and spatial distances; *socio-political*, in that all social organisations place an extraordinary premium upon games, which effect and sustain essential mediations between different regimes and orders of the social body; *psychological*, in that play serves to bind trauma, to enable development and support varied

---

[42] Peter Galison, 'The Ontology of the Enemy: Norbert Wiener and the Cybernetic Vision', *Critical Inquiry*, vol. 21, no. 1 (1994), 231.

mediations that are at once sub- and supra-personal; *ethical*, in the sense that games and play are differentiated compositions of languages and bodies in an expanded field of activity; and *technomilitaristic*, in which the reinscription of all action according to a model of wargaming is submitted to ceaseless development and implementation across the diversity of the socius itself. The conceptions of games and play developed in these modes of thought are stringently limited by their own disciplinary foci, yet cannot help but push towards their own limits. These orientations are not only irreducible to each other – in some cases, quite deliberately so – but establish a kind of force field of extreme tensions regarding the status of games and play that conditions the entire post-World War II situation.

Translation Issues

Axelos expresses this context and its torsions *in extremis*. Axelos is highly attentive to all the currents that we have enumerated in his own account of the destiny of play, the play of the game of the world. A reader unfamiliar with this book will be struck by its sheer physical size, its scope and ambition. It is like an encyclopaedia – or anti-encyclopaedia – of quasi- or non-concepts, composed of aphorisms that both detach themselves from and agglutinate themselves into a whole that they at once affirm and undermine. Moreover, these aphorisms often hypertrophy, become too large, too unwieldy, to function as pithy or condensed bursts of *Witz*, mutating into monstrous paragraph-sentences that run over several pages, sustaining a mode of sense in its disruption through extraordinary syntactical subordinations and adhesions. Axelos deploys a set of keywords that insistently recur – game/play (*jeu*), errancy (*errance*), the planetary (*planétaire*), mondialisation (*mondialisation*) and so on – which he interrogates according to his unique vision. Maintaining Axelos's syntax is often do-able in English, if at the cost of a certain ease: although we have tried not to either reduce or complicate Axelos's stylistic singularity, it is often at once as lucid and as entangled in French as is the case here, simultaneously brilliant, captivating and frustrating.

We should say a few words about Axelos's words. First and foremost, the word '*jeu*'. It is, although the term is misleading, perhaps the keyword of Axelos's entire enterprise. Just like the German *Spiel*, which similarly troubles the translation of Fink,[43] *jeu* lacks the separated English interplay of 'game' and 'play'. It signifies *both*, a circumstance which has incalculable

---

[43] Moore and Turner, 'Translator's Introduction', 9–12.

consequences for this text. As Lydia H. Liu has observed regarding the decisive and de facto suppression of the cybernetic context in the anglophone translation of late twentieth-century French philosophy:

> French mathematicians rendered game as *jeu* and created a heterolinguistic supersign *jeu*/game in the course of introducing John von Neumann and Oskar Morgenstern's mathematical theory of games applicable to economics and nuclear warfare. When this supersign crossed the Atlantic in the guise of French theory, the English signified of *jeu*/game fell by the wayside and the word *jeu* reentered English as a different supersign, play/ *jeu*, to authorize something like a free play of signifiers to the American literary critic.[44]

One of the frustrations of this situation is that von Neumann and Morgenstern had already indicated in a footnote that 'the French terminology is tolerably unambiguous: "game" = "jeu," "play" = "partie."'[45]

For Axelos himself, however – who was very aware, as the reader of this book will soon also be, of the impact and implications of cybernetics, game theory, and their associated technologies – the confounding ambivalence of the French *jeu* is part of the point. This renders the play of *play* and *game* in French absolutely impossible to render consistently into English. There is often no way to decide whether 'play' or 'game' is the better reading. To attempt – as we initially considered – something like *gameplay* or *game/play* is also misleading, too decisive. And an entire semantic network of terms, such as *enjeu* (stakes, prize), *enjoué* (cheerful, playful), *déjouer* (to thwart, to outmanoeuvre, to evade), *en joue!* (take aim!), *mettre en joue* (take aim at) and so on, remain both active and lost in translation. The reader should then keep in mind that almost every instance of 'play' or 'game' that appears in this translation may well also have been rendered by its absent counterpart.

Comparable difficulties go for other keywords. Take *le monde*, the world. Throughout this book Axelos plays heavily on this word and its associates, such as *mondialisation* (which is often used as a synonym for globalisation in French, but which needs to be distinguished from the latter and which we have accordingly simply transliterated), *mondial* (worldwide), *immonde* (dirty, filthy, vile, squalid), *émonder* (to prune, trim), *monder* (to blanch

---

[44] Lydia H. Liu, 'The Cybernetic Unconscious: Rethinking Lacan, Poe, and French Theory', *Critical Inquiry*, vol. 36, no. 2 (2010), 291–2.

[45] Neumann and Morgenstern, *Theory of Games*, 49, n. 1.

or bleach) and so on.[46] The expression 'tout le monde' – literally 'all the world', 'the whole world' – simply means 'everyone' in French, but given Axelos's penchant for using wordplay to indicate and reinforce historical, linguistic and philosophical relations, we have sometimes chosen to keep the reference to the world in English. We have also done so in our translation of 'immonde' as 'unworldly', precisely because Axelos's homophonic point would otherwise be lost, for example, 'le monde immonde' as 'the unworldly world', though a more literal and legitimate translation would give something like 'the unclean world'. Axelos, moreover, is drawing his own thinking on world from Heidegger, for whom the question of 'being-in-the-world' is absolutely fundamental, and which is still further complicated when the vicissitudes of the relationship between 'earth' and 'world' start to become central for the latter from the mid-1930s, not least in the characterisation of the work of art as establishing itself in and as the rift between the two. Yet we cannot reduce Axelos's use to Heidegger's. So what *is* the 'world' for Axelos? Is it the totality of phenomena? Is it 'all that is the case', as Wittgenstein famously notes? An active verbing? A fundamental labour or place of taking-place of *Dasein*? All or none of these? The problem of the World, Axelos writes, is what at once founds and surpasses metaphysics. As the reader will quickly find, there is no immediate answer to be given to these questions, precisely because the crucial orientation is given by the book's title: the world and game/play are indissociable, the world itself is game and play and unworks such received distinction as phenomena and noumena, the possible and the actual, the fragment and the totality, all and nothing.

We need also note, again following Heidegger, the play between '*L'être*' and '*l'étant*', between *being* and *beings*. Sometimes Axelos capitalises the former, sometimes not. In Heidegger's German in his 1927 magnum opus *Being and Time* (*Sein und Zeit*), *Sein* as being is always the being of beings or existents, *Seiendes*, the former relating to the latter as the ontological to the ontical. If being must be shared by everything that exists (which are themselves beings, existents), not one of these beings or existents, no matter how great or powerful, is able to provide the key to being itself: after all, privileging one particular being as the proper model of being is one of the distorted hallmarks of metaphysics itself, and, at the very least, argumentatively untenable. In Heidegger's treatise, it is by means of *Dasein* (literally

---

[46] As Elden puts it: '*Mondialisation* is the process of becoming-worldly, something which relates to the Anglophone term "globalization" but cannot be simply equated with it'; 'Introduction', 18.

'there-being') that being for which being itself is a question (crudely put, human beings), that the disjunction between beings and being has to be broached. The translation of *Sein* as *L'être* and *Seiend* as *l'étant* was already standard in French philosophy when Axelos was writing; since German nouns are always capitalised, however, there seems to be the temptation to try to fix or unfix the terminological difference in languages such as French (or indeed English) by alternatively capitalising or even de-capitalising the substantives. Given this simultaneous clarity and uncertainty, we have basi-cally followed the letter of Axelos's text here – being for *L'être*, Being for *L'Être*, being for *l'étant*, beings for *l'étants* and so on, if the significance, if any, of some of these variants is sometimes difficult to ascertain. Axelos even occasionally seems to use *être* where elsewhere he might use *étant*, and vice versa. Sometimes we have resorted to 'existent' for *l'étant*, as a result of a particularly dense sequence of word- and thought-play *in situ*. An asso-ciated difficulty turns on how to translate such terms as *tout/e* – all, every, any – which so often modify 'being' and 'play/game' for Axelos. Again, and although we have sought to inflect our translation according to contextual indications, the losses are insuperable. In any case, it is crucial to underline that Axelos himself considers his emphasis on game and play to be more primordial than being and beings, Being and beings, existence and existents, however we wish to cash these terms out.

Given that Heidegger's thinking of technology is also so important for Axelos, we have had to think very carefully about all the different terms the latter uses that are in this semantic ballpark, including *technique*, *tech-nicisme*, *technicité*, *technologique*. Axelos plays on little differences – *la tech-nique* and *des techniques*, for instance – whose senses are often quite hard to render directly. Although we believe the decisions we have made are defensible in this regard, there is still nevertheless a question mark hanging over their heads and their hearts: we trust the reader will treat our deci-sions with healthy suspicion. Something similar goes for our translation of *echaufaudage* – literally, scaffold, scaffolding – which also is a kind of trans-position of Heidegger's *Gestell*, a 'set-up' or, as a standard Englishing puts it, 'enframing'. It is perhaps also worth mentioning that *Gestell* has elsewhere been rendered in French as *dispositif* ('apparatus', 'device'), sometimes as *arraisonnement* (this latter word is rarely used by Axelos).

Other difficulties perhaps already familiar to the English reader of late twentieth-century French philosophy might include those with such words as *pouvoir* ('to be able', but also 'power') as against *puissance* (potency, force). Here, we have simply translated Axelos's phrase '*les grandes puissances et les forces élémentaires du monde*' as 'the great powers and elemental forces of the world'. There is the hoary chestnut of how to translate *connaissance* (rec-ognition, knowing, familiarity) as opposed to *savoir* (science, knowledge): we have sometimes marked this explicitly, but at other times, taking the risk that the phrase and its context don't seem to inflect the term one way or another, we have silently translated it. We have also tended to translate *dépassement* as 'surpassing', with an eye to the Hegelian reference of *Aufheben* (often translated in English as 'sublation'). In Hegel's text, *Aufheben* is an operation that is simultaneously a cancelling and a preserving, whereby what is surpassed is not for that destroyed, but continues to be differently effective in a transmogrified, integrated form. A number of other words have also had to be nuanced accordingly. *Actualité*, for example, has an everyday sense of 'news', 'current affairs' or 'topicality', but also a more philosophical sense of 'actuality', 'reality', not least because the ordinary German word/ Hegelian technical term *Wirklichkeit* (whose standard English translations are 'reality' and 'actuality') is very often also at play within it.

There are a number of words less difficult to translate, but which are given singular inflections by their part in the Axelos armature. The adjective *planétaire* is one of these. While it is directly rendered as 'planetary', it also retains a cosmic reference with Heideggerean connotations. The French word is linked to plans, planes, flattenings, platitude and many other terms of import to Axelos. The planets in Greek are literally wanderers, errant superlunary bodies, which has the further bond in Axelos's thought to what he calls *errance* (errancy), the levelling errancy of being and thought in the game of the world.

Although there are many other noteworthy aspects of Axelos's vocabu-lary and style that might be mentioned, there are two further issues of crucial importance. The first is our translation of '*Cela*', which titles and orients a significant section of this book. *Cela* is a pronoun that could be rendered either as 'this' or as 'that'. We considered, as the German translation of the book gives it, turning *cela* into It (*Es*). However, in French *Ça* is the stand-ard translation for Freud's It (Id in English), and so is misleading here.[47] So should *cela* be *this* rather than *that*? The standard French translation of the term *das Diese* ('the this') in Hegel's *Phenomenology of Spirit* provides: *le ceci*. If these considerations may seem otiose to the common reader (if such indeed exists), the Italian philosopher Giorgio Agamben has dedicated an important study to the role of the demonstrative pronoun in German phenomenology. He writes:

[47] See Jean Laplanche and Jean-Bertrand Pontalis, *Vocabulaire de la psychanalyse* (Paris: PUF, 1967).

Da and *diese* (like *ci* and *questo* in Italian, like *hic* the adverb of place and *hic* the demonstrative pronoun in Latin, and also like *there* and *this* in English) are morphologically and etymologically connected. Both stem from the Greek root *to*, which has the form *pa* in Gothic. From a grammatical point of view, these particles belong to the sphere of the pronoun (more precisely the demonstrative pronoun) – that is, to a grammatical category whose definition is always a point of controversy for theorists of language.[48]

Agamben points to these particles as critical to the Western philosophical attempts to articulate the negativity of the taking-place of language itself: an incontrovertibly central concern for the thinking of the relation of language and being. In the present context, then, this word *cela* should be understood as referring to Hegel, Heidegger and Freud's uses of *Diese* (this), *Da* (there) and *Es* (it), but is irreducible to them. Hence we have decided on the 'That'.

Another translation issue stems from an encyclopaedic encryption: despite at times directly quoting other world-historic thinkers, Axelos tends not to disclose his sources. What presents for us translators a 'merciful absence of references', as our amicable advisor Dr Robert Boncardo put it, is for the reader almost a rite of passage: those who ask do not need to know. Some passages appear to speak to an initiated circle of those who know the key texts for the themes discussed without the need to spell it out. Although we started to uncover the hidden references by adding footnotes, we choose to side with Axelos to let the reader play this game. However, when we found Axelos disclosing the source and citing lengthier passages, we chose existing English translations.[49] Like the original text, our translation has only one footnote, linked to the very last sentence of the book.

Adding to the enigma, Axelos, who acted as Heidegger's translator and himself published in German, scatters isolated German sentences across the chapters. For the English reader's ease we have provided our own translations of German phrases in parentheses immediately following.

One final but very delicate point concerns our decision to render Axelos's French in as gender-neutral a fashion as we could. In French, all nouns

---

[48] Giorgio Agamben, *Language and Death: The Place of Negativity*, trans. Karen E. Pinkus with Michael Hardt (Minneapolis: University of Minnesota Press, 1991), 19.

[49] For Plato, we have drawn on the texts in *Plato: Complete Works*, ed. John M. Cooper and Douglas S. Hutchinson (Indianapolis and Cambridge: Hackett Publishing, 1997), and for Nietzsche, *The Gay Science*, ed. Bernard Williams, trans. Jeff Nauckhoff (Cambridge: Cambridge University Press, 2002). We also note that the unnamed 'Christian and minor poet' cited in the chapter 'God-Problem' is Charles Péguy.

are gendered male or female, and at the time at which Axelos was writing '*l'homme*', man, could still function as a quasi-synonym for the human being per se. Should we simply and directly translate *homme* as man – with absolute fidelity to the existing text – and be done with it? This would probably be the most straightforward and justifiable route. Yet it is necessary to affirm that the English language of the early twenty-first century has fundamentally shifted in its relationship to gender. 'Man' can no longer masquerade or impose itself as an abstract universal, and cannot under any reasonable description today be given such a function – even if in this case we pleaded the priority of grammar or textual fidelity. We felt that we could no longer take the historical markers of the politics of grammar and grammatical gender as secondary or marginal. We did not take this decision lightly; on the contrary, it has proven to be an ongoing anxiety for the entirety of our work on this translation.

It is not as if Axelos was not already considering the import and consequences of the sexual revolution under way – his writings expressly seek to affirm the necessity of the transformation of 'man', of humanity – although he was still in a world in which the grammar could be deployed without the current urgent intense planetary questioning of the status and stability of gender. Yet Axelos was in his own way already very attentive to the sexuation of language too. We have therefore made the decision to translate 'man' throughout in such terms as 'human', 'people' or otherwise as far as that was possible without undue falsification, given Axelos at these moments himself tends to use *humain* and *homme* in free variation. As a result, we have also opted mostly for an accompanying 'their' and 'they', 'them' and 'it' – barbarisms from the point of traditional English grammar, but a solution which hopefully still functions adequately enough here. This is of course far from an ideal situation and solution. It raised (and raises) many further questions. What about the monotheistic patriarchal God, for example, not least because God is grammatically masculine in French? As the reader will see, we have kept the gendered language when the context requires it.[50]

---

[50] This translation dilemma is now evidently of a planetary nature. To give another example of a comparable although not identical approach, we might cite David Maruzzella and Gil Morejón in their 'Notes on Translation and Acknowledgements' to their translation of Alexandre Matheron, *Politics, Ontology and Knowledge in Spinoza* (Edinburgh: Edinburgh University Press, 2020): 'We strove to render everything using gender-neutral language as much as possible. For the most part, this has meant turning *homme* into "human being" and utilising "they" as a generic singular pronoun. We consistently make Spinoza's God an "it", which is, incidentally, preferable on purely philosophical grounds' (x).

Caillois has made the critical point that: 'a game which one would be forced to play would at once cease being play. It would become constraint, drudgery from which one would strive to be freed.'[51] This is certainly one of the features of play that sets Axelos at once inside and against the cybernetic closure, for which not only is there a stringent distinction between 'game' and 'play', but gaming is mandatory – there are everywhere only games – and such games are all ultimately organised according to the principles of economic warfare. In our own time – the plague-times of late capitalism – the managerialism of the multinational capitalist corporation has, merging techniques drawn from the history of slavery and of extermination with those drawn from the history of play, forged what is essentially a new paradigm in the control of labour-relations: what is now widely called 'gamification'. Norbert Wiener's fever dream of 'the human use of human beings' has become nightmarish in its coupling of capital surplus-extraction with new forms of technical expropriation under the heading of play itself.

The Game of the World: A Timely Topic

The Game of the World conceives of the dawn of the twenty-first century, in which technological transformations generate a world of playable worlds. Forced by a pandemic, we invest in ways to play a part in the world without leaving our homes. We can observe that playing games is not only for leisure any more. It is also for work, health and wealth. Even war and love become played online through games in cyberspace. The play of who wins and who loses becomes widely played among the competitors contesting polemical elections, court cases, gambling casinos, beauty pageants, school assignments, television shows, research grant applications, performance reviews, stock market exchanges, and awards of noble and desired prizes. Radio, television, film, games; it all plays. Playful users play their audio, video and multimedia players. All our games are globally played on the World Wide Web and streamed on our displays ready to play. As if in generalised indifference, all becomes virtually and actually playable via Google Play, YouTube's play button, and other global players. When we play our games in the metaverse, what becomes of the universe? Where are we moving to when we are scrolling and clicking? Are we continually falling when we are continually swiping? Are we homeless on our homepages and playless at our PlayStations when moving backwards, forwards, upwards, downwards,

---

[51] Caillois, *Man, Play and Games*, 7.

inwards, outwards, in all directions? Aren't we erring as through an endless playground? Isn't the illuminated display breathing at us, chilling us? In our erring, in our playing, we are searching for the worldwide game, but are we finding the unfindable play? What *holy games* did we invent for ourselves and do those games obscure from us our play? Is worldwide gamification played by the play of the world? Is the display of the worldwide worldlessness a play? While the gamer thinks to play worlds, it is the play of the world that games the gamer. Does the worldwide unification that fragmentises the world into the play of bits and bytes demand a worldwide thinking of fragmentary wholeness? Can this way of play place its focus on the play of plays? Humans, global players and worldwide gamers of planetary and virtual worlds in the metaverse – playing with as they are played by the post-human and the inhuman from which they cannot ever be fully distinguished – have yet to mature in the game of the world.

This English translation of *Le jeu du monde* seeks to contribute to the current research in games and play by rendering Axelos's thought more accessible for an English audience in an age where games of all kinds dominate the structuring of experience at every scale from the pre-personal to the super-planetary. Through an active thinking of the becoming-planetary of the world as the fragmentary totality of being-in-becoming that deploys itself as play, and tracing such thought from the Presocratics through Socrates and Plato to contemporary philosophy, Axelos offers a unique perspective on the vicissitudes of our life and times. If *habent sua fata libelli*, perhaps ours is a moment in and for which Axelos's unique book might enable us to play differently, to reconsider our fates as fêtes.

As Axelos may have said: *we are all planetary thought now.*

Acknowledgements

The translation of this book was accomplished mainly under the conditions of an uncanny global plague – a plague of *mondialisation*, of the errant becoming-planetary of all experience, as Axelos might say – that is now universally named COVID-19. This obviously had an enormous impact upon our working conditions. It slowed the process enormously, physically separating the translators from each other, and forced us to rely upon now-nearly-naturalised forms of communication almost unimaginable only a few decades earlier (e.g. Google Drive, email) under variable conditions of local and national lockdowns. Yet this disruption also induced us to attend to what would previously have been indiscernible or less notable aspects of Axelos's work (to us at least).

While it has been an honour and a privilege to work on this translation together, it has not been an unmitigatedly positive experience. Luckily, we have had the extraordinary support of Katherina Daskalaki, Professor Stuart Elden and the (very understanding) team at Edinburgh University Press, who persisted with the project despite our seemingly endless interruptions and delays. The translation could simply not have happened without their interest and assistance, for which we are extremely grateful. There are probably not sufficient words of gratitude for Dr Robert Boncardo, whose generosity in reading the manuscript and providing detailed feedback and references has entirely improved the translation as a whole, as well as saving us from embarrassing errors. Knox Peden and Joe Hughes have also provided further indispensable advice.

The translators were first introduced to each other in 2018 in Melbourne, Australia, by Dr Adam Nash from RMIT University, who, for a variety of reasons, was unable to continue to contribute to the translation himself. Although we regret Adam's absence, this project would never have happened without him. Monz is a Lecturer at RMIT University in Vietnam; Clemens is an Associate Professor at the University of Melbourne. We would like to thank both institutions for their support for such a project in such a difficult time.

Disrupted by a planetary pandemic, as well as the accompanying manifold institutional, social and political disturbances that everyone now living will be aware of in their own way, these difficulties were perhaps less overwhelming than the difficulties in Englishing this unique masterpiece. *Le jeu du monde* took Axelos fifteen years to write and us five years to translate – too long, in its way, but perhaps, in another, not nearly long enough.

Prelude

There is no impassable abyss separating the thought of the great systematic thinkers – Plato, Aristotle, Thomas Aquinas, Descartes, Kant, Hegel, Marx, who each determine an epoch in the history of thought and, altogether, the course of the world thought – from the thought of the great fragmentary thinkers – Heraclitus, Pascal, Novalis, Nietzsche, who, with their aphorisms, pass like meteors between heaven and earth. Today we take the former as 'classical', logical and more settled, and envisage the latter as intuitive and more tortured, even 'accursed'. The former is considered more discursive, even scientific, the other more elliptical and poetic. What however escapes this classification are the intimate bonds that always unite, in an open and fragmentary system, continuity and discontinuity, all the thoughts delimiting the horizon with boundaries and limits, marching and jumping on the path they follow because it imposes itself on them. Open to the blows of death, all the thinkers, guided by and guiding words, tend to approach a language that would englobe all languages, yet do not arrive at noting, lifting, recording, classifying, cataloguing, coordinating and elucidating everything in their words and in their writings. Partial-total moments of thought, they give themselves to the word, to thought and to writing, and appeal to past, present and future interlocutors and readers. The question *for whom does one write?* remains suspended, and, although governed by and obsessed by the here and now, we envision a future. Which does not mean that we write for the pleasure of a restoration which would be happy to discover you in x years. In this work of the discursive and accomplished and the aphoristic and elliptical, the two streams join again and compose a unique course, the perceptible [*sensible*] finding itself passably sacrificed, only managing to emerge with great pain.

The discursive – the continuous – is nonetheless also fragmentary, and the aphoristic – the discontinuous – is equally total, provided that we do not confuse aphorisms and sentences. The illusions of the systematic and the aphoristic – separated from one another – prevent us from comprehending the secret of the aphoristic systematic, always exploded, neither systematic nor aphoristic, and both systematic and aphoristic. Thus the systematic and aphoristic encyclopaedias, integrating and interrogative, affirmative and questioning, are constructed in the game of continuity and discontinuity that poses us the question of the fragmentary system and the fragments of the totality, in the space of errant coherence, that is to say, a certain coherence. Incompleteness remains the lot of humans. Everything can be registered, commented on, explained, interpreted indefinitely – the corrections, the amendments, the additions are also unlimited – and all remains unfinished, even – if not above all – finite. There is therefore no total expression. In every way, one does not say all that passes through one's head – and the rest – and one does not succeed in organising all the materials.

When can one then say that a book – after multiple readings – is completed, achieved, finished? Wanting – essaying – to put into the world a thought that is neither simply (and illusorily) systematic nor aphoristic, neither total nor fragmentary, but encyclopaedic and elliptical, the author incites the reader to a reversible and polyscopic, relational and combinational, permutational and productive reading with many entrances and exits, and invites the reader to this work – to this play – where the book writes and reads itself, in the becoming of time, through the author and readers. So each fragment of the open totality requires multiple connections and applications, because the ensemble of the fragments does not constitute a chaotic and arbitrary mixture, but is coherent, leaving open the question of contingency in the combinatory play of writing and reading, consequently opening itself to mobile and aleatory readings.

In the centre of typhoons, there are zones of calm, where movement and rest gather. It is from there that thought which surpasses convenient distinctions takes its impulse and opens itself to the world in opening it, overturning the classifications.

There are books which are written above all to be written, and there are others which before all offer themselves for reading. The book explodes. The book, which was the guarantor of the tradition and the prototype of intelligibility, has already exploded, although it continues to haunt us.

One nevertheless continues to write. For what? To the search of the author corresponds the search of readers, and to the assimilations are opposed the differences. The book of all books, the total book, does not exist and cannot exist. The dream of an automatic and global writing which would quasi-simultaneously say everything, which would unroll the whole film of thought, the course of thought saying the course of the world, and would construct the whole pyramid of what is, remains a dream for awakened sleepers. Every book obeys a structure, an ordering, in its ensemble as in its details, partakes in a rootedness and deploys itself on the horizon, contains what one could say, what one has said, and what is grasped by its readers. It implicates all the undertones and the misunderstandings, the provocation and the encouragement to read between the lines, to enter into the circle that opens and breaks itself. The end of readers is not yet consummated.

Opening.
The Great Powers and the Elementary
Forces of the World

The human accesses the world through the intermediary of mediating *great powers*, fundamental powers that establish the relationship human–world and take charge of it through institutions. Fundamentally activated by the elemental forces – *language* and *thought*, *work* and *struggle*, *love* and *death*, *play* – of which they constitute elaborations edifying us from the outset of the play, these powers are called:

> *magic*, *myths* (and mythology), *religion*,
> *poetry* and *art*,
> *politics*,
> *philosophy*, *sciences* and *technology*.

They open us to the world and open it to us, constitute it for us and form us for it. It can be that they manifest themselves simultaneously, proceeding from the same source – which? – as is the case for the great epochs of world history. It also happens that one or many of them are lacking, by retreating so to speak from the increased and stifling power of the other or other powers. But none of them alone exhausts the being in becoming of the totality – no more than their ensemble exhausts it. None is separately the first foundation and none is the servant of the other. Without being autonomous or separate, even though specific, each referring to all the others, impregnating them, implicating them more or less explicitly but without artificial symmetries, the great powers – dimensions, openings and routes – all emerge from the same problematic centre. Their saying and their making are penetrated by the being of all that is; they make it be and call it. Particular and total totalities at the heart of the totality, each is a total aspect of the totality of the world, a constituent of the totality. They are not isolated elements of a whole, simple parts of an ensemble. They communicate with each other, interpenetrate, fight and fertilise each other, connect, but not through relationships of cause and effect. Because specific 'objects' or 'subjective' modes of an approach do not correspond to them. Each of them specifically approaches and fragmentarily expresses the totality of what is and is done, by imprinting its mark on it.

The great powers of the world, born from the original violence of the architectonic logos and poetic praxis, emanating from a common centre – a working totality composed not of levels but of domains – are carried and supported each time by great humans and great peoples and give the measure of historical time. They are not always all present. For the sacred to become religion, for speech to become poetry, for phenomena to become art, for the community to become political, for thought to become philosophy and science, there must be the decisive contest of the great powers. Once constituted – they do not form simultaneously – they are all at work, but sometimes one slumbers, sometimes the other awakes. When one or more of them do not manifest, others take over. During very great epochs they are all present, proceeding from their unnameable and unique source. Very often, however, more vague and original movements substitute for the great formative and formed powers: for what inspires religion, poetry and art, politics, philosophy and the sciences does not always deploy itself as religion, poetry, art, politics, philosophy, science. Sometimes we can even go so far as to suspect that divinity, poeticity, plasticity, the organisation of the community, thought and research are withdrawing.

If all the great powers derive from the same centre, what is and where is this centre? It is easier to delineate it negatively than positively. This centre is not the spirit of an epoch, a people, a society or a time, for where would this spirit arise from? It does not reside in economic and political history, the development of the productive and structuring forces, for where would the source of this dialectical movement reside? It is not the *idea* or absolute or historic spirit, nor cosmic *matter* or the material of human labour, without being for that the junction of spirit and matter, idea and reality. The one focus, from which the great multiple powers develop, hides, so to speak, behind and in them, though it renders them visible and they render it 'visible' but unavoidable. If religion, art, politics, philosophy and the sciences have a common structure for the totality of an epoch and a society of which they are actualisations of a certain register, from whence then comes the so-called global structure that makes correspondences emerge or gather? To privilege one or the other of these powers, to see it as determining – sometimes in a general manner, sometimes according to cases – can and does happen, affirming and invalidating itself. This does not however solve the problem, does not even pose it, and remains too unilateral. Once more: from whence comes the 'spirit of the time', over which no one can jump? And even if all or each of the powers express the epoch, how does the epoch impress itself?

The great powers form a totality in progress, without centre or focus, origin or motor, source or kernel, foundation or principle that would limit the play of their structure. This non-centre – non-existent or non-disclosable, if the question follows this formulation – is not a lack or a loss, but the play itself that also plays in the search for the centre.

Is the centre of every *epoch* that conceals itself in the suspension of the *epoché* something like a cause of the structure of the whole – an absent cause?

It is that or who that is closest to a centre that is at the same time that or who which is furthest away from it. The philologist is as far away from poetic and thinking speech as the philosopher is from thought, and the man of the Church from the sacred; the physicist is no nearer to nature than the psychologist is to the human soul, and the historian to historicity; a ditch difficult to cross separates the politician from the city, and the technician from the secret of technology. Yet it is in the proximity of their exponential functions – if not their functionaries – that there hides the distant presence of what 'tries' to broach a path.

Must everything enter into 'its' time so that it can enter into time? And all that one epoch cannot assume and rejects, others take up and make resound.

Being of its time, of its epoch? Being it [*L'être*]. – Being of its time, of its epoch? Not being it. – Being of its time, of its epoch? How not to be it?

What is that which is in the air?

The defenders of yesterday and those of tomorrow are always embarrassed by today.

It is the epoch that belongs to the principle that dominates it more than the principle belongs to the epoch, and this also concerns our epoch – epoch of compromise. At the same time, this epoch cannot find its dominant configuration, since we are already marching towards a beyond of figuration.

Relationships know [*connaissent*] a history, even when they misrecognise [*meconnaissent*] it, erecting a comprehension into an absolute norm: our relationship to the Greeks, for example, our comprehension of the Greeks, is very different from the relationship they had with themselves, their comprehension of the – and their – world.

Tradition resides at once in the transmission and the forgetting of origins.

Maintaining and cultivating the heritage bequeathed by tradition, playing at the relay race, is part of the highest habits.

What marks, regarding an epoch, a break introducing a future approach, can precisely not be captured by the epoch, epochally insensitive to this rupture.

What is highly revealing is not such or such great power, its forms, contents and works, but what is revealed and produced through each, through its mediation.

Every great work contains its own critique.

Magic, or what is very problematically called such, opens the cycle of great powers and – before disappearing as such – passes into them. It is unitarily what will then manifest itself differently as religion and art, politics, technique and knowledge. It offers us an example of the eclipse of a great power.

The mask is the face of the magical, mythical, mimic, cultural and liturgical game: it figures the simulacrum, mobilises prestige, provokes trances, fixes and unchains vertigo; it makes the revelation pass – masked.

Does all that is profound advance masked?

The play of primitive, savage, archaic masks provokes phenomena of possession and dispossession, panics and ecstasies, with the help of spells and enchantments, in a demonic universe that one tries to exorcise by demonic means. Later the mask will become face and uniform, mimicry will become politics, sorcery will become knowledge and power, the cultic play cultural play.

Throughout the millennia, the human plays not with but through the mask.

Long before dualism, the magical, mystical, cultic and cultural game uses the mask, the double, duplication, duplicity.

The animist conception, supposing an agent behind every event, has a hard life. It is only much later that one understands that behind the mask of the world – *persona* – there is no one.

The magical and mythical, poetic and artistic, political, juridical and technical, are in their beginnings one. They function with formative and restrictive rules.

What remains, among other things, of the magical attitude is the temptation and the practice of conjuration, exorcism, spells and enchantments, up to and including superstitions.

The technique of the scapegoat survived primitive magical practices.

Magic – repetitive and inventive – as a source of art – an initiatory, collective and ritualised, occult and occulted source – has ceased to be. Art has become like the religion of the modern world – a problematic priesthood – which does not exclude, quite on the contrary, the flood of the cultural industry in radical and generalised democracy, in the commencing socialisation, the deployment of the reign of production-consumption and the total exploitation of all that is and is done.

Magic – collective phenomenon – will have already disappeared when the democratic and tyrannical reign of the individual, which will be succeeded by the socialist collectivity, manifests. Neither the individual nor the socialised can be called magical.

Have myths above all been – and are they still – in the powers of the imaginary, overcompensations for actual weaknesses, for theoretical and practical powerlessness, or imaginary projections announcing technical real-isations? Is not this reading, already and again, a little mythological and technological? For myths only later became mythology, while technique [*technique*] always awaits its technological [*technologique*] deployment, which is not exempt from mythological elements.

Myths are a sort of primary presence that is already veiled, because when we believe we find ourselves in their presence, they have already gone through an elaboration, have become mythology: we only deal with mythologies.

All that, which is, is mythologically invested.

The myth is a saying that recounts and orients an action, a legend, almost inseparable from what is designated by the term 'reality', since it inhabits it.

The myth states a story. The rite reproduces it. The liturgy celebrates it, that is, plays it.

In all myths, does not a playful propensity intervene?

In the mythical universe, the lot of the human is bound by spells that fix the part play.

The myth prefigures and condenses what will effectuate and monetise it.

Behind us, in us, before us, sparkle mythical – that is, mythological – constellations, like nebulae or galaxies, in which our ideological constellations take part.

Our future is taken with a nameless mythology in which it is caught and lost.

To religion belong the speaking or silent games of mystical interiority as much as the spectacular and cultic games of ecclesiastical exteriority. Each of them is inseparable from others. Thus, religion can play unitarily on both tableaux.

Religion both hides its game and shows it: it plays on and with the presence-absence of presences, of absences and representations.

Religion justifies and confirms the existing order, denies it and refuses it. It fights on the side of the strongest and appeases the weak. So, it plays on two tableaux at once.

Is the origin of play cultic? Is the origin of cult ludic? What is their common root?

In the cultic play, the play becomes sacred and the sacred finds itself played.

Magical, mystical, cultic action – ritual play – is participation in the demonic powers and reaction against them, in human play and as divine play.

The original cult play, playing the tragicomedy of the play of the world, becomes tragic play and comic play.

Does not every religion imply awaiting the miracle and salvation? Is not the human always in search of supreme rescue, of a redemptive denouement?

It is on all levels that we await the miracle (more prosaically: the very exceptional).

Did the saints propelled by historical legend exist? Did they expose them-selves to mortal propulsion? Soldiers of the divine being, did they not betray Being and, by leading the (divine) word into victory, did they not betray the logos? Their doing, finally, was it not 'too' crystallised?

Mystery possesses a strongly attractive power.

Mysticism turns around sex and death. Which does not stop the mysteries of mysticism from being highly mystifying.

The sacred is particularised in the sacrifice.

A great power emanates from the one who sacrifices. Even greater than the one who sacrifices themself.

Every religion that presents itself as sacred – or as profane – and every secondary religiosity have their heretics: those who announce that the promise did not take place; those who denounce imperfect realisations;

those who are overthrown by the orthodoxies of power; those who can raise something in some future.

Belief and doubt refer to each other, mutually condition each other, drink from the same source whose current they channel.

A very subtle play connects belief, credulity, deceit, in all kinds of ceremonies.

Religion is already an alienation of faith.

Was it only after a certain usage of beings and things, when these and those were overused, that the sacred began to prevail over the profane, becoming a sphere and a particular activity? That time preceding the distinction between the sacred and the profane and the banalisation of the course of life, did it exist otherwise than in the eyes of our nostalgia for a golden age, a lost paradise?

The sacred is inseparable from the prohibitions it enacts and its delimitation regarding the profane. Will the era which would like to be post-Christian be able to stop the human from needing any more prohibitions, if only to have the pleasure of violating them? And how will it manage celebratory rites?

Faith and belief determining intellect and thought – with or without conflict – characterise not only religion but all the great powers, practised more or less religiously.

How convenient and touching the distinction that saw in religion hope and faith, and in philosophy and science knowledge.

Already the primary form of knowledge is sacerdotal.

Religion, which has forbidden knowledge [savoir] as sin – preaching distance from the tree of knowledge [connaissance], sin being knowledge – does it succumb to knowing [savoir], even though it belatedly strives to integrate the knowledge [connaissance] that suits it?

Everything becomes secular and the centuries become drops in the ocean of time.

The desire for a sort of community of lay monks, living and thinking the transformation of the sacred into the profane in relatively protected places and moments, is more tenacious than one imagines.

Art and politics, philosophy, the sciences and technique do not only carry religious elements that themselves carry magical, mythical and mythological elements, but also constitute the religion of art and an artistic religion (or a religious art), the religion of politics and a political religion (or religious politics), the religion of philosophy and a philosophical religion (or a religious philosophy), the religion of science and a scientific religion (or a religious science), the religion of technique and a technical religion (or religious technique) – up to the irreligious religion of everyday banality and the search for sensations.

Is poetry the secret and the creative force – poetic – of any art? But in what sense of the term 'poiesis'? And in what web of relations with *logos*, *praxis* and *techné*? Impossible to exit the initial confusion, prolix in distinctions. One separates the theoretical (and contemplative) from the practical (and active), without specifying whether this communicating separation is itself principally theoretical or practical, or even if each of these two powers, their opposition and composition, arise principally from the theoretical or practical. One then separates the practical and active (the praxic) from the poietic (and creating) – subordinating in value poiesis to praxis (especially political), while placing poiesis at the summit from which it falls into the city to let itself be more or less excluded, since it does not theoretically say the truth nor practically act, but poetically makes up its own with fabrications and fictions – as if practice were not equally creative and the poietic active, not to mention the metaphysic-logic-politic-aesthetic fixation of the true and the good and the beautiful. Finally, one leaves technique powerful in shadow, which is skilled at making, art and fabrication, process and expedient. From this will result the later confusions, the subtle distinctions and the gross separations between art and artistry, creation and production, fabrication and action, in the theoretical, practical, poietic and technical melee.

Poetry and art, that is to say poetry and prose and all the arts, do they operate principally by means of an intuition more or less sensible or noetic? To pose the question in a striking manner comes back to knowing what intuition is.

Poetry, does it fit into the prose of the world like an enclave, or is it prose that is part of poeticity? The language of prose, dominant language, imagines that poetic language is vague and imprecise, ambiguous and equivocal, prevents communication: as if prosaic language effected it. It could also be that prose and poetry are a bifurcated language. This does not solve the problem of the links between thought and poetry.

The profound kinship between art and play has often been noticed. But it is not only art that is of play.

For a long time there has existed an aspiration – fairly mythical – for a complete and total work of art, integrating all the arts and integrating itself into life. All realisations, however, remain partial. It is another aspiration, for a poetry and an art made by all. Is it less mythical?

Each work and each type of art is a proposition of life, a behaviour and a gap.

Every artistic work – and every work at all – contains a bit of imposture.

Politics does not take precedence, as think those for whom politics is *the* destiny; nor is it simply an affair of organisation and institutions, administration and agitation. Politics is what institutes and constitutes the polis, that is to say the city or the empire, the State or universal history. When it is great. Great politics is more and something other than the putting-into-action of thought; it is like the master of its domain; and the greatest thinkers cannot be the greatest politicians, any more than great persons of action are not the greatest persons of thought. Politics is not only the art of governing humans and administering things; it is what permits the world to reveal itself to humans, social beings, by permitting them at the same time to reach it and to bring it violence, living and working in community and in struggle, fighting, building and demolishing.

The place of politics is the State and the revolutionary movements aiming at power. The poetry of the seizure of power then grapples with the prose of the government and the administration.

Politics realises a governmental synthesis between the polis and the police.

The bonds of the ethical and the juridical are woven so that they can be torn from each side, while remaining a single fabric with various and intertwined threads.

Determined by economic and political technique, and overdetermining it, every established right is conservative, and every call for a revolutionary right becomes it.

The organisation of laws, rights and justice tightly depends on economic and political necessities, while masking them. By the way – by where? – no society can do without repressive organisms.

The juridical is there to supplement the ethical.

Can the game of politics not override restriction, planning and compromise, even when it exceeds tactical manoeuvres?

All politics is tactical. It is the total, unveiling and falsifying half of a totalising totality, although always partisan and partial. Thus even the politics that proclaims 'anarchism' as final goal cannot do without, along the way and in every order, repressive power.

Can politics avoid the lie? Is the question itself political?

The apolitical contributes to the adventures of local and world politics.

Institutions tolerate very well the refusal of institutions, assimilate this refusal, and can go as far as establishing the institution of refusal.

Institutions and what transgresses them as institutions, and which is only their transgression, are part of the same game. As for the transgression of transgression?

Knowledge as well as power cannot do without solid organisation, which is however liquefied.

Once upon a time, saints and heroes made believe that the combat was already won in heaven or on earth.

Philosophical thought, coming after the formation of the other great powers, often flows into their moulds and borrows their language: it is thus sometimes above all religious or poetic or political thought. In its high places it is ontological (logical and metaphysical) thought. Subsequently, it becomes above all scientific and technical thought.

Philosophy is not the whole of thought. When it thought this, it locked itself into its closure whose era is closed.

Inextricably mixed with non-thought, the thought that dominated under the name of philosophy, later called metaphysics, purported to account for what is and lost itself in this enterprise of accounting.

Philosophy has been, throughout its course, both a questioning and a justification of what is.

Philosophy and aphilosophy, problematic and aproblematic, confront each other and interpenetrate.

Philosophical thought is born from the play of the enigma for which life and death are at stake, and tries to pose the enigma of being, without daring to grasp it as a game. To formulate the supreme enigma, to which no one can answer, is that the game of supreme wisdom?

As for the exploration of the sources of philosophical thought, we have hardly advanced.

Philosophical thought – almost always torn between its poetic and prophetic tendency and its professorial, logical and scientific tendency – is made to distinguish three phases and levels in life and knowledge: first, a pre-philosophical mode, naive and mythological; second, a philosophical and scientific mode; third and finally, an absolute mode, somehow metaphilosophical, more or less positive, rather more than less, assuming negativity, marking an end and inaugurating a beginning.

The history of philosophy, in its ensemble and in its moments, which in flashes gives 'free' course to thought, is constantly left to rethink productively and await integration into a vaster history of thought. The thought which precedes, traverses and follows philosophy, at equal (?) distance from intuitive poetry, completed philosophy and conquering science and in dialogue with them, can begin again, and begin to think, by accepting its 'nongrasp' on the world governed by the technicised sciences and by tirelessly pursuing its questioning in the direction of the opening of a horizon. (This thought must not be confused with the various theories that amalgamate all sorts of contributions, with the different critiques, social, literary and otherwise, with the multiple discourses that only monetise it – insensible to its exigency and its rigour –, vulgarise it, or render it precious.) The technicised sciences which, emerging from philosophy, render effective the continuous end of philosophy and relay it, have to come up against their own successes and limits and will thus become perhaps a little more problematic, that is, thinking.

In the indistinction between the history of thought and the history of philosophy, the common understanding and the professorial understanding unroll the scroll: *oriental* thought or philosophy: thought dawns in the East – especially in India and China – and it then passes to the West to constitute *occidental* thought or philosophy which knows great epochs: the first of these 'epochs' bears the archaeological title of *ancient* thought or philosophy (Greek, Roman, Hellenistic) and goes from the Presocratic to the Neoplatonists. One does not know well where, how and when the second begins: with the Old Testament and the Jews, with the Gospels, with the Fathers of the Christian Church (Greek and Latin), with Saint Augustine? In any case this epoch is called *medieval* thought or philosophy and principally embraces occidental Christian thought, with some references to Byzantium, to Jews, to Islam. The third epoch is formed by *modern European* thought or philosophy that goes from the Renaissance to our days; to try to see a little more clearly what, before their eyes, is happening, historians call the very last episodes of this third epoch: *contemporary* thought or philosophy. So everyone is supposed to be found again and to find themselves again. Rare are those that suspect the irony of thought and its history.

The being of the world having been thought of as *physis-logos*, by the Greeks, as *god-logos*, by the Judaeo-Christians, as *subject*, by the Moderns, the thought of the planetary era is in search of a thought that would think the unitary and combined *play* of all 'that' in the direction of a play that would assume and exceed it.

Thought or rather philosophy is subdivided into 'disciplines': propaedeutic or ontological *logic*, formal, dialectical or formalised, theory of knowledge and science, methodology and epistemology; first or general philosophy, *metaphysics*, ontotheology: *theology*; *cosmology*; *anthropology*, pedagogy, ethics, psychology; *philosophy of history*, social and political philosophy, sociology; *poetics* and *aesthetics*. Rare are those who know how to read this articulation.

Entire centuries live on a great thought that they retell and contradict in developing it theoretically and practically.

The great thinkers of a certain tradition constitute through their march the history of philosophy; the history of ideas is a vulgarising version.

The system of the history of thought, even of the history of philosophy, cannot easily be established without reductive schematisations.

The nascent philosophy, born and accomplishing itself as a play of youth grappling with old age, as both leisure occupation and school exercise – *scholé* – unfolds itself in a mixed space composed of sacred elements, playful and pedantic systematisation. It succeeds mystical wisdom and the games of sophistry, namely prophetic, visionary and thaumaturgical, poetic and hieratic language, and rhetorical competition and emulation in the agonal play of antagonistic arguments. By succeeding the magician, the priest and the 'charlatan', the philosopher moves into the dimension of the enigma – the adversaries capture each other in a net of discourse – the play of questions and answers, of controversy, of dialectical play.

Philosophy is born in Greece, tied to pederasty. *Philia* and *eros*, which are coextensive with it, give birth, in a sort of tragic joy, to the children of thought and of humanity. A genesis and a youthfulness are united with a maturity at the gates of old age.

Homosexual – pederastic or lesbian – *eros* is also an instigator of the search for Being through being-with. Numerous are the great thinkers, great poets and great artists who were explicitly homosexual. The greatest woman-poet was lesbian. Rather numerous are the great religious types and great politicians and warriors who were implicitly homosexual.

Philosophy appears from the outset as stillborn; domineering and evanescent, since its Platonic foundation, it is the light of a shadow. When it speaks of reality, it is an ideally elaborated reality that is in question, according to a metaphysical model that puts to work the terrible spiritual power – and not only spiritual – of the negative, which then turns against the ontological wheel to reverse its movement. Materialism as a philosophical doctrine possesses its own truth and remains grounded by the same torture.

Metaphysical philosophy or ontotheology, that is to say, Platonism, its contradictors, its avatars and its reversals: sophistry, sensualism, empiricism, scepticism, and all that flows from the mainstream.

Idealism and materialism are the two streams of philosophy, that is to say, of idealism.

Even after the collapse of idealism and dualism, the reign of ideas and duality survives: ideas become pieces of ideology and ideals; all that, which is, remains at least double.

Philosophy existed in – and as – a vicious circle: it posited logos, thought, spirit, dialectic, at the start – reign of the beginning ruling the development – and it (re)found them at a certain end. Is it, however, only philosophy that succumbs circularly to this vice?

With Descartes and Pascal, the destiny of modern philosophy plays out right from its beginnings and before its consequent completion. Both try, grappling with Christian theology, to reconcile reason and faith, thought, science and religion, human subjectivity and divine transcendence. The first puts to work the reason of understanding that aims at the mastery and possession of (external) nature and (internal) human nature, and transforms doubt into certainty. The second puts into action the reason of the heart, listening to interiority, aspiring, too, to a beatific certainty. With Hegel and Kierkegaard this play is resumed, closing modern philosophy. The first wants to think in its totality the world-historical spirit, the second tries to make individual existence speak in its paradoxical particularity.

The motto of Descartes, herald of rationalist modernity, was *larvatus prodeo*.

All Pascal's research, the rearguard of theology and avant-garde of modern mysticism, aimed at *Deus absconditus*.

To see in Hegel only Christianity put into concepts and in Nietzsche a lamed Antichristianity is correct but denotes short-sightedness.

If philosophical thought had only been – at its high points – the consciousness that the culture of an epoch has of itself – as common sense and beautiful souls represent it – it would have been only the servant of cultural affairs, not to mention the fact that the consciousness that an epoch has of itself bathes in the *epochal* unconsciousness of withdrawal. It certainly comes historically *after* an epoch: 'As thought of the world, it only appears in time, after reality has accomplished its process of formation and has completed itself. What the concept teaches, history shows with the same necessity: it is only in the maturity of reality that the ideal appears before the real and after having grasped the same world in its substance reconstructs it in the form of an intellectual empire. When philosophy paints its grey in grey, then a form of life has aged and with this grey over grey it does not let itself be rejuvenated but only recognized. The owl of Minerva only takes flight at dusk' (Hegel). But at the same time, philosophy that thinks is an anticipatory thought that thinks *ahead*, not only what has been accomplished, but above all what will be accomplished, because prefigured. It is not for that 'prophetic', except in the sense that it speaks ahead. Hegel's philosophy is thus at the same time a completion and a thought – in advance – of what will unroll after it, under its aegis or against it. It continues to prefigure what 'thought' and 'reality' have yet to accomplish – even through the Marxist schema that wants to invert it.

For great philosophy, learning to die and learning to live are one. What it wasn't able to do: learn to play.

The great Greek and German idealistic systems – ontological and epistemological – have something definitive about them.

Alongside the great masters, mobilised by the great powers, there are the little masters, and to these geniuses and great talents are added, celebrating them, denigrating them and vulgarising them, the pack of scholars, journalists, professors. Not to mention epigones that operate eclectically in the survivals and variations, maintaining thus certain currents of tradition.

The professor of philosophy, the writer and the journalist are the servants of the unthinking and unthought thought that darkens into specialised and general culture.

The nineteenth century experienced the unfolding and collapse of German idealism and romanticism and the entrance into the epoch of anti-idealism with great thinkers. But the next century could not support this tension and this level, and engaged, without listening to some great voices or by banalising them immediately, on paths located on several levels lower and much flatter, fascinated by positivism and logical, psychological and sociological neo-positivism.

Since the historic-systematic completion of philosophy, in Hegel's system of knowledge, all thought (post-Hegelian) is reactive, while another style of thought seeks its way, a way that must not lead 'only' to a system of *knowledge*.

Every great thinker thinks – and misses – the sense of the totality of the world (which founds and exceeds the problem of the 'natural' and 'historical' world), and advancing a one- and multidimensional thought, deploys a range of major themes linked among themselves and referring to the central core of their vision, and breaks finally against their own conquest. Nietzsche's thought has a centre: *the death of God*, the murder of transcendent, spiritual and eternal significations, the reversal of the super-sensible and Christian world by temporal mortals, instruments of the *will to power* that aim to render humans masters of the planet, opens the way – after a long march through the desert of *nihilism* destined to spread – to the enigmatic *superhuman* (this Caesar with the soul of Jesus) knowing how to say yes to the *eternal return of the same* – so also to negativity – and daring to experience the *innocence of becoming*, since the world of non-total totality, being inseparable from nothingness, has no ground, 'is' play.

Academic philosophy, after a long period of silence, journalistic literature and political ideologies (of national socialism, democratic socialism and bureaucratic socialism) – all that Nietzsche loathed – seized upon it. By rendering it scholarly, literary, reactionary, progressive. The purpose of this was to put an end to disquieting interrogations, the putting in question. Nietzsche, however, will begin to be present to whoever will want and will be able to hear his voice saying that the answer to the fundamental *why* is lacking in the modern world – an era of the beginning, transition, exhaustion? – and cannot be granted technically or ideologically.

If Hegel marks the end of a very great stage of philosophy (infinitely more than occidental) and announces the overcoming of philosophy in favour of absolute knowledge, if Marx advocates the suppression of philosophy by its realisation in total technique and practice, Nietzsche, obsessed with Christianity, went to war against metaphysics – Platonic and especially Christian, Cartesian, Kantian, Hegelian, and against the world issued from it – even though motivated by it. His thought is much more than a reversal of Platonism-Christianity, which it also is. He radically questions the reality and thought of the Christian and modern world, world without thought and thought without world. He puts truth and error face to face, up to their fusion and confusion. He exposes the crisis of modernity thrown into a precarious and conquering march. Without any doubt, modernity, if not every epoch, is perpetually in crisis and in a state of passage. Nietzsche, with all his own misery and biographical naivety, deepens the crisis, renders it even

more serious and derisory, discovers the abysses, goes back to the foundations, interrogates the future. Beyond the crisis of the contemporary world –
bourgeois and socialist, individualist and collectivist – he preludes the crisis
of the *future world*.

Before the nineteenth century there were particular kinds of knowledge –
the sciences – that had to justify themselves before the systematics and
methodologies of speculative thought, that is to say of philosophy, to constitute and integrate themselves. Since then, it is thought that must justify
itself before the sciences – mathematics, physics, biochemistry, psychology,
sociology – that nevertheless depend on it, function with concepts borrowed
from it, but want to leave the cut soil from which they have grown. It is for
thought, therefore, to recover itself and put them back into question, that is
to say metaphilosophical thought which knows how to renounce a circular
and too harmoniously articulated system of the totality of knowledge.

On the basis of concepts elaborated by forgotten and/or parenthesised
philosophical thought, a terminological tower of Babel is erected, a conceptual confusion and imprecision that wish to operate with a vague precision,
babbling about the rigour of the concept, innocent of the problem of the
enlargement and fluidification of concepts, if not of their destruction.

Philosophical thought explodes and is expressed in the sciences:
logico-mathematical, physico-chemical, biological, psychologico-
sociological and historical. The world no longer needs it because it implicates it, whereas the sciences explicate it. And the sciences think less
than they operate. What formed the trunk and branches of philosophy –
ontological logic and the theory of knowledge, ontology (general metaphysics), theology, cosmology (philosophy of nature) and anthropology
(the three branches of *metaphysica specialis*), the latter as a psychology
and philosophy of history, ethics, poetics and aesthetics – all are taken
charge of and sublated by the various techno-scientific activities, which,
starting from them all – by taking their departure from them and leaving
them – bring them before the democratic-scientific tribunal that wants to
possess its own laws and judgements (without being free from prejudices).
Through – and throughout – this process there manifests the need for a
thought that is grounded and questioning, historical and systematic, flexible and firm, for a metaphilosophical thought that with rigour and vigour
interrogates all the logical, ethical, political, etc., criteria, both to show
their governmental character and to put them into question. And the

answers? Doesn't the very rhythm and style of an accepting and transgressive thought open a horizon to answers?

In philosophy, one can always advance a replica, pertinent or not.

All the theses and hypotheses, all the options and opinions, all the points of view and all *isms* – both theoretical and practical – are collected and prefigured in the history of philosophy, from which one takes them from time to time, combining them, updating them.

Thought – and even more philosophy – accommodates itself to the world as it is, far more than it puts it in question.

Has philosophy been the search for the first and ultimate reason, the attempt to account for it, the major totalisation? Was it not also worked up by untenable suspicion?

In its starry hours philosophy was also the *bad conscience* of its time.

'Philosophy reveals lacks, a decentred being, the expectation of an overcoming; it prepares, without necessitating and presupposing them, positive options. It is the negative of a certain positive, not some nondescript void . . . The negative has its positive, the positive its negative, and it is precisely because each has in itself its contrary that they are able to pass into each other and perpetually play in history the role of enemy brothers. Is it forever?' These thoughts of a good intelligence, why are they not radical enough?

The philosophy that wanted to be establishing and contestatory is now contested as justificatory.

Was the instrument par excellence of philosophy the concept, its fundamental function a tribunal pronouncing judgements, did its principal task consist in reasoning? It is reassuring to represent things like this, whether to praise or blame.

Law and philosophy manifest a latent and manifest agreement, interrogating, interpreting, judging, justifying, acquitting and condemning according to the rules of an almost common tribunal in which disagreements do not fail to erupt.

Philosophy walks on its head in the eyes of those who themselves walk on their heads, trusting themselves to naive consciousness. At the moment where the task is fixed: making it walk on its feet, it is already beheaded.

The death of philosophy was celebrated for a very long time, by philosophy institutionalising and ritualising itself, organising and technicising itself and by trying to bring back to it every thought that had already surpassed it. Thus 'philosophy' presents itself for today and tomorrow, in its dominant closure, next to the *history of philosophy*, as a combination of *logistics* and *epistemology*, of *psychoanalysis* (more or less Freudian) and *sociology* (more or less Marxist).

All the great philosophers wanted to inaugurate, found, begin to properly speak philosophy and put an end to it. Philosophy, like the Phoenix, was reborn from its ashes and recuperated even thoughts that were not properly its own. Will it continue to be so? Philosophy – essentially Platonic – thought – in the metaphysical or anti-metaphysical dimension – the whole of being, of becoming, of the world, in fixing its being, its foundation, its sense – logico-ontologically – as an absolute, leaving it nonetheless unthought and making of it a being. At the same time, it circumscribed the different domains of beings and opened the field to regional ontologies: nature, humanity, history, etc. Under the yoke of the true, the good and the beautiful, configurations of the unitary and signifying absolute, philosophy lived until Hegel, who historically and systematically reprised its realisations, its principles, its possibilities. Then, through the efforts to reverse Platonic, Christian and Hegelian philosophy – Marx, Nietzsche – and despite the epigonal uprisings, the brilliant, talented or vulgarly professorial attempts, we entered the terminal stage, the continuing death, the continued end, the non-perfect completion of philosophy. What passage is then effectuated and imposes itself on us? What passes with philosophy? Firstly, philosophy is gathered into the *history of philosophy* that we constantly have to take up again to disengage in it what had been thought and left unthought. Secondly, a horizon opens to the *thought* that precedes, traverses and follows philosophy, a thought that is differently open, adventurous and rigorous, that no longer justifies the world, but questions it. Thirdly, philosophy breaks out in *technicised sciences, in scientific techniques*, made possible by it, but that deny the philosophy which is at their base without being able to totally reject it. These three aspects of a single passage offer themselves as a decomposition and an assembly and do not exclude overlaps and interpenetrations. Philosophical thought takes shelter in the history of philosophy, gives birth to a metaphilosophical thought that restores the juncture with pre-philosophic thought, generates the – logical, linguistic, logistical, semantic, physico-mathematic, biochemical, anthropological, psychological, historical, sociological and cultural – sciences-and-techniques that take it over. The love of wisdom does not become absolute knowledge, as Hegel claimed, but structural and effective knowledge and power. It is above all the human sciences that take charge of this succession, that is to say the sciences and the techniques of the human, who leaves for the technical and scientific conquest of their natural and social milieu, of the universe and of the place occupied by the human, who collectively wants to govern all according to the science of government or cybernetics. Thus, humanity, whose being and becoming reside in a social and socialising activity – theoretical and practical – although crushed by the production that produces it and that it produces, remains, if not ontologically, at least anthropologically and methodologically, the decentred centre of the sciences and human sciences that also prepare its overcoming.

The putting into question of metaphysical philosophy poses the problem of the thought that succeeds metaphysics, the problem of the succession of philosophy, the problem of what exceeds it. If pre-philosophy and philosophy thought being in the dimension of *eternity*, on metaphilosophy is imposed the play of *time*.

Its children and its close relatives progressively abandon philosophy: first mathematics and the natural sciences, next the human sciences, psychology and sociology, and, finally, logic (mathematics). Of its old organism only the history of philosophy subsists – that ever more scientificises and technicises itself – and the remains of general philosophy, to which must be added the philosophy of this or that domain: politics, morals, art, etc.

The language of philosophy also perpetuates itself in foreign lands.

To lead back to philosophy (metaphysics) the attempts that attempt to escape it or that forget that they arise from it.

Metaphysics escapes both the cut and the continuity between the so-called banal life and the so-called superior life.

To unite the contribution of metaphysics and the contribution of anti-metaphysics is a programmatic task to accomplish.

Metaphysics still governs where one pretends to surpass it; the most outrageous tendencies aiming at transgression still relate to it; it reigns in a rather inapparent manner over what wishes to exceed and succeed it; it is necessary to know how to bring back to it what believes itself to be escaping it. Philosophy, in exiting itself, effecting an exit outside itself, still remains determining in its (alleged) heirs and successors. The outside of metaphysical philosophy or ontotheology roughly repeats its inside.

Throughout all the extraordinarily long reign of the succession of metaphysics, it cannot be a question of returning to something less than metaphysics.

Metaphysics sacrifices physical life, people always say. As if physical life could do without it.

The suspicion is persistent: is metaphysics part of the physis of the human?

To what extent is metaphysics, posing the real as the sensible, and ideality and the ideal as the non-sensible (the supersensible), and provoking all the anti-metaphysical turnarounds and reversals, part of the nature – of the physis – of the human, since it is also in human nature to change this nature and thus to deny metaphysical negation?

Actuality no longer knows where to go: resume and relearn the classics or promote its own modernity?

Surpassing of philosophy (= metaphysics) signifies above all a productive recovery of the thought of the great thinkers, a profound 'comprehension' of their thought (because we treat them with an arrogance that is matched only by our inability to surpass them).

Metaphilosophical thought tries to engage in dialogue with prephilosophic thought, while listening to philosophical symphonies.

Also the surpassing of philosophy-metaphysics remains highly problematic. It is not about surpassing the gains but, at most, about the effort aiming for the surpassing of the metaphysical mode of thinking.

If art intuits, religion represents, philosophy conceptualises – which is already not so certain – science operates, constructs, connects, decomposes, scaffolds, what, in any case, it does effectively.

Between thought and knowledge, science and consciousness, bridges are thrown and abysses lie. One cannot pass these by walking but by jumping – and by breaking one's neck.

Knowledge, critique and science techno-scientifically replace religion and philosophy, wanting to monopolise the One-All and the One-Multiple, accomplishing glorious conquests and wishing their praises always to be sung louder and more often.

Science is based on the metaphysical and anti-metaphysical faith of Platonism, Christianity and their reversals: it believes in the truth that, from the divine, has become human.

It was only on the basis of Greek philosophy and Christian theology that science could be built.

Not less than philosophy, and even more, since it already implies it, 'the' science draws a good part of its directing schemas and evidence from religious and theological myths that constitute its implicit underpinnings.

So the sciences continue to speak the language of metaphysics even when they pretend to overflow and overstep it.

There is no science: there are particular sciences and a scientific approach characterised by its language, its theory, its methodology and its ideology – always unilateral, particular and partial, even when totalising and totalitarian. When someone affirms to you: it's scientific, retort: relative to what science?

Each science delimits a field, traces its method, fixes its objective (and not its object) and its aim, on the basis of a segmentation previously worked out by thought. So 'it constitutes itself as a perspective and operation' on and above all in the world, not grasping the world, but an aspect of all that is. Even the ensemble of sciences does not grasp the world in its ensemble. The hidden resource, and now making itself visible, of science is technique, which manages to upset the world from top to bottom – from mathematical technique to the technique of the imaginary.

The sciences do not elucidate their (philosophical) presuppositions, the content of their concepts, nor even their operative approaches.

Science and the sciences only do business – in a delimited field and with relatively precise aims – with relationships. Highly problematic, even in their constraining experiments.

The sciences refer always to a tomorrow.

Science – the product of the will to science – lives in incessant incompleteness.

In turns, and often competing with others, one knowledge pretends itself science of sciences.

Everything has already become the material of science: the sciences of nature and/or the sciences called human.

Much stronger than science, its research and its results, is the scientific – techno-scientific – method, which dominates the sciences and not only the sciences.

Science, that is, its attempt and temptation to scientific explanation, dangerously brushes, that is to say plainly, against scientism.

The methodological properness of the sciences – their methodological properties – means they cannot pose questions which overstep their jurisdiction, not being their responsibility.

In science, questioning necessarily stops within the limits of scientific activity, which therefore blocks the incessant interrogation in the name of better answering its limited fields of questions. The ensemble of the sciences does not know anymore what to make of problems that it can neither pose nor solve. The scientific constellation remains partial and partisan.

The theory of science is not itself scientific.

Science must also be, if not principally, comprehended in the manner it comprehends itself, that is to say, less according to what it is than according to what it believes itself to be. It presents itself as . . .; we must therefore also take it for what it presents itself as.

Science is a manner that becomes more and more decisive, in which all that, which is, presents itself, is provoked and transformed – scientifically. From Greek and occidental, European and modern, it becomes planetary.

Scientific rigour fails to suspect the rigour of thought and the content of the non-concept of rigour.

Thought can only ever learn to think again in the midst of the sciences, without mistaking itself in them and without despising them, without contempt for its own task, and without letting itself be intimidated by the contempt shown it.

As there is a thought that precedes science, which opens horizons and fields to it, there is a thought that comes after science.

Progressive, victorious, conquering, glorious science also nourishes thought.

There was the time of *magic*, *myths* and *mythology*, there was the time of *religion*, great *art* and *philosophy*, there was the time of *politics*. All these powers are still active. The course of time – the course being only the most grossly visible aspect of time – leads us however to the era of *technics*, in which our world enters belatedly and with difficulty.

Everything seems henceforth to require a technical, particular and general solution. In everything, there is technical progress to be made.

Is technics something like thought solidified-yet-fluid, or does it intimately inhabit thought itself? Do we interpret technical production reflexively or productive thought technically? What kind of play connects thought and technics?

Technics is almost ready to replace politics; at most, politics still proposes, while technics disposes. Technics is getting ready to administer the globe, to promote and manage the world economy in the framework of a capitalo-socialism of State and bureaucratic collectivism, in the name of moralism and in a generalised petit-bourgeois and planned style. The difference between democracy and autocracy is becoming more and more inexistent in totalitarian democracy, as are many other differences. What will happen next? Let us look first at what is happening before our eyes.

Technics far surpasses every instrumentalism and every technicism, even technicity.

More than an instrument of the human marching towards the mastery of the world, technics makes the human the instrument of a process which is expressed through technical and technological development.

If humans let themselves be dominated by the play of technics and techniques – the techniques of technics and the technics of techniques – they could then back up to take a better jump.

Within the techno-scientific set-up that seizes the world, there is no longer the sovereign good, nor even the happiness of humanity, its well-being and comfort. Humans have and will have to live and die without comprehending what is happening, why it is happening, how it is happening.

Are accidents in the world of technics not destined to multiply? The peaceful more so than the warfaring. How important, for example, are a few thousand deaths around the world during peaceful car trips on weekends? How could it be that auto- and hetero-mobiles not also transport death?

Dominance henceforth belongs to – theoretical and practical – *techno-scientific* activity (which carries out the fusion of science and technics under the impulsion of technics) and to *technocratic* and *techno-bureaucratic* power (which carries out the fusion of economy, administration and politics under the impulsion of technics).

If the struggle for the technical domination of the world can take place in the name of doctrines of philosophical origin, this is due to the fact that philosophy, extinct, had already, with infirmity, named what comes.

By logos becoming technics, logic becomes technics, cosmology cosmo-technics, biology biotechnics, psychology and sociology psychotechnics and sociotechnics. And technology?

The technics of the imaginary are also technics of usage.

Technology and ideology are enemies and allies. The era of triumphant technology corresponds to militant and suffering ideology.

Thought, theory, consciousness and knowledge contain ideological elements, that is to say camouflaging and non-revealing, which reverse the relationships of force rather than render them transparent. Nevertheless, any critique, which denounces the ideology in the other, also itself contains as many ideological elements and does not make its principles, its starting points and its aims explicit. In its turn, reversed reversal, it succumbs to thought.

It is the titles, uncontrollable appellations, *isms* and slogans that today form the fabric of ideologies and worldviews. Intellectuals are their dealers.

Contestatory ideology is now englobed in certifying and dominant ideology.

Science and technics are not exempt from ideology. Their rationality, even their rationalisations, denote the connection between knowledges and transformative practices, pressures and dominant interests.

With technics seizing everything, will it also seize its putting-into-question, by technically reducing it to silence or making it speak only technically?

Unhinged machines reveal a part of the horizon.

For the moment, the stopping of techno-scientific development is not foreseeable.

The metatechnological zone is still far from opening up to us.

The priest and the artist, the politician and the philosopher, the scientist and the technician are the servants of the great powers, ruling – and ruled by – those who speak and think, work, love and die, struggle and play.

In saying of religion – whether brought back to the *religare* or to the *religere* – that it is extended towards the divine, and that cult, prayer and sacrifice are the signs of this tension, in saying that poetry speaks of the world, life, love, combat and death, in saying that art represents in a perceptible manner what is presented to it, in saying of politics that it consists in the government of humans and things, in saying that philosophy was the thinking search for being, in saying that technics grasps and transforms what is, in saying all this and by putting all these sayings into communication, we have still hardly said anything.

What matters is not the religion but the problem of the sacred. It is the voice and the silence, the light and the shadow of beings that are more important than poetry and art. What matters is not politics but the historical destiny – or the metahistorical play – of humans. It is thinking utterance that is more important than philosophy.

The great powers fix the errancy of the world and propose the rules of the game, construct dwellings and edify works, consolidate institutions and build worlds, traversed and shaken by the elementary forces that channel and overflow them. Families and cult games, Churches and works of art, States and parties, Universities and techno-scientific set-ups are the forts that mark out the maze of the world and succumb to their weaknesses, while the human travels the labyrinth of the game, seeking forms and norms to be able to pose and repose, adhering to them and taking off; every maximal approximation complying to the greatest common denominator and none-theless remaining allusive.

Violence is the removable spring of great powers.

The genius being 'all' world, they let themselves be penetrated by the human – even the too human – and connect the world and the human and not the human and the world. They thus grasp the world in the dimensions of logos and of being in becoming, the divine and the cosmic, the human and the historical, the poetic and the artistic, in all that transgresses these dimensions.

Hidden in the 'depths', another ingenuity can be at work and open and propagate what opens to it. This ingenuity, of a reckless modesty, unable to be situated within or beyond established openings, would not lead to directly vis-ible works. There are – among others – inspiring geniuses, who themselves put 'nothing' 'into work', but rather set in motion those who will put into work.

The most brutal and vociferous ingenuity never ceases to implicate the silence of the unspeakable.

Relating apparently distant reference points is what is proper to the productive genius.

The genius comes to suspect that totality is not totality nor fragments fragments; being becomes evasive without nothingness becoming a point of support.

Ingenuity relates what would remain separated without it (at the level of the said).

Grasping prophetically the past, living the contemporaneity of what has been and continues to be, existing in the present and being caught by the future, letting oneself carry and be carried away by this movement that grabs the attention and feeds the tension, finding oneself precipitated into the break: all this supreme effort of donation and abandoning is in no way bearable for effective talents or for humans who are only out of the ordinary.

For humans to be able to say and to do something great, there must be a greatness and misery to what interpellates and affects them vitally and mortally. What corresponds to this call must be for them a question of life or death. When they cannot say and do otherwise, their winged freedom coincides with levelling necessity. Every genius is striking because thunderstruck.

To upset and illuminate the average, the mediocrity and the greyness, the honourable and dull successes, beautiful accomplishments and bloodless conformisms, to darken the superficial illuminations, usual and gloomy or flashy and brilliant – that is one of the tasks of the genius. Why, however, is every poetic – namely, creative – genius profoundly sad?

We speak of 'great humans', of famous humans whose glory indicates a permanence in time. Their own being is part of the historical becoming of humanity of which they are the summits. Every great human is either a great human of religion, or a great artist, or a great politician, or a great thinker, or great sage. Are there other great ones? Who would not be captured by one of these grandeurs? Who would convey what? Can the movement of saying and doing be expressed brilliantly without going through major mediations? Is there a totally great human, that is to say, being of the opening and not of one of the openings?

The great powers and the elemental forces return to the – double? single? – play of *myth*, of *logos*, of *theoria*, of *speech*, of *thought*, and of poetic and creative *praxis*, of *action*, of *production*; they return to the play of *saying* and *thinking* (logos) and of *making* and *doing* (praxis) that pass into one another, all theorising and all activity being speaking and active, the saying and the doing forming the modalities of all language and all production; the saying-and-doing of the great powers seems to return to the great power of the play of technics – theoretical and practical.

If the great powers emerge more and more from the power of technics, the elemental forces which command them emerge from the play of the human – for which technique is only the dominant constellation – which itself emerges from the play of the world.

The great powers, returned to *saying* and *thinking* and to *making* and *doing* of the play of technics, join again the elementary forces – still more powerful – from which they derive and that, also, reside in a *saying* and a *doing*, returning to the polymorphic play through which the play of the world unfolds among humans.

Elemental forces and great powers do not stay immobile. They moult.

The great founding powers rely on the *elemental forces* that they express, organise, channel and regulate. Elemental forces, much more primordial than the great powers, are called:
language and *thought*,
work and *struggle*,
love and *death*,
play.

They reveal and shape – equally shaped by it – the being in becoming of the fragmentary and fragmented totality of the multidimensional and open world, whose most fundamental approaches and major approximations they form. Each of them is tied to all the others and illuminates them, integrates them, penetrates them. Each of them may appear to englobe the others, which it *also* does, in making itself equally englobed, but none of them, separated from others, although necessary, is sufficient to constitute the play of the human and the world, which makes them appear and that they make appear.

Each of the great powers and elemental forces maintains a decisive rela-tionship with *all* the others, and concerns all that is, in its parts and its whole. All together form a multiple unity – in various positions. Because they need one another.

Great powers and elemental forces demand to be studied for themselves and with reference to what they themselves are not.

Each of the great powers and elemental forces of the world served as a model to form conceptions – or visions – of the world.

Although overdetermined by the great powers, elemental forces – themselves decomposable? – animate them and make them explode.

The great powers manifest themselves either by their presence or by their absence, that is to say, by the combined play of presence and absence. The elemental forces of the world that work them – and of which they constitute the elaborations – seem to need these major mediations. The human is a being of mediation. The great powers artic- ulate the being of the human on the being of the world, while 'alien- ating' both the being of the human and 'Being'. The elementary forces accord with the great cosmic rhythms, model human actions, passions and omissions, are modelled by historical, social and cultural structures, become the play of language and action, in the play of this discordant accord.

Who posted the posts?

Elemental forces are based on links and ruptures.

Undoubtedly less composite than the great powers, the elementary forces are nevertheless not in a bare state: mediated, they enclose us in their system of mediations.

All the great powers reduce language, thought and writing, work and struggle, love and death, and especially play.

Is language the driving force of thought?

We speak the language that speaks us.

Words work: on whose account?

Words guide the thought that guides them.

Language is almost the possibility, always limited, through which the totality, unlimited and unspeakable, speaks fragmentarily.

Language speaks. It speaks us. We speak it.

Language already thinks in itself and through itself. Then we think – it – it that thinks us and passes us by, that is to say we think in itself and through itself, without being able to pass it by. This does not solve the problem of thought and – or 'and' – language, identical and not identical, in any case said and thought in the same language.

It is the play of the structured ensemble that, out of phonic elements, makes words.

Words are said in a proper sense and a figurative sense. What obliteration do they know at the times when they are about to decline figures?

One has first to learn to read and to speak in a language that one will have to forget.

One can think of one thing and say another. Who then realises this non-coincidence? Its individual bearer?

One does not necessarily think thoughts at the moment one speaks them.

Anyone who tries to think and say the strength and weakness of speech and of thought succumbs to the same power and impotence.

Between spoken language and written language lies a profound difference. Although both obey specific structures, words, syntagms and rhythms remain different. Would it be possible to write as one speaks and speak as one writes? If spoken language is rather spontaneous and flowing, is not written language more concentrated and elaborated? In any case, the difference between the two languages does not cease to be a problem, a problem that encounters and overlaps with that which concerns the language of the everyday and of everyone and the highly articulated language of great moments. Here too – despite and with all the attempts of juncture – is the fault insurmountable? For even pre-philosophic and metaphilosophic language, language which does not separate in a trenchant manner thought and poetry, remains separated from everyday and trivial language that its great spokespeople themselves speak in everyday life.

The verb can go so far as to recognise and say the devaluation of the verb.

There is hardly any full discourse; in every discourse there are voids.

Language is, in the strong sense of the term, limiting and hierarchical.

It is only by pursuing a discourse and an experience for a long time that one has a chance of success. Indeed.

Speech transforms into a legend all that it transmits and without which it would not exist.

More important than speech and actions, inhabiting them, revealing and hiding them, gestures remain. Learn – as far as possible – to control them – yours and those of others.

What complicity connects conjuring, knowing, calling, engendering, in the course of rounds of hide-and-seek and brilliant successes that burst under our noses?

What to do with the anodyne saying that comes in floods, what to do when beings have nothing more to say to each other and with moments when there is nothing more to say?

Often words resound in a world without an echo.

Is it the discourse or the violence that separates and unites discourse and violence?

How often do we speak and act with an almost perfect somnambulant assurance, which passes by the disquieting abyss and troubling problems?

Speech *seems* to pass from the adult and mature man, individual, white, conscious (or supposed to be), sane, civilised, and more or less linked to the dominant classes, to the proletarians (or ex-proletarians), to the peoples of colour, to the colonised and dominated (or ex-), to the masses, to children and adolescents, to women, to the unconscious, to the neurotics and the insane of all kinds (psychically, mentally, racially, ethnically, religiously, socially). Thanks to this dialectical *reversal*, as they say, those who have not yet spoken speak and enter *into action*. Is it however speech they take, from where and from whom do they *take* it and to say *what*, in the theoretical and practical mixture that is in the process of universalising itself?

The place of the word and thought, where is it? It is not the school or the university – it once was – it is only very partially the book and writing. The language of thought pursues its non-topological march.

It is in the labyrinth of the world and in the maze of language that the enigma arises, the word of the oracle and initiatory ordeal at its origins, rites of passage, pronounced to be divine and requiring divination, speculative problem and then philosophical question, innocuous board game and proof of aptitude for exams at last.

Did the Sphinx that grasps not already know that there is no word for the riddle?

Often that which presents itself at first sight as a riddle, is not one.

Does the riddle find its transient solution in a flash or short circuit of thought?

The word of the riddle found, interrogator and interrogated imagine themselves no longer enchained by the question, having posed the question and replied according to the rules of the game. Because it was not the game itself that was in question.

The solution of riddles becomes enigmatic again.

Who poses the questions? Who answers? In the tremor of indecision appears the 'fundamental' and 'superficial' ambiguity of what breaks itself and breaks us, poses and imposes itself, leaving death unexplained.

The thought that poses questions should all the same also propose answers. Undoubtedly. However, without isolating them from each other.

If all certainties refer to interrogations, all the interrogations refer to certainties.

Thinking poses questions and proposes responses. These correspond to and miss each other. Thought concludes and opens. Each thought, confined equally in a present. Words and sense are filling and emptying, convincing or not. Words can change sense and their senses say otherwise. In the round. Partial significations are imposed and collapse; the signification of the whole, although often proposed, no longer imposes itself. This does not prevent the whole, strangely connected to its parts, from subsisting and wishing to continue. If a thought appears to you too questioning and interrogative, call for another, more affirmative and positive – and vice versa.

Thought is interrogative and questioning, because it is put in motion and into question by that of which it is the thought.

To great questions correspond questioning answers.

Humans encounter great questions by trying to avoid them or by believing them soluble.

Many problems depend on a previous question. Every question and every problem encompass in their fullness the ensemble of the problematic. They pose themselves each time as the ensemble itself.

Most often the answers precede the questions. Neither the question nor the answer has an absolute beginning; each drifts, by successive differentiations and thanks to leaps, from earlier questions and answers; step by step and with the help of mediations, we go back to the enigmatic start that we know – or suspect – only through the development by which it took place.

On the fields of language and thought there are quite a few questions without answers and answers without questions.

Often the answer has a different content than the question.

Humans suppress problems rather than resolve them (when problems do not suppress their bearers).

Does putting into question and into action not also signify putting into peril?

Yet the contestation is far from being ineffective. Because the interrogation – the putting into question – can combine itself with the putting into action.

The putting into question is both forward-looking and precocious, conclusive and tardy. It arises too soon and everything seems to postpone it until much later. The usual answers do everything to avoid it.

The putting into question must not be separated from the putting into action. The doubt, the uncertainty, the fluidity and the contestation of one are not so far from the certainty, the fixity and the construction of the other. Rivals, they are each the condition of the other.

What answers can be offered to children, the young, crowds, trapped in crepuscular questions and opening interrogations?

How far can humans push the power of interrogation?

For everyone to verify: before every burning problem everyone flees.

Most great problems are cancelled and bypassed, pass into other problems, without being resolved.

It often appears that *the* answer (by the way impossible) is not even desired.

Demanding the other make demands.

One never questions radically enough. It is only later that one remembers the questions that one should have asked at the time. This moreover concerns not just questions.

Certain apparently stupid questions are often the best.

Let's learn to pose questions coming from an unexpected horizon and on a terrain that discomforts what or whom is questioned. Let's practise questioning on all terrains.

Advance in life by advancing affirmations that implicate questions. Stepping back towards the answers to jump better.

Most often solving the problems and the difficulties consists in making them disappear, revoking them.

Frequently the questioner is put into question by the questioned.

Undoubtedly the habit of asking questions may very well be lost.

Trigger the counter-questions following the questions.

The human doesn't like too often to ask why, nor too often to give answers. It wants both to calm and to excite itself.

Being cured from the question, no longer seeking the absolute, this is not easy, because it is impossible to forget.

Don't *settle* into questioning, interrogation, don't make the problematic and problematisation a kind of absolute principle.

Putting into question even basic principles does not stop being troubling, disturbing. This is why this provocation never goes far enough.

What follows the putting into question?

Thought – that is not necessarily arid – likes to lean on a more passionate youth and beauty.

Passing through a school is inevitable, 'therefore' desirable.

'Wisdom' gives the impression of seeking youth, youth seeking to be educated by what it imagines to be wisdom.

There are always several apprenticeships to do and redo and return to the point. There are also a lot of things to constantly unlearn.

Learning to learn is a late acquisition. Learning to teach is unfortunately not done in the ardour of youth, but in the renunciation of maturity.

Students will become teachers to educate, as they say, other students, who, in turn, will become teachers. The teachers who were students educate students aspiring to become teachers. Whoever administers to the other a teaching – due to administering it or due to the teaching? – sows among those that it fecundates and to those it bears violence an ironic contempt that does not always come to light.

By what means can one meet a formative master in this polycentrism of the explosion that dissimulates its unity?

The master questions and formulates responses. The student demands and waits for responses. They can in their turn become a master when they learn to pose questions.

Teachers should be able to self-criticise their relationships with those being taught.

The master can only learn to also disappoint their student.

That the disciple leaves the master must be foreseen by the latter.

At certain times and in certain places, thought settled into propitious places. The Presocratics grouped around them students and disciples, but none of them formed a school: in the shadow of temples or at the heart of the city they spoke their thoughts. The sophists, the first who sold thoughts as masters of thinking and acting, dispensed their teaching in the midst of the agora; their place remained open. Socrates disdained teaching and writing and, interrogated by his demon, he interrogated. Plato and Aristotle inaugurate the era of philosophy and are the first and most brilliant teachers of philosophy, founding schools, the first schools of thought. A long history begins with the Academy and the Lyceum, where total knowledge is organised on the basis of philosophy, ramifying into *logic, physics, ethics* (and *politics*). Nevertheless, in all Greek thought – including Scepticism, Stoicism, Epicureanism, Neoplatonism – the polis remained the place of thought, the place where being in becoming (πέλειν) goes, the place of the gathering of the thinkers and the poets, priests and politicians, artists and athletes, hetaerae and ephebes. The polis, however, turned towards the Empire and cosmopolitanism: teachers and writers succeed the thinkers. Until the theologians, mystics and doctors of the Church emerge. Christian and medieval thought develops within the place formed by cloisters, places of religious communities. From this situation universities gradually develop. The university is and remains – until further notice – a medieval edifice: an edifice embracing in knowledge the whole pyramid – the sum – of knowledge and of the being; this knowledge is universal and ramified. *Theology, art, law, medicine* grow like advancing branches, ready to become autonomous. In the pyramid of the existent in its totality and located in the light of God-Being, to the theological summa, to the cathedrals and to the *Divina Comedia* the *Universitas* corresponds. Nascent European modernity (renaissance, one says, without knowing of what) had nothing to do at the beginning with scholastic universities, bastions of what it wanted to take by storm, even though it still moved on the same rails. The first thinkers of this third epoch are quite simply thinkers and not professors or doctors. They explore the world, established or wandering. This goes on until the French Revolution, which finally took by storm, in a certain way, what it wanted, what it could take with its own badly chipped forces. The bastion taken, the 'medieval' tradition of the university was resumed, and the universities – secular – shone – some of them – in brand new and worldly brightness. A new universality embedded in the old began. Philosophy became again – albeit differently – a matter of teaching, the foundation of all teachings: it affirmed itself as total knowledge, encyclopaedia, critical system. During the eighteenth and nineteenth centuries, philosophical thought found in universities its place and its formula – although it did not lack for mavericks – in those schools which linked masters to students. Almost the whole movement we so flatly call German idealism organically inhabited the universities as places of the universal and meditated more and more on the nature of the academic institution. The fall of this empire of spirit rendered many things problematic and displaced centres. Hegel, who had already understood himself as the last philosopher, conceiving his philosophy – historical and systematic – as the – historical and systematic – culmination of philosophy, is akin to Plato and remains the last great philosopher professor of philosophy, by closing – as the Aristotle of the modern world – a great epoch. Those who succeeded Hegel turned away from the emptied universities: Marx, Kierkegaard, Nietzsche . . . Universities continue however to exist, bourgeois or socialist, in the Occident and in the Orient, and more are ceaselessly being created. All these universities dispense thought and culture, cultivate language and literature, study history, the sciences, the arts and techniques. They form the future elites of countries – of all countries. No one can ignore them and they do not want to ignore anything, assimilating their opponents. From them all teachings depart, towards them all information converges. Each in its 'totality' organises into a system – quite decentred – the totality of knowledge, by erecting the historical course and the encyclopaedic edifice. However, unity is lacking, and the universe of the universality can no longer be built as sum by universities. Philosophy is still taught in these universities until its different 'disciplines' leave its corpus by making themselves autonomous. The current university – factory and cemetery – seems (still?) unavoidable. It is the school and the university that make young people fit to earn their living, theoretically or practically. The university, by falling under the juris-diction of technics, functions technically, operates technically, produces technicians of all kinds. There is no doubt that thought still circulates in universities – in privileged moments and places – but thought no longer feels at ease, and thinkers, those displaced (ἄτοποι) par excellence, are no longer at their place in the *alma mater*, without being elsewhere. Deprived of high places, must they think everywhere and nowhere, for everybody and nobody? Or have they even lost their consistency as displaced beings, in the places and during the hours that do more than trouble the bonds of 'inside' and 'outside'? Insults and curses, polemics or sighs of dissatisfaction, con-formisms, compromises and reforms can do nothing to solve the problem since they do not even pose it. It remains, however, posed. Nothing pre-vents us from dreaming of other forms of communities or colleges, schools or institutes, where masters would confront students. What would their practical and public utility be? A question that poses itself, if these insti-tutions cannot be satisfied with setting up chapels or retreats. This dream apparently does not unblock. But dreams follow their course. If thinkers are not simply employees of the universal, enlightened or amateurs, they could tend towards a 'place' – a place of questioning and problematic teaching – without fear and without cowardice, without aggressiveness and without pusillanimity, without wanting to replace or imitate the other schools. A place that would be extremely attentive to the noise and fury of the powers of the world without succumbing: is such a place something else and more than an unrealisable dream, struck with inanity? For the moment, and not only for the moment, thinkers stand up as topologists of the non-place.

Life and thought: each perpetuates and kills the other.

Thinking, isn't it like holding oneself back from living? However, there is hardly human life without thought.

The inequality of what is lived and said and thought makes reconciliation difficult.

Do not look for agreements and disagreements between writings and lives. This is inappropriate and you will be blamed.

The application of theories, their uptake in life as assumed and lived theories, constitutes a highly problematic task. Can one speak and think, act and write unconsciously and on purpose at the same time?

Living one's thoughts and thinking one's life does not come by itself. Extremely rare are the thinkers who live their thoughts and people who think their lives.

Thinking the most profound, loving the most living, is yet another way of manifesting the differentiated unity of thought and being.

The verb is also an action, the logos is also praxis, the verb is the action word. And all action is passion.

The different pieces of the planetary play – the play of the world – cannot be thought by detached thoughts but by thoughts attached to what gives thinking – even if the theoretical status of speculative and theoretical 'discourse', non-formalisable and non-conceptual, cannot be fixed for the moment – what gives thinking nevertheless remaining the least thought, if not the unthought.

Every experience contains thought and all thought experience. Nothing comes only from experience or only from thought. The same goes for theory and practice, and does not go differently for logos and praxis, speech and action, saying and doing. Nevertheless the problem remains whole, although or because it is already cut in two. The two constituents of the totality are neither one nor two; and one and the other, neither one nor the other, succeed in constituting themselves and constituting their co-belonging. The very distinction between theory and practice, logos and praxis, entangled with poiesis and techné, does it derive from theory or practice or above all from a technical interpretation of theory and practice? Is it about abolishing the distinction between theory and practice – by surpassing it, of course – theoretically, practically, in theory, in practice or on another neutral terrain, at once single and double, on which one advances hesitantly? Usually, one juggles very skilfully with the concepts (?) of theory and practice, with all their possible combinations, their unity and their differences. Holes, breaks, inadequacies and incoherencies however do not cease to manifest themselves – theoretically and practically – in the interference of the 'empirical' and the sensible and the 'transcendental' and the intelligible. For it is in the light of the intelligible and the transcendental that the sensible and the empirical appear, fall into sense, enter into the meanderings of sense, and it is in the course of an empirical and sensible progress that the transcendental and the intelligible are developed and fall apart.

The relationships – in whatever manner one establishes them – between the *theoretical* and the *practical* are extremely embarrassing. Do both – their unity and their separation – have a common root – which? – that determines them together much more than each of them determines the other?

Is it possible not to sacrifice the *vita contemplativa* to the *vita activa*, nor to flee from the one to the other, but to participate in both, each requiring nonetheless a specific, if not exclusive, orientation?

Sometimes the theory is adjusted to account for facts, sometimes the facts are fiddled with to justify the theory. Thus, without distinguishing the various plans, it is quite easy to be right, either at the 'right' moment, or, as is the most frequent case, too early or too late, in the multiple prospectives and retrospectives. Regarding an article in the *New York Tribune*, Marx wrote to Engels on 15 August 1857: 'Perhaps I rendered myself ridiculous. But one can always get away with a little dialectics. Naturally, I have presented my opinions in such a way that, even if things turn out differently, I will be right.'

Practicism is only the completion of logicism.

Can the thought and activity of humans rigorously assemble, with knowledge and know-how, all the combinatorial possibilities whose realisation is offered to theory and practice?

Who most misrecognised the aforementioned concrete reality? The theorist or the practitioner?

To speak and to act requires that we privilege only certain aspects.

Doing the thing and its theory requires two different times.

Very often the force of a thought, of an action, resides in its advance in a single direction.

Every action comprises its corresponding omissions.

Action presupposes a stubborn, limited and certain will, with the minimum of humour and distance, a compact adherence. The moment of action seizes all forces and silences all oppositions, striving towards its goal that, once approximately reached, will reveal the weaknesses of the action, already revealed in the eyes of a clairvoyant thought.

Consciousness – a certain consciousness in any case, even if strongly tinged with unconsciousness and ideology – is necessary for action. A slightly too full consciousness risks being paralysing at the decisive moment.

Humans and societies detest applying their theories to their practices, to explore somewhat the full play of contradictions inherent in their theories, their practices and even more so the relationship between the two. They detest even more applying to themselves the irony they exert towards others. Even when they recognise this, they do not practise it and denounce as a scandal those who strive for this exploration and denunciation.

To reach an end, if not its end, action unfolds with more violence than elegance, and it mobilises a certain fanaticism to thwart, during the heated hours, any questioning that surpasses urgent tasks.

There is not on one side logos, thought, language, poetry, theory, sight, hearing, knowledge and, on the other, praxis, action, touching, production. We can say at the most that these are two streams deriving from the same source and flowing into the same ocean. The problematic unity – and not the identity in the indifferentiation – of *saying* and *doing* has nothing to do with all the words – how derivative! – that speak the language of spiritualism or materialism, idealism or realism. The conquest of the earth and the march to the stars, the terrible and often almost silent action of speech and the power of creativity manifest this poetically productive unity, at the heart of which prosaic forces do not cease to surge.

Is every theory grey compared to the verdant tree of life? Does this colouration concern the forest itself, where life and theory intertwine, both bushy, and, against a ground of greyness, joyous with lightning?

The logos does not prescribe us to say: Ἐν ἀρχῇ ἦν ὁ λόγος [In the beginning was the word]. Praxis does not make us say: *Am Anfang war die*

Tat [In the beginning was the deed]. The logos is inseparable from praxis and praxis is said by the logos.

What *in theory* is glimpsed, contemplated or even clearly conceived still has a long way to go until it is *practically* accomplished by winding roads, with struggles, relapses and approximations. This is why the world, humans and societies give us the impression of still having so much to do.

If abstract knowledge ends in failure, then what does concrete doing do?

What is *said*, what is *thought*, what is *done* . . . How to disentangle them, attentive to their specificities and their differences, their relatives and their dissimilarities?

Could we not subordinate praxis to poetry without reversing their 'relationship'? Would it be possible not to decide which of the pathways of speech-and-action – poetic, thoughtful, practical – is the most decisive? Would we accept not cutting the mystery and mechanics of interiority, the mechanics and the mystery of exteriority, to try to surpass – in what direction? – their dialectical link? Would we be ready to stop seeing in the poem the place of poetry, by finding our rhythm according to the poetry that breaks into the world – the poeticity of the world – but without experiencing it as a perpetually given mode of being? Would we support no longer understanding poetry as a meteor that traverses the sky to fall on earth, without wishing to make it our daily bread? Do we already sense how little original and future is the distinction between (fixed) installation and (vagabond) errancy?

What does experience prove, grasped in the combined play of prolegomena and epilogomena?

Is it foreseeable to think and say that perhaps one day the protean force of language and doing will take over, after the internal exhaustion of religion, poetry and art, politics and philosophy, after the full accomplishment of their possibilities? At this level humans would speak and sing, meet, create, manage and think, without passing through these mediations that are open to them so that they open up to what exceeds them (humans and mediations).

An act of faith, most often implicit – act and faith – is at the base of every act of thought, of any act in short.

Thought cannot cover everything: other powers and forces that precede or accompany it are also uncovering and covering. Nevertheless, thought thinks the game of being in becoming of the totality of the world, or does almost nothing.

The force of thought penetrates what is, inhabits it, until it becomes inseparable from it.

It is only at rare moments that thought becomes a behaviour assumed in its own right.

In short, the thought responsible for itself, assumed, explicit, bathes in a vague, general, implicit thought.

The origin of all great thought is lost in time.

How to think the thought that does not yet think itself, wild thought? Is it already the thought itself as an other?

To find the initiatory, aristocratic, buried lodes is one of the duties incumbent upon us.

It is today essential to go and interrogate the ancient magical, mystical, occult and esoteric traditions and make them talk. Taking up again, after the passing of leftism, the old secrets of dexterity. Revolutionarily. Continuously.

Accepting and shaking the heritage and tradition from which our thought proceeds is a task always to be accomplished.

Traditions and orders cannot be shaken like the dust of a rug so that humans, or rugs, get a new look. Animated by the great powers and informing elemental forces, the intertwining of old-and-new traditions and orders command the words and actions, the thoughts and passions, the games and omissions of *homo faber*, *homo sapiens*, *homo ludens*.

Thought emerges from the depths of immense anonymous symbolic activity and becomes the discourse of this or that thinker, before going to die, like all the particular rivers, in the great ocean.

The theme of the common structure of the human spirit and the relatively reduced number of its themes demands to be specified.

We are looking for the diversified unity of the human spirit.

Will we ever succeed in constructing the typology of development and the universal and differential manifestations of thought?

All thought remains suspended in the mythological tremor of sense.

Since most of those who are presumed to be adults are presumed to be specialists in particular domains, is the thinker the specialist of presumed universality?

The thought of a thinker is offered both as a whole and in its evolution.

There are people who have played a great role in the history of thought without actually making themselves part of it.

Every thought inscribes itself into a pre-existing history and systematic. As we cannot think *the* absolutely initial and primary thought, we are always in the presence of thoughts that follow one another. The *history of thought*, punctuated by great thinkers (who always end up as postage stamps), encompasses the history of philosophy, if one understands by philosophy – equally metaphysics – the movement that calls itself that and goes from Plato to Hegel. The history of thought, continuous and discontinuous, offers a succession of emergences, without one being able to tell whether they are or are not 'dialectically' linked. The history of thought begins with 'pre-philosophical', poetic and mystical forms, and continues with metaphilosophical thoughts. Properly speaking, it only begins with the logos that names and names itself.

It is very disconcerting that the history of thought forms neither a rigorous dialectical concatenation nor a free and arbitrary march.

Behind and between the glittering stars that dominate the visible scene of the theatre of thought, evolve less visible stars that often benefit from the glitter of the former.

The logic of the history of thought is unique and multiple.

Every great thinker thinks a great central thought, alone and encompassing. This is exactly what the thinker leaves unthought (and which is, perhaps, unthinkable). The question it poses is not in them, although one could make the latter enter into it.

Through lightning flashes and moments, thinkers succeed in grasping what is – or seems to them – contrary to their thought.

What the author meant to say surpasses them and surpasses the commentators, who offer angular interpretations.

No thinker can say all their thought, still less those who follow them.

We can no longer represent what old thoughts and lives represented; we live the closure – the end and the continuation – of representation.

Even so, the transmission of texts in the history of thought has been made with remarkable continuity.

Hinduism and *Buddhism. Taoism* and *Confucianism. Prophetism. Zoroastrianism* (which survived in *Manichaeism*). These are the great 'visions of the world', mystical and ethical, which ruled the Orient and Asia, sometimes fertilising the Occident – if only by the Bible – and shattered against it. *Around* 500 BC, history begins to become global. In all the high places of the planet voices emerge. In India, after the Vedas, the Upanishads and yoga, the Buddha. In China, Lao-tzu and Confucius. In Palestine, the Prophets. In Persia, after the Gathas of the Avesta, Zoroaster. In Greece, the tragic poets and Presocratic thinkers. Different voices, simultaneous but apparently without an actual link between them, seem to converge, even when divergent. Do the parallels meet or not meet each other? At the heart of the Same?

Orphism and *Pythagoreanism* are like a hub connecting Orient and Occident. Then it will be Christianity's turn.

Between Heraclitus and Parmenides 'something' remained in suspense.

Nothing great is done without a certain cold passion.

Nothing great is done, it seems, with humour and irony. Yet Socrates . . .

Since then, it is incumbent on us to constantly put to work the frank play of a dissimulated and midwifing Socratic irony.

To burn passionately with the least possible signs of passion indicates an excess of force, a faculty of concentration.

Thought seems to imply a certain humour and a certain irony, humour and irony that depend neither on certainty nor on uncertainty, nor on consciousness nor on unconsciousness. This irony and humour would be corrosive to other thoughts and to themselves.

There are also those who want to generalise 'correct thought', who are deprived of any sense of humour and persuaded that the 'truth' has a single face, no one having the right to move away from it.

The humour and accuracy of thought do not have to solve all the enigmas of the world.

No one is yet initiated into the play of an extraordinarily ironic argumentation.

Irony requires that certain words and actions must be at the same time – without apparently being under the same relation – ironic and not.

An 'excessive', that is to say, insufficient and presumptuous, dose of humour can prevent living as well as thinking.

Could we push the irony to the point where it would go unnoticed?

The great thinkers who interpellate us are few and are called: Heraclitus and Parmenides; Plato and Aristotle; [Augustine and Thomas]; Descartes, [Spinoza, Leibniz], Kant, Hegel; Marx and Nietzsche.

Platonism. Aristotelianism. Christianity (sometimes platonising, sometimes aristotelianising). *Cartesianism. Hegelian-Marxism.* These are the great visions of the world and the attitudes towards what is – which rule the history of the Occident and Europe, and the tendency for global expansion. Will we finally begin to comprehend that these thoughts became visions and realities of the world, *-isms* and ideologies, blazons of an eclectic, syncretic, ecumenical and planetary confusion, that all these types of thought are dead, although strongly surviving, for us to give in to a planetary thought which, more than nostalgic or backward-looking, modernist or contemporary, anticipatory or futuristic, will be *thought*?

Do aspirations and realisations intersect more than they counter each other? Let us accustom ourselves to record all the brilliant discoveries of Marx and Freud – revealing particularly and partially almost all social and individual determinations – to record and situate them within a larger thinking and thought, lived and alive, active and acting whole.

Marx, Nietzsche and Freud will remain the masters of suspicion as long as we do not begin to suspect them themselves.

The case of Freud is extremely embarrassing. Without being a great thinker, Freud upsets mental structures and discovers omnipresent motivations and themes, releases forces of the unconscious, shows the driving role of life drives and death drives, demonstrates certain mechanisms of *eros* and *thanatos*, tries to unmask the face of the disease under the mask of health. Psychologist and doctor, certainly, social critic in his moments, he is *more than all that* and, although a great man, he is nevertheless less than a great thinker.

Every thinker and author also creates their readers and detractors.

The great so-called classical texts offer an inexhaustible resistance and always inspire new explorations and interpretations.

Every text offers itself to readings and interpretations, additions and retrenchments, as a pretext.

To the writings of great thinkers are joined the writings of interpreters and commentators. In the becoming of the thought marked by the great thinkers is superimposed, juxtaposed or opposed the whole history of their great and small interpreters and commentators. Every thinker is encircled by commentators who open paths to them and obscure them more, always make them speak again and conceal – that is, disguise – their thought. All these works accomplish a role, perpetuate a tradition, exhaust a mission.

Even the exposition of the work of great thinkers, the exposition of their thought in a 'systematic' manner or the most authoritative commentaries of their texts most often transform them into superb cadavers ordered in a vast cemetery.

One never restores the thought of a thinker as they thought it (they thought it, moreover, unitarily but multiply).

We can no longer represent what ancient thoughts, historical lives and constellations represented, and this is consistent with the continuous end of the area of representation.

The great thinkers were hardly functionaries, studious professors, schoolmasters (they were also that, but it is another aspect of the same history). They erred greatly.

Systems of thought can be reduced to the personal life of their authors and to the different totalities of the epoch.

The biography of thinkers, the historical conditions of their appearance and social context, explored historically, psychologically and sociologically, have the disadvantage of not exposing us to the danger of a 'dialogue' with their thought, to the possibility of an encounter. The life of a thinker cannot be so easily grasped. What is living? What is thinking? Biography covers up life as schoolchildren cover their notebooks; the immense misery and the parcel of grandeur that hides in it would shake too violently those who pretend to establish the balance sheet of an existence, which, however, also demands to be considered. Sociological explorations, as important as the problem may be that touches them, habitually stop short or drown in evidence and banalities.

Very schematically, the three phases of the expansion of a thought can be described thus: the thought is ignored, fought, trivialised.

The great historically determining thinkers leave behind a summary portrait, a coin circulating in public, a bust for parks in front of which children play and the elderly rest.

The great thoughts which rule the world can only act through *misunderstandings* – in a banalising and unilateral way or in many confused and eclectic multilateral ways.

Every thought transforms preceding thoughts into a prelude to its own play: by distorting and illuminating the history of thought.

The most massive thoughts are those that carry historically.

It is not enough for thinkers to be great; they must promote a direction of the world.

However, in the domain of thought also sometimes the task is: to take power (very problematical by the way).

With each thought, old and/or new, the question is posed and poses itself again: what to make of it and with it – in thought and in action?

In the vast reserve of planetary doxography we find all the defended opinions – each 'point of view' seems to encompass all the others – which means we still have to combine them. Because all were 'true'. But we, having finally arrived on the other coast to indiscriminately recognise that there is neither a course of a river nor a shore, we still have before us a good number of combines and combinations.

At the height of the time of planetary technique, disturbing in itself, will a planetary thought of the play of the world succeed in deploying its polyphonic and atonal, precise and stochastic rhythm, speaking the planetary era and circumventing the uncircumventable?

Two thousand five hundred years after the first polycentric blossoming of a prefiguration of the world thought, are we capable, by disarming the rivalries between belief and faith, knowledge and thought, action and practice, and with all the techno-scientific armature, of acceding to a planetary thought?

The planetary thought of the play of the world should also elucidate, in and through praxis, the relations between theoretical knowledge and effective action, relations that are extremely complex and in general rich in contradictions and counterfeits.

Planetary thought, speaking the play of errancy and opening itself up to the planetary era, can only attempt to be at the highest poetic and thinking point – surpassing even what could be the alternative – archaeological and retroceding, historical and observational, prophetic – namely, speaking forth – and pre-emptive. Nostalgic, contemporary and, even more, anticipatory, this thought will essay itself as a globalisable and encyclopaedic thought, in dialogue with the sciences, animating practices and being fertilised by them; a systematic and at the same time fragmentary thought, an overview and grasp of details, it may be able to connect parts and totalities, in the thinking words, the deciphering reading and the problematising writing, affirming and questioning, proving and testing, provoking and troubling, relaxing and soothing, serenely and harmoniously; it will endeavour to relate contraries to their unity, to their reciprocity, to their wavering, to their oscillation, to their struggle, and to their connection, by recording the simultaneities, the breaks and the displacements of equilibrium; without privileging absolutely one plan in relation to another, since each great centre constitutes a point of departure, liquefying everything – and the All out of nothing – and, scrutinising its enigma, it will butt against the unnameable and the unplayable – always a sketch in development – constrained to assume its successes and to accept its failures, touched by the suspicion that the unsuspected is escaping it and not even suspecting it.

The planetary thought of the play of the world does not tend to create a (more or less closed) system but aims at the elaboration of an open (coherent and exploded) systematic, a methodological (polyscopic and unitary) problematic and not a doctrine; it opens itself to all questions and, questioning indifference, it encounters difference.

Trample on planetary thought. You are planetary thought.

It is when it becomes a question of life or death that thought thinks.

How could thought liberate itself, not only from philosophy, but also from thought – to think wider, deeper, closer and further?

When thought thinks it is at the same time, while being neither one nor the other, governmental and oppositional, central and marginal, accepting and transgressive, visible and invisible.

Rivers disappear into the sea. The thinker – liberated – in 'the' thought.

The thinker is this displaced (*atopos*) being who addresses themself to everyone and no one.

Does not the thinker who is in accord with the world that transforms itself – but what is the secret of the mix that engulfs acceptance, renunciation, resignation, revolt and revolution? – let themself be overtaken on the left? On condition that they are extremely vigilant and thrown into the future.

Isn't it a kind of unconscious collective thought, mythological and technological – individually and world-historically – that seems to lead the world?

If thought were and remained 'consequential' and anticipatory, nothing would be constructed: not churches, not revolutions, not states, not families, not systems. The thought that kills the lucidity that kills, can it be founding and foundational beyond the foundation?

How to make coexist what cohabits anyway: critique and acceptance?

Thought recedes before what would render it impossible, humanly and socially.

Those who let themselves be manipulated by thoughts then manipulate explosives themselves.

Does the sacrifice that is presently required of thought aim at an augmentation of resistance to a new test?

Thought retrocedes, tramples, advances.

Work begins by being this productive and producing, positive and concrete negativity, which extorts nature by using mediations and instruments, which is necessary for the production and reproduction of human life. It tends to become an abstract negativity in and through which humans exteriorise their life by alienating it and gaining it by losing it. Taken as a quasi-autonomous dimension, it builds works that the human, tool-fabricating animal and worker, produces and consumes, by covering the world through the network and scaffolding of its technical fabrications. Being a species of play right from the start, could work – beyond the distinction of working time and free time, interested activity and leisure – become a hard game?

How do needs – natural and produced – move humans, how do they open to them dimensions and orientations (or are opened by them) and how do they enter, as soon as the human enters the world, into the world of the productive work of the world?

In original and elementary work, know-how, knowing and doing already coincide and separate.

To be moved by a work, an orientation, a goal, a task, passes for necessary, so it is necessary to know that one cannot pass it by.

Work resides in a production that involves reflection.

We work so we can rest, and we rest so we can work.

Marx departs from a radical analysis of the alienation of work and workers to bring his critique into the vision of a completely non-alienated society. Without explicitly asking himself whether this prediction itself is not part of alienation, he recognises that 'the suppression of self-alienation follows the same path as self-alienation' and that 'communism is not as such the goal of human evolution, the form of human society'. 'This movement,' he adds, 'that *in thought* we already know as self-suppressing, will traverse in reality a very hard and extensive process. But we must consider as real progress that we have, from the beginning, acquired an awareness as much of the limited character as of the purpose of the historical movement, and a consciousness that surpasses this movement' (*Political Economy and Philosophy*). Practical materialism wants to be materialistic and practical; it makes economic motivation the predominant motivation of all human history; does not his theory and action aim at liberation from reigning materialism and the liberation of the human as material of work? 'The reign of liberty begins in fact only where work conditioned by necessity and external finality ceases; it is therefore, according to its nature, beyond the sphere of material production . . . The shortening of the working day is the fundamental condition' (*Capital*). Thus opening the doors to a 'beyond of the sphere of material production' – although this beyond was always characterised, for the whole history, history of alienation, as an idealistic and ideological complement – doesn't Marx advocate a kind of work, that has never yet existed, permitting the generic human and worker to 'find pleasure in the play of their own bodily and intellectual forces' (ibid.)?

In short, is not the ideal of workers idleness and play?

Will the noblest creations of the human spirit, as they are pompously called, born in leisure and superabundance, moult and be reborn in a post-industrial civilisation of abundance and leisure? To pose the problem in this way is to rather artificially dissociate work and leisure, abundance and indigence.

Production no longer imitates prototypes or models, no longer creates according to them. It produces – not without fluctuation – beyond realism and idealism, forms or the formless, modes of being and exploiting, 'objects' of any kind, momentarily frozen and fundamentally unpredictable. In general, moreover, there are no more evident frameworks for human activity.

That creations, productions and games can surpass and subjugate creators, producers and players remains always and again to be relearned and experienced.

Why does the human, each human, want to dominate?

Do all interhuman relations remain relations of force? Based on the struggle that aspires to power?

The 'dialectic' that opposes and unites force and weakness – strong and weak – gives victory to the strong worked by the weak, to the weak that possess immense force.

Very frequently two partner-adversaries mutually intimidate each other.

Letting go can constitute an excellent offensive and defensive weapon, prompting the other to advance into the desert to break against its own force.

The human has not only to struggle against others, but also against itself.

All the combats of humans are destined to satisfy insatiable and generally unacknowledged desires.

Both defenders and attackers are bound to the same game. Of two adversaries in presence and struggle, both can partially and partly reveal the game that holds them through their dialogue and their contradictory combat. Nevertheless, each party does not simply bring to light a part of the total game.

Combat and struggle, polemical and agonistic, aim at power over the other, an acknowledged victory, engage in a competition that respects and breaks the rules of the game, appeal to the public and come crashing against their own success.

The master-slave couple confront each other, under different names, throughout universal history, on the terrain of work and power, management, direction and execution.

To recognise the warlike beauty of the enemy army that is advancing against you and that will bring you down, or that you are going to bring down, is not given to everyone.

There is never and nowhere an absolute winner and a definitive victory.

Imbeciles believe themselves victorious after every debate or combat.

One triumphs over an adversary – if one ever triumphs – not by leaving them outside, as an independent power, but if one succeeds in dissolving and assimilating the adverse force by transforming it.

What we elude takes its revenge and then eludes us.

Being *for* or being *against* someone or something means staying riveted to the same power that sometimes demands, with a particular insistence, to be defended or fought – attacks always supposing defenders and the defences of the attackers.

The play of unleashed violence and one-upmanship, the fanaticism of the new, the maximalism of the most and the ultra, the precipitation and haste permit what must arise by arising in breaking what enchains it; once arisen, it will become a link in the chain.

The play of the most fatalistic passivity, the fixation on what appears unchangeable contribute greatly to the provocation of the contrary, although they accomplish the role of the guardian of what is, guardian who helps to transport what they have to guard to somewhere else when the house is about to collapse.

Do all 'consciousness' and all 'will' aim at the death of others? Others that we need so much?

If your defence system is limited to a single side, woe to you.

Offensive and defensive are inextricably combined, every struggle needing both, for frontal battle and guerrilla warfare.

The desire for vengeance keeps the human turned to resentment and avenges itself even where one believes to have overcome it.

Declared war is the most exoteric – and often anecdotal – aspect of the much more elemental and powerful forces of struggle and conflict, antagonism and combat.

The law of the strongest and that of the weakest are interwoven into one another.

There is never a full settling of all accounts.

Does single combat, in or 'out' of the general melee, and 'total' conflicts, seek above all glory?

The struggle for prestige is one of the most stubborn struggles.

Culpability and aggressiveness are connected by a common play.

To govern, it is necessary to be possessed by an active and extroverted force, to be inhabited without too much questioning by goals and ends to be realised – through compromises and approximations – by being turned towards success, not repudiating any means – especially violent ones – for imperfectly achieving it.

The contestation of all that is and revolt, negation and revolutions, the questioning and the dreams of an alterity, cover a surface and advance into depth, and, without departing from a certain naivety and certain illusions whose need dwells in humans, moved even by the propellers of utopia, possess their 'truth', 'beauty' and 'goodness'.

Love-eroticism-sexuality remain caught in the net of a finite combinatory.

It is to the totality – in all its forms – that sexuality, eroticism and love, as well as their children and their children's children, aspire.

Nowadays the need for tenderness seems more frustrated than that of sexuality.

The need for tenderness, affection, human warmth, love is matched only by the contrary need.

It is necessary to recognise: the association of calm tenderness and violent desire is dissociative.

Without the movement of tenderness and its corollary, aggressive movement, two people could not encounter or love each other, not even make love.

Love feeds on the fundamental contrariety that opposes and binds.

In all small and great adventures, in the small and big world, there will be availability and its loss, accomplishment and privation, fixation and renewal.

Love itself is stronger than the person loved; however, it needs a polariser and a catalyst.

Love is not deceptive because it does not keep what it promised. As we hope, wait, always watch for *love*, it disabuses us and forces us to experience it as sexual violence, affective tenderness, fraternal friendship, separating opposition. It is it and the situation to which it compels us that are much stronger than the characters who meet and separate.

For a human encounter, friendly, erotic, to be liveable and, in time, durable, it must be based on a common language and practice and inscribed in the perspective of the future.

With each new love one retells and reshapes one's life.

One must know not to sacrifice too much to the myth of total transparency between the members of the couple.

Having the generosity to give the other the attention they deserve.

To open oneself to love, one has to overcome self-love a little.

Seduction is more and different than a little psychological game.

Man and woman join and disjoin, struck by the powers of *eros* and *thanatos*, forces that are much more than human, joining peace and discord, harmony and war. The search for being, however, only encounters beings.

The desire of the other being aims at the suppression of a lack of being.

Copulation unites the members of a couple, makes them be together, is the *is* of the couple, the copula that proposes itself. Every being is infinitive and transitive. The sexual act, coitus (*synousia*), union in the 'presence', tends to become a doing and an affair of representation in the face of absence.

Eroticism wanders/errs: for a long time, the class struggle has encountered the struggle of the sexes. Today, woman is becoming more and more virilised and man is feminised. It is the woman who seems to be at the forefront of the contemporary world. Will the play of the sexes lead to a community without sexes, to the introduction of the androgynous (bisexual), the establishment of a neutral being (asexual), or the reign of 'gynaecoid' beings?

Marx, the thinker of historical nature becoming technics, went so far as to consider love as a form of labour; according to him 'the division of labour was originally only the division of labour in the sexual act' (*German Ideology*). Marx advocates the sublation of work and the division of work as they have existed; the biological future of humanity should therefore be ensured by other activities; sexuality, too, can only be surpassed.

Love has become a doing centred on representation. It surpasses all presence. The reproduction of the species falls under the blows of the general rhythm of production. It is to be expected that *production* – producing 'material' goods and 'spiritual' goods (good being inseparable from bad, as well as the material from the spiritual) – will also extend to the production of human beings. *Eros* and eroticism seem surpassed. After the disintegration and liberation of the energetic kernel of 'matter', the artificial production of 'life' must – that is to say will – come. Technical production will take charge of the reproduction of the species. Technics – which may not be a simple human creation – will technically create sentient beings endowed with reason. Will they be metaphysical animals?

Women are still a means of communication between men.

Girls with sad eyes and slightly heavy thighs still attract non-chivalrous knights on the quest for the Grail.

The Don Juanian quest, marked by its different components – 'impotence', 'homosexuality', etc. – is at once nostalgia for distance, decentring, renewed ecstasy, and hope for the encounter of a close partner, in the constant change of partners. In any case, it is grappling with the masks of death.

What unites a couple? Sexuality? No. Affection? No. Intelligence? No. The three together? No. So?

What ties and unties beings [*les êtres*] escapes them completely.

So man and woman managed not to hate each other too much, in their joining uniting them with the world that separates by uniting.

Will a kind of complicity in duplicity, a certain warm friendship, a tender and certain companionship, succeed in surmounting love-passion and the marriage of reason, by surviving them?

Friendship, harmony in *philia*, is much less a nostalgic tension than *eros*.

Instead of dreaming of an unparalleled couple, is it possible to construct a couple – a way of 'sharing' the world – slowly and efficiently? Since the myth and the fabric of love-passion tend to be surpassed by love-friendship, love-companionship.

We are always seeking the realisation of unrealisable erotic and sexual figures.

We would aspire to externalise our most secret desires, were it not . . .

The call for erotic follies does not eliminate the contrary decrees.

It is always an inaccessible imaginary that we pursue erotically that pursues us.

The first contact with a woman or with a city is filled with trouble and enchantment. Attraction can also take on other aspects.

Desire is always inscribed in a hollow mould: it wants to repair a lack and lacks it. One wants what one no longer has or not at all, and one misses it.

This derision that strikes the sexual is part of its game.

It is as a wonderful misunderstanding that love is understood to provoke agreement and disagreement.

Love remains torn between unity, duplicity, multiplicity.

As no being can be the whole of being – being in its entirety, the whole of the world – all people – all beings – encounter only partial beings, parcels of being, which leads to the erotic combinatory which demands new games, especially today, where new rules of the erotic game are waiting.

Does eroticism exceed human forces?

Exercise of anxiety and exercise of sexuality feed off each other.

Sexual anguish gives us wings and pulls the rug out from under our feet.

Humans don't only seek out sexuality, almost all also flee and avoid it.

Prostitution, under the guise of the most wanton mercantilism, conceals the powers of exchange and of gift; what is exchanged is hardly love for money: the prostitute does not give herself, she refuses herself.

In the sexual act, desire is liberated and 'one' liberates oneself.

The peaceful coexistence of two beings who have surpassed their nervousness can constitute a fertile terrain for their blossoming, or even the blossoming of their divergences.

Once women have surmounted this phase of revolt, they will become open partners.

Life is bigger than love. The world is bigger than life.

Every erotic point sends us back to a counterpoint.

The separated halves hopelessly and hopefully seek each other.

Eccentric love can also, for a greater or lesser period, turn around a central pivot.

No man – no woman – can love all women – all men – a single one of them – at the same instant.

Woman possesses, namely is possessed by, that chasm where every erection will perish victoriously, in tumbling downwards.

Woman transports and supports in the heart of her body the nourishing and murderous opening. She wants to be more actively masculine. Man advances and penetrates: his prominence is forceful and fragile. He wants to be able to abandon himself to female passivity.

Man is forced to confront within his own being his own femininity, the woman her own masculinity.

Desire being maddening, it is dammed up.

So many embellishments of need, desire, envy. Not that they are perfectly superfluous.

In erotic life, as elsewhere, one can only lose possibilities, occasions.

Erotic discomfort causes this trembling and these inhibitions that fuel erotic life, this accomplishment of always delayed desire. Awaiting the surprise and a better tomorrow.

They were seeking excitement insofar as it was tolerable to them.

Can love realise desire remaining desire?

Within the movements of sex lie the section and the separation.

Even two beings who believe they love each other do not know what passes between them, through them.

Love, eroticism, sexuality, while seeking the exception, fail to escape the ordinances of seriality.

We are all torn between nostalgia and the attraction of home (unifying, stable, secure and sometimes stifling) and the anticipation and the attraction of adventure (fluid, opening and often dispersing and spreading).

Home and adventure can both become moving and emotional [mouvants et émouvants], escape or routine.

Love, relation between private persons, appears most often antagonistic towards public things.

Could man and woman meet and live erotically and amicably as brother and sister? But how would the other attractions of the woman play out: the mother and the little girl, the lover, the prostitute and the comrade?

Do they stay with the same partner until they have found 'better'?

One always marries into the family: the man marries his mother, his sister or his daughter, or a combination of them.

Sex appears as the last refuge of adventure and convenience – all in all – opening. Even when it bores us, it forces us to pursue it, without us knowing what rules agree with its game.

It is in the course of time that love must be born and die and be reborn in other forms. A shared love dies: of satiety? Does contrariety permit fulfilment and saturation? An unshared love dies too: of starvation? Is not contrariety also nourishing?

The couple has become the fanatically problematic preoccupation and obsession of the modern world – an abstract and mediated, if not inverted world, in relation to what base? – it has become a small world of problems opening and closing the partners and adversaries whom it unbinds and rebinds – really and imaginarily, more or less passing or enduring, by centring and decentring them – to the problem of the world, vitalising them and stifling them. But another constellation has not yet emerged.

The couple often wants to be a kind of fortress protecting them against the world, underestimating the fact that the two flanks that form its bastion reinforce and weaken it. As if there could be bastions that could withstand the world. The world animates and mines from the inside more than from the outside – if this distinction can still be made – all the fortifications, reinforces and weakens their defenders and their attackers, who are all as much inside as outside of strong castles – castles of cards.

The couple and little family suffer modern instability, disquiet, dissatisfaction and at the same time constitute the refuge against this instability, this disquiet, this dissatisfaction.

The familiar and the obscene attract us equally.

Each member of a couple wants to affirm itself at the expense of the other.

The difficulty for the couple – relative remedy for massive solitude – consists of being free with and not against the other.

Confrontation, the ordeal fortifying and weakening the couple, subjects it to the attraction and control of the elsewhere.

The couple 'redeems' its coupling if they do something together.

There is no prototype of a successful couple, no paradigmatic couple.

Social and societal, socialist and communal forms that can offer refuge to love-eroticism-sexuality have not yet been found.

Sexuality – the weak point of the human structure – does not aim so much at a positive satisfaction as to liberate itself from a need, to abolish a state of tension.

Is curiosity the precious instrument – of high precision – of eroticism? Goaded by and goading this inextinguishable desire that we do not know and yet we hope to accomplish.

Erotic errancy, pursuing its sexual and imaginary quest physically, psychically and mentally, manifests a need for dazzling sensuality, mollifying tenderness, communicative speech. By experimenting with barriers and barred roads on which barred subjects engage.

The child as well as the man and the woman desire to possess the phallus. But no one is or has the phallus. Because it is not empirical.

Love is stronger than us: in attacking and withdrawing.

Sex and corporality in general have multiple equivalences.

Often one wants to do everything with a particular being.

Jealousy is one of the forms of excitement and homosexuality.

There is a part of exoticism in eroticism.

Is there a normal sexuality?

Erotic investigations are also a matter of vocabulary and syntax.

Can a man, a woman, a child bring salvation? They can in any case contribute, in time, to the unstable equilibrium, in a moving system of complex coordinates.

Is woman the central problem for man and vice versa?

If man is *the* problem for woman and woman for man, it could lead us on the path to another confrontation of the sexual problem.

The ballet steps of the erotic game are strictly regulated. When one advances, the other moves back, and vice versa.

One loves love as one wants the will.

Life does not stop at the number two.

Loving also means helping.

The obsession with death incites the sexual obsession that makes it momentarily forgotten. Arrhythmic erotic practices leave a taste of ash.

In love beings wait to attain what they are and, even more, what they are not. Love denies limited beings. Death will render them into brutal negation, to the unlimited void, skinning them.

The greatest power of love implies the greatest power of death.

The quest for faith becomes religion and church, creativity work of art, revolution party and state, questioning thought system, amorous conquest family. What becomes of the movement of death?

Love desires totality and stumbles against particularity. Death makes particularity and totality coincide.

The place of love is the couple, the family, the adventure. What is the place of death?

Death can never be looked in the face. Doesn't it have one?

Tons of toneless things were written about death. To hold what is dead is otherwise difficult.

What to think and what to say about death, which remains unthinkable and unsayable – once one were not content with the generalities and particularities by approaching it from the angle of exteriority, of otherness – snatching us from every directly living, speaking and thinking dwelling, to plunge us into a dwelling from which others live and die, speak and think?

Even death aims for survival. The cult of the dead and of memory are its forms.

It is less death that preoccupies us than the time that leads to it.

Life is only possible by destroying what destroys the appetite for life.

The human being, once born, aspires to life: it seems to desire and want to conserve and propagate it. Carried away by vitality. Hunger and love lead to the production and reproduction of life, binding, through the play of ambivalent love (attraction) and hate (repulsion), each human to others and to other humans, in the agreement and the antagonism between self-conservation and conservation of the species. So manifests the drive – or the drives – of life. The human, however, also aspires to return to a state anterior and posterior to life: drawn in by death, it also aspires to it. Carried away by mortality. Aggressiveness – already bound to the effort of the conservation of life and accompanying love – leads to the destruction of other lives and the destruction of the human by itself. So manifests the drive – or the drives – of death. The human is consequently seized by the desire to be and to persevere in being, and by the desire not to be and of non-being, these desires combining and also falling into their opposite: fear, refusal. Is the human, then, crossed by two – or two groups of – drives, one vital and conservative, the other mortuary and destructive (Freud), plaything of a bipolar play? Or is the self- and hetero-destructive drive only the reverse, the negative, the wounded result of the conservative and positive drive, life itself turning against itself? (Conservative, moreover, they both are: progressively moving forwards, they are no less reactionary, effecting a return to what precedes and follows the deployment aiming at the satisfaction of the need – either the need posed as vital, or from need tending to rest in death – that is to say, a return to the lack of need and the tension it creates.) We can admit the duality of drives or seek to establish their unity – ramified and circular – or try to subsume each under the other. We can see life and death; we can grasp the unifying process, the closed circuit, life-death-life, etc. (life being in death and vice versa); we can comprehend life, which includes death and continues stronger than it, or death which includes life and continues stronger than it. Is it not better to try to elucidate the junction and the difference, the agreements and the antagonisms, the combinations and the reversals, the fusions and the complementarities, the action, the reaction and the interaction of life drives (which also signify their contrary) and death drives (which shake the living), inextricably entangled – though often differentiated – within the organism, the psychism and organisation of signs that constitute, vivify, mortalise and kill the human being?

Whether the death drive is an autonomous drive, or an opposing and powerful derivative of the life drive, is ultimately secondary, since it powerfully manifests itself.

To privilege only the surging of presence, the compact, the solid, the ascending current, appears as playing the game of life, without for that escaping death. To privilege the rupture, the crack, the break, the fault, appears as playing the game of death, without ceasing for that to belong to life. It's up to us to extract the necessary learnings and lessons. It is up to us to link the different aspects and the multiple functions of the unique game – with several variants – which links life and death.

Quite often one would not want to be. In any case one could not be nothing.

Nostalgia for prenatal life and life close to the mother's breast, the desire to fuse with the One-All, the desire for the extinction of all desire, the abolition of tensions, the obtaining of a state of serene saturation, the solution of all disquiet and all struggle, in quietude, in peace and in salutary dissolution, the anticipation of future absorption in being-nothingness, move the double-and-unique play of life-and-death.

Everyone would like to die to rest and be reborn regenerated. Like the Phoenix.

Dying without dying so as not to have to live and to die resolves strictly nothing.

By bringing the hatred of the world against oneself or self-hatred against the world, one opens the door to suicide.

To a certain point it is necessary to kill in oneself life and desire to continue living. By avoiding killing oneself – 'existentially' – to no longer risk living and dying. Death as protection escapes just as much as life.

By desiring, the human desires to suppress its desire, to abolish tension, to find satisfaction. The desire for omnipotence is by far the most tenacious, and aspires equally, but very obscurely, for its annihilation.

It may be that the attachment to life becomes gradually a little more problematic.

Humans do not choose their entry into the game. Can they decide to leave it, if they cannot endure the hardness of existence? Must every human live? Without being able to answer the question: for what? Is there only one – philosophically and more than philosophically – serious problem: suicide? This one, who claims however to surpass life, can they not also be surpassed? Do they not remain too attached to life, do they not show too much disappointment and greed, do they not remain a prisoner of the vicious and infernal circle by which overvaluation and devaluation, appetite for and fear of life and death join, complementing each other and cancelling each other out? Don't they hypostasise hope and despair at the same time? For serene suicides are extremely rare, after a life lived with its fullnesses and emptinesses, at the moment where lassitude takes over and where any future is blocked. To quit life voluntarily without extreme tension can be a high possibility after a trip on the high seas, as a deserved rest. But this type of chosen death is not yet on the agenda. The days that we have to live, no one can actually live them as living among the dead or as dead among the living, for our experience of death is 'infinitely' more approximative and illusory than that of life. Even aspiring for a prenatal and posthumous life – sucked up by them – we are still prisoners of life. Even when living upside down. Every human being can only experience – like everyone else, or almost – the difficulty of being, passing ups and downs, trying to overstep one's unhappy consciousness and assailed by one's unconscious. Would it be better to learn to live – and die – without *reason* to live? In this case, it would not be a question of affirming or denying existence, of supporting it or not, but of being carried away by it.

'Voluntary' death, suicide, is the example of the extreme point of the unity of contraries, the strongest ambivalence towards life and death, fears and desires. Would the suicide have desired not to have to die? But could they desire the desire of life?

If one were totally, that is to say as much as possible, ready to die, one would also be ready to live.

Strange, this feeling that conquers humans: to live and to cease living are experienced as imaginary solutions, existence being elsewhere. What is called life imposes itself and withdraws. The human can neither live nor cease living.

Memento mori is a call launched to be often forgotten.

One dies already, before dying for good, in a provisory manner, performing as a test, in this play of repetition that precedes the play played for good.

Convinced that we experience life, how then do we experience death?

Life watches over death.

The prestige of those who will die soon exists.

The point where life coincides with death is always fleeting.

It exists as a contemporaneity of the living and the dead.

The dead being is not nothing or rather it is something with which we maintain a relation.

Was it principally death and the dead that fuelled the dreams of demonic revenants?

Death kills both the particular as well as the absolute, and lets wounded life continue its course.

Death is a closure of chance, although it can present the very opposite of misfortune.

There were soldiers in the old days who went on the attack, in the opposing camps, to the cry of: *Viva la muerte!*

The point of view of life on death and the point of view of death on life communicate.

By losing it, it's not just about earning a living but also death.

Behind and in all powers and forces stands, disguised, death.

The already dead can die once again, if not several times, and resuscitate in different ways.

The living and the survivors believe they are right and take revenge on those who are no longer alive, the dead take revenge on those who are not yet dead.

Great powers and elemental forces are not born as play, nor of play, but in the play.

From games of language to human games, games of love and death, from natural games to political, bloody and boring games, from sacred games to artistic games, everything signals to us 'the' game.

The play of each game of elemental forces and great powers is regulated – up to and including its transgressions, except perhaps those that are extremely rare and unheard of –, conforms to typical structures, likely to be classified within a coherent structure that underpins all games, constitutes an ensemble of conventions and a combination of possibilities. Also, language and thought, work and struggle, love and death, as well as special games, all of them, as well as magic, myths and religion, poetry and art, politics, philosophy, science and technology, rules and openings of games that are played through them and above all the game which contains them and which slips away.

The game plays itself, through the diversity of acceptations of this term, in ambiguity. What is its specific difference? Precisely its globality and its multivocity, since it embraces all the great powers and all the elementary forces of the world. With radicality, steadiness and flexibility, the style of the game, its general look, can be graspable by an oriented and methodical thought that accepts experiencing it, as an ensemble composed of several elements, multiple combinations; to carry it to articulated language it is necessary to grasp it as a whole, without neglecting its parts and its aspects, its faces and its backs.

The place and the time of the game are not only situated on the lands and locales of the games, at the level of all the particular games, but are placed and glide through the world and, still more precisely, give site and rhythm to the game of the world, commanded by 'it'.

To play also means to move, to function easily: the key plays well in the lock, what does not join exactly: the woodwork has play.

There is no common Indo-European name for designating the game. Among the Greeks, culture, education and training – *paideia* – and child's play – *paidia* – were associated and not only as the highest leisure activities of free humans. The play was first called *ludus* – training for study, combat, competition – among the Latins (see ludic, allusion, illusion, collusion), to follow the drift of lightness and to be supplanted by *jocus* – play of words, joke – which gave the French *jeu* – game. In the group of Germanic languages, Anglo-Saxon knows the words *plega* and *spelian*: see English *play* and German *Spiel*. The word 'game' and the game itself imply a very large semantic multivalence and an immense field of application, transposing and transcribing themselves on several, on all registers, obliging us to take into consideration and to keep in sight all the play of the game and games, all the collusions, everything that unfolds, everything that can unfold and is conceived as unfolding as a game, that is, everything.

The play of the same word, which names two contraries, is frequent: *scholé* signifies in Greek *school* (studious) and *leisure* (idle), *ludus* designates the *play* and the *school*.

Play is not the inverse of work, the other of the serious; it encompasses both.

The game is a struggle for and representation of, struggle and representation can be combined, the game containing every struggle and every representation and surpassing them, being at the source of every combat, every production, every reproduction.

Children imitate adults and adults children. So everyone enters the game: by illusion (*in-lusio*)?

It is through play that the child – the father of the man – is individualised and socialised. Play is the work of the child and could become that of the human. Animals also play, but our decoding of their play is still very crude.

Is not all education a formative process in which the child is taught what games it can or should play and how?

The play of the child possesses at the highest point spontaneity and exuberance, fantasy and gravity, creative impulse and destructive force, poeticity and artistic gifts, intuition and sense of questioning. Few know how to safeguard and develop these qualities in banalised, socialised adulthood, without falling into infantilism.

Children's games are similar to those of time, or rather time plays as children play, which Heraclitus already knew. The play is also related to the fire that can be lit, extinguished and lit again. Children play forbidden games. In playing they are afraid and love to be afraid. They believe in their games without believing entirely. They take them seriously, adhere to them, and at the same time they mock them, make fun of them, remain distanced.

Children and humans – little humans and big children – open their playthings to see what is inside, break them, break themselves and mature in incompletion.

Children are irresistibly drawn to forbidden games.

It is not only children, lovers, fighters, poets, artists and thinkers who know the starry hours. Even those without star participate in the play that connects us to the stars and provokes disasters.

The child who plays is not necessarily infantile. Infantilism is a trait of big children and adults, which our epoch accentuates with a mortal seriousness, both in banter and in fanaticism.

Play involves sociality and cooperation and reinforces them.

Simulation is one of the components of play.

The balance of justice and the balance of chance distribute shares and fates, rights and wrongs, ruled by laws.

Play involves persons 'and' masks, masquerades and disguises, roles and functions, imitations and models, simulacra and scenery, intrigues and rules; it does not distort the play of reality: it plays it.

Civilisation is a ritualised and codified game. Certain games predominate and are epochally imposed.

Sacred at its origins, the play establishes little by little its own sacredness.

The game is not only expenditure: it is above all productive.

Does not playing come back to betting on a piece of hope?

All societies regulate games, encouraging some, tolerating or banning others, themselves obeying a gaming system.

All play aims for more, to obtain and lead to less.

The game – agonal and polygonal and bringing out *agon* and *agonia*, struggle and anguish – mixes, to their confusion, the superfluous and the necessary. The threads that connect the players, the springs and the secrets of the game, put them into play and into question and no one can withdraw from the play. And does not every play imply feint?

In play, spontaneity and organisation are inextricably linked at the heart of a governing code.

The game is a trial.

To take the wrong role is part of the play. Whatever one does, one plays.

Mischance only consumes chance.

Is play necessarily a fast action, circumscribed in space-time? Is it not rather a rhythmic, rhythming and rhythmed movement?

The game can conjugate the tensest effort with the greatest indifference.

All institutions function as a game. All the gears are playing.

Game wreckers are only playing an 'other' game.

Not respecting *fair play*, distorting the play, is in the eyes of communities much more forgivable than breaking the play, namely a play.

We do not renounce any game; we exchange one game for another.

The game plays with the difference of the worthy and the unworthy by confusing their roles; it even plays on their specificities and, recognising them, confuses us, that is to say, strikes us with astonishment.

There are socially accepted games, tolerated games, provided they are not played in public, and forbidden games; the latter, played to their final consequence, end catastrophically.

One can also play inside a play.

Competitive and sporting games, games of chance and skill, games and festivals based on the simulacrum, games that dominate vertigo and the call of the void – these games can be combined – are the most broadly visible forms of games and play.

The game is most often considered a secondary power. But compared to what primary power?

The play unites partners and opponents, the cautious and the reckless, and often confuses them.

Isn't one playing to risk rather than to win? One certainly wants to win, but at the same time one loves to be around the danger of losing. Play is oriented towards success and fascinated by failure.

The game unites what counts and what does not count.

The game embraces wisdom and stupidity, 'true' and 'false', 'good' and 'bad', 'beautiful' and 'ugly'. From the outset, it transcends logic, ethics and aesthetics, by implicating them.

In the play that keeps the players tied together, they try to calculate their chances, provoke destiny, while waiting for the deadline.

The collective humanity of tomorrow will principally have to play five games: the cybernetisation of thought, the domestication of atomic energy, the artificial creation of life, the biopsychic restructuring of the human, the fitting out of the planet. With much back and forth – setting in motion the play of reactive formations – the big children will continue to play with technically exploited thought and natural powers, with life, psychism and historical societies. Who will be able to say if it is playing with fire?

How do chance and necessity meet? A throw of the dice and a great number of dice throws, don't they at once follow chance [*hasard*] – a word that comes from the Arab name for dice, *an-zah* – and necessity? For if each throw is completely independent from the next or from the previous one, in the long run all possible cases appear the same number of times, all chances tending to equalise according to the – probabilistic – law of large numbers.

Primally, many future [*futur*] games served to predict the future [*avenir*], the game of time. Initially divinatory, these activities only then became games, in the restricted sense of the term, by which one tries to predict the aleatory flow with the calculation of probabilities.

Play a little – until exhaustion – with the possible combinations of *searching* and *finding*, not searching, not finding, etc., etc.

Those who contemplate the wheel of fortune, and those who base their hopes on it, generally ignore those calculations of the calculation of probabilities that are called the theory – mathematical – of the ruin of the players.

Games of skill and chance, tactical and strategic games, codified, obeying rules – where one can trick, bluff and even cheat – rely on an exchange of information and aim for a gain. The calculation of probabilities and aleatory combinatorics can seize them, their offensive and defensive combats can be measured and to some extent predicted, any approach to games remains nevertheless stochastic, that is, conjectural, and every decision aleatory. Thus, what depends on the players and what does not depend on them, meets and intertwines, to form the knot of the game. Certainly, one can build machines that would play certain games against any adversary and win through calculation. But if one complicates the rules of the play to the extreme, one would checkmate the calculation.

In every play there is an aleatory partition that can sometimes be calculated mathematically.

The game or rather the games are supported by the calculation of probabilities, which studies the possibilities and combinations using matrices, vectors and permutations. The games, if not the game, are equally taken charge of by the strategy that studies and calculates the chances of games, fair or not, determined or not. These two kinds of calculation, one calculating, the other calculated by the adversaries who use it, aim to block chance as much as possible, to control the aleatory: they thus play to dominate the games, dominated by the game which shows and hides itself, dwells and passes.

After having played so many effective games, parents of children will perhaps be able to devote themselves to some fictional games.

Believing, desiring and most often wanting to win, humans, deprived of the hopes that they believed well founded, do not know, when they lose, to whom to impute their bad luck and imagine that there was a misdeal in the distribution of cards. Winning also makes you lose your head and losing makes you stupid (the inverse is not totally excluded).

Playing ball and bowls, with balls and balloons, on the surface of the sphere, in the air and in the water, making hoops spin, children playing adults and adults playing children experience the cyclic power of the round and the ring and are knotted by the same knot of the coiled strap that grips them in its play.

To see only play is to play badly, that is to say, very little. To see only error is to err greatly, that is to say, meanly.

Luck plays itself – loses itself and wins itself – in the play.

Every human activity is not pure play but impure play.

Among all the fascinations, the fascination of the game is particularly fascinating.

In the game is not only manifested the desire to win but also, if not more strongly, there emerges a need to lose. Because if one plays for a long time, the chance of losing one's winnings increases, and the loss relieves the player.

What manifests as free must be rooted in a much larger network of games.

The player respects and despises conventions. With a tense casualness.

Not content with the given or the product, the game claims the excessive.

For the play to be thrilling – if it has to be – it has to be almost equally aleatory for the parties involved. In this sense, bullfighting is an unequal play, a rigged spectacle where the human – with minimal risks and without being able to lose in general – puts the beast to death in a cowardly way.

Winning on two, if not on several, tables at a time strongly tempts humans.

Are there plays more serious and decisive than others? Those that directly concern life and death?

The decision serves the play which also serves indecision.

Chance escapes will and knowledge. It is what is not (yet).

Nobody can pull the pin on the game – killing game.

The play also includes disillusion, disenchantment.

Combining calculation and chance, expectation of luck and conjuration of bad luck, the play, whether played with passion or coldness, aims to win – and it happens to lose – parts and totalities.

In the game of life, rules, moves and ripostes are much more confused than in other – more codified – games.

Almost as much as bad luck, luck is hard to bear. Would the place of play be the interweaving of forgetting and waiting, the suspense?

The thirst for risk throws us into the play that provokes always 'new' feelings.

When there are nine chances out of ten to miss, one can count on the tenth.

Prestidigitators and fairground juggles also participate in the play of the world.

After the era of creation and genius came the era of production, reproduc-ibility and suspicion; will the era of play come next?

Religion and poetics, politics and ethics, logic and ludic rules claim to normatively govern what pertains to them – and the rest – demanding the subjection, freely agreed, to the application of the system.

If we do not learn to read the play that connects the effective and fictive, useful and futile, we will understand nothing about the play of the human, partner of the play of the world. Not only is play neither – uniquely – a particular activity – playful, ludic – nor is it – principally – a particular modal-ity of every human activity, which it also is. The tendencies that engender it in the human and that are read biologically, psychologically, sociologically, etc., demand a broad and deep comprehension, envisaging the players as a function of play in all the varieties of its deployment. If the play is a regulated activity having its end in itself, then it is only the play of the world that fully deserves this definition, commanding all the particular species of the play that essay to join it. And if you think that the seriousness is otherwise dramatic, remember, please, that dramatic play is part of the play.

Humanity plays the order of nature, the birth and death of the divine, its own destiny, its future succession.

Certain games will go by losing their precise rules.

The world of the game is only a prelude to the game of the world.

The great powers and elemental forces hold each of their plays in the partition of the whole and support the whole of the play that holds them.

Each of the great powers and elemental forces – whose plays with all others are to be explored and re-explored – each of the great words, great thoughts, great actions, great operations and great constructions propose a formative reading, a regulation and an edification of the play of the world, readings, regulations and edifications remaining inner-worldly, whatever they do, never being able to fly over, regulate or edify the world itself. For even their totality does not manage to exhaust the play of the world.

All human works – are there any that are not? –, passed and situated behind us, have their future in front of them, constantly remade by those who come in contact with them to form and transform them. In this sense, they are all open.

Who above all makes the great powers and elementary forces *speak*? The play of logos, obviously.

I

Logos.
The Language and Thought of Man and the World

We have made logos the *beginning*, the supreme *principle* and *power*, the *arche* leading to cosmic nature and, through it, to human and world history, which develops the discourse that grasps the logos and expresses it. Thus, everything begins and ends with it. It exists, so to speak, before being and knowing, and we find it afterwards. No one has dared to lean over the abyss of this logos pre-existing all and then dominating all.

What precedes language and thought remains the crucial problem.

Every genealogy of the logos leaves vague its own genea*logical* origin. To be brutal: where to situate the origin of the logos?

If the logos is there from the start of the game, how does it develop and become logos properly speaking?

The relation human-and-world, 'preceding' each of its two terms, only finding the terms of their language in this co-presence, is this 'dialogue' that confuses its partners. There is neither primacy of language and the thought of the human, nor of language and the thought of the world; language and thought start, so to speak, from the outset at the second power, detach themselves from the first unity and the first cut, raise their voices and emit signs, made and unmade from a ground that escapes – what one can call the play that provokes all plays.

There is not thought and world, but the thought of the world.

From the start of the play, it is at the broken heart of the human and world and world and human dialogue that thought arises, since it has fallen like a catastrophe upon a particular species of beings, human beings, who think, think themselves and think the being of the world. Thought, that is to say from the outset, language speaking, thinking and acting, opens itself to silence, to obnubilation, to what activates and outplays it.

The broadest binary relationship, which involves all the others, binds human and world.

The logos – speech and thought of the world and of the human in a 'dialogue' that surpasses any dialectic – appears as the very first moment and – chrono-logical – and topological – place, where and from which is said and thought what gives and withdraws itself from language and thought. The logos is, however, only one of the instants and spaces of that which would remain mute without it.

For the world to become thought, was it not necessary for it to already be?

What becomes thought that does not become world?

For a logos to be imposed, it must be codified in technique. Another sort of logos circulates underground and opens other horizons.

Logos has been made the divine light of physis, the language and the order of the world. We have made it one and God, Idea, Spirit. We have envisioned it as one and as the faculty of the human, progressively acquired. We have made it into a complex secretion or an evolved product of matter. We are currently reducing it to a gigantic network of information and communication, with several stages, inputs and outputs, in a combinatorial circuit. But who or what produces the logos so that it can be so reduced?

The world 'precedes' the thought that thinks 'it' and thinks inner-worldly things. All thought is preceded by a sort of belief, which never ceases to accompany it. The intertwining of belief, thought and knowledge is infinitely more tight and complex than we believe, think or know. Is not philosophy itself always linked to its theological-religious presuppositions, even when denying them?

Everything does not begin with the logos, although it is only from it and through it that one can speak – even of what precedes it, accompanies it as an alterity or as a (illuminating) shadow and surpasses it.

Are there 'things' outside of logos?

Logos is the generic and detailed assemblage, the reunion and, more so, the unity of all approaches; it is itself the target of various and varied approaches and interpretations.

Logos is the violence and weakness of the Occident.

Whether it tries to think itself or tries to think what it is not and also what contradicts it, the logos remains always at the heart of the supreme tautology, the Same, respecting the princely and governing principle of non-contradiction, even under democratic and socialist forms: for it is impossible for the same to belong and not to belong, at the same time, in the same way, and *under the same relation*. It is this Same, which maintains a very troubled relationship with the like-wise and the identical, the different and the other, which also demands surpassing.

Would the logos of the human and the logos of the world constitute – in and through analogy and homology – tautology par excellence, the Same? In an open equation?

Every primordial ontological logic, even if it is dialectical, exposes the frames of what is (thoughts and things) before the Creation – Hegel recog-nised this – although it only makes itself known afterwards, at the end of a development.

By deploying itself, a language deploys the world.

For two thousand five hundred years, all that is and becomes appears in the light of the logos: through logos and as logos.

Very quickly the logos forks: in the direction of words and speech, tongue and language (supported by grammar and syntax, rhetoric and logic, litera-ture and phonological and semantic linguistics) and in the direction of fig-ures, numbers and (geometric and mathematical) relations. Both paths tend to rejoin in formalisations, structurations, axiomatisations, although these two paths of the logos do not come into dialogue.

Logos is a verb-word, while grounding and exceeding its becoming-verb.

The exigency of logos surpasses in fullness and depth the logos itself.

Can the logos only remain imprisoned in the logos?

What is stronger than the logos?

The thought. This does not exist.

The play of thought aims at the invisible world power.

Every logos delivers many contradictory and confusing messages.

Logos is at once concentration, recollection, and dispersion, bursting.

Logos separates in binding, binds in separating.

Through the logos, the same is said and resaid in other words and in many ways, samewise and otherwise, and even the 'same' things are said multiply.

Is all logos monologic? Only the logos speaks, but does it speak alone?

The logos can also move at the limit of two or more territories, between day and night.

Logos thinks and speaks being, beings and things with all its being. That is, with cosmic forces, the body and the perceptible, emotions and affectivity, images and schemas of representation, social and historical powers, words, intuitions, notions, concepts, speculative entities and abstracting thoughts. How to establish a hierarchy in all this? Receptive, affective, imaginative thought, conceptual and speculative thought – individually and socially – go together and recognise articulations, jump over and fall apart because they are equally disarticulated. At once concrete and abstract, thought reassembles the scattered and scatters itself, illuminates and burns, seeks and seeks itself.

More than symbols, signs and signals, messages, metaphors and metonymies, the logos operates analogically.

Who speaks? To whom is it speaking? From where does it speak? When and how does it speak? What does it say? Why does it say it? These are the questions awaiting their surpassing, for that which will suppress them and surpass them, abolish and elevate them to a 'superior' power.

Avoid getting to the big words too fast.

Null and nothing *seem* to be at the origin of discourse as a whole.

Do we know, can we *speak*? How *to say* this question?

How to say that of which one does not speak?

What does this mean: what exceeds everything that can be formulated (of it)?

Strictly speaking, one does not comprehend perfectly what one says.

They want, it seems, to bring all to language. Where then was *all that is* before?

Logos circulates just as much in vague and imprecise words as in those that want to be decisive and precise.

All legends, all messages and all information transform in the course of transmitting.

Does whoever speaks, in the entanglement of symphonic and cacophonic words and voices, suddenly take power and are they for a moment the strongest?

The language of thought fails to liberate itself from the power and weakness of images.

It is overwhelming, but that's how it is: the word, words, are successive and not simultaneous; thought and gestures seem to escape this limitation.

From the time – past – of the original common language – hypothetical – will we be led, through the problems raised by time and language, to the time – future – of a universal language?

More and more one can say whatever; and one does not deprive oneself of it.

Many parallel discourses are articulated, apparently without much relation between them, all aspirated by the whole of what is said, which does not entirely cover what there is to say.

The play that links a group of sounds and a word or concept – a sign – is purely conventional.

What lesson will ever tell the play that connects sound and sense?

Every word pronounced engages the whole course of the game.

Does not all that is – as such, grasped – have a name?

What passes through the meshes of all nets, the radically other, remains nameless.

How can we know what we are unable to name?

Words are not things and things are not without their names, that is to say, they are not stated and called, named and said.

Call things by their name, we often hear said. By what names? Say things as they are, you are asked. How are they?

Were words 'concrete' before becoming abstracting and 'abstract'? What is then the concretion of the verb and the substantive to be?

Words change sense in the course of the ellipse that draws our life – individual and generic.

Words freeze experience; but it implicates them and they 'explicate' it.

What do useless words indicate?

Are not all words as if already burned?

All the words in the dictionary are in great need of being explained and thought.

An intelligent Indo-European dictionary of all grouped keyword-concepts would be highly desirable for the planetary and disoriented Occident and for the shaken Orient.

At most, one can shed some light on the central words which we use.

Words explain each other.

All the words of the language have become extremely difficult to employ. They lack definition and contours: they are used-up and clichéd, emptied of their (?) sense and full of misunderstandings. No thought, however, can thematically elucidate all the words of language and its language. Anchored and adrift, the words, all together and altogether, are fixed and errant. A new *lexicon* or *dictionary* that would historically and systematically scrutinise the sense and senses of each word, giving at the same time relational and questioning definitions that would indicate the relations and fit into a hollow mould, would be more than necessary and would close and open many debates. But it equally manifests the need for a new *grammar*, examining and ventilating language formations, attentive to time.

The whole history and system of grammatical time demands to be clarified. Grammar and syntax in general require a different formalisation and approach.

Very often we have the impression that we lack words that would be apt to express certain fluid and elusive, mixed and multiple states.

It is more experienced than expressed and said. It is not about converting the lived into words, but making it speak.

'One' can only speak with the other about what they can comprehend.

In leaving the era of the word to enter that of the sign, does the escapade of speech and writing know a change, a transformation, an evolution, a revolution, a mutation?

It would be necessary to take a sentence and analyse it 'completely' – right up to the exhaustion of the analysis, if not the sentence.

Practical works: take a sentence – whatever it may be – and analyse it from the angle of the greatest possible number of 'points of view', term by term and in its ensembles. Complementary exercise: how to halt, finish a speculative sentence, where to finish with the elucidations?

Every thinking utterance says and takes back what it says. It speaks without contradicting itself, nevertheless making a sign towards another direction. It is perhaps the same, but not the one we thought.

When we speak a thought, another trots through the head.

Does not all that is said demand to be resaid? In which language?

Does one ever hear all the harmonics of a sentence simultaneously?

What matters is not only what I say, but also, if not equally, what I do not say.

Frankly: what does or can it mean to speak frankly?

Language as information and as an expression presupposes pre-existing content. Also we commonly speak of language without knowing what speaking can say.

Midas can only want to tell his secret in order that it be known.

The most fertile speech, the most agile thought, the most subtle understanding, the most vigilant consciousness, emerge on the compact and fragile ground of the untold, unthought, unknown, unconscious.

The logos in us aspires to be said – spoken and written – in many ways and simultaneously. Who would not want to be able to speak with several mouths at once, write on several lines at once, as on a musical score, with even more possibilities?

The signs of every language – verbal and non-verbal – benefit and suffer from this radical – and thus arbitrary – contingency that mobilises them in the games of language (in the interior of the game of the world) and the games of writing (in the interior of the game of language).

Does language double the world which without it would not be spoken and said?

Language is constrained to think its saying, and to say.

The mistakes of language, the errors of the tongue, pose a brutal and delicate question, and can introduce us to a general and specific problematic. It would be necessary to let them play, in view of a richer development of language possibilities, for a finer articulation of the combination of sounds and senses.

Are you looking for the word that carries the decisive moment? You know, however, that everything comes too early or too late. What is then the right time?

Is the need to speak stronger than that of saying?

In all verses and controversies are at play language mechanics, stereotypical articulations, metaphors and comparisons, tics and clichés, nontransparent grammatical, syntactic and semantic structures.

Alliterations are parts of the play – and traps – of speech and thought.

It is not only a matter of saying definite things, but of saying what there is between and around definite things.

Is there some discourse that knows what it says?

The discourse founded on itself has the limits of its own will and above all: of its power.

Dialogue is a useful and futile verbal play. Within it are clashing and always confronting methodological abstractions, which express ontological particularities, necessarily unilateral arguments, parting and partial points of view. In any case, it tends towards its abolition.

Should thought aim less at the 'dialogue' than the echo?

The play of thought engaged in speech consists of taking up positions and retaking what surpasses any discussion, any dialogue, any controversy, any dialectic.

We also need to learn to unspeak.

Not speaking can constitute an effective weapon.

But do not neglect – when necessary – to cleanly break the dialogue.

What can the saying and thinking of untranslatable words and locutions do?

With the translation from Greek into Latin begins the great history of uprooting in relation to language.

A decisive thought can pass into all languages, by crashing into them.

When, where and how does the proposition manage to express itself at the propitious moment: apropos? Because at the same time it also speaks of something else: always apropos.

Theoretically and practically, one always lacks the a-propos. Good ideas and good words generally come after. By taking the service staircase.

A tongue and a language, reaching their peak in a historical epoch of the life of people and having offered up poetic and thinking possibilities, the keys of speech and their possible combinations, don't they then find themselves exhausted, imitated to emptiness, restored and modernised, exploited, decomposed?

Even in the desert, speaking is preferable to preaching.

They hear most often the loudest and not the most decisive voices.

How to measure the utility and futility of words?

Some, if not most, voices become more and more neutral, sinister, slow yet hasty, often interrupting themselves.

Language also marches towards its self-destruction.

All our language – lexicon, grammar, syntax, logic – is impregnated by a history that it has equally impregnated. The destruction rises upon those buildings which make it possible. This is why major destructions give the impression of destroying each other.

It is henceforth a matter of hoisting language off its hinges.

Saying everything is impossible. Saying as much as possible is possible. Saying what one usually hides, and what tries to make a, if not its, path, can be, if it becomes relevant, necessary.

How does discourse even manage to surpass categorical fragmentation without becoming for all that this univocal message of theories and practices of information and communication?

To hear also the tone in which what is said is said.

Modernity passes more and more – antiquity pursued the same path – from the reign of *ideas* (idealism) to the reign of *words* (rhetoric and various formalisms).

The sign is much more indication than expression.

Language has so much or so little importance, we hear peremptorily stated. Since logos speaks and is silent, takes place in language that annihilates itself, it is as chiaroscuro that speech emits words and chatter. Situated on several planes, it can be high and clear, but, as if its own altitude was untenable to it, it rather often crawls or flies off in abstract clouds in the course of everyday language.

Everything can also be treated as language, which one does nowadays by remaining in the orbit of a metaphysical logos, which one imagines surpassing, by making science succeed philosophy. The reign of metaphysical philosophy is no less strong where it is most unapparent.

We do not succeed in clarifying the obscurities of 'internal' thought, the not said, the interior monologue, the unfolding of thought not spoken aloud and not written.

The light that illuminates a word comes from another word.

Language is and remains metaphorical – whatever it does.

The pertinent word – continuous and fragmentary – knows how to be impertinent and conclusive and open.

Word games make the game of the world speak.

Everything is discussable, since it renders discussion possible.

The nagging impression of the already said does not leave us easily.

Analysing or completely elucidating a sentence or a proposition would come down to – through the play of references – analysing and elucidating all that is.

Sonorous signals emitted and captured by speaking beings can appear as a language that passes through loud- and low-speakers in a network of transmitters and receivers.

The word says at most more or less what links the unnameable and the unnamed to the named.

The bearers of a thinking and poetic speech of high flight cannot have a victoriously happy face.

That of which we speak is also what acts.

It is as if we always speak and write a foreign language.

Gestures and 'signs' preceded speech and thought, reflected 'then' in and by them.

Beings, things and signs of the world can only be said and resaid.

Everything is in turn subsumed under a word.

The speech that orients is neither rebellious nor established: vigilant.

The dominant figure of all rhetoric – and not just rhetoric – is it repetition? Is there discourse without redundancy?

In any keyword or concept, one can detect an ontic-ontological sliding, that is to say, a back and forth between what is more or less empirical and visible and what is more or less speculative and invisible.

Suddenly, certain things become perceptible, speaking, sayable.

Examples are at once the crutches and the infirmity of thought.

What signifies having – to be possessed by – too much or not enough of speech and thought, what do slow rhythms and fast rhythms signify?

The genealogy of concepts, their archaeology, their teleology: always in transition (whether they are regulative or constitutive or both at once).

How can one learn what somehow one already knew? Isn't all cognition a recognition? The circle that links thought and experience, given and projected, *a priori* and *a posteriori*, is decidedly infernal and vicious.

How to operate cuttings in the flow of the spoken, the thought, the written?

No question is only terminological, although everything is said with the same and other words, in the same way and otherwise, and no speech – attentively heard – is uniquely necrological.

Nobody doesn't know it: the game of thought wants to engender, and sometimes does so, positive knowledge. And then problematise it.

The method is a path, a route and a routing, an extremely precious instrument of orientation, discovery and invention, thanks to which one finds what one was seeking, thanks to which one re-searches for what one has already found. Methods must be crossed with each other and reversed to generate new results, no methodology alone opens the royal road; we have to go back to their presuppositions and also practise the method devoid of method – or surmounting the method. Knowing that there is always an implicit method – and that a method never succeeds in dismantling the machinations behind the scenes and setting of the world's theatre, which change with the new – and the same – play.

We want, you want, they want a method, a methodical logos, a methodology, a route and a routing, to approach, situate, examine and solve problems. For method is an effective weapon and there are, indeed, armed methods; it wants a sure direction, precise discipline, fertile orientation, productive exploration. The various existing methods prove their validity and demonstrate – to the prudent – their ambiguities and their infirmities, combat and combine with each other, rule and are replaced. What can we, what can you, what can they think and do with a questioning and interrogative, problematising and combinatorial, multidimensional and self-critical, holistic and fragmentary new method?

The method of research and labour possesses an extremely productive and reductive force generates results, provokes discoveries and inventions, but remains a double-edged sword, usable in multiple ways, that can be turned against itself because, in this domain as well, there is no absolute and total weapon.

Because in the game of thought, not only does the result count but just as much, if not more, the path, the route, the routing, the *methodos*.

There are also more hidden, veiled methods, which one must know how to discover, themselves seeking to discover the hidden, the veiled, all methodically.

Yet there is no sovereign method. Each of the methods is apt and none of the methods are apt to illuminate their quarry, as hunter and quarry are intimately linked. Of course, there are always and momentarily more efficient methods than others. In the clattering of opinions, points of view, arguments, ideas and theoretical constructions, it is not about opposing truths to other truths – or errors – but about putting into question, interrogating, destroying the certainties by recognising them, by knowing how to stay in the absence of an answer, daring to give up a certain armour for thinking and speaking better. Why do all this? In view of an interrogation conducted otherwise, of another taking root and another horizon, of a different proximity and distance. Since all points of view and all theses and hypotheses destroy themselves, one against the other and, above all, each against itself, since abstract negation has no other import and every fixed position is ridiculous, so that thought finally dares to play its own play and that of the world, with extreme flexibility and finesse, with the most rigour and the most vigour. Recognising with humility that, neither in theory nor in practice, there is no supreme instance and no contesting power is indisputable, thought could perhaps set out towards a very problematic and tense, weary and kaleido-scopic wisdom.

No method can therefore be fully codified. With the same method, one reaches very different results, as one can achieve similar results from differ-ent formulations.

Can a methodological question be answered by throwing a pebble into a lake?

The most open, the most inquisitive, the most adventurous thought must also be the most solid, the most articulate, the most rigorous.

Effective thoughts move on rails, effecting passages and going to rest in garages, from where we take them – sometimes – to restart them, renovated.

What intuition urges is later often observed, and this observation crea-tively and retroactively strengthens the premonition.

Renouncing to regain everything results from a gift and an apprenticeship and is not easily given. Above all in a time that does not leave much time for meditation and is often content with summary, sophisticated and sen-tentious thoughts.

A great deal of the decodings of old messages are presented as original messages.

What is this power that maintains the power of logic – so fissured?

Metaphor plays the game of metaphysics. Both hold impregnable power at the heart and in the course of language.

Thought never manages to think anything to the end – if end there is. It is even strictly impossible to think and push a thought to its extreme consequences. It is equally impossible to comprehend completely a deep and ample thought, to keep to its height, to follow its depth. Thoughts that follow and are inspired by a great thought can hardly prevent themselves from undermining their movement by promoting their own direction.

Anxious to establish and explore the ultimate foundations, all thoughts stop short before a so-called first – and last – foundation.

Thoughts fanatically focused on determinations forget to interrogate the foundations of determinations.

Formulated thought does not die with the individual human; its message continues to be transmitted and captured.

In every logical and dialectical edifice, there are ruptures of level, changes of plan, discontinuities, leaps.

The relations between the logic called formal and the logic called dialectical are almost inextricable, and the second possesses no formalisation. Do these relations effect a junction in the disjunction? Which of the two encompasses the other, when we have reached the threshold of a 'metadialectic' language? What to make of the principle of non-contradiction, which was charged with founding the possibility of discourse? Can we only conserve it by surpassing it? Must we annihilate it as a principle, to respect effective contradiction? Is it possible for us, however, to not also respect it in discourse? Undoubtedly all thought is inscribed in a 'system' without which we can say neither words nor things, which nevertheless elude us. But is it about thinking the dialectic or thinking dialectically? Thus arises the question: can we think non-dialectically, if dialectics is the rhythm of language and thought? What does it nonetheless say about the rhythm of the 'real' and the relation of logic and the real? What dreams and realisations, constructions and destructions, sayings and resayings, backtrackings and forward steps! What efforts to say the same otherwise! What torments to surpass and not dodge or resolve the contradiction! Contraries, opposites, contradictions pass into one another. Do they also surpass themselves in a third – excluded in principle – that occurs in and through breakage, as much as, if not more than, through and in unity? What terms define the relation between inclusion and exclusion? How to see clearly into the relations of inverse and complementary powers, and how to face the very light in which bathe all these edifices and their reversible and irreversible deconstructions?

Antagonism and reconciliation, contraries, contradictions and mediations, opposed in a mutual conjunction, do not realise a synthesis in a third
surpassing power, but adjoin themselves in a certain unifying presence, at
the heart of the tearing that makes them exist and coexist and that mortal-
ises each of the struggling positions and their juncture. Need for tension and
relaxation goes together.

There are thoughts expressly open to negation, made for the negative,
assuming the full weight of affirmation, proclaiming the identity of identity
and of non-identity.

Every interpretation is at least ambivalent, ambiguous, equivocal, dialectical, everyone signifying itself and its contrary which inhabits it.

The system of contraries, opposites, antagonisms and contradictions is to
be shaken from the ground up by a language and a thought attentive to the
common presence of the axes of the world.

All oppositions are symmetrical and proportionally inverse: they are both
oppositions and poles of a unity. In the famous unity of contraries, one must
capture both the unity and the contraries, without forgetting, however, how
all harmonies are warlike, for it is in spite of itself that a term fuses with its
contrary.

The junction, the accord, the complementarity, the antagonism and the
reversals of contraries and contradictories, of opposites and radical differences, all play to lead to the unity and the struggle of opposites as well as
to the – reassuring and irritating – fact that everything also signifies its
contrary.

Usually, contraries – unilateral – wear out each other, and apparently
antinomic themes unite in the same imbrication.

There is much more to the 'surpassing' of contradictions than their resolution or synthesis.

A very large number of couples of opposites is destined to leap.

There are contraries which stay calm, as there are acute antagonisms.

To surpass – to conserve and to suppress – the *ontological* principle of non-contradiction can mean: to recognise and respect, to integrate the effective contradiction, and to recognise its surpassing power.

The most extreme form of the transformation of an entity into its contrary, of negation and effective contradiction, is annihilation.

We function with oppositions which we cannot do without and which we cannot credit.

Every unity dislocates itself, every position tears itself into dominant and secondary oppositions, each of which generates new positions and oppositions. In theory and in practice.

The complementarity of opposites will never be sufficiently comprehended.

Do you want to remain attentive to the contrary poles without reducing them to one another or rapidly effectuating their assumption into a third synthetic power, do you want to respect each negating possibility of the other without losing sight of an ultimate convergence, do you want to pose the question asking if the solution of an internal contradiction is internal or passes through an external mediation? Do you want to accept not only dialectical reversals and harmonies, but the reversibility of all aspects?

Contraries unite and struggle with each other. Above all, they play with each other and in others and with their premises and their results.

Where does the 'solution' of a conflict come from? Which power vouchsafes it?

When one says pompously: of two things one, it is the third which is established.

Let us try to maintain the two terms of opposition as well as their common origin and destination.

Let us exercise ourselves to ask for more and more precision from thought.

In any discourse, except in strictly formalised discourses (and again), one can add and subtract.

As you know well: everything explains itself after the fact, once realised and nearly collapsed; then one finds all the reasons that constitute its weave and explain our explanations.

To the multiplicity of theoretical formulations of a question corresponds its unfolding on several planes, on which we think and live.

Thought can put into motion – because actioned by it – the terrible power of negativity capable of denying all, and not only 'in thought'.

Thought creeps and flies over, picks up and sweeps. It always has to relearn the overview without overview, the sweeping without sweeping.

Getting used to bringing explanations and interpretations back to their implicit unstated principles.

How far can we succeed in not becoming prisoners of our formulations?

We have to admit it: a certain stupidity is, for individuals and portions of world history, fascinating.

Let's get accustomed to perceiving almost imperceptible phenomena.

Are there messages that pass neither in the epoch nor in the world?

If one does not first raise the problematic of the thing to a status of the question putting itself into question, one cannot study anything.

It takes multiple tools, simultaneously put to work, to grasp the different prisms of all that is and is done.

The concept struggles to triumph over intuition; but, finding again the immediacy that does not precede intuition but succeeds it, after a long course, thought reacquires the character of intuition.

From precategorical thought we pass – little by little, through jumps, evolutionarily and revolutionarily – to the categorical phase. Bravo!

The more one works also with the unconscious, the more one reaches a wide and deep result.

The locution: 'hardly equivocal' is itself equivocal; it says: very little equivocally and rather equivocally.

Thinking thoughts are linked to each other, not through – so-called free – associations, but through variations and combinations.

Being against does not shake what holds, and does not advance.

In their turn all refutations are refutable. Do we then refute whatever is?

If we don't recapture what is given to us, we lose it.

Increased lucidity is linked to the dynamic of designification.

Since Epimenides the Cretan said 'All Cretans are liars', we henceforth don't know whether he tells the truth or if he is lying. The logical paradox becomes paradoxical logic, discourse turns against itself and loses its 'truth'. The act of speaking thus enters into errancy – don't we also call habitual processes errors – adorned with all the distinguished artifices, etc.

Logic instructs and destroys according to premises and conclusions that it presupposes and that escape it. But – particular reading of thought – it is not only a formalisation of the frames and arrangements of an implicit and prior discourse. Logically, it perfects a work of edification and annihilation. Logically. What a paradoxical adverb. Paradoxical. What a logical adjective.

Reason, rationality and rationalism, which corner all, leave their presuppositions and their conclusions in emptiness and vagueness, and keep their eyes closed before their shadow: irreason, unreason, the absurd, irrationalism.

Like the 'I think', the 'why?' mutely accompanies all our thoughts and actions.

Disposing of cases and rubrics to classify materials is highly necessary for every recording and forecasting enterprise.

Informatics and programming open the way for what will be distorted and outplay the forecasts.

When we think that we think, without thinking, we stop ourselves half-way up the backstairs.

It would all the same be revealing to discover the naivety and the ruses of the notions, concepts and schemes with which we think or believe we think.

A new myth speaks and says: surpass the myth of depth, clear it from the surface of planet earth. The hidden depth of superficiality and platitude still remains to be discovered.

How does sense come to humans?

Thought questions all authorities, but it cannot take off without relying on the authorities.

All depth becomes supposedly and actually measured.

The work of embarkation can only be done by a thought that retrocedes, actualises, anticipates.

The hidden force of logical aporias, dilemmas and paradoxes resides in the traps of a logos trapped from the outset of the play.

Just as logic is only an interpretation of thought – incontestably the most governing – all sense is only a reading of its components within a system, a structure, the system of systems or the structure of structures, having no more sense than it lacks. In this sense, please, note the dominance, but do not be blinded by it.

It is the cold-bloodedness and the heat of attack that are important for thought and not pretended objectivity.

It is hardly enough that things are; they must be recognised to be known.

The path of knowledge is not the same as that of the order of the appearance of phenomena.

Everything can receive multiple and contradictory explanations and interpretations amongst them. All explanations and interpretations that would give themselves as objective are selective. Some – or sometimes, and for a moment, one of them – particularly impose themselves and show themselves as operative and active.

Inscription is not transcription.

Sincerely: have you ever seen a primordial signifier at work?

What is against . . . leans on . . . and opposes . . .

Knowledge is not free of all morals.

First plane: unproblematic adherence. Second plane: challenge. Third plane: adherence or accepting questioning.

Signposts and reference systems always contain a personal equation within the historical and global orientation table.

How sinuous the path of thought which tries to untangle the skein of implications and explanations.

Does the route of thought lead from metaphor and symbol to abstractions and signs?

Each discipline tends to be doubled by its metadiscipline. We are attracted by the metadiscipline of all disciplines, as by the metalanguage of all metalanguages.

One apprehends and comprehends in some way only what one already knows. Bizarre knowledge [savoir].

Every theory of knowledge as reflection – even when it would be materialist – remains a prisoner of the Platonic theory of the reflection, thus enclosed in the cave and inverting only the relations of shadow and light. It is however this shadow-light dichotomy that is the problem.

What do symbols symbolise?

To make the bases of what is solid tremble a little. Is this still a utopian programme?

If the morning sobers up [*dégrise*], the owls of Minerva see clearly at evening.

The rational is built on the non-rational which is not irrational.

Whenever someone gives you an example to illustrate a rule, look for the contrary example.

To be flat-out right is often less productive than erring.

Unconscious are those who do not see how their concepts float.

Every message is transmitted by a code establishing a system of communications and instituting an order of permutations. Thus receiver and transmitter are linked together. Will this completely overturn consciousness as presence to self, will it open the era to the iconoclasts, will it take charge of the perceptible, the imaginary and the speculative?

Will synchronic thought, mathematically structured, and its formalised schemas, as well as diachronic, anthropological and historical thought with its schemas of movement and change, fuse – under the aegis of the one? the other? in a synthetic and ramified unity? – leading then to the unification of knowledge?

One neither comprehends nor explains oneself, and yet one 'communicates'.

Every great thought is at once island and empire.

Breaking the habit of wanting to comprehend could well constitute one of the next habits.

Theoretical matrices dilate. We can get everything into grand systems and large structures, and treat everything specifically. Theoretical matrices contract.

The methodological plane and the plane of what methodologically effectuated the seizure are neither identical nor separated by an insurmountable distance. They fuse momentarily in what is seized each time.

One thinks neither in all times nor in all places and one does not think of everything and of the all.

Thinking consists as much in watching and seeing as in hearing and listening.

All that is, whether we like it or not, letting itself be compressed, classified, subsumed under types, is put to the test by various typologies, themselves being put to the test. If 'reality' does not correspond exactly to our schemas, it does not any more exist for us outside every schema and the ensemble of schemas.

A thought with a fine and piercing point, clear and sharp as the blade of a knife with a massive handle, is a disarming weapon which will also be disarmed.

The logistical logos leads with – or rather without – mastering operational research and informatics towards the non-mastered mastery of heavens and earth.

By interrogating the errant truth of the lie, of dissimulation, of false consciousness and bad faith, of unconsciousness, subconsciousness and preconsciousness, we are caught in the very nets with which we hoped to capture the true error.

One can only formalise a knowledge by holding it accomplished, provisionally.

In all sorts of analysis, diagnostics, critique, calculation, prognostics, let us also calculate the personal equation – the coefficient – however impersonal it appears.

A certain opacity exerts its attractive force.

A current of ideas does not necessarily carry thoughts.

How many denials are only affirmations disguised as their contrary.

Rest assured: no one supervises everything.

The difficulty consists in this (and the novelty): attacking from another angle.

Even the most daring critics and analysts do not apply their research to their own ideals.

The free spirit: the truth of the alienated life that forgets itself.

It is on the high plateaux of the uncertain that doubts and certainties settle.

What carries the name of consciousness risks its life to be recognised by the other consciousness as being more than this life that it risks. No particular satisfaction can appease it, nor can it, once launched on its course, find appeasement by denying itself.

What one recognises only intellectually is very little. It does not touch us, we do not touch it.

Terms – designations and limits – are assigned to beings and things as a share (moïra) and not as destiny. This lot, this fate, constitutes, however, their destination.

Thought does not always know very well how to separate contestation, interrogation, doubt, uncertainty, hesitation.

Everything perceived detaches itself from the ground of the unperceived. In a flash, certain 'things' become visible.

What is surpassed does not necessarily remain presupposed.

What happens to that which is supposedly surpassed without having been attained and exhausted?

We are novices in the knowledge of the functioning of the 'mechanisms' of thought.

All sectors of thought, and what it is not, communicate and are supposed to be separated by thresholds.

If a method, interpretation, explanation were not fragmentarily total but exhaustive, it would exclude others or include them in its unity to itself. It does this too, but by letting itself be equally encompassed by others.

If all that is and is told, in one way or another, did not possess a kind of logical – axiomatic and internal – coherence, it could not be – even fictitiously – probable.

The risk of a too-negative intelligence is to be compensated and surpassed through an incisive and decisive – productive – contribution.

Everything is a sign of what?

It is in and through the clouds, the nebulae, the galaxies of thoughts, which, in density and rarefaction, order and clear themselves chrono-topo-logically, that thought 'must' try to orient itself.

Rationalism, even rationality, would they not be surpassed by a thought that would burn its bridges?

All that is relativised by scepticism does not cease for that to be equally maintained.

And all the knowledge prior to the recognition that we have of things?

Burn the necessary stages? Is this feasible?

Sometimes two incompatible signs are both effective.

In which direction points the fact that we can feel without knowing?

The imaginary, its theoretical seizure, remains the stumbling block of any theory and criticism of 'reason': it disturbs – and is disturbed by – the sensible and the abstract, their duality and their unity.

How nourishing the imaginary can nonetheless be.

Ingenious thought also proceeds through enormous simplifications.

How many 'things' are hidden in a sort of semi-consciousness, already ready to emerge, almost known, repressed, without yet cropping up, neither conscious nor unconscious, more and less than preconscious.

What we miss in any case: the word of the beginning, the word of the end.

The game of explanation must be played at least in two senses: explaining – illuminating – the superior through the inferior and vice versa.

The most fugitive vision remains vision and fugitive.

Proximity does not help us see better. Distance, not necessarily either.

We recognise things above all by their aura.

Persuasion in the domain of thought is not the only resort of thought: charm and violence, suggestion, interests, schemes, etc., play their role.

Thought never prevails in 'realising' itself fully with the human and in history.

If thought, recognition and knowledge absorb everything – is this possible? – what remains for the rest?

Doesn't everything depend, not on the point of view, but on exigency and possibilities?

This or that also. But not only.

All interpretations become more and more possible in the gap of the opening where diverse individuations arise.

After the ruin, which persists, different *isms* do not go on to forge a new one: problematism.

Thought cannot, because hindered by the wind, fly into the void.

Since Greek thought we know that humans can be ignorant of what they know and pretend to know what they are ignorant of.

In the varied games of diverse explanations, each explanation can explain – situate and explicate – the others, and be explained by each of them.

Is synthesis always governmental?

Does not thought remain much more rapid than language and all the rest?

To approach things without prejudice or better: without a preliminary project that encompasses us as much as them – this is hardly possible. From the outset, it is in a sort of hierarchical vision that beings and things are perceived.

Aim a little less at pseudo-consciousness and a little more at thought.

Do we ever comprehend how 'things' have happened, are happening, will happen?

Those who think concrete thinking generally move in the abstract. Only abstracting thought assumes and thinks the concrete.

Each time a tone – or a set of tones – predominates.

One can opt for one or the other, for one and the other, for neither one nor the other.

The thinker 'is the tip of a spear'; they take charge of pointed thought, the point of thought; or rather, 'it takes charge of them, picks them up and throws them . . . to pierce the horizon'.

How to retain too-fleeting thoughts?

Great thinking does not directly touch every point of the world. It touches the world above all, so also all its points.

No thought can effect, as you have been taught, regression to the 'infinite'. It necessarily halts.

In turn and simultaneously, each person is judging and judged.

Great thought remains for a long time without definition. At the end of the development of thought in which one believes, one no longer believes in it.

A certain drunkenness helps to think better.

From where, from when, can logos say the repetitive and differentiated becoming of the Same?

The explosion of significations could show us that there are many – and none of them.

Future thought presupposes and implies other pre-existing thoughts.

Since individual work is failing, should we not resort to interdisciplinary and synthetic teamwork? That teams are constituted as such or that diverse researchers meet, empirically or otherwise, matters little, if all are working in the same direction.

In some way, and so to speak, everyone obscurely feels and knows everything.

Deformations accompany forms and formations.

Innovative thinking – recognising the necessity of the adverse, the extremes calling to each other and also to a centre, the decentred centre provoking the extremes – will not be a mother, nor a sister, nor a wife, nor a mistress, barely a friend who will accompany us, since a friend of the world.

The wisdom of nations does not retreat from banality or contradictions. This is why its limited view is often right, though insufficient, if not dominant, on the flat plane of current triviality. Common sense, being common by definition (and not universal), good sense – 'the power to judge well and distinguish truth from falsehood' – is entirely correct in the belief that it is the most shared thing in the world.

Can a thought manage to criticise itself, to give thoughts and not contrary arguments?

It is in the power of thought to proceed by striking shortcuts.

Behind and in the absurd hide the networks of reasons.

Humans are not masters of their thoughts and their thoughts fail to master them.

A thought of extreme flexibility and plasticity. Constantly performing jumps and collecting the places and times from which it jumps, to which it jumps, without being forgetful of the jumps themselves. Wouldn't you want it?

How to take charge of or leave alone neither the unconscious, repressed and censored, which doesn't reach the light, nor the preconscious that only asks to come to consciousness despite all the resistance, but the non-conscious, the extra-conscious? Doesn't the play of muscular and nervous structures intervene in the formation and execution of our movements and gestures without being either conscious or repressed?

There is scarcely any possible statement of a decisive judgement recognised as conclusive.

All thought is prismatic, all experience polyphasic.

The facts themselves are fabricated: without sorting and interpretation (from which they are inseparable), they provide no explanation or comprehension.

The mutations of thought are much rarer than one thinks.

All thoughts proceed through the slippage of sense.

How, in the ensemble of the game, do and will these things play: intuitive thought, originally giving and visionary, speculative thought that far surpasses the reflection of understanding, dialectical thought rich in antagonistic mediations, formalised and codified thought, techno-scientific thought?

A certain intelligent and dissolving functionalism could make everything appear in the play of diverse functions that everything fulfils in a multiple way, which would not be so bad, even and especially if it went as far as to establish and break the moulds of the various functions and prototypes of functionalism itself.

What we least comprehend: what does comprehending signify?

Could the logic of each 'regional ontology' and of each particular scientific discipline constitute itself in a specific panlogic, by encompassing special logics as in the case of species? Like the pangeometry that embraces Euclidean geometry and the others? Thus a pancosmology, a panbiology, a panpsychology, a pansociology would form, unitarily containing the different methods, approaches and doctrines. Could the union of these different particular and total totalisations lead to a universal and differential panlogic, by totalising the fragmentary totalities in a global, detotalising and open, unifying and multivalent manner?

The enormous power of this vast reservoir that is common opinion – usual theories and practices, that is to say, errant, habitual processes – has never yet been fundamentally dismantled.

It remains to promote diagonal thoughts, which would traverse several types of thought.

In the processes of thought and consciousness, the roles of sensible or visionary intuition, of representation, of analytic and reflexive understanding, of synthetic and dialectical reason, and of speculative thought, can only be analytically distinguished, even though a certain type or style of thought is, in general, dominant and thought is rare.

Thought unfolds itself on various planes and comprises several degrees. One can bring everything back to each plane – linguistic, semantic, biocosmic, psychophysiological, unconscious, affective, historical, socio-cultural, etc., seeking to establish correlations between several planes, without being able to establish – supposing that one ever is – a theory of the whole. In the same way, thought thinks, more than it reflects itself or speculatively speculates, at diverse degrees, by being able to pass from the first degree to the second, to recover the third – even without the obsession of the thesis, antithesis, synthesis – up to the *n*th degree.

Is all 'consciousness' necessarily and as such linked to lack and negativity, therefore 'unhappy'? What about this aspiration towards a beyond of unhappy consciousness?

Hard-hitting thinking proceeds by breaking and entering.

The games of the intuition of games are very subtle.

The human mind – and not only its mind – always seeks both identity and alterity.

From the reserve or the 'system' of the totality of principles, each principle emerges anew with its specific development.

Intermediaries play a fairly important role. They are links in the chain, transmission belts, means of transport.

Each question, each problem embraces the ensemble of the problematic, of the question. They are each time the partial-total ensemble itself.

Every call for fidelity towards a thought must foresee 'treason'.

The result is generally achieved before the completion of the whole process.

Between individual stupidity and world-historical stupidity lies a ditch surmounted by a bridge.

What happens in our 'head' before we fall asleep deserves supplementary attention.

Everything is also a question of terminology.

The recognised is rarely known.

Does not every thought begin in and by the cut, since the constituted which it wants to (re)constitute precedes it?

The unthought and the thought illuminate each other under the dominance of the unthought.

A thought transcribes itself, translates itself, multiply.

Interpretations have no limit.

Every theory meets its ruin when it is pushed to its 'term'. Then it abolishes itself.

Thought, and not thought uniquely, functions with unclear evidence, erecting itself on unfounded foundations.

In the facts of the most decisive empiricism, interpretations already hide.

Every logical edifice, logic itself being only one of the constructions and interpretations of thought, even though its dominant constellation, in the form of the thought of thought, presupposes a philosophical orientation.

Thought obeys a sort of balancing: it is sometimes thought cantered on the totality (of the world), sometimes thought cantered on the human (empirical or transcendental, individual or collective).

Thought always keeps grappling with what it is not and with non-thought.

Every thought comprises a reductive power.

Speculation and positive knowledge, speculative recognition and positive science coexist and succeed each other over time, when the excesses of one call the other.

Nothing is posed or resolved once and for all.

A reversed proposition continues to maintain the inverted position.

A thought 'must' not start from too many presuppositions, silently considered as evident.

One tends to forget that principles – hypotheses, axioms, postulates – do not demonstrate themselves, they serve to demonstrate.

There where the system does not immediately appear in the open, it is necessary, without too much system spirit, to know how to unblock it patiently.

The imaginary opens doors to us through which we cannot pass.

The same problems comprise different aspects: a thought characterised by its elasticity knows how to recognise this – without despair and without hope – by exploring the links between everything.

No thought is the measure of all thought.

Transformed sensations and neurophysiological energy, affects, needs and fears, desires and prohibitions nourish the most abstract speculations.

Alternating coordinates constantly come into play, with diverse parameters, on diverse planes, caught in the nets of logical rationality, even if we do not consider logic and reason as the only interpretation and exposition of thought, however militant and triumphant they may be.

Often, through thought, the suppression of all thought is aimed at, said, realised and annihilated in language and action. Yet absolutely anything can be a pretext to thought, from a wall poster to a tune of a song.

There is implicit thought in all that is and is done. It becomes thought, properly speaking, when it is made explicit.

All lucidity is insufficient. To enlighten, it is necessary that lighting *receives* its enlightening and shattering force.

Most recognitions are obtained through a sort of osmosis.

The unthinkable comprises many aspects.

All our modes of reasoning that we hold imperious – intuitive and/or syllogistic – so often presenting themselves to us as tacit conventions, do they not offer the framing and the rules of the game for knowledge to grapple with 'the' rules of the game of the world? All innovative thinking cracks the old frames and overturns accepted rules to propose others.

Every logos seems to demand, and we seem to demand from it, a proposition that would be more than logical.

'The' thought and the thoughts dispose of a great number of points of view, types of interpretation, explicative models, reference systems, coordinate axes, marker points, sets of operations, schemas and methods, readings of the internal correlations of a problem and correlations with other sets, by aiming at the theoretical and practical comprehension, explanation and transformation of everything. This does not prevent certain questions from slipping through all these grates. Usually one isolates one or several models by opposing them to others, as if every step were necessarily selective. Intricacies hide themselves quite well in and between the different networks. Following the same method, varied interpretations, adaptations and results can be established. Methodology and epistemology are therefore not rigorous sciences, and even the cybernetics of thought cannot avoid offering its flank to critique.

Very often arguments cannot be proved; contrary arguments neither.

All that, which is, is done, allowing itself to be deciphered, implies an ensemble of entangled, often contradictory reasons, which one tries to make explicit, explicate or comprehend, while privileging some of them more or less, the others remaining in shadow. No reading and no operation can account for the ensemble of connections.

All thought proceeds through cuttings, analyses, and by totalisations, syntheses. The ensemble of thoughts wants an almost complete apprehension of almost all differentiations. The classifications and the establishment of hierarchies are necessary for the operating and operational approaches that mount and dismount structures, ordinances, armatures. At the same time, speculative thinking, scientific research and technical action construct coherent ensembles and want to play the constituent elements and determining factors through a comprehension and a practice as global, relational and multifunctional as possible. Division and specialisation increase efficiency; otherwise, all remains in all and vice versa. Nevertheless every logos and every praxis, relational as desired, escape many displacements and inversions, implications and reversals, causes and consequences, passages and mixtures, mixtures and incoherencies.

What presentiment and prospective thinking foresee in chiaroscuro realises itself effectively, clearly and obscurely, with gaps. But, as you well know, one cannot foresee and imagine in detail what will come, even if one organises it carefully.

Knowing that one does not know what one knows is a non-negligible result that one can achieve after hard work.

Launched in its errant course as a will for truth, the logos doesn't stop carrying error, lie and unconsciousness, dissimulation, disguise, bad faith and false consciousness.

What can the most advanced thought take on, before it is, professorially and journalistically, brought into line, to use it partially and partly, to make it a philosophy and a commonplace thought?

Anchored and innovative thought is neither traditionalist nor avant-gardist. It is neither for the people nor for some elect. (Often extreme, yet fecund with futurity, thoughts give the impression of being reactionary, right-wing, because of their criticism of all aspects of the present time and their lack of faith in progressivism.) Does the hour approach when thought will be made by all, will become collective? Happy hour!

There is no longer any new principle. This 'absence' of principle is precisely the novelty.

Logicism, rhetoric and epistemological rage. Scientism: naturalistic, physicalist, structuralist and, above all, technicist. Psychologism. Historicism and sociologism. Aestheticism. Behold what *begins* to replace philosophical thought, dead to its supreme destination, but continuing to drag, propagate and generalise the sound and fury of its bloodless existence. What will become of thinking speech, the permanent interrogation, the incessant question? Planetary thought recording the decline of sages and master thinkers, and daring to recognise the fundamental and global errancy of truth and truths, how will it make its way through governments and oppositions fastened to what they combat?

Logicism, intellectualism and methodological shambles, as well as dialectics and logistics, cybernetics, 'thinking' machines and electronic brains, will extend their great but leaden power over the entire surface of the planet and will enter, conjointly, into the phase of what will overcome them. Yet the wasting away is extremely slow.

Are not machines and devices (of any kind) logically what necessarily go haywire?

It is not enough that affectivity tends towards thought; it is also necessary for thought to traverse an affectivity able to support it.

The concept is the residue of what?

Does sense occur to the human, in the intertwining of affirmations and negations, propositions and critiques, or does the human consider as sense what escapes them in alphabets and syntaxes, rules and codes?

The 'point of view' does not clear, as such, any view.

Thinking implies thinking what is and its inverse.

Consciousness dies its death, killed by thought and the world.

All analyses, all interpretations, all schemas are in some part correct, but remain insufficient.

We, you, they – in a personal, collective and neutral manner and according to all modes and times – are in search of the system of all systems, on the quest for the interpretation of interpretations, eager for genealogy and evolutionary logic, no less eager for logical structures and articulated ensembles always already present, struggling with the inside and the outside, doing things and making up theories about things, unable to decide where and how things and theories coincide or separate, shaken and fatigued by the – problematic – movement and inertia of the world, put into play as much by dominant structures and differential histories as by differential structures and dominant histories, mobilising – and mobilised by – our sensibility, our intuition, our imagination, our reflection and our thought that make us participate in the play, while also keeping us out of play.

All speech, all thought, are said and thought in a preliminary frame, a structured 'system', plunged into historical becoming and forming it.

The system of all principles and all viewpoints is theoretically and practically edified: what remains is to tweak its combinatorics.

One usually thinks inside schemas already produced.

The force of the system – in everything – is enormous: it is an ensemble of powers and relations that maintain and transform themselves as independent of the beings and things they reunite.

Do we know how we know? Do we recognise the systems and processes of our recognitions? Do we all think 'our' thoughts? Are we conscious of the articulations of our consciousness?

The absolute schema of all thought assails us and steals away.

Logos becomes technology. Logic becomes logistics. Computing machines, electronic brains, intelligence models will function according to organisations and automatisms more and more advanced, planned, programmed, cybernetised. Information and decisions obey a calculus – at once logical and laughable, integral and disintegrating – and operationally govern in the horizon of another kind of language and thought, by obeying a particular and total schema. The usage and the will to power of the old logos generate the will of will and the use of combinatorial logistics of today and tomorrow. So everything ceases to be signification and becomes a message to codify, to decode, charged by the process aiming at programming, global domination. Adjustments and compositions instituting an arrangement of a new type will not fail to correspond to malfunctions and decompositions of an antique and future type.

Without any doubt, until now, organisms and organisations have developed themselves, vitally, logically and historically, albeit with necessity and under the blows of chance, according to one possible type among others. Don't other possibilities and systems, in part calculable, also ask to be developed in the finite synthesis of all potential combinations? But even they, or the whole of their complex network, will play only one part or a larger, total and partial arrangement of the play of thought. That 'the' play of thought can be included in the arrangement of various types of communications does not disturb it.

Each thought feeds on other thoughts.

Never can the integral chain of signifiers be decomposed.

Thoughts develop themselves less according to successive periods and platforms than in often superimposed phases, to proper epochal dominants that do not exclude overlaps and recurrences. The question of the intertwining of global structure (now of simultaneities) and diachronic history demands a common ground on which it could be posed.

Every thought thinks at once historically – according to the thread of a tradition – and systematically – according to the order and aspect of problems. So every great thought takes up all the successively given interpretations and takes a position regarding the articulated ensemble of questions that are given it. All thought is fragmentary – making only dark and clear cuts into what is to be thought – and *at the same time* global – since saying and aiming at what is in its ensemble. All thought is *simultaneously* interrogative – putting into question what is – and affirmative, naming it. The thought which dares to grasp truth and truths as triumphal forms of errancy, planetary thought, multidimensional and worldly thought, the thought which can comprehend all interpretations and hermeneutics – historical and systematic, fragmentary and global, questioning and positive – as past-present-future constellations of the game, broaches a way from which all or almost all the ways depart and towards which they converge, especially if it knows that all the ways and the way will be put into question – the same and other figures of the game.

Everything can be thought in many ways – up to mental vertigo. All available or created points of view, all schemas and all their combinatorial liaisons as well as interpretations of interpretations offer unlimited – but not infinite – possibilities for grasping whatever there is. Multidimensional interlacings, interpenetrations, stackings, pyramidal edifices, analyses and syntheses, reductions and totalisations – we need all these and many other perspectives and connections to think the simplest of phenomena. It is rather the labour that consists in isolating the most determining factors that is the most difficult. An enormous volume would not be enough for a simple bouquet of flowers to be grasped multifocally. Neurophysiology, optics, botany, psychology of the conscious and the unconscious, the sociology of human work, aesthetics, mythology and history of religions, literary history and art history, lexicology, etc., etc., would not be sufficient; not to speak of all the crossings: the psychoanalytic interpretation of the bouquet in such a picture and then the sociological interpretation of the psychoanalytic interpretation and so on, indefinitely. To grasp totally, that is to say through all the means at our disposal, a simple little flower, would be equivalent to the comprehension of the entire universe. This is why research makes the task much easier.

Neither the logos of generalists nor the logoi of specialists manage to recover everything.

Neither voluntarily nor involuntarily, semi-voluntarily semi-involuntarily, thought discards what troubles it.

Humans often think, omit and act with a somnambulistic certitude.

The montage of games and decisions, strategies and tactics, the reversible linkage of elements, the management of hazards, the devices of cyclic structure, the ensembles where all possible liaisons – within the given programme – are arranged as a function of the operating schema and the goal to be achieved (it is only in conforming to it that one can pose accepted questions), the efficient calculations arranged in the most economical manner, the models of demountable and demonstrable behaviours, the matrices of the game, the frames of conduct, questions and answers, tasks to be accomplished and regulations, are built at the heart of a gigantic scaffolding – which they equally build – where biological and logical, mathematical and mechanical, cybernetic and economic automatisms, organisms, organisations and regulations are combined. The mechanics of logic and the logic of mechanics join in this programming and these behaviours. Thus, once the axioms and initial and non-contradictory postulates deductive process and processes, which must also be non-contradictory, have been positioned and constructed, in other words, once the givens of the game, which one will – or with which one will – play, are set, a game with defined rules, a lot of problems can be solved, many questions can be dealt with, a large number of operations – with statistically blocked probabilities – can be accomplished. What remains in suspense is the problematic character of the problems themselves; what leads to another game is the problem as problem.

Does all ultimate knowledge lead to mediated and meditated ignorance, to non-knowing thought?

As I write this or that, what becomes of all that traverses my sensations, my sensibility, my perception, my imagination, my memories, my thoughts? How is all this included and/or excluded? And what happens when you are reading this or that?

Each thought, by articulating itself, plays other thoughts.

Almost nothing is less rigorous than the 'concept' of rigour.

A preliminary orientation guides all research. By searching one almost already knows what one is searching for, and then one finds it, therefore one had already found it, but not yet discovered or invented. The relation of the questioner and the questioned does not link two separate things, for it precedes, so to speak, as relation, what is brought together and differentiated in its play.

Thought draws its strength from the opposition.

Rationality and irrationality of the ensemble, irrationality and rationality of the detail correspond to and counteract each other.

In regard to everything, immediately the whole fan of human opinions opens – contradictory among themselves – often then to be revised, which pronounce and drop judgements: very good, good, very bad, bad, without forgetting all the middling assessments. Which gives rise to ardent and tire-some discussions where only points of view clash.

The love of wisdom – or the search for wisdom – can it not lead to wisdom itself?

Any judgement is based on clues.

To repudiate the alternatives is very tempting. But insufficiently decisive if another way is not open.

Disjunction and reunion, conjunction and intersection, negation and complementarity are unmastered operations of thought, which does not know how to relate each to each other and to their common core.

Basic banality: thought being thought of being in becoming is itself a constant unfinished becoming.

Tactical thought orients itself through the games in the world, strategic thinking aims at the game of the world.

Let's learn to welcome unthinkable thoughts.

Specialisation is called to generalise.

Are not natural, sensible, immediate, evident recognitions, as it were, mediated from the outset, long before their theoretical elaboration and formulation? At the same time, recognitions passing for certainties, do they not impose themselves almost naturally with their specific procession of the sensible, the sane, the insane and the supersensible? A rigorous order cannot be established, all being held in the play between levels of analysis and those of reality. For all evidence implies – with or without evidence – its putting in question.

It is absolutely consequential that completed thought (*skepsis*) completes itself as scepticism completing itself.

A logos allying meditation and contemplation with psychic exercises and disciplines and physical training could mobilise and stabilise thought-heart-body and avoid some of their dark dysfunctions.

What is maladroitly called a symbol can very frequently be much more real than what it symbolises and what one calls real.

How to distinguish what is metaphorically, conceptually, ontically and effectively confused?

'Consciousness' is maimed and murderous.

In the generalised methodological jingling, everything can be said multiply, and says itself amphibologically, points of view reversing, arguments clashing; while we deduce from the general concept what is implied in the particular case and we try to climb back up from particular exemplifications to the universal formula, specificities and generality intermingling under our illegitimately amazed eyes.

Entirely definable concepts do not exist.

A single dialectic links shooter and target.

The explanation and the explicable change into their contraries.

They have known it for a long time: analysis never exhausts the concrete and the particular.

Open and multidimensional hermeneutics, polyscopic and with several variables, binding as much as possible everything with all relations, interpreting everything multiply, would provoke an unbearable mental vertigo. That is why one fixes certain explanations and interpretations, one follows rules, one consolidates mechanisms, one establishes signalisations, one builds circuits, one blocks roads, one throws certain bridges. Woe to those who are blinded by lightning tearing the sky in every direction – and none.

All expressed thought escapes whoever conceived it, gets caught in the nets of aleatory interpretations and escapes them, as it has already escaped its own author.

Between the initial project and the final result lies a chasm crossed by a walkway. The initial project, however, makes the first step.

It happens that thought is drunk from sangfroid.

From intuition to knowledge, which, without being identical, pass into each other with a constant back and forth.

Different thoughts, which appear distant and isolated from each other, join each other, thought a little further, differentially and tangentially.

Productive thought – observational and contestatory, accepting and transgressing – is never simply programmatic; it seeks the – solid and mobile – pivot points to launch itself forwards; it seeks to be integral, so more and other than totalitarian, and differential, able to think specifically this or that; it knows how to recognise all the power of traditions and permanence and opens itself to the call of fertilising novelty. Knowing that posterities are multiple and contradictory.

Thinking signifies thinking 'onto-logically' and beyond; epistemology is the thought of the poor. Theory is, generally, a para- and pseudo-philosophy, more or less correct and dogmatic; when it is not theory, it is thought.

How many theoretical debates, which excite curiosity for a moment, are – and with less poetry – only storms in a children's pool.

Even though thought is worldly, it seems that everyone has to do it for themselves.

It is always attempted by a sole and total thought. Although nothing can be thought and done only according to it.

The camels of culture, the – replacement – runners who relay, those who manage and those who are the transmission belts populate, often usefully, the overcrowded, ideological, technological, cultivated and cultural desert.

Are there thoughts that are unacceptable and untenable because they are too strong?

Does not the logos also remain mytho-logical?

Is the logos the quest, foundation and legitimation of *sense*? Seeking *the* signification and the direction of the great All and of all, we only encounter signs.

If one dismantles and 'demystifies' the reasons of reasons, does one find the *nothing*?

Thought that runs ahead must be of a terrible sobriety, keeping in poetic exaltation all its sangfroid.

The thought to come will have to shake from top to bottom the entire grammatical and syntactic, logical and dialectical structure of the language of thought to better grasp the game of the world. The verb 'to be' is destined to be surpassed as copula and judgement, auxiliary verb or substantive. To be/being will rejoin becoming in time, ceasing *to be* not *to become* something or to sink into empty nothingness. The becoming of being will have the world as horizon, and the *world* will hardly imply any immanent or transcendent sense without being, for that, senseless. And the invisible world will contain the visible world.

The thought to come must also think platitude, conventions, clichés, stereotypes, superficiality, insignificance and imbecility (whose wingbeat does and will do more than pass over the foreheads of humans), present and future forces, in their daily and official, individual and collective, journalistic and academic, talkative and silent, light and erudite forms. Since everything progresses, how could it be that platitude does not progress too? Humanity – including its avant-garde – seems to have a great need for the force of inertia and gravity.

The most distant perspectives are in general – and in particular – here. It is enough to grasp what 'is'. The hypotheses concerning the future already hide themselves in the thetically given present, a present full of antitheses. The past and the future exist only in the movement of the always negatory present. It is not the unbridled imagination that can construct images of future times. (Except if the imaginary proved to be the privileged place . . .) Time is futurition and it dislocates all images, all idols and all ideas. It is not about hovering above what becomes, but about attentively flying over fields like the birds – children of heaven and earth.

The totality of what is, the sense of being in becoming of the totality of the world, lies fragmented and its fragments fail to close over their wounds. However, the world becomes planetary: plain [plat] and plane [aplani], planned [planifié] and errant, engaged in the shucking of an incessant rotation; without centre and without circumference, our little planet errs in space and time, knowing neither for-what nor towards-what. How to think it and say it, live it and act it, in and through a poetic and praxic logos, itself taken up in the planetary, namely errant course? Because planetary also signifies (as masculine noun and according to the dictionaries): a kind of technical mechanism, a special gearing.

Is thought the enemy of victory?

How do humans pass from one thought to another?

To grasp the extreme and decisive importance of constraining circumstances and conditioned conditionings, positive and negative determinations and encompassing situations, always remains a crucial task for the play of thought – and that of action.

How and why bind – chains and links being themselves also produced and liquidated – the production and the product?

What constitutes the gestures capable of saying and doing planetary thought, open to the poetry and prose of the Sphere, engaging with the labyrinth of the world, without being imprisoned in the Circle and while recognising it? What would be its place and time and play?

A thought that maintains suspicion in the project, tension in the building, that exposes itself methodically, that explores the structure of all structures, that accomplishes and betrays its programmatic declarations, that announces and renounces, that feels, knows and ignores; a thought that plays with principles, that opens itself to aggression – triggering it and undergoing it – aims at a certain harmony of opposing tensions, supports its contradictors; a thought that moves according to the always moving and remaining possibility of thought: to think what offers itself to thought by withdrawing from it – it is in this that the tasks – never completed and accomplished – of planetary thought could consist.

In principle, has human thought reached its limits? Has it deployed its possibilities? Is its horizon unlimited, but finite? Will it be forced to say and to say again, to do and to do again, to pass and to pass again all along a spherical or spiral trajectory? Will the combinatorics of connections and interpretations know boundaries? And how will thinking humans meet their borders?

In the midst of the ruins abandoned by the various thoughts that were deployed, we have to elaborate, while continuing their work and innovating, a thought of continuous flexibility, fundamentally, amply and profoundly aleatory, all at once *methodical* and *visionary*, assuming the general banality that is at play and problematising it, a thought confronting the agony of a world that trembles on its bases, itself agonic, firm and fluent, also knowing how to isolate a point as well as to plunge it into the spiral of the totality, multiplying the equivocations and permitting certain of them to lift, maintaining and liquefying unity, totality and difference, playing with the opposed terms, at once maintained and abolished.

A childish aporia: What is reflected in the mirror when nobody looks into it?

The hermeneutic circle turns too round. How does it manage to always isolate an interpretation – sometimes actually effective – in the rich and complex network, and propose it for interpretation?

It may be that the – that is to say a – thought manages to grasp facts and interpretations stochastically, to encompass the largest ensemble of points of view, recurrent plays, to disassemble the mechanisms of causes and effects, to make – with humour, irony and toughness – a trip around the world, that is to say a world. What then remains for it to think and do?

We would like at the same time to be able to trigger the movement of thought, control the unrolling of thought and know how to stop the activity of thought so we can rest.

Sometimes we want to talk without really knowing what. Sometimes we think, without really knowing what. Often we want to write, without really knowing what. Sometimes we want to live something, without really knowing what. Often we want to play, without really knowing what and for what.

Today – but only today? – distinctions between *systematic language-and-thought* (more or less open or closed) and *fragmentary language-and-thought* (more or less coherent or aphoristic) tend to be erased. Beyond systems of all kinds, having existed or still existing, by surpassing them, that is to say by preserving them, by suppressing them and elevating them to a multidimensional level, it is a matter of elaborating an articulated and open, liquefying and problematising, questioning and interrogative language and thought, able to grasp and transform poetic, literary and artistic, political, scientific and technical, lived and dreamed activities, in short, the style and the pace of the planetary epoch, namely itinerant because of the *erring*.

The essay and the aphorism seem better suited for contemporary thought, provided that they are structured as a (holistic or totalist) synthetic ensemble and polyvalent combinatory, embracing fragmenting and fragmented ensembles, without succumbing to complacency and literary mannerism.

Starting from our situation, this is the inevitable journey of thought that goes back far into the past and the future anterior, to insert itself into an actual present, but not immediately consumable, and working for the future. By starting from – and leaving – what is ours and is not. We are a passage, we are already and not yet past.

Any position of a problem – therefore this one too – is and remains ambiguous, and its ramifications leave us unsatisfied. Reasons assail us, impose themselves on us and withdraw themselves. Any power and any challenge, any *why?* and any *because* . . . cannot have the last word, because all the words said and unsaid enter the networks of misunderstanding, thanks to which the game of the world accomplishes and misses itself.

The play of writing – prepared through the play of grammar and logic becoming language – inscribes itself immediately into the world of the play of technique.

For two thousand five hundred years, humanity has been living with the obsession of the *Book*. Book sacred and profane, book of laws and poems. Everything comes from the book, everything goes towards the book. Words, thoughts, lives exist, so to speak, through it and for it. Doesn't everything find itself written down in books and continues to be so? Would not one want to have written and read all the books – the great ones – each book being able to be comprehended multiply according to this or that grille of reading? The tension, the agreement and disagreements between word, thought, writing and life inscribe themselves into writing and emanate from it. Logos and praxis, poetic and thinking word and constituting action, deci- pherings and readings of the book of the World are engulfed in the world of the Book. Books animate the world and are nourished by it. Books enter into the course of beings and things, are part of it, and want to monopolise it. Bookish worlds and worlds of life get confused. The civilisation of books and print generalise themselves in it, at the same time preparing for the surpassing of the book as well as for a certain cultural formation. When the whole world reads, writes and prints, a threshold will be reached. The book itself will be transformed. Computational and combinatorial machines will open other possibilities of games with writing. Will we begin in this respect to be unbooked?

How to effect the reading of every book between the lines? Like the saying that speaks in half-words?

The two words and lives that most profoundly marked the Mediterranean- European and, by this, world history: Socrates and Christ. They did not write. They lived and died their words, which then were transformed by the disciples into books.

In every book, provided it is productively read, there is some good. For the book requires the collaboration of the reader. Just as one does not know what one is going to say, think and write, except in saying it, thinking it and writing it – despite and because of the generally distorted interferences between intention and realisation – so also the result remains in an incompleteness – appealing to several levels of reading – in the conjunction of involuntary dissimulation and voluntary publication. What one writes and the way one writes it – this unity of style – encounters rigid and open readings – different styles of reading – that make the book a completed and never fully finished work. The greatest density of writing – and reading – calls for diverse times.

A singular history is that of the book, and for whoever writes it, and whoever reads it. What does writing a book signify? Each book can be added to and subtracted from. The total book that haunts every author does not exist: no book can say everything, although the greatest say everything fragmentarily. By means of erasures and additions, the book would become like that painting of the Balzacian *Unknown Masterpiece*: a painter wanted to paint the absolute painting and showed no one his work: it was indeed a painting so overloaded that it offered the spectacle of a shapeless shambles. What does drafting a text that gives itself as a work signify? And rewriting the 'same' book forever? What does reading a book signify? Does one ever read a book from page to page by *comprehending* it? Is it possible to follow all its lines and also read between them? Every text disappears under the light and weight of the interpretations it arouses, becoming a pretext for other texts.

Writers like to measure others by their acts and ask for themselves to be measured by their suppositions and projects.

For whom do we write? For oneself and for others, for the worlds and the world? For those who by miserable means – erotic, religious, political, artistic, poetic, philosophical, scientific, technical and mainly unseen – have playfully shaken, shake and will shake the plane and plain surface of the little planet? For those who are and will be everywhere and nowhere: for everyone and for no one?

The total writing which we hoped to achieve does not exist.

For what generation do we write? For that which, plunging its roots into the past and jumping over the present – how passing and obsessive – will be born in the future?

Even so: nothing is exhaustive and everything is selective. In the era of the end of readers one writes for writers.

Habent sua fata libelli, the enchanted and disenchanted fabricators of books always think.

A simple daily newspaper implicitly contains several treatises on philosophy and something else.

Written thought is only thought if it advances, if it sees 'its' century from afar. In this sense, it must be more than speculative, a little liberated from the *speculum*, and without mad hopes of traversing the mirrors. One lives, one speaks, one thinks and one writes among one's contemporaries. Without question. But in dialogue with one's predecessors and in addressing oneself to future generations.

Sometimes, the impression of the already said, the already written, arises obsessively. One could imagine children, adults and the elderly taking books by chance from the bookshelves of a library and copying passages – indefinitely.

On every word of a book, there are books.

The astonishment before the thaumaturgy of speech and writing is only like the disenchantment with regard to the said and the written.

The logos is and remains the speaking face and the concealing mask. Metaphysics – ontotheological – reduces language to writing and that to continuity.

On the one hand, thought is supposed to precede the speech that translates it by betraying it, and speech the writing that translates it more or less imperfectly. On the other hand, and conjointly – by a counter-action – writing is, that is to say, has become, the mould of thought and speech.

It may be that a book offers itself less to the comprehension of the reader than it helps the evolution of the thought of the (productive) reader.

The book tends to contain the counter-book.

The community of speech and silence which we inhabit can be neither clearly said nor silenced.

The links between language and thought ultimately remain as inextricable as those that unite speech and silence.

It is the logos that speaks silence. Let's listen to 'them': both logos and silence.

The moments when humans have nothing left to say and to say to themselves – nor, consequently, to do together – do not necessarily coincide with silence.

It is indispensable to know how to respect the moments when one has nothing more to say to each other.

Silence speaks too. And one can make it speak.

That the logos takes refuge in the silence of the world and the world in the silence of the logos is not surprising.

At the very moment when everything becomes language, silence extends its domination.

In the course of the logos we meet silences that speak and speeches that are silent.

For a very long time and undoubtedly forever, the logos says in being silent, and is silent in saying.

And all that one keeps quiet, forgets, betrays, leaves aside, does not express and does not imprint, all that one cannot assume or take charge of . . .

In any case, we will have to learn to let a certain silence hover.

How does the logos comport itself in regard to its own eclipse?

Without too much chattering about errancy and play, about oneself and silence, and by uttering words and sayings that carry, what does the logos think and say? The play of That.

II

That.
The Play of the Being in Becoming of the Fragmentary and Fragmented Totality of the Multidimensional and Open World

That 'is': *being* of all that is, and *nothingness, becoming, movement, positivity* and *negativity, space-time, unity, multiplicity* and *totality, world* open or closed, finite or infinite or indefinite.

That 'is': *the being in becoming of the fragmentary and fragmented totality of the multidimensional and open world* – to name it in a not too dissociative language – as it constitutes itself in and through its encounter with the human being; it is rather inside this encounter that the *Same* says and makes itself. For we can neither depart from the being of the human to reach being in becoming, nor do the inverse. We are always on the way to the heart of the Same – always problematic – always in the interlude.

That 'is': the play of all its unveilings and all its occultations, all the readings and interpretations it arouses and troubles, all the machinations it provokes and breaks. This *play* is the One-All, the One-Multiple, Being-Nothingness, the All-Nothing.

That 'is': the horizon of horizons that withdraws; one could call it simply *World.* You call that a world? The human is not without the world and the world is not – that is to say, is not said and done, is not a problem – without the human. None of them is the other and none of them goes without the other. They make neither one nor two. How, then, do they institute the Same? Behold the *game.*

That 'is': *logos* as language and thought of the world said by the human, *spirit, idea,* start and end of all that is, *God,* measure of creation, and *physis* as cosmic totality, universe of universes, energetic *matter* in mechanical and/or dialectical movement, historical *humanity*, producer and transformer of what it is and what it is not, *technical* scaffolding of reasons, actions, networks and passions that assemble and combine beings and things.

Each of the great designations of That, being, nothingness and becoming, space-time, unity, totality and world, God, nature, human and play, is not what it is and is what it is not.

That has been said and named, called and invoked, by remaining unthought and unprecedented in terms of enigma, of secrecy, of mystery, to become like a question and a problem, without escaping the unspeakable and the unnameable.

That neither escapes the finitude – the unique rather than double finitude – of the being of the world and the being of the human, finitude of time. In this major finitude, the finitudes that are not simply particular are gathered, and proceed from it: in particular the finitude and the limitation of the imaginary (utopias and uchronias), which is not an infinite or even unlimited dump of possibilities and alterities, nostalgias and anticipations, desires and dreams – the finitude of history, the finitude of all the games.

Each of the dimensions of That is encompassing and encompassed, is implicated in all the others and implies them; it is at once moment and totality.

Do all aspects of That reveal – and do they arise from – alliances and mis-alliances, relations of weakness and power? Are all the worlds of the world unsatisfactory? Are all forms of the game rigged?

It is not only the horizon of That and That as the horizon, it is even any idea of the horizon that has become problematic.

Each of the great circles, each of the great equivalences of That, comprises several aspects and versions.

It is That which happens when something – that – happens, even if what happens looks like nothing.

Most often That remains vague, vague, vague.

That can only remain the Unnamed, although requiring certain names.

That is caught in the meshes of an increasingly mediatised network of mediations. This is why everything is more and more complicated, making impossible any more or less immediate, evident, unproblematic attitude. Yet how persistent is the temptation to recover everything.

That is not neutral, although it neutralises everything, making everything possible, animating it, killing it, letting it return. It always remains in suspense.

That has also been taken in charge by the mystics and the esotericisms that discovered as-yet uncounted treasures, custodians of a tradition that plays with us as much as we play with it, itself rather mystified, believing ourselves dismantling it quickly. Situated and situating, silent and speaking, does this esoteric and mystical tradition, several thousands of years old, await its hour?

That, which is there, does not always and everywhere happen as an antiphanic epiphany.

The search for That, the theme of first philosophy or metaphysics or ontotheology, remained a science without a name, a sought-for science, an unfindable science.

That was also poured into the hollow mould of the world. We are always in a relationship of half-full half-empty comprehension with the all and the nothing 'before' thinking them. A *tension towards*, a *relation to* and an *attraction by* precede thought. Metaphysics and anti-metaphysics have grasped the being of the world as full and present in its totality. The intuitions, concepts, categories and ideas expressed it or cautiously put it into question. It is that which no longer goes.

This relation that is open to the ensemble of what is, communication – by instants – with the splendour of the world, the rhythm of totality, being swept away by the flow of life, that itself which can at certain moments leave traces that accord us with That, also exists and coexists with its contrary.

All contact is a function of an acquiescence and a resistance.

Similarities and dissimilarities attract and repel themselves.

All the elucidations of That comprise oscillations and pendulum movements, accomplish themselves through slanting leaps.

That cannot be read simply as a text offered by the Book of the World. There is no unique reading of the Book of the World, nor of any text what-soever, though the world does not constitute a text.

That requires polarisations and polarisers.

We encircle That which encircles us.

It is That which is there: it unveils and veils itself, shows and hides itself, offers and withdraws itself, lets itself be grasped and remains ungraspable.

The game of 'That' itself allows us to call it provisionally, in considering all terms as equivalents, provided that one explicates them differentially: *being, nothingness, becoming, totality, world, play*.

What is being? That is *the* question. It does not, however, comprise a positive answer, for as soon as one fixes Being by saying that it is this or that, one makes of it a particular being; this is how all philosophy later called metaphysics operates. Being reduces itself neither to the verbal infinitive nor to the verb becoming substantive, although it is closer to its verbal than to its nominal look. It does not reduce itself to copula and judgement. It is not even something that is, nor the foundation or the totality of everything that is. So? It *is*, but it does not *exist* as being. Implying nothingness and implicated by it, being is in becoming, is the becoming of the totality of the world, the play of errancy.

Being was grasped from the start – that is to say, with the Greeks who named it – in and through the ontological, analogical and metaphorical logos. Moreover: it was identified with thought. Since then, the fundamen-tal equation of ontological thought formulates itself: being = thought. What happens to the difference?

The-unity-and-the-difference between what is and what is said and thought *of it* remains troubling. What is *this* that resists the diverse approaches?

For metaphysical thought, being is presence or, in a derivative way, absence; presence grasped in modern metaphysics by consciousness pres-ent to itself in self-consciousness, in the representation that prolongs its action to become, at the threshold of its completion, representation of the representation.

As absent does not mean: absent.

Representation strikes presence, reigns over it and maintains conjointly the radiance and the obsession of the presence that thus perpetuates itself, even in the form of absence. So it suppresses and conserves – by exacerbating – presence-absence. It wants to render things present in their absence. Because 'absence' calls for an original presence, effectively existing and/or existing in representation.

Absence is only the reverse of presence. It is the reign of presence with barely reversed signs. It is the same orientation and the same nostalgia.

Most often one criticises the metaphysics of representation with the weapons of the philosophy of reflection.

To think That, philosophico-metaphysical thought appealed to the luminous and illuminated gaze and to clear hearing, scotomising opposing powers and neglecting the chiaroscuro and the silent and often inaudible noise of the sensible, and subordinating the world to the light and the word of Being. Being posited as thought became the focus of theoria, the logically discursive or logically intuitive vision, the central theme of representation and spectacle. The entire history of onto-theo-logy is a history of the eye and, even when it becomes anthropological history – thus completing metaphysics – this same history remains history of the eye, now human, until it stops looking without seeing and loses sight of itself. Regarding the ear – called external or internal, depending on the case – one never knew too well what it was listening to, or what to do with it: does it hear or not, and what?

What punctures the eyes and deafens the ears is no longer present.

What is present in itself is 'indissociable' from what is present to the human – within and beyond its representation.

Neither presence nor absence is: there is only their combined play and the play of which they are signs.

It is in the heat of dialogue, that is to say, 'by playing a laborious game', as he calls it himself, that the Platonic *Parmenides* poses his first hypothesis of the One (that is Being).

Usually, not knowing where to head among beings, we do not search for being. Exceptionally, the latter, that is, the being of the world, starts to shine on particular inner-worldly beings. Searching for being, we meet only sparks of fragmented being, which, sparkling or dull, are said by the sparks of words and thoughts.

Is it on the basis of the original fold between being and the being that nothing goes without fold?

Metaphysics sees and does not see the difference between being and a being.

Metaphysics makes Being a being, fixes it and subordinates it, and, at the same time, sinks every being into a second-rate reality, subordinating it to Being par excellence.

Roughly asked, the question formulates itself: what exists?

How does that exist which no longer exists or not yet, and, in general, the 'inexistent'?

To 'being' belongs what is no longer and what is not yet.

Being and appearing are mortally linked, each one vivifying and mortalising the other, animating and cancelling each other mutually and conjointly, because we can no longer save either essences or appearances.

What is, shaken by imbalance, instability, disorder, drowned in the unfinished and the unlimited, can reach the clearing of appearing only in a certain equilibrium combining stability and fixity, particular order and provisional completion, limits and limitations.

The path towards the appearance and the disappearance of the being is one and the same – and different.

Is it in our power to grasp the phenomenon as surpassing its conditions of appearance, that is to say, not reducing it to them or substituting them for it?

Metaphysics privileges light and the visible, although it relies on the invisible.

All that appears manifests itself, has invisible roots.

Vision has been clearly privileged at the expense of hearing: it is true that through it are conveyed so many opinions and platitudes, gratuitous and non-engaging things; but someone is not listening who simply listens without understanding anything, or who understands vaguely without listening.

To face the light, we use visors.

We mainly see, of all that is, only the side turned towards us – the side towards which we direct our gaze.

The eyes were seen as the windows of being.

Are there things that one sees and that do not exist and others that one does not see and that exist?

We see more of what emerges and less of what it emerges from.

What has not yet lived and what is already dead can sometimes almost be glimpsed. A buried and invisible treasure *exists* only on the day it is discovered. Where was it before?

When rays of light compose a beam, the hour of a certain clarity has arrived. A too brilliant and burning transparency would consume all.

Does 'everything' become clear, when 'everything' is finished?

Except at noon – where being and appearing coincide – each being and each thing that advances or recedes is preceded or followed by its shadow, and one always asks for a light from elsewhere to dispel it.

The law of the day and the passion of the night divide and share the being devolved to human being. Can it agree with the night without hating the day, and with the day without fearing the night? Does the agreement proceed from disagreement, or vice versa? Would there be an agreement with being, which, forgetting itself, would refuse to agree?

Has everything emerged from a dark abyss to which it will return?

Darknesses are only completely dark when they don't know what they are. But *are* they then? From the moment they are recognised as such, what becomes of them – for us?

Light and obscurity, illuminations and darknesses take hold of all the foundations emerging from the without-ground.

Being has been posed as the fundamental position, the thesis par excellence, from which the other positions and oppositions are thetically and antithetically, analytically and synthetically derived. First and supreme hypothesis – wanting to be true and not just true-ish – *it is*, that is to say, comprehends itself at the same time as anhypothetical. It is also the fundamental proposition, itself subject, copula, attribute and predicate in speculative judgement: the being is being, the being is the being, or better: the being is (being, the being); so its placement in parentheses is prepared.

From the moment they are named, sense and being are barred, erased. Same goes for the foundation and the origin.

Every chain of questionings comes to butt against an initial question, variously said and enclosed by replies that eliminate it. *What is being and why is it there?* seems to be this ultimate question that surpasses all others in the direction of the interrogation that blocks and opens the play.

The fundamental search for a *primus agens*, for a prime being or *mover*, activates all thought and renders it reactive.

Everything, at every time and everywhere, obscurely or clearly asks why? and does not receive an answer. Is this an indication of the path leading to a cure from the question?

The principle of sufficient reason says: all that is has its reason (or foundation) for being, or, nothing is without reason (or foundation) for being. Except 'Being' itself, it would be necessary to add.

Between the given and the founded the bonds remain enigmatic. What one does not comprehend, even in saying so, plays several roles at once, blurs the tracks, in the general confusion, does not manage to dispel misunderstandings.

The call of the foundational remains extremely strong. Even if it cannot receive any foundation, a foundation opening and assigning the diverse signs of human and historical life their mobile place, thus to different structures of the ensemble, is always, and always again, expected.

Always the first and supreme foundation is itself founding and without foundation, without ground [*fond*].

Self-foundation and self-suppression of the foundation go together.

There is no master of being, being itself not being the master.

Thus, from now on, the 'fundamental' will remain without foundation; not that it possessed it before.

It is from the anonymity of being that words and names, gestures and actions, beings and things emerge.

Ontology, speculative theory of what is – what has been, what will be – already contains implicitly what will develop from it while also controlling it: a deontology, normative and more or less practical and ethical, of what must be. Theory of being and theory of must-be are mutually conditioning.

Into the nets woven by ontology and deontology – nets that weave them too – a certain axiology is always woven: a valorisation of beings and a theory of beings and things as values. But it is especially through the ontological tearing – more than through the holes of the nets – that these valorisations appear and are torn in turn.

About the mode of articulation of the 'ontological' and the 'anthropological', we cannot yet articulate a discourse.

To methodological abstractions supposedly correspond ontico-ontological domains.

The sensible, subordinated to the intelligible by metaphysics, therefore neglected, magnified at the expense of the supersensible by anti-metaphysics – the question of the link uniting the senses and sense always remaining in suspense, even and especially when it receives unilateral, bilateral or multilateral responses – is what shows itself by hiding itself.

All those who participate in the assault of the fissured ramparts of being that do not protect anything, lose themselves in the undergrounds and bastions full of sense which assail the assailants – sense produced by them or by their kind? – and, in the fury of combat, neglect the sensitive and the sensible.

There are differentiations that remain when differences are suppressed in and through indifference.

What is is in realising itself and in unrealising itself.

What is supposes an access to it – being for us.

More important than beings and signs are the relations and the relations between relations.

What is possesses and takes root and grows – sometimes – into a vast horizon. Even small horizons are plunged into immensity.

Seeking the unique and closed or total and open being, we meet only the unfinished and the incomplete.

What is near is usually far away, what is familiar does not cease being strange.

What is holds itself in danger; is it always necessary to face it?

Would an 'ultimate' attraction of being orient a thought that would open itself to the meditation of being in its withdrawal, withdrawal of being in the manifestation of the being, withdrawal itself withdrawing?

There is no longer an ultimate name of the origin and the end in an ultimate ontology.

Is there some strictly individual and particular, and if so, is it expressible and speakable?

All the readings of what 'is' appear more and more like equivalents. Will text and experiences equally become more and more indifferent and interchangeable?

Those who proclaim, state or murmur the invisibility of being do not comprehend how and why *this* Being-itself, its sense or its truth, is already barred, erased, deleted, crossed out, the erasure still rendering visible and readable what it erases and its own action. It is an index, if not the index.

To be and not to be, this is the horizon of the 'ontological' and central anthropological response.

Why would being aspire to become mobile, to be mobilised, after having been posed as immobile – moving without being moved – as denying movement?

For the moment, 'being' is so ingrained in our language – 'our' grammar, 'our' syntax, 'our' logic – that another possibility, which would not be entirely ours, is not yet clearly apparent.

Also pay attention, please, to the aura of what is.

Is being a hole – clear and/or obscure – in nothingness? Is nothingness a hole – clear and/or obscure – in being? All being true and nothing being true? All being false and nothing being false? In the obscurity of the presence-gap?

Nothingness – nothingness or the thought that thinks it? – is it some 'thing' derived, secondary, in relation to being that it presupposes? Is *void* the negative of the full? Is *disorder* only a different, incomplete, unexpected order? Is the *possible* only and principally what has been? Is it lack, absence, that hits the given and the thought so that these negative entities can emerge? So goes all philosophy – thought of light, of (compact) being, of presence. It will now devolve to us to experience the opposite. How not to see double?

Nothingness: would it be the invisible knocking on our doors?

Nothingness emits signs, without which it would not be, would not attract us.

Is it on and in the empty horizon that beings and things are outlined?

Negativity cannot only be reduced to returned positivity or simply affected by the minus sign.

Sometimes with clairvoyance and sometimes almost blindly, usually in a mixed manner, negativity continues its work as a mole that undermines all terrains and collapses buildings. The moles gnaw at and also cut the roots.

Negativity puts into action and into question. It errs and it fixates.

The development of what is is accompanied by its negation.

What is contrary must also be inventoried inventively.

Always and everywhere the worm is in the fruit.

Being: non-being; becoming. – Past; present; future. – Presence; absence; hope.

If hope is misleading, disappointment is no less misleading.

That deploys itself in the space-time of the world, where everything appears, disappears, reappears . . . It is not the world that is in space, but space that is in the world as space of the world where the various locations and the different places are situated, as well as all the movements and all the displacements. It is at degree zero that every place can be occupied; what occupies it then being denied by time.

Space knows both expansion and shrinkage. In it places and locations are built and it is by them that it is experienced.

Is not space a play of relations where time is in play?

The play of the space-time of the world 'is' the world itself.

In the space-time of the world, no one can move without an orientation available that avails of them – of the human more than of the world.

Extension and duration manifest the unity of the gaping fork of space and time where everything is engulfed.

Could not all particular 'geometries', of all kinds, be integrated into a global pangeometry that would not sacrifice the unitary perspective to the integration of plurality, or vice versa?

We must finally build the topology of the non-place.

Time is also spacing, and movement in space is time. In extension-duration.

Becoming is becoming of being, of totality, of the world; it is the play of time whose temporality constitutes productive positivity and negativity, movement, historicity. It is in and through history that all manifests and institutes itself. The secret of the movement seems unfathomable: on what does the movement rest? Why and how all that is, therefore also us humans, seems to aspire only to rest, to a state so to speak anterior and posterior to movement, while being moved and provoking movement? Would time in its totality rest in immobility, and would it be that in which everything will gather itself and rest? Becoming is itself this oriented and global errancy – this determining and determined itinerancy – fundamental – though without foundation – pursuing a trajectory, but not including an answer to the question of why, rendering the question itself almost useless. Errancy signifies that one cannot assign a truth to the becoming of being, for it is in and through errancy itself that all truths and errors appear and disappear. It is precisely the deployment of the play having no foundation external to it.

In time and by fracturing it, humans elaborate a legend that they take for the history of their life and for their life itself, and history elaborates legends that give themselves as segments of the becoming of universal history, a major legend giving itself as universal history itself, the greatest legend taking itself for history – the becoming – of being.

Continuous becoming is equally discontinuous.

Even discontinuous, becoming continues and remains continuing and continued.

It is not only the beginning that is inchoate; the end too is inchoate.

Everything is pushed towards its non-definitive end.

We constantly have to go back over the steps of becoming.

What does not change, dies. What does change, dies also.

Watch out for the turns and detours of surpassing: what is surpassed, when, where and how, what has surpassed it, when, where and how, what has become of the surpassed and the surpassing?

What is surpassed remains 'somewhere' and goes back in time, because there is a past that is gone and a past to come, constantly recreated.

Can humans ever overcome both their obsession with duration and the haste to end it?

On the ground of the world without grounds, all that is must be grasped as the ensemble of its history: the little tree of the forest becomes a Christmas Tree and then the mast of a child's boat, later providing the material for the pencils that serve to write the drafts of these children's stories.

Time does not flow.

Is not time essentially, namely temporally, rhythm? Neither circular and repetitive, nor rectilinear and progressive, at once circular and repetitive, rectilinear and progressive, does not time in its entirety contain the whole of time and times, the totality of temporal development? What has been, is and will be. But how will be what has not already been in the finitude of the entirety of time? Logically and ontologically, the beginning as well as the development and the emergence of the new are somehow impossible: the beginning implies unfolding and ending that are nevertheless unforeseen; it is the end that reveals the beginning and the unfolding there where there is, there where one considers that there is an end. The becoming and the motive negativity, positive and annihilating, the time of the world – the play of time governs us and escapes us. Time unfolds itself multiply: it makes be and it makes disappear; it gets experienced and measured in many ways. It poses us the problem of its irreversibility and its reversibility, for we humans who never know too well with what time we are dealing. With so-called real-time? With lived time, which governs our memory and our memories, our confrontation with the present, our projections and anticipations, in the three-dimensional play of the past-present-future? With the time of techno-scientific calculation? With the time of representation? With the time of thought or the thought of time?

Everything seems to accomplish itself in time according to a pendulum movement, where lack and excess provoke the contrary movement, swinging the balance, marked by its scourge.

In any case, time will do its work, accomplish its labour. Strive, without too many contradictions, to see for whom and for what – and not why – time labours.

All the same: why does it produce almost always what we did not expect in this way, what we did not foresee exactly?

Do not over-isolate a moment; not to isolate it at all is impossible.

Very often, the past was not a present and often the future will not become one.

Inexorable and inglorious, becoming records the different needs of order and puts them into question: (it also raises the question: with what concepts is the putting into question done?).

To know how to wait, even the day after tomorrow, gaining and losing 'one's' time, labouring and passing with time, seems and is difficult. Are we not all, as long as we are, precipitated, not bearing our weak share of freedom?

In the river of time, if one maintains this spatial imagery, the waters of the future are behind us and the past has already overtaken us.

The most radical contingency of 'being', is it time?

Was not all rest, first of all, movement?

Time is always in suspense and history unfinished: even when it reaches its end, it remains to pursue, without attaining it – without 'end'.

A deaf struggle enchains actuality – which imposes itself – on immense temporality.

That is in time: both the more or less durable and the more or less fleeting.

The human can only seek to occupy – to structure – time through activity and imagination, to flee boredom and the flight of time.

How are the various movements contained in the 'unique' movement, the play of all that is?

The 'ground' of worlds gathers time and is gathered in the time that all philosophical (and idealistic) thought wants to abolish since Plato (out of time) up to Hegel (the victory of the spirit over time).

Time makes everything cease. What makes it cease? With stubbornness, humans would like a glimpse 'out of time' that would contain time.

Do not build only on sand, but with the sand of time.

One would like to keep in memory more than it can bear.

In the centre of the movement of whirlwinds and cyclones there is always a zone of calm.

Time takes revenge on all that seems to violate it.

Repetitions and constant changes compose being in becoming (the being of becoming, the becoming of being).

There is hardly any unique direction. The direction which gives itself as unique – and may effectively be – is the triumphant direction.

No path of becoming is quite straight: ellipse or spiral, it is usually warped.

We are always dealing with a semi-spiral.

What passes is, generally, the passage.

Omnitemporal becoming 'well' understood can only mean: being in becoming of the world in – and as – *time* – not in eternity – errant course of the totality of non-totality, *play* of the open world, multidimensional *world* without graspable origin and without foreseeable completion.

We grasp not so much the becoming as the become.

The end as such cannot be dominated. The polyphony of origins masks the aphony of the origin. There is no ultimate word of origin, if it is not the play of its unapparent apparition.

The origin that has not ceased to be and which always is, belongs again and always to the future. Thus the present is at once the most dominant mode and the most suspended mode of time.

The beginnings of the end are, when they are decisive, destined to reign interminably. It is as if the end doesn't end ending.

When will we construct a chronology at once synchronic and diachronic, open to the succession and simultaneity of the three dimensions of time, each of which also counts three dimensions (past-present-future) that ceaselessly create and recreate?

Permanence, succession and simultaneity of the ecstasies of time inscribe themselves in the same totality.

Every past is mythical; the present becomes it; the future is it already.

There are only provisional completions. And the constancy of myths and rhythms of time.

Unable to pose, if not resolve, the question of reversibility and – above all – the irreversibility of time, according to the various plans and different approaches, humans desire a modifiable past, a present omnipresent throughout time and a future synonymous with eternity, for which they invented and imagined various histories.

It is in the fire of the play that the ephemeral and the durable appear, are lit up, consume themselves, as suits the game of all the antagonistic and complementary movements.

There are, incontestably, moments more opening than others. The distinction is however difficult to establish.

The relations between memory and time make the game of time that collects and undoes memories. For it is not memory that is the place of time, it is time that is the non-topological place of memory, always blurred.

Memories seek us and flee us.

Memories are as patchy as omissions.

In the course of time, let us take care not to forget the extreme power of oblivion.

No day, right until the last, is unique; there will be a following.

Why do we always have the sensation that everything that happens happens too soon and, above all, too late? How does the question of the right time pose itself?

Very intense beings, things and signs – apparently – do not last very long.

The play of time and the play with time, this bifurcated temporal play, temporarily and artificially permits the presenting, gathering at a precise moment of time other moments of time and times.

We strive to kill the time that kills us.

Stopping the 'march' of time is one of the strongest human obsessions. As if to avenge ourselves for it, humans have nostalgia for a past that could have been other than it was, and project a future radically different from the past and the present.

Time passes and makes pass, but just as it arises and makes arise. Countless histories are woven and told in the fable of time.

Everything matures quite slowly and consumes itself rather quickly.

Scrupulously examine the before-signs, which, for the most part, remain indiscernible.

One wants to organise time so it both passes and does not pass. One wants everything to finish quickly and everything to last as long as possible. One wants stability and passage.

Will we ever learn what we do anyway: gaining and losing 'our' time?

The habitual three-dimensionality of time cut into a good original past, a critical and bad present and an eschatological future good once again, feeds on experiences and can receive cosmic, psychophysiological, psychological, historical illumination: thought, a catastrophe befallen some higher animals, humans; the ice age; the foetal state and the desire to return to it; the golden age of infancy; naive and 'natural' primitivity.

Measured time, cosmic and natural time, psychological and historical time, all these times compose the fabric of time without exhausting it, because it is not in our power to take time – segmented or total – under our protection.

Over time, will we get used not only to feverishly counting time, but to counting a little more serenely with and on time?

Haste and precipitation, impatience, as much as slowness and waiting, patience, give time rhythm.

Time seems to impose a time when we have less and less time.

We comprehend backwards, the past comprehends us, and we live nevertheless forwards, in the future we do not comprehend.

Human time agrees more with the becoming than with the coming.

Diverse machines and machinations venture to dismantle time, and time dismantles them. That is in time and, moreover, that is, in the game, time itself.

How to distinguish between what changes, becomes other, differs, is or appears as new, transforms itself more or less radically, marks a revolution, what evolves, renews itself, blossoms and collapses, transforms itself gradually, and that which remains the same to itself, identical, joins itself, repeats itself, returns? Are the differences between radical and revolutionary change, jump and bound, and evolutionary transformation, step by step, differences in degree or in nature, and are the differences in degree and in nature differences in degree or in nature?

What returns in time – changed and the same, more different than identical, often with inverted signs – does not return from the side where one expected it.

What repeats itself is not so much the identical as the difference. It and its limits have no end. They have just a circular limit at the interior of which repeats indefinitely – and not infinitely – the repetition of difference.

The Same is not identical to itself.

Eternal return – that is to say temporal – of the same implying the other could indicate this: to assume all *as if* it had to return.

The temporal return of the same does not return the identical infinitely. Other is the enigma of repetition and rotation, the cycle of productivity and reproduction. Why, from the origin, does all seem already played? Where does the explosive force of the presentiment come from?

The new produces itself within the cycle of advancing repetition.

In the name of the Same, it is permissible for several adversaries to fight each other.

The same, in its history, is divided against itself.

The same has several terrains of application.

The return of the same changes and transforms itself in returning to the same.

Different interpretations of the same text can be openings.

Reborn from the ashes. This wish is part of the ashes. Is the temporal return of the same not comprehended in it?

Patiently practising accentuating the same in the other, the other in the same.

Order and questioning compose the 'two' sides of the same.

In the intersecting fires and games of resemblance and difference, a rather glacial separation sometimes emerges.

Moreover, how to unite or separate the other and the same, as well as what is and what is seen so or otherwise? Do the identical and the different rejoin themselves, not in indifferentiation, but in the One-All, which maintains all the differences in the indifference of the differentiated one?

The new that always arises new again – obeying what need? – borrows its clothes and its disguises from the old that thus renews itself.

The differentiated unity of being, of the Same – and not the indifferentiation of the identical where all sinks into indifference – is constituted by a network of relations that it constitutes at the same time.

Following the spirals that go from the similar to the same, let's be attentive, more than to the nuance, to the *specific difference* and its play with *indifference*. In all domains. On all registers.

The totality is not the sum or synthesis of all that is, it is not a closed set. It contains all the totalities, it is and remains open to time, constitutes itself as a play of time. Already every totality has characteristics that are not parts. Every structure is more than the set of its constituents. No process is entirely reducible to one of its sectors and factors. All the more so *the* 'totality'. It always remains fragmentary, because we are dealing only with its fragments, ourselves fragments of it, and we fragment it more to grasp it.

The whole of being *and* the totality of beings manifest themselves in the attraction, the withdrawal, and the secret of appearing – 'in' becoming – as neither identical nor separable.

The perspective of totality is in general grasped through the partiality of different particular optics. But each dimension encompasses and is encompassed by others, all the points of view – historical and systematic – communicate, their mobile ensemble (as well as all the multilateral crossovers between ensembles) and the nested plays making a part of the totality of our access to the totality, if not the totality of aspects of the totality of the world.

The whole world is never given, neither as original nor otherwise.

Since the whole 'gives' itself in the part, isn't it then possible to act on the whole by acting on the part?

Does 'all' that is 'sin' through excess and/or through flaw?

All that, which is, is so singular and so linked to the rest.

None of the circles of the totality is completed, none possesses total autarky, none succeeds in excluding or securing the other circles.

There are no pure beings, in fact, no pure event. All that, which is, weaves more links with the rest than it destroys. Every fragment is part of an ensemble and every ensemble part of a larger ensemble.

Every isolated system fluidifies itself, liquefies itself: this provokes its playful experimentation.

The totality must not be comprehended in this manner: what is *in* all of the world. We again and always name the total movement of the world after particular movements.

All is structured, organic or organised; all that, which is, comprises, and is envisaged as comprising, rules. Formalised structure is a case in point of structure in general.

All that is and all the particular totalities know a *genesis*, a *becoming*, a *history*, are in a *process*, possess a *system*, a *logic*, a *structure*. All forms are formed and constitute formations, changing and persisting throughout permanences and changes. There is no genesis, no becoming, no history without structure, and there is no structure, logic, system, formation without genesis. Which, however, commands the other, how do they imply each other, and thanks to what do these transformations operate? The logical and systematic, formed and constituted structure knows a historical genesis, a becoming, a process. These know that. That is to say: it is we who are in the process and the structures, by erecting knowledge and recognising them, in the totality that perpetually makes itself and that we make. The development, the genea*logical* and phenomeno*logical* becoming, the dia*lectical* and historical process, lead to a logical and systematic structure of the ensemble, this development itself being the becoming of a kind of initial and total structure. Thus the circle seems to turn, making us turn with it and leaving us in the plan, since we do not succeed in composing or decomposing the differentiated unity linking historical becoming and logical structure.

Does the structure of the ensemble find itself in the parts, or can we consider the parts as capable of making us find in them the structure of the ensemble?

This structure of structures, whether fanatically or half-heartedly sought, persists in not showing itself, although it is around us – and we in it.

All that, which is, seems to require a rhythm, a delimitation and a frame: word and thought, writing and typography, painting and architecture, human life and diverse games. This frame enframes and delimits what is carried by a rhythm and, in its interior and the frames of frames, everything is 'worth' itself, all keeps together. Even what appears as arrhythmic and overflows the frames. Revolutions themselves – never total – follow a rhythm, delimit themselves and are delimited, unfold themselves in the interior of a frame and mobilise frames. Whether the rhythm appears fixed, given or unchained, whether delimitation is respected or transgressed towards another delimitation, whether the frame is called order, organism, organisation, system, ensemble of rules and relations or structure, has secondary importance. No overflying thought can disassemble these times of the world and these worlds in the world, and no so-called rigorous and detailed analysis that traverses the corridors with the pace of (blind) rats can account for it.

We must look nowhere else than everywhere.

The origins will always steal away, my child (and the questions will overflow the frames).

All that is granted to us comprises the other face: what is refused to us.

How does one manage to isolate whatever there is of the whole?

There are no simple details, if they are treated according to a plan of the ensemble.

Are there defects of detail or are all the defects the defects of the ensemble?

The totality that is fragmentary (ontologically, so to speak) and fragmented (by us and our graspings that decompose it into aspects), the fragments that are totalitarian (in 'themselves') and totalised (by us) are always apprehended in an angular manner, because it is envisaged from a certain angle that everything shows itself and plays, totalitarianally, fragmentarily, angularly.

How is the difference of what reunites itself anew preceded in the whole?

What determines the human and what the human determines is preceded by a relation to the whole world, which seems to precede, and in any case include, the relation to beings.

Can everything become a *said* fragment of the totality?

One can enter a system through a particular point.

Unification and diversification impose themselves on all that is, and expose it to the danger of the opening and the closure.

Everything appears as cut out from a foundation of a horizon previously cut out.

Each thinker thinks one thought and all think the One-All: all the central intuitions, oriental and occidental, mythical or discursive.

What happens at the level of the 'totality' also happens on all planes, at all levels.

The totality is formed by sums *and* differences.

Everything, once 'posed', we can explore certain of its details.

Every totality, every system, every structure is stronger than its components, even though one of their constituents can make them explode.

Know that in every system or network a variable never functions alone, even though every systematisation or operation isolates one.

The open whole and the closed one do not constitute an alternative.

Everything fragments itself always more.

The intramundane fragments of the totality are not parts that would be in the same relation to the whole world as the fragment of something particular to the ensemble of this same thing.

The fragment: this collaboration of human and death.

The phenomena which burst out [*éclatent*] in broad daylight are splinters [*éclats*], possess a brilliance [*éclat*].

Some fragments are more total than others.

Each fragment of the universal comprises several specifications.

The agglomerated and the compact disintegrate themselves differentially, the scattered and the dispersed reassemble themselves. Everything tends towards unity, everything tends towards separation.

Big organisations are chaotic, and chaos is as already organised.

Distinctions, once established, play then as such.

Nothing is attacked frontally; everything is approached aslant.

All that is becomes sign. Signs, beings and things mix so inextricably that they become inseparable.

All that is appears, becomes, is done, comprises residues and waste.

We never meet a given totality: the totality is what is indicated in the play of presence-absence and beyond them.

The comings and goings between the partial, the particular and the singular and the total, the general and the universal often lose their way, remain on course, miss the departure or return.

The totality is not this or another circle, this or another spiral movement; the being in becoming of the totality is not 'the being in becoming of the totality' printed in italics or not, with or without quotation marks, yet printed black on white.

When the whole puts itself into motion, does the rest necessarily follow?

The totality of the expressions of a thing, is it the thing itself?

If one says that the concrete can only be grasped through the intermediary of the abstract and the whole through the intermediary of the part, one is tempted to add: and inversely.

In every part, is there 'everything', or can one find everything?

Is the whole not in its parts? From each angle, one grasps the whole, to a certain extent. Nevertheless, one always deals with parts. And even all the biases through which one can approach the same phenomenon do not exhaust it. Is it not, therefore, identical to the totality of its entries?

All can be considered more or less autonomous – possessing its own logic and particular dynamic – and as linked to the all and the rest, to the logic of the ensemble that escapes – the logic and the ensemble.

We never confront the total face of the world, calm, smiling or sad, uncovered or masked. We never see the total face of whatever is.

There is no totaliser of totalisations.

In turn or simultaneously, the totality can be subsumed under each of its moments – which it contains. The whole illuminates and implicates the part and the part the whole.

Nothing reduces itself entirely to the constellation of which it is a part, even if it entirely depends on it.

It is only an image of the totality: the serpent that bites its tail. All the circles remain sketched.

What relations maintain the totality of the world and the totality of our access to it?

What is impossible as totality can be possible as moment.

What's paradoxical: the totality is more than the sum of its parts, and the set of subsets of a set possess a power superior to that of the set itself.

Everything that is given as total and universal is at the same time fragmentary and particular, and, for it to be able to appear, illuminate and fertilise an aspect of everything, it must, it seems, want to manifest as total.

Everything is as immediately mediatised.

Everything is to be reinvented, as one ceaselessly repeats. But everything is also thus used up, including its reinventions.

Everything tends to become mass and quantity, measurable and measured, accounted and computed, calculated, at the same time as everything tends to become number, figure, sign possessing its own, more and more symbolic, mediatised, formalised and fleeting reality. Thus all constitutes a total account in formation. A *throw of the dice will never abolish chance*, Mallarmé thought, his eyes directed towards:

A constellation,
cold with forgetting and disuse
                    not so much
            that it not number
on some vacant and superior surface
            the successive impact
                        sidereally
of a total account in formation . . .

There is nothing outside of totality; strictly speaking, there is not even totality.

Everything and nothing: each keeps itself 'behind' the other.

Its limits delimit all that is.

Every system has its weak point.

All that is adjacent or subjacent traverses all the compossibles, of which a single formation will become effective.

Everything can be questioned: because limited or because unlimited.

Every function has its dysfunction: usually the phenomenon is not excessively serious.

To order and orders correspond counter-orders, to currents counter-currents.

The need for order, norms, forms, rules, laws, measurement, in short, hierarchy, who does not feel it, without the need for the reversal of hierarchies arising sooner or later?

Most often, systems and structures try not to exclude but include (what is excluded and what is included in any case are ordered reciprocally). What happens, however, to what exceeds structures and systems, their closure and opening?

All that is appears as fixed by (arbitrary and/or necessary) conventions.

The life of all that is – of organisms and of organisations – does not seem to be able to unfold itself without certain self-regulating automatisms.

Everything resides in a melange of extreme or rather attenuated oppositions.

It is not so easy to distinguish between the melange, the compromise and the mixture.

All the great powers and elemental forces, the regions of the world, and the dimensions of thought partially constitute a total aspect of the total relation to the totality of the opening.

Does all that is leave a trace? Perceptible by whom?

'Somewhere' all is strangely balanced.

And if all that is knew sometimes, somewhere, like a type of assumption?

Below the existing world, there is a pre-existing world.

We are missing several pages of world history.

That can also be called World. That is to say, its mode of being is to be World and to world itself [*mondialiser*]. Never, however, do we meet the World itself; we ourselves, and all that we are dealing with, beings and things, never stop being intramundane. What is the world? For whom? For the Greeks, it is the deployment of logos-physis, uncreated and eternal in its beautiful order, a jewel (*cosmos*). For the Romans, *mundus* is at once an ornament and a pit, a mortal abyss open to subterranean darkness and to daylight, an abyss of light, a gorge of shadow, a hole. For Christians, the world and all that is worldly, creation in its ensemble, the universe, is that which is in time in opposition to the divine and eternal spirit. For the Moderns, it is all of what is, being in its totality, the all of becoming and the becoming of all, such that it exists for and reveals itself to human subjectivity, because there is no world without humans and no humans without world. The world refers to the human without being dependent on it. In the same way, the totality of thought, the totality of nature and the totality of history, without being under the domination of the human, do not occur without it. 'The man of the world participates in the great game of life' (Kant). Secondarily, world and worldly signify the great life of high society, the great world of the privileged, and distinguish themselves from the little world and the demi-monde of the inferior or declassed classes, with equivocal morals. What is then the world? The open, non-empirical totality of all that manifests itself and is grasped, experienced or produced through the human, in time. It is the supreme horizon, which encompasses what appears as *thought*, as *god*, as *nature* and as *human history*, in and as the play of time, the being in becoming of the totality. It is like a circle – or better: a spiral – infinite and finite, whose centre and circumference are everywhere and nowhere. It contains all the significations that one attributes to it, the faces and masks of its game. It surpasses all the dimensions according to which it grasps us and we grasp it, because it remains open. The human, who already through being born comes to the world, aspires to become a citizen of the world, although the human remains always a stranger to itself and to the world. In the interior of the world, worlds, particular ensembles, networks stretched over the world, various foci are consolidated and disintegrate. The world is at the same time unworldly. Heraclitus, the Greek poet-thinker, tells us that 'the time of the world is a child that plays with pawns; the kingship of a child'; he also tells us that 'such a pile of garbage scattered at random appears the most beautiful order in the world'. Augustine, the Christian theologian, declares: *mundus est immundus*.

The concept of the world is intramundane; only the world as a horizon is not it, while being it always and again.

The world seen as existing – as a problem – only through thought or envisaged as existing independently of thought, these two positions fall under thought and are carried by the world.

What to call the discordant accord between the human and the world, thought and things? Coincidence? Simultaneity? Encounter? Harmony? Isomorphism? Co-ownership? Equation? Exchange? Correlation? Dialogue? Homology? Analogy? Reciprocal play? What is the common root, the original unity, prior to the distinct and portentous manifestations of a future fusion – and confusion?

According to an old – and future – word, everything that arises and particularises itself – all intramundane things – joins again the universal cradle from which it came and is also its tomb, that is to say, the *world*. So the world rolls with an open tomb. This process, however, doesn't permit itself to be entirely measured and calculated.

The world as it presents itself at each moment and to the individuals and societies of each epoch, marks and masks the World, whose world of being is being world, masked and revealed, proposed and refused, while one strives to uncover the afterthoughts of after-worlds.

No intramundane thing is integrated and integral. The world itself is not it, despite the unspeakable power of the whole.

The world, which always worlds itself, becomes now worldwide, is worlded and curtailed [*mondé et émondé*]. As becoming-thought of the world – becoming-world of thought. What worlds itself? Platonism-Aristotelianism, Judaeo-Christianity, Cartesianism, Hegelian-Marxism. Together with the surging and dominating process of technique that Marx began to foresee. This domination accomplishes itself in a techno-scientific and techno-bureaucratic way. So begin to govern – cybernetically – logic and logistics, metaphysics, physics and mathematics, in short, technique. Hegelian-Marxism worlds itself thanks to its partisans and adversaries, who cannot ignore it, and it is thus put into question: economically and politically, anthropologically and ideologically. While the technical, industrial and statistical society establishes itself and is almost able to digest its crises and critics, Nietzsche says that European nihilism is also worlding itself. The technical world and the human as subject and object of technique find themselves launched into the planetary course – the errancy – where multiple machinations consolidate and disintegrate themselves. Seriously and ridiculously, this global adventure fails to give – and to give itself – a rhythm and a style to all that is produced and reduced, consummated and consumed. Everyone in the world is judge and judged, about to sue and about to be sued, but there is no final or supreme judgement. Excising signifies to cut, to rid of the superfluous. Worlding signifies to clean, prune, eliminate. What will happen to the encounter of production, reduction, provocation, consumption, usage, consummation?

What triumphs and what does not succeed in proposing or imposing itself within a world, itself a constellation visible to the naked eye and with the use of devices inside the world, is acted rather than acting. Computers, programmers and planners are taking over what passes and what remains in time. Universal errancy seems to abolish a good number of errors. So the worldwide and planetary errancy tries to correspond to the errant time of the world, to the errancy of the being in becoming of the totality. The flat, plane, global and errant world offers its finitude to experience through human finitude. Is there a finality in the unlimited deployment of limitation and finitude? What is planetary and global is at the same time parcelled, partial and particular. Planetary thought tries to think of That in its itinerancy, otherwise called the play of the world. We other passengers on this congested planet no longer have a last resort, no supreme, theoretical, practical or technical instance. In the play, which plays itself between the human and the world, the human is the player, the played, the plaything. The question of the gamble still remains unclear. Both constituting and contesting thought, as well as constructive and destructive experience, fail to overcome this englobing, which is the human, englobed by what it is not, namely the world. World and human, all at once partners and adversaries, judges and parties, parts and totalities, return the ball to themselves in the course of the same play; they are what they are not and are not what they are. No doubt there will be neither an – immediate – apocalyptic catastrophe nor a mediated and distant eschatological salvation. Neither black nor grey pessimism nor pink or pale optimism can trace a route of decipherment. Utopia and uchronia close space and time to us. The world rolls and will roll. Like a tumbril. Can 'it' pass without the human, being passing, being passenger?

One seeks to fix the vertigo. Is there a supreme chance? By playing with the earth ball – ball of frozen fire – will we burst it? Neither voluntarily nor involuntarily? Will errancy wish that by a trick, the planet shatters through an error in calculation, through erring of technique? And what about the prospects of managing the planet and human life on it? Or the conquest of other stars? Will we go from the similar to the same? Everything fluidifies itself, unrealises itself, at the same time that everything consolidates itself, realises itself. So-called stable structures and revolutionary events accomplish a rotary, traditional and revolutionary movement, which in its immobile mobility traverses a finite curve, successively passes through the same points and returns to the point from where it left. Progress and repetition, advance and temporal return of the same, change and recovery, frenzy and stagnation go hand in hand. What do we regard and what regards us? In French, *regard* also signifies – according to the Littré dictionary – the situation of two stars that orbit each other. The occidental obsession, currently becoming worldwide, the indefinite search for happiness, for organised and indefinite well-being, is in full swing and succumbs to the attraction, to the fulfilment and to the fear of the void. With the maximum, or almost, of rationality and absurdity.

Something follows its course and seeks itself. All the established and/or revolutionary powers provoke it and turn their back on it. The game played is extremely complicated. The thought that tries to think it remains unheard. It appears in contradiction with everything, even though it belongs to it. Faithful and transgressing thought, it tries to see, to hear, to say, to do. Everything seems to indicate that its suspicion is untenable. Even if it had to appear so clearly in the constellation of the planetary world, it would be only for it to be quickly ejected, flattened, levelled, eclectically amalgamated, sunken into the inevitable worldwide and planetary confusionism – to be comprehended as a dominant ideology 'similar' to Asian and oriental Confucianism, a sort of reunion if not a universal reconciliation of thoughts, beliefs and experiences. One will restore it in rank and order, this thought, for the need for order and rank is imperious. Not thinking for thinking, nor practice for practice, nor activist and monoideatic, nor unilateral, nor abstractly general, nor narrowly regional, nor vaguely multilateral and total, the play of the thought of the play of the planetary world, enrooted speaking and thinking activity, should concretely and meditatively confront the world as a problem and the problems of the world, should shape the ensemble and the details. By apprehending the differences and the oppositions that exclude each other by plunging them into a kind of neutralising indifference, in a sort of englobing unity, through not misrecognising the complementarity of irreconcilables, the conjunction and not the synthesis of opposites, the play of thought would not offer us all-access keys that open only open doors, would not arm the mouths of spokespeople of advertising slogans, would not run away into the myth of the world, *quodlibet in quodlibet,* but would try to orient and experience what, beyond the world of the Orient where the sun rises and that of the Occident where the sun sets, forms and traverses the world, pursues its itinerancy, with a terrible and somnambulant precision, in an open horizon which contains the 'given' world contained in the opening of the World.

Just as the totality is more than the sum of its parts, the ensemble more than all of its components, the world is more than the ensemble of intra-mundane beings.

The closure of the human to the world is only a mode of its relation to the world; the opening of the human to the world as such effectuates itself more rarely.

All that, which is, is of the world more than in the world, since the world is not a spatial englobing.

The world perceptible to the five senses is a tiny fraction of what, in becoming, is in its entirety.

In the world, one lives or inhabits several worlds.

Every world is forged with the materials available.

There are worlds that communicate only with great difficulty.

It is the speaking world that makes the 'silent world' speak.

To the putting into question of every word and every thought responds or corresponds to the density of the being-there of the world.

No world can be the whole – open – of the world.

All the worlds in the world know ebb and flow, contraction and dilation.

The world empirically offered, given, produced, is only one of the faces of the world.

Is the world finite because the human is finite? Does it not remain indefinite?

The *world* – more than the being of the world or the world of being – is never integrally apprehended: neither immediately, nor thanks to mediations. The worlds that form themselves in it can be neither confused nor distinguished; they are given together but apart. Fragmentarily offered and elaborated, they do not permit us to affirm that the world is unsayable or that it can say itself or can be said. The world keeps itself neither in language nor out of it; we pursue ceaselessly – and with much distraction – it, the world, which is not something to say, which has not pursued someone, the human, to say it.

The unlimited play of interpretations constitutes the world. This play sweeps through the human.

It is the world that is the enigma and the *solution* to all enigmas through the reunion – fragmentary – of all the elements – fragmentary – which have been separated in an ensemble – fragmentary – which forces thought, speech and writing to be and to remain fragmentary and to differ incessantly. This does not prevent the world – quite the contrary – from remaining enigmatic.

To the amplification of the world corresponds its reduction. To its complexification, its simplification.

There are not two worlds: one visible and apparent and another hidden and concealed, one superficial, the other profound. It is in the interior of the same world that these differences exist – even though their differentiation is problematic – show and hide themselves.

There is no other world: one must recognise the plenitude and the desert side of 'this one'.

In any expenditure of energy, there is inevitably waste, the rhythm of the world proceeding by elimination of the human contributions.

New horizons succeed and superimpose lost horizons: openings and closures.

What metaphysical philosophy left unthought and what it even evacuated is the problem of the world.

The suspicion of the other dimension of the world – the abandoned – is not only suspicion of the other dimension.

To build a world of the World is always tempting.

The world is always richer than one imagines.

The world is not a whole but the whole.

Everything is torn from 'its' world and thrown into the world, while dwellings, which crumble and renovate themselves, remain 'habitable', and while a rather traditional life, between consistency and inconsistency, continues its course.

The world is at once a world of rarity and profusion.

Does a world only withdraw into the appearance of another – of a new – world, which it makes be and that it bears – secretly – through its own withdrawal and its own disappearance? And does the new eclosion not belong to its own – and new – withdrawal?

Beware impasses: one often ends up there, and new passages open themselves.

What was given until now as the end of the world was only the end of a world.

The total refusal of the existing world is a very insufficient step. Being against is inoperative.

What is the world when it 'keeps quiet'? *What* keeps quiet?

When the world is obscured, there are those who hope that the flame will be maintained by someone somewhere. Yet it is never an entire flame that conserves itself. Many carry a scrap of this flame.

Monstrous formations, apt or not to survive, are part of the world.

About everything, that is, whatever, can't we reconstruct the history of the world?

Does the question of the sense of the world, 'therefore' also of life, have a sense? And if there are senses, is there a sense?

Having no destiny as a destiny contributes to transforming the world into an anti-world.

Who leads the world? Those who answer the question or those who close it?

There is no solution to the problem of the world. Because it embraces all the solutions and shatters them – in surpassing them.

The unity of the human and of the world can be neither established nor re-established.

More than in the world, we are always in the between-world.

You already know it: it is about the problematic that is the world, the *world-problem*, more than about the problematic of the world, as long as that is a problem.

To the hollow world correspond the hollows of the world.

In the combat with the world, who to privilege?

Why does the world constantly ask for something new? Because the old and the existing are unsatisfactory? To fill what gaps and propose what additions?

'Too much' problematising dislocates everything. But where to stop?

The entire world is an enormous interrogation.

In any case, the human is a citizen of the world and a deserter of the world.

At the moment that the world becomes planetary, let us beware of launching planetarism on the world market.

The everyday world possesses usually and in public opinion a perceptible and symbolic certainty made of evidences; it is when its reassuring and customary aspect disappears that problems arise.

Everydayness is a land where all that is weaves itself. Its consideration, examination and criticism must be extremely attentive to all its folds and refolds. For it is equally on its terrain – if not primarily – that the great formative powers and the elementary forces of the world are situated, that the destiny of language and thought, of openings to the world, of the divine and of nature, of the human and history, poetry and art, play out. It is that which absorbs and resorbs all that is, it is that which poses itself as a problem requiring a change and that opposes the change, it is that which teaches us daily – banally and fatally – that one should neither overestimate it, nor – especially – underestimate it. Cradle and tomb of all that is, it makes all take off from the earth of the earthlings where all will come to earth.

Everyday life could offer an almost limitless field to criticism and transformation, to play, if its play were not more blocked than it appears, preventing fair play and rendering extremely difficult – and nonetheless facilely tempting – more complex plays.

The one. The one identity. The identical. The undivided. The unique. The united. The unitary. The unifying. The universe. The universal. The unequivocal. The same. The tautology. They always throw at us their founding and fracturing call.

The identical, the equivalent, the tautological try to master the powers of the same and the other, opening wide the door to banished contradiction. Identity and unity were never thought and distinguished or united.

The primitive uroboric unity, how does it develop next?

The duality. The double. The doubling. The duplication. The duplicity. The bipolarity. The alterity. The contrariety. The opposition. The contradiction. The breaking. The binary. The one and the other. The being and the appearing. The true and the false. The good and the bad. The beautiful and the ugly. The life and the death. The light and the obscurity. The high and the low. The here and the elsewhere. The presence and the absence. The male and the female. The before and the after. The positive and the negative. The sensible and the intelligible. The physical and the moral.

The soul and the body. The heart and the reason. The inside and the outside. The surface and the depth. The front and the behind (or the back). The right and the left. These antagonistic forces are all at work, have a singular and common origin, demand to be united, do not tolerate remaining separated, but cannot be artificially surpassed, do not let themselves be taken up into an identity, because they are adjoined as two aspects and moments of reversibility.

Being, non-being, becoming. The three dimensions of space and those of time. The body, the soul, the spirit. The beginning (the *arche*), the development (the growth), the final outcome (the *telos*). The male trinity. The female triangle. The Father, Son and Holy Spirit. The man, the woman and the child. The man, the woman and the other. The man, the woman and death. The ternary dialectic: the thesis (position), the antithesis (negation), the synthesis (negation of the negation). Each thing, its contrary, the unity of itself and its contrary. The action, the reaction (backlash) and the result. The enigma of the triad – combining itself with the enigma: what is, is it so, or is it seen to be so? – never stops guiding and troubling us.

The four elements: earth, water, air, fire. The four dimensions: length, width, height, time. The four moments of time: the future anterior, the past, the present, the future. The four kingdoms: the mineral kingdom, the vegetable kingdom, the animal kingdom, the human kingdom. The four seasons: spring, summer, autumn, winter. The four stages of the day: morning, afternoon, evening, night. The four cardinal points: north, south, east, west. The four ages: childhood, youth, maturity, seniority. The four angles and directions of every cross. The x. These 'square' powers – meeting with triangular configurations, duals and unitary aspirations – present themselves and are much more fruitful than they appear through mythological, symbolic, allegorical or scientifically natural representations. Their presence is immediate and mediated, acting and poetic. It fertilises works and days, animates being, appearing, disappearing, and the rebirth of beings and things. It manifests itself in the becoming of the world – neither rectilinear and progressive, nor circular and repetitive, nor the one and the other – what carries and carries off the human.

The multiple. The plurality. The diversity. The variety. The sparks. The fragments. In all parts and particles, is there the whole of the world that manifests itself through its aspects and regions and according to our divisions and perspectives? Does not each person apprehend it in many ways and on many planes, according to multiple mediations and multiple segmentations, according to various functions and variables, the One-All, the One-Multiple, never integral and never integrally decomposed? Will the combat, if it nevertheless imposes itself between polycentrism and unity, be engaged?

All that is can be transposed and transcribed on several registers.

Never anything is or is done for one reason alone.

Monotony and polyphony combine their voices. So monochrome and polychrome combine grey and colours. Is grey the philosophical colour of the world, the barely visible pictorial dominant of spectral movement?

In the midst of the One-Multiple – of the multiplicity of the one, of the unity of the multiple – all splits itself – at least – in two – in all the domains – the two separated elements reuniting themselves.

In each figure a polygonal problem is dissimulated.

The multiple protects us from the one, the one structures the multiple. A discordant accord knots the destiny of the university to that of the multiversity.

Plurality and multiplicity plunge us into embarrassment.

How to unite to distinguish, to distinguish to unite, what ceases, stops, dies, finishes, accomplishes, ends, incompletes itself?

We always play one – and on one – plan against another and others.

Do not trim angles and see their districts.

The sphere of being and of spheres. The ring of the being that holds, maintains, contains, encloses. The circularity of becoming. The circle of the totality and concentric circles. The open and delimited, empty and gaping circle. The hole. The zero. The rotation of time. The cycle of the beginning and the end (that enigmatically and mutually presuppose each other, referring to each other). The wheel of stars and that of history. (The wheel is at once mobile and immobile; it is motive, motor of movement, and its movement rests in immobility.) The planet that turns. The revolution of all movement. The circus of human games. The circulation. The rounding. The repetitions. The tours. What turns and/or does not turn around and in a round. The game already played must be played until the end and resumed. Why do we fail to think of time – the gulf of experience and openness – as omnitemporality and not as limited or eternal time, as a unity of the old and the new and not as a fleeting instant or as duration that flows, as time of the world and not as world in time?

Every circle is magical, vicious, infernal. How to get out? By breaking it? Is this possible? Or by entering more resolutely within?

Is the gulf an unlimited hole and not an encircled opening? In the heart of the circle of every opening, is there not a hole?

In the centre stands this invisible void that maintains everything that springs from it and converges towards it, focus of light that renders everything visible, abyss that engulfs everything, broken circle from which straight and curved, conquering and broken lines radiate and return.

Every opening to the world does not lack corresponding closures. Every opening is delimited by a closure.

The opening of all that is constitutes at the same time its wound and its tearing.

Through tears and tearing a field of vision is also offered.

How many gaps and even openings are not barred?

Is it in the interior of concentric circles that everything redoubles itself, multiplies itself variously, unifies itself?

Entering the round already indicates that one will leave this one to enter another, even larger.

We are both in the interior of the enclosure and in what exceeds it.

In the spiral of spirals, one goes from the periphery to the centre and from the centre to the periphery, periphery and centre being everywhere and nowhere.

Every beyond of the world is built on the below.

The being of the world has been taken over by *onto-logic* – mystical and/or discursive – itself taken over, in turns and conjointly, by *theology, cosmology, anthropology, technology*. Each expresses and betrays Being, none exhaust the ontological question, none even confront That. It contracts and expands, falls and shines out among all the particular beings and all the privileged beings, supposed to be, successively or simultaneously, Being, itself, which is neither personal nor neutral, neither being nor non-being, not becoming nor always identical, letting itself be said negatively, and positively shaking all that is, traversing all the fragments of the totality – it also not being what contains it.

First philosophy, or general philosophy, metaphysics or ontotheology, lets a schema be deployed through it. Thus, we all depart, as long as we are, or almost, believers and unbelievers, initiates or laypeople, from a 'total' representation of the being in becoming of the totality of the world. Absolutely from the origin, in the beginning, there is the arche, the dominant power and principle: it is the *logos* or the *spirit* or the *idea* or *god*, that traverses *nature, creation* or *matter-energy* (that is to say the evolutionary dynamic or the dialectical movement, thus implying the logos), to end up with the human, who, through its history, elaborates them, recognises them, expresses them. The loop is thus looped, the movement is circular, and one can operate, either starting from the logos or starting from god or starting from nature or starting from the human, to arrive at the same result. Both spiritualism and idealism as well as materialism and realism, whether they recognise it or not, inscribe themselves in this rotating schema. Monism and dualism do the same. A being (ideal or material, divine or natural or human) is said to be the source and the sense of Being as being and of the being of all that, in its becoming, is.

From this first position, the totality of the world lets itself be reconstructed or constructed by thought. Everything holds itself in three acts (all thought seems ruled at once by the obsession of unity, that of duality and that of the trinity). First act: there is a divine, cosmic or human *logos*, which is the sense and rhythm of all that is, that renders everything intelligible, because it already is. Act two: what is manifests as *nature, universe, cosmic system*, earth. After the material kingdom of inorganic matter, the mineral kingdom, succeeds the vegetable kingdom. From simple matter-energy and plants come the animal kingdom and finally the human emerges, beginning of the third act. These reigns are supposed to take place one after another in space and time (logically, providentially, evolutionarily or dialectically). The process ends in the human, master of matter-energy, plants, animals and itself. Each realm of this curious kingdom possesses its own laws and princi-ples, each level of this total pyramid rests on the level below, is conditioned by it, although every level also constitutes a specific *novum* in relation to the inferior level, and its own novelty renders it almost autonomous. The *human* continues to become. Its body, soul and spirit develop themselves in the historical community (whether it progresses, tramples, regresses or is already – theoretically or practically – almost complete, is little important here). It is only with the human that there is *history* strictly speaking. This history embraces and empassions individuals, peoples and societies, states, civilisations and cultures, and inscribes human subjectivity – through magic, myths and religion, politics, poetry and the arts, philosophy, science and technique – in the historical process leading from prehistory – across Orient and Occident – to the current phase of universal history, the planetary era of humanity. The humans in history look at what they are and at what they are not, and grasp through thought – at the end of becoming – the whole process. The human collective will do this even better tomorrow. The ser-pent bites its tail, all is recovered, the start implies and joins the end, the end contains the total movement and contains itself. The piece can be played starting with any of its three acts – which constitute a single piece – or even by any of its scenes or actions. It can be played in a rough or very subtle way. It always remain the same, and it also encompasses opponents, deviants, antagonists and contestants, letting them participate in the same game.

Logically and *onto*-logically, to each principle or to each way of being cor-responds a grasping or a way of knowing. To Logos-god or to God-logos, to cosmic Nature and History, to human consciousness and unconsciousness, correspond, colour for colour and unit for unit, the adequate graspings. To Logos-god or to God-logos correspond – on the basis of *onto-theo-logy, first and general philosophy* or *metaphysics*, which is a kind of *prephysics* – *logic* as speculative knowledge or formalised ensemble, unapplied *mathematics*. Ontologically, logically and paradoxically, being as being, rather the being of all that is, the being-logos and the being-god, that is to say, the being of the totality which ontotheology, logic and mathematics deal with, also reveals itself as nothingness and nothing that the named approaches do not recognise but fill up. Because ontotheology, logic and mathematics deal with being-nothingness, the all-nothing. Human language thinks it expresses the logos of being. The human being imagines itself, itself being the aim, or the mediation, to grasp the original and dominant logos, from which it comes and of which it is the outcome. To cosmic nature correspond, after the philosophy of nature founded on pre- and meta-physics, the *natural sciences*, which always derive their origin from a philosophy equal to metaphysics. Mathematical physics, astronomy, cosmogony, geology, chemistry and biology explore, experiment and transform the heaven and earth, the stars, the material, vegetable, animal and (physiologically) human world. To nature therefore physics corresponds. So the human apprehends and comprehends, thanks to knowledge, what preceded their birth. The human also wants to grasp their own being, their history, their works. Polymorphic anthropology, psychology, sociology and the social sciences, the various histories and historical, philological, archaeological, etc., sciences, in short, the *human sciences* (are there inhuman ones?) tackle magic, myths and religions, economics and politics, poetry and the arts, philosophy, science and technique – historically and systematically, and drawing several intersections – and grasp, so to speak, in the second degree the being, the becoming and the works of the human, the way in which they come into contact with the All and with all, by transforming it.

'That' is consequently unitarily, dually and trinitarily taken over, and the somewhat mysterious logos of the 'beginning', simple logos, logos of being, divine logos, cosmic logos, flashes up at the end, that is to say, is known and recognised, assembled and scattered, as human logos, that, in addition, examines itself; one can also, if one wants, make of the human logos the beginning and the end of That, its aspects, dimensions and modalities of being grasped. Each of the great powers, which link the human and the world, takes hold in its own way of logos, god, nature and human history. *Philosophy*, *science* and *technique* want to express them and shape them thematically. When philosophy precedes science, technique is at once their growth, their engine and their outcome. Because technique also grabs hold of all that composes the World. Logical and logistical, linguistic and mathematical techniques want to grab hold of the logos. Physical techniques of all kinds want to seize nature. Psychological, historical and social techniques want to seize the human, wanting to signify in all these cases: effectively doing it by playing their roles with brio.

Philosophy, before its eruption and its explication into the sciences, wanted to embrace the all of That and all that. Now it remains a little behind, at the same time raising the need for a global and concrete thought. Thus philosophy, science and technique speak, explore and transform what is and becomes, whether of the order of logos, of nature, of the human. The all is unitarily cut into three: domain of *onto-theo-logical* and *mathematical* beings and perspectives, domain of *physical* beings and perspectives, domain of *anthropological* and *historical* beings and perspectives. This tri-partition is then reduced to a bi-partition, the world finding itself cut in two: into cosmic Nature and human history, cosmic universe and social universe, more or less corresponding to the split in two: matter and spirit, physical and moral, sensible and intelligible. The university itself, pillar of knowledge, sciences and universal techniques, distributes the cards of the game.

How can the harmony and the concerns that lead to fruitful research, how can the distribution of roles in and through the theatre of the world, be problematised or even be straightaway problematic? Does not the 'non'-scientific and 'non'-technical and, moreover, metaphilosophical interrogation lose all its rights? From the beginning, at the initial moment, beyond which nothing and no one can ever go back, at the very start of all that is and has been (strange and persistent confusion of being and having), the *Logos* or the idea, the spirit functioning *a priori*, or the divine logos, or the cosmic logos or the human logos (functioning *a posteriori* and recognising the *a priori* afterwards), or *God* or *Nature* as energetic matter or the *Human* who reconstitutes it, this first moment, through its consciousness and its science, leads to – renders intelligible, creates, produces, founds or institutes, either in the order of presence or in that of representation – the *Universe*, that is to say, the energetic matter, the minerals, the plants, the animals, the humans, prolonging and being recognised by *human History*, which lives the deployment of economy, magic, myths and religions, morality, poetry and arts, politics, philosophy, sciences and techniques, from prehistory to today, the days of *History*, for the first time effectively *worldwide*, of collective humanity, which, in its turn, grasps all that has been, is and is produced, says it, thinks it, explores it, transforms it, since in their turn – works of humanity in its historical becoming – philosophy, onto-theo-logical and metaphysical, logic and mathematics, the ancient philosophy of nature – now explicated in cosmogony, astronomy, geology, mineralogy, botany, physics, chemistry, zoology, biology and medicine – ethnology, history and various histories, psychology, law, sociology and social sciences as well as philology and archaeology, which take up the ancient philosophical anthropology and philosophy of history, living on them – the problem of *ethics* remains in suspense – correspond step by step and by performing a grandiose flashback after the arrival, to all that in its being and its becoming is highly appropriate to them, while powerful techniques operate in all the domains and all disciplines, marching, briskly but surely, to a gigantic and total technology that grabs the entire scaffolding of the world and all the particular scaffolds. Because the force of technique and its technological explanation resides in the fact that the logical powers, formerly divine, cosmic and human, social and historical, thereby find themselves bound.

On being as being – as one says still out of habit, to not say that of this being one makes a being – on the logos, which is coextensive with this being, on god, of whom one speaks so much, dodging the problem of the sacred and the divine, on the original spirit or matter, on the sense – the signification and the direction – of the total and particularly historical and human becoming, on these some specialists of the universal, professorial or brilliant professors, gifted or domiciled mavericks, writers or journalists, illuminated or dull autodidacts are still leaning. All these types lean on and speak of 'That', through very little troubling themselves to think. Others reflect from time to time on the 'highest questions', declared unsolvable, useless and idle by strong minds. But imbeciles are also part of That. While an open thought still remains in the state of waiting and sketchiness, not assimilated even when it manifests itself. If indeed high-level thought can ever be radical enough not to make itself, God, nature or the human the last instance, recognising that all so-called logical thought emerges from a physiological humus, namely organic and biocosmic, psychological, namely psychic and affective, and sociological, namely historical and social, and that it can only obey the play of the world, which it says, thinks and shapes.

To say it again: the *logos* is the condition for speaking-and-thinking, it expresses and says the sense of being in becoming; the logos says certainly the being of the world, but it is as if its saying rests on the base of a pre-liminary call and a preliminary reading of this being, moreover: being and thought are supposed to be and to be thought identical; the logos says itself and thinks itself, says and thinks the being in becoming of the world – what calls it and whose logos it is – what has manifested itself as *god-logos* (creator of all that is or the human creature), as *cosmic nature* generating the human that evolves in the space-time of *human history* – in the course of which language, thought and action (logos and praxis) develop that say all that is, transform and organise it practically and technically – and that itself ends in philosophy systematising the circle, which turns from where we begin it – also turning in the opposite direction – beginning and end joining each other. This circle of the – fragmentary and fragmented, even though global – totality of the multidimensional and open world, consti-tutes ontico-onto-logically – that is to say, both at the level of experience and beings as well as at the level of the logos of the Being of all that is and that manifests itself unitarily and differentially – the system of knowledge and the light of practice, all 'flowing' from each of its points, every particular approach leading to all, pursued right to the 'end', each case always remaining to refill anew, although there is nothing more – philosophically – to know. Philosophy – love of wisdom – was in its historic-systematic becoming, and became especially in its completion, the *onto-theo-cosmo-anthropo-historico-logical* system – if not wisdom – and it gave the system of world each time its 'sense'. This historic-and-systematic ensemble of these senses – is that wisdom? – forms precisely the system of completed philosophy – by having reached its term, its goal and its end, theoretically at least – that lets itself be replaced by techno-scientific activity and that 'must' open the field to the thought which precedes it, traverses it and succeeds it, this thought no longer obeying the being in becoming of the world – by the logos and the praxis of the social being of the human – said, thought and done according to a sense, but by experimenting, speaking and thinking *That* as game, structuring and structured, one and unique, in all the possibilities of its permutational combinatorics.

Strong is the temptation for a kind of global interpretation of the world, comporting specific interpretations of its diverse modes of being. The *logos* of the world would be brought to language by a thought and a language, namely a *dialectical logic* that would imply formal logic, would analyse and order the production of languages, knowledges, ideologies, would tend to lead if possible to a formalisation capable of fertilising the methodological and epistemological searches and systematisations, and to give life to a polyvalent and generalised semantics and combinatorics inscribed in electronic machines. *The being in becoming of the totality of the world, That*, should be expressed through a subtle *dialectical materialism* essaying to surpass ontological idealism and materialism and discover what the world in time is and becomes thanks to the theory and the practice of humans. The *cosmic world*, nature, would be grasped through a scientific *cosmology* and through the physico-mathematical and experimental *natural sciences*, which would strive to decode all messages. The *human* and *history* would be explored by an *anthropology* and a *theory of history*, psychologically and sociologically, psychosociologically, by means of a whole group of approaches ranging from psychophysiology and depth psychology, though the theorisations and techniques of a historical materialism at several levels, up to different sociological explorations. Finally, all the spiritual productions of historical humans – mythological, artistic, ideological, theoretical and practical, in a word, cultural – would be dismantled and structured according to ensembles combinatorially linking diverse possibilities and realisations, arranging into sense what without them would remain without. This total explanation of the world and these different graspings, which would be integrated into it – unitarily and multidimensionally – would become, speculatively and philosophically, more and more cybernetically techno-scientific, the theoretical and scientific knowledge not so much generating practical and technical transformation, but rather being moved by it. What would it lack so that this map, dynamically exposing the ensemble and the ensembles, be complete and satisfactory, the very dissatisfactions that would provoke it conferring on it the dynamism of its progression? Certainly, the map is not the territory; this everyone, or almost everyone, knows. This total picture that would represent, beyond the reign of the representation, the famous total reality and the particular realities, constituting and constituted, would not be blameworthy as a picture, orientation table and programming schema. Where would its lack reside, if it lacked? Wherein would it lack and what would it lack, provided that every lack has not already been taken over by it? Would it not offer a non-figurative, serious and decisive configuration of the game of the world and a unified scaffolding of multiple games? Certainly. The game of the world loves dashboards, and the table of tables guiding the knowledge and action of humans is one of its favourite playthings.

Everything, in the domain of thought and action or in that of the world, can be reduced to one of the great foci, from which all flows, and with whose aid everything can be envisaged, explored and practised. Everything can be reduced to each of the *elemental forces* and *great powers* of the world, from which all that is apprehends itself and constructs itself, any of the great foci co-producing, so to speak, the totality of the world. Everything can be situated in the schema of *world history* and plunged into its historical process. Dimensions and orientations of thought and regions, aspects and sectors of the world correspond, systematically and historically, to any circle of what is or what is grasped – speculatively and *techno-theoretically*, *techno-scientifically* and practically – leading to all the others: everything can consequently find its place on the basis of a certain implicit or explicit ontology, in the schema of dimensions and regions of the world, of thought and other approaches, according to the manner and the manners of appearing and being grasped. The order is certainly mobile, and the schematisation permits logical, ontological and ontic permutations; this is why one can find the same themes multiply grouped and diversely regrouped according to the angle of approach, of exposition, according to the articulation. Elemental forces, for example, precede the great powers, but it is only from the latter that they become more visible. We begin to speak and think from the logos, which is like a prologue and a propaedeutics to encyclopaedic systematisation, although the logos is already an interpretation of the play of the being in becoming of the totality of the world. All the great centres emerge from the grand whole and lead to it, form aspects or approaches of the being in its entirety – *fragmentary*-total aspects and approaches – can be linked, combined, seen as starting points or links in the chain, all the particular plays orienting us towards other plays and towards the play of the world, each one of them serving to decode all the others at the centre of a table with several entries: ontological and systematic, genetic and historical, logical and methodological, ontic and theoretical, techno-scientific and practically transformative, multidimensional and total, the total schema itself not exhausting the world in its entirety, world open and in becoming.

The global logico-ontological schema – thought, nature, history – corresponds, since the Platonic Academy, to the tri-partition of philosophy into *logic*, *physics* and *ethics*.

After the three fundamental thoughts, God, Nature, Human, said by and in the Logos, will there be others, or will the same be grasped otherwise? Watch out for the Game.

Thus, alternately and conjointly the world has been said as *logos*, as *god*, as *nature*, as *historical humanity*. For, effectively, all is also in any case logos, god, nature, human, appearing – simultaneously – as such, which should prevent us from saying that logos or god or nature or human precedes or constitutes all. It goes without saying that all combinations are possible or have been effected: *logos*-god, *god*-logos, *logos*-nature, *nature*-logos, *logos*-human, *human*-logos, *god*-nature, *nature*-god, *god*-human, *human*-god, *nature*-human, *human*-nature. Etc. The wider and deeper a thought is, the more it thinks, at once and according to an order, logos and god, nature and the human, history and art.

If one of the links in the chain logos-god-nature-human is dislocated and disappears, does it drag down all the others? On which register?

All that, which is, is also – and fundamentally – logos, nature, human, history, play.

Usually the world is subsumed by logic, physics, ethics, psychology, sociology, aesthetics.

The temptation of an intelligent empiricism, positivism and pluralism is always tenacious. However, they are assumed and integrated, rather than assuming and integrating.

The three articulations: *logos, spirit* or *idea* – onto-theo-logical – that says being-nothingness-becoming (spatio-temporal), the one-multiple-all, by posing and presupposing the logos that speaks, that is said and that says the world and its worlds, conceptually or otherwise; *cosmic nature,* or *universe* – constituted through matter-energy-life in motion in space-time – whose realities are measured objectively (by inter- and pan-human subjectivity) – and that is supposed to constitute objective reality; *human and history,* whose spirit and phenomena unfold themselves almost empirically in space and time, seem to require more and more three types of approaches: a *speculative, meta-onto-logical* and *meta-dialectical* approach; a *physical, objective, measurable* and *calculating, experimental* approach; a *meta-phenomenological, ontic* and *empirical, psychological, historical, sociological* and *poetic* approach that accounts for whoever speaks (of themself and the 'rest'), for the world where they speak and that of which they speak. It goes without saying that the problem of tri-unity and difference remains unelucidated.

The world has been maintained for a very long time under the triple yoke of the *true* (logical), the *good* (ethical), the *beautiful* (aesthetic), and often shaken by efforts to be liberated from them or liberate them. Would it be better now to surpass them, even if we would have the suspicion that nothing is ever finished and surpassed?

Nonetheless, humans remain under the yoke of the *true,* the *good,* the *beautiful.*

The world does not belong to anyone.

Is the solution of non-solution a solution?

It is not forbidden to examine autonomies, that is to say, to consider them as specific.

This problematic inertia of the world, it is us who shake it, it is it which shakes us.

The play between the enchantment and the disenchantment of the world consists of a constant back-and-forth.

Following the easy slope, if not without difficulty, in certain contexts, times and places of the world, thought, the human and history, has reached the lowest level.

Everything is well held in place, logically, physically, biochemically, psychologically, historically, sociologically, and still plays the game of movable and, to a limit, surpassable frontiers.

The moving ensemble of networks and bundles that group what is and its ensembles, as well as our explanations, comprehensions (concerning which we obviously do not understand each other), constructions, explorations and interpretations; logico-ontologically, methodologically and epistemologically. The structured and decomposed processions. The – inexhaustible? – combinatorics of factors, sectors, vectors. The 'totality' of all that sinks like a wedge into the world. The rings of totalities, totalisations, detotalisations and residues. Rigid and fluid order of access routes and means. The strategic and tactical ordination of targeted aims and fixed objectives – near and far. The order of aspects, flashes, angles of attack, sightings. The organisation of viewpoints and visions, optics and revisions, dimensions and directions, perspectives and forecasts. The more-than-problematic hierarchy of stages, planes, levels. The conceptual apparatus and apparatus of inherences, inferences and interferences, inductions and deductions. The – integral and differential – calculus of variables, probabilities and possibilities. The computation of spaces and times. The schematisations of disorder and orders. The schemas and channels of trajectories of continuous and discontinuous movements. The global configurations and local constellations. The enchaining and unchaining of potencies and impotencies. The actions, the interactions and the chain reactions. The retrospective considerations, the retroactive effects, the feedbacks and the programming, the planning, the projects, the rejects, the projections, the prospectives, the anticipations. The functions and the dysfunctions of tendrils and grilles. The inversions and the reversals of signs, significations, signals. The treatment of information. The regulation of governments and organic and organised, automatic and cybernetic regulations. The more or less dynamic models and the more or less moving rules of diverse plays. The scaffoldings of determinations, conditions, motives and reasons, and multiple groundings. The forms and the contents of forms and contents. The demonstrations, the argumentations, the experiences and the shipwrecks, and the ships that did not go to sea. The detection of poles, areas and auras, and everything that didn't cast off. The anatomies of the normal, the analyses of the pathological and the therapeutic remedies. The circular processes linking cohesion and dislocation, coherence and incoherence, correspondences and non-correspondences, relations and cuts, passages and correlations, circuits and short circuits. The rhythms and the measures of evolutions and involutions. The indices of inclusions and exclusions, the emergence of questions, problematic solutions, conscious and intended (and especially unconscious and involuntary) eliminations, and the non-registration of what happens unnoticed or is not even perceived. The classifications, the typologies, the structurings that at once want to isolate entities and make them communicate with each other, coordinate unities and differences, variants and invariances. The classes of commutations and permutations, nestings and transfers, transitions and translations, implications and explications. The analytic or synthetic abstractions and the exemplary or arbitrary concretisations. The convergent series and the divergences. The groups of equivalences and alternations, words and things, figures and numbers, signs, sigils and symbols. The grouping of centres and decentrings, formations, information and malformations. The fields entangled in each other, delimited and elusive, dominant and/or underlying. The more or less durable or transient systems. The systematics of images and intuitions, representations and schematisations, reasoning and formulations, codifications and formalisations, decodings and decryptions. The systematisations of intersections, interrelations, correlations, connections, interlockings. The entangled spirals deploying themselves in the spiral of spirals that 'embraces' all. All these non-figurative figures, all these operational, operative and operated – handled and obscured – operations compose and decompose the maze and labyrinth of the world. All this grasps perspectively and prospectively, effectively shapes and transforms logico-ontologically, epistemologically and technologically aspects, sectors and all the world.

Putting it into order is something to celebrate.

Watch out, too, for the particular, the conditioned, the determined, the concrete, the circumstantial.

Between the extremes, intermediaries, melanges, mixtures, compromises, conciliations, excluded thirds, are realised.

The world does not personally assume all the world's reasons, all being somewhere right, all finding a kind of justification.

The last *figure* of the world is the universal empire of *representation*, in and through which presence and presences exist, move, are grasped, being become appearing more than apparition and falling, as being and beings, under the hold of representation posed as the equal of being: being thus equals presence of appearing, equals representation. No point of view can overview this situation, because all points of view, as such, are engulfed in this egalitarian and visual but not visionary realm. That is why the last humans, who are the ones who last the longest, invent happiness and look at everything – without seeing – by blinking their eyes.

What is the truth? It is surely the play of *unveiling* and *veiling* (ἀλήθεια) of all that is. It is, no less surely, as *veritas*, the adequation between *intellectus* and *res*, at once an agreement of thought with itself and with the reality of being and appearing, in the name of thought or reality, an adequation between what one thinks and says with what is and what one does. The truth is therefore the contrary of error, of falsity, of the lie. Having been all that and still being it, will it not continue its path that illuminates every path? Undoubtedly its shadows enchain it: it does not know very well how to clear itself from error, concealment, falsity, lie, deception, illusion. Even more: it itself becomes more and more problematic. Declaring everything true is tempting and true. Declaring all untrue also is, even though this proposition negates itself. Establishing the criteria of truth – whether one situates them on the side of the senses or on the side of thought, in reality or in its intel-lection, in experience or in ideas – puts us before the question of the truth of these criteria and so on, every foundation or ensemble of axioms, postulates or basic positions shaking in its very foundations. There remains the other way: to see and make in truth and truths *figureheads* of *errancy*, *triumphal constellations* of *erring*, *signalisations* of *itinerancy*. Universal errancy takes over and overcomes both truths and errors. It and its figures and constellations do not replace the truth and its forms and contents. Errancy contains them, assigns them an emplacement, because their foundations are unfounded. The truth and the truths maintain and abolish themselves, becoming con-sequently problems and questions, foci and dwellings of the erring of the world. What corresponds to it illuminates and darkens, because it does not correspond to anything, anywhere, anytime, anyhow. The *corresponding* powers are the moments dominating the visible scene or the subterranean course of its play and time.

An active comprehension of the ensemble of (coordinated) 'truths' and 'truth' (situating and situated horizon) – in the play of errancy – disarticulating disciplinary specificities and articulating globality, a comprehension of the differential and total historical system of the 'true' – constitutive of the play of errancy, constituted in it – could it lead – thanks to a learned mixture of words and silence, after having effected a 'tour of the horizon', traversed nihilism, accomplished an enormous and patient effort – to 'absolute knowledge' and not total knowledge (knowledge which would open perspectives on partial knowledge and partial actions)? The *schema* of *great powers* and *elemental forces*, whose play coordinates itself with the errant play of truth, the *schema* of *world history* that performs this knowledge through the *journey* of *world-historical* thought, belong to the open circle of the play of the world. This contains all the schemas and the whole journey, offering us the ensemble and regions of all that is, becomes, is thought, known, done: it 'is' the '*circle*' of '*absolute knowledge*'. Provided one comprehends it in time, as time, finite and unlimited, open to the past-present-future.

NON-SCHEMATIC SCHEMA
AND PROBLEMATICALLY CIRCULAR CIRCLE
OF THE PLAY OF ERRANCY, OF 'THAT',
GRASPED THROUGH ITS CONSTELLATIONS
AND ITS ITINERANCY, OUR ITINERANCIES
AND OUR REITERATIONS.

SCHEMA OF THE ELEMENTARY FORCES
AND THE GREAT POWERS OF THE WORLD
in the play of logos-praxis

LANGUAGE AND THOUGHT.
WORK (animating the economy) and STRUGGLE (for power).
LOVE (institutionalising itself in the family) and DEATH.
PLAY.

MAGIC, MYTH, RELIGION (institutionalising itself as Church).
POETRY and ART.
POLITICS (institutionalising itself as State).
PHILOSOPHY (institutionalising itself as University), SCIENCES and TECHNIQUE.

SCHEMA OF WORLD HISTORY
the becoming-world of logos-praxis

PREHISTORY.
[OUTSIDE OF HISTORY: wild, primitive, archaic.]
ORIENT: Mesopotamia. Egypt. India. China. Iran. Palestine.
[PARAHISTORY: Barbarians. America. Africa.]

OCCIDENT: *Greek and Roman antiquity. Judaeo-Christianity* [and Islam]:
Oriental – Byzantine – and Occidental (Middle Ages). *European modernity.*
USA. USSR.
PLANETARY ERA.

PATH OF WORLD-HISTORIC THOUGHT
the becoming-logos of the world and praxis

HERACLITUS and PARMENIDES.
PLATO and ARISTOTLE.
[AUGUSTINE and ST. THOMAS.]
DESCARTES, [SPINOZA, LEIBNIZ], KANT, HEGEL.
MARX and NIETZSCHE.

(THE PLAY OF) THE BEING IN BECOMING OF THE TOTALITY
OF THE WORLD
First and general philosophy; metaphysics; ontology

	Speculative and techno-theoretical approach	Techno-scientific approach
LOGOS	Grammar. Rhetoric. Theory of language. Semiotics. Logic; dialectic. Theory of knowledge and science; methodology; epistemology.	Linguistics. Mathematics. Logistics. Cybernetics. Game theory.
GOD	Mythology. Theology.	
PHYSIS	Mythology and cosmogonic religions. Philosophy of nature and life.	Mechanics. Astronomy. Physics. Chemistry. Geology. Mineralogy. Botany. Zoology. Physiology. Biology.
HUMAN	Philosophical anthropology. Ethics. Pedagogy.	Psychology. Psychotherapy. Psychosomatic medicine.
HISTORY	Philosophy of history. Social and political philosophy.	Ethnology. History. Human geography. Demography. Economy. Law. Political sciences. Sociology.
POETRY AND ART	Poetics. Aesthetics. Theory of particular arts.	Philology. Literary history. Archaeology. History and technique of the arts.

The play of errancy, taken over by knowledge, must be understood, not without irony and humour, in its unity, its duality, its trinity, its multiplicity, its totality – angular and global – its 'circularity', its *spiral*.

The error has been considered almost as a moment of truth, the un-true (the false) passing into the true (Hegel). The truth has been considered as a genre of error, the true passing into the un-true (Nietzsche). It remains for us to consider errancy as the opening, in which appear the truths, figures which correspond to it, and the errors, figures which move away from it and move apart.

What was and is true was and is held as and recognised as true by ordinary mortals and by superior humans. We remain in this optic even when we write and think that 'The truth is in its essence untruth' (Heidegger).

Does not the play between truth and lie resemble a battle of darknesses in a dark tunnel?

What corresponds to errancy should not be understood as another type of 'truth'.

Never has there been an anteriority of truth to all the means of its errant inscription.

Know how to greet, whenever you can afford it, what liberates (us) (from) the error dressed as truth.

Certain fair and flat truths are far less effective than certain forceful and flamboyant errors.

Truth, a triumphant and weakening figure of errancy, a symbolic function of it, can let us sense that errancy – which itself is *also* a symbolic function – and manifests itself and conceals itself only through this truth and these truths. The problem of the hierarchy of its truth and truths can only remain gaping; only particular, oriented and perspectivist, functional and operatory hierarchies can be established.

Ferments and catalysts reveal the truth, namely what is recognised or misrecognised as such by eliciting adhesions and polemics.

From truth to truth, we discover little by little the errancy which abolishes a good number of errors.

Errancy lets us comprehend that the truths of the past were errant.

For almost two and a half millennia, one tries to think the truth. The task
imposes itself: to think fiction, is it still too arduous?

Do error, fault, injustice, crime, sin, guilt consist in a certain isolating
separation, an insolent particularisation in regard to logos and physis, God
and other humans?

Error and lie are – voluntarily or involuntarily – what does not correspond
to the deployment and unveiling of errancy, what falsifies it or conceals it,
what disguises it, even though they always express it in a distorted form.

The arcana of errancy are to be explored concretely, judiciously and
meticulously.

The deployment of errancy is not just the movement of a planet whose
orbit is fixed, calculable and known.

The errancy of the world is installed, arranged, inhabited, in the course of
the errancy of the human that also knows dwelling.

The ludics of illusion, empirical and transcendental, is transfiguration.

Where does one encounter reality? Are we not always grappling with
the *res* that themselves make arise the *nothing* from which they arise? Why
is it the *accusative* of the word *res* in French that gives the *nothing* (*rien*)?
How to separate and/or unite things, words and thoughts? Would reality
be a mode of being and grasping, in the dimension of presence, representation, experience and objectivity (that also encompasses subjectivities),
effected by the practical and theoretical activity of objective subjectivity?
Through where passes the dividing line between what is real and what
is not? To what extent, when, where and how, are thoughts and dreams,
words and visions, part of reality? To think, to dream of a large glass of
water, to say it and to see it in imagination, does not accord it with reality
for whoever is dying of thirst. On the other hand, several soft or violent
thoughts, reveries, words and visions really change the face of the world.

From what threshold did they become real? Is the difference between being and existing real? How to apprehend unreality? Weren't angels and demons for centuries as angels and demons said, painted, carved, experienced as real? To say that everything is real, including phantasies and phantoms, would be the equivalent of saying that nothing is. Would real be what is active, acting, forming and transforming? In what space, what time and for which worlds? Reality, really, as well as truth, truly, couldn't they indicate problematically what *corresponds* to the errancy of being in becoming, in time and in times?

A very large part of what is called external reality is constituted through our *projection*. Correlatively, the most interior and intimate reality is constituted through the *introjection* of natural and social powers acting as from the exterior.

For a long time, humans thought and believed that what they were calling reality – since the Latins – was mostly resistant and frustrating; they will realise, little by little, that imagination is no less so.

Is not the belief in the sensible, empirical, material, objective immediately given or constructed reality, thanks to techno-scientific mediations, part of the myth and the imaginary of modern humans?

What humans call reality is one with so-called symbols and what are also called signs and significations. All signals include diverse variables, fill several functions, and are to be interpreted multiply. And humans always 'think' that reality is elsewhere.

Sincerity consists in the correspondence to errancy: to say what one thinks and does, to think what one says and does, to do what one thinks and says.

Truth and reality are supposed to be common and universal. They are *part* of everything it takes to make a world – if it takes everything to make a world, until the end of the world.

The two aspects of the world, sensible matter and suprasensible and intelligible truth, are caught in errancy from their separated and conjugated appearing in the nascent philosophy and despite their intentions. In the Platonic *Timaeus* matter is called *errant cause* and in the Socratic *Cratylus* the truth is designated as *divine errancy*. Plato went so far as to speak of a *true lie*.

The world, both *ontologically* and *gnoseologically*, has been seen as unique (spirit or matter, thought or empirical experience) and double (dualism). The problem thus posed is inextricable and lacks precise formulation. *Unity* comes up against a certain *dualism*: in what is and what we grasp (*being* and *knowing*). *Dualism* comes up against the unity that seems to encompass everything. And there is no middle way. The oppositions appear to us effective: between the sensible and the intelligible, the senses and the sense (signification and direction), the empirical and the metaphysical (transcendent and/or transcendental), the physical and the moral, the soul and the body, the innate and the acquired, the theoretical and the practical, the interior and the exterior; each being and each thing project something like their double. They manifest on several planes. Not privileging one of the two terms that call the other can still be done. But to abolish or to overcome duality itself, without spiriting away the problem and without dialectical prestidigitation, to unite the two poles of dialogue, is it thinkable and feasible? Sometimes we think yes, sometimes we think no. We can certainly tell ourselves that the pendulum movement takes place on the same clock, but we cannot get out of the circle. Perhaps it would be necessary then to enter it resolutely and see how it turns. For all global thought is and remains circular, as if That itself, its regions and our access to it were and remained circular.

Yet none of the five positions is satisfactory. Each of them, however, is very tempting. Reducing everything to the movement and complexities of matter, sense or reality, from the origin of all that is to ourselves and all that concerns us, is tempting. To seize everything in terms of 'ideals' is no less so. Great also is the temptation of dualism, of the binary structure that separates and unites, and no less great is the call of unity containing – somewhat problematically – the diverse modes of being and making different worlds that communicate (how?). Finally, circularity offers and imposes itself on us and carries us along as it carries everything in its movement. Human thought and experience pursuing each of these schemas and paths, and all at the same time, always get into an impasse, nevertheless effecting a passage and sometimes a jump.

All materialism, realism, positivism is underpinned by idealism, which is one of its configurations. Idealism and romanticism crumble; at the same time every ideal falls: ideal of an ideal and real truth, ideal of a knowing speaking being, ideal of the ideal man or woman, ideal of an ideal life, ideal of an ideal society – it would call itself real – ideal of ideal poetry and art. But to the idealism suppressed, erased, deleted, barred, crossed and crucified – sign that indicates the cross that we put on every cross, the four dimensions of the horizon and the unknowable x – necessarily corresponds to the conjoint suppression of realism, particular reading of the 'real'. Dualism opposed them; the two poles must fall. Where to? Idealism – with mythology, religion, poetry, philosophy – enlightened one half. The other total half? And – at the beginning of a new decentring – ontological, epistemological, ethical unity?

Are not all speculative thought, all mysticism, even that of empirical practice, all high poetry, tearing away from the sensible, idealist team? Is not language itself already, as such, at once a sensible activity and an idealising action? The fact that the world and its diverse aspects can be said, thought and practised, thus or otherwise, bears all the inversions of signs, does not change anything of this unbearable intertwining of the two 'halves' of the 'totality', its two manners of being unitary.

The *subject-object* relationship is not sempiternal. In the eyes of the Greeks, there are *beings* and *phenomena* (*manifestations* and *appearances*) of the cosmic and divine *physis* revealing themselves and remaining invisible through and in the *logos*, the ὄντα and the φαινόμενα, the forms of what is, its visages and faces through which we think, the *ideas*, and the products of human activity, the poetic and practical *techné*, the *erga*, which inscribe themselves in the same rhythm of the being in becoming of logos and of the physis (not created and eternal) to which they do not do violence. The Greek world does not know the subject-object split. Υπο-κείμενον is the foundation, the substratum; what has become *subjectum* then is, for the Greeks, infinitely more 'object' (non-objective) than 'subject'. It is with the Romans that the notion of *res* enters the scene. From now on, the (human) *persona* opposes *res*. Thus personalisation and reification, the rights of the person and the *res publica* are born simultaneously and conjointly. But the Romans do not confront *objects*. In the Hebraic-Christian and, subsequently, rather Christian perspective, there emerges the conception of what is as *ens creatum*. The world is the ensemble of *entia creata*, created *ex nihilo* by God (supreme creator) and dedicated to the final Apocalypse and/or Redemption. In this perspective, a new project comes to light, an unprecedented task: to struggle against created nature to make the eternal Spirit triumph. Humans, creators within Creation, can 'create' *entia*, because even in creating they recreate, populating the earth with new creations. They march for the dominion of the earth, fulfilling the *plans* of providence. It is only with European modernity that the position of the subject and the object – and their opposition – enters into the world and upsets it from bottom to top. Descartes is the founder of this theory and this reality of (intimately linked, if not indissoluble) subjectivity and objectivity. In this dualism are caught: the subject, the *ego cogito*, the foundation of what is and does, and the object, the *res extensa*, the things that face us, that we grasp and shape. The two poles of this relation are, strictly speaking, the *res cogitans* (the thinking and active subject being comprehended both as subjectivity and as thing) and the *res extensa* (the field of the theoretical and practical activity of the human, the world as an object). The face of what is faced (*Gegenstand*) loses itself and sharpens itself in becoming an apprehended object (*Objekt*). Philosophical thinking, science of nature and history, technics engage in the conquest and transformation of the world. The modern epoch is the epoch of subjectivity (Cartesian ego, Kantian transcendental self, absolute and spiritual subject in the Hegelian optic, objective, material and socialised subjectivity in the Marxist view) and, at the same time, the epoch of objectivity (of objectification, the grasping all that is as object for a subject, of realism and reification). For the foundation of objectivity is nevertheless (objective and human) subjectivity and its objectives. The subject and the object depend on each other, can reverse their roles through the fact that a subject can make another subject an object, etc., and the question of their foundation remains open, is not even explicitly posed. Modern and European thought and technics surpass the confines of the Occident: they put the whole planet into motion, ideologically and technologically invading every region of the globe. Humanity wants to pose as a subject and as an ensemble of freed and free subjects, to rationally dominate and economically exploit the totality of the so-called objective world. All humans aspire to subjectivity, all things are caught in the nets of objectivity. This march, when it has reached its goals and when these will be realised and generalised – at the level of individuals and at the level of socialisation – will lead nevertheless further.

We are already on the threshold of a new epoch: the planetary era. It mondialises what is and what produces itself, unifies – through technics – the globe, throws humans and things into a becoming that, to tend to universalisation and *globality*, is no less *errant* and does not exclude *platitude*. The earth, an errant star, becomes in its ensemble the theatre of human activity, and *planning* and *planetary* technics seems to launch itself on the conquest of the universe. The links between subjects and objects become inextricable, precisely because all humans aspire to become subjects making

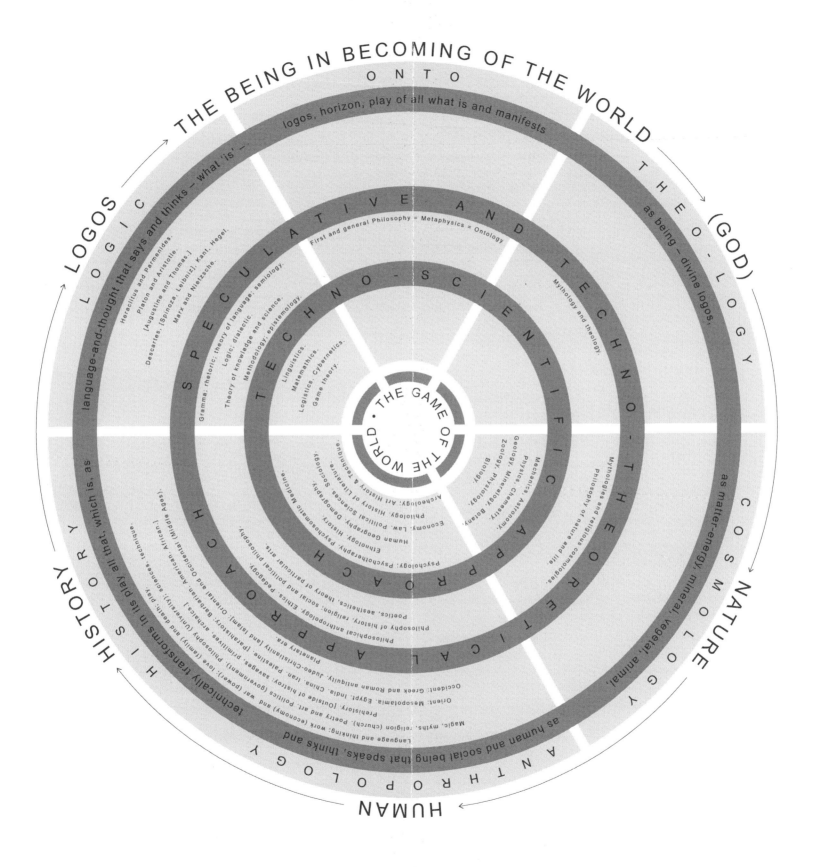

THE BEING IN BECOMING OF THE WORLD

ONTO

LOGOS

LOGIC

THEO-LOGY (GOD)

logos, horizon, play of all what is and manifests

language-and-thought that says and thinks – what 'is' –

as being – divine logos,

Heraclitus and Parmenides.
Platon and Aristotle.
[Augustine and Thomas.]
Descartes. [Spinoza, Leibniz] Kant, Hegel.
Marx and Nietzsche.

First and general Philosophy = Metaphysics = Ontology

Mythology and theology.

SPECULATIVE AND TECHNO-SCIENTIFIC

Gramma, rhetoric; theory of language; semiology.
Logic; dialectic.
Theory of knowledge; epistemology.
Methodology; epistemology.

TECHNO-

Linguistics.
Mathematics.
Logistics. Cybernetics.
Game theory.

THE GAME OF THE WORLD

Physics; Astronomy.
Geology; Mineralogy.
Zoology; Physiology; Botany.
Biology.

Mechanics.
Chemistry.

SCIENTIFIC

COSMOLOGY

NATURE

as matter-energy, mineral,
vegetal, animal,

Mythologies and religious cosmologies.
Philosophy of nature and life.

THEORETICAL

APPROACH

Psychology; Psychotherapy; psychosomatic Medicine.
Ethnology; History.
Human Geography; Demography.
Economy; Law; Political Sciences; Sociology.
Philology. History of Literature.
Archeology. Art History & Technique.

APPROACH

Philosophical anthropology; Ethics; pedagogy.
Philosophy of history; religion; social and political philosophy
Poetics, aesthetics, theory of particular arts.

HISTORY

Occident: Greek and Roman antiquity. Judeo-Christianity [and Islam].
Orient: Mesopotamia. Egypt. India. China. Iran. Palestine. [Oriental and
planetary era.
Prehistory. [outside of history; savages, primitives, archaics.]
Philosophy (university) [Barbarian, American, African.]
love (family) and death; play.
sciences, technique]
technically transforms in its play all that, which is, as

which is, as

as human and social being that speaks, thinks and

Language and thinking: work (economy) and war (power) and
Politics (government). Politics (government).
Magic, myths, religion (church).

ANTHROPOLOGY

HUMAN

all beings objects. Everything is caught in this play of mirrors between the subject and the object that reflect each other; no one can distinguish between what is and is received, what is put into and interpreted into. Is there still external or internal evidence, or a place of their encounter? The circle of hermeneutics, analytical, synthetic, explanatory, comprehensive and everything one would want, keeps us glued to it and prevents us from stopping time. In this total becoming, both the subjects as subjects, as well as the objects as objects, and the opposition subject-object enter the phase of their radical transformation, their suppression, their supersession. Everything consolidates and liquefies itself (at once), everything is caught up in the cycle of production and consumption, fabrication and usage, *planning* and *annihilation*. In language and literature, in science and painting, in politics and in everyday life, we are already witnessing – by participating in – this process of surpassing the subject and the object. Another worldliness appears and is produced, beyond subjectivity and objectivity (of an idealist or realist type). The productive dialogue between the being in becoming of the human and the being in becoming of the world – through the annihilation of old entities and the strange production of new structures – begins to unfold itself in a new horizon.

Production, consummation and consumption allow the human to accord itself to the world. If the destiny of the world is a 'useless' and unlimited accomplishment, the human – limited being, acquiring, expending and squandering all kinds of riches – is the player and plaything of this accomplishment for nothing. Subjects and objects going towards what will surpass them, will we soon see subjects without consciousness and a consciousness without subjects, a consciousness no longer having anything for object?

The problem of the *limit* invites us to crossings and keeps us nailed on the spot.

Distinctions, genera, species, cases, modalities, entities, in their ontological and methodological imbrications and differences, pose delicate problems.

What is *cause* and what is *reaction*? How to unravel in entanglement, other than in an operational and functionally segmental fashion? The search for causality remains affected by a coefficient of culpability: one wants to track down, liberate or domesticate the culpable or capable cause. In this and that, in the slippages of sense, a certain finality pursues its path, rushing through and getting caught in the nets of the rules of the game.

The secret or complete causes of things slip away to make place for operative apprehensions and effective calculations.

Knowing above all effects and results, we bring back to the causes the certainty concerning them.

Causality *uses* many determinations. The relation primes the cause.

In a still simple schema of causality, A acts on B and B on A. A and B act on each other and both on a first and a third product that acts and reacts on them. In the schema of causality, the complementary and circular path, marked by the interaction of fields, functions and multiple variables, is treated with more than just neglect.

The analysis of the play of determinations is inexhaustible. In the bundle of causal explanations and comprehensive interpretations, how to determine the most determining factors?

Let us suppose that a cause determines an effect, which, in turn, is the caused becoming the causing, and determines a third product: is it caused by the first cause or the effect becomes cause (insofar as one can isolate them)?

Only one possibility of the fan is realised? Where are and what becomes of unrealised possibilities? If the possibility is what renders possible its actualisation, what can then indicate, if they exist, the unrealised possibilities?

The *possible* is a way in which the present comprehends the past: it constitutes what was necessary and effective.

At the heart of what is, making a sign towards what is not, in the melee where the possible manifests what renders possible its actualisation and the possible which does not actualise itself, stands the impossible hoping against all hope.

There are always certain possibles that are realised and combined, others finding themselves excluded.

Chance – with or without quotation marks – remains troubling in the eyes of whoever envisages it without losing sight of necessity and probabilities.

The play between the necessary and the arbitrary – to diverse readings – loses itself in the arcana of its own constructions. The same goes for chance and destiny.

Chances – encounters – strongly resemble necessities.

Quantity and quality belong to what is. Does quantity change into quality, even when it extends its grip – quantitatively? Is the combat between the quantitative and the qualitative a question of quantitative or qualitative debate, if the distinction can be maintained?

Everything is relative, conditioned, determined, circumstantial, situated, depending on its place and time and on the point of view according to which one envisages it and, at the same time, everything is, in all its fragmentarity, absolute, partially absolute.

Go recognise yourself in the muddled game of the 'essential' and the 'occasional' that mutates the one into the other.

Chase this or that; it returns at a gallop.

What are the principal figures of the play of That? Evidently, God, nature, the human.

III

God-Problem

How could a meditation articulate itself with a loud or a quiet voice, a thinking or praying voice, an accepting or challenging voice, an extremely fragile and hardly convincing meditation on the God-problem? Speaking *on* already denotes a certain relationship of externality, which, far from facilitating our access to the problematic, makes it even more difficult for us, especially if one does not fall for one of the convenient solutions – in fact, dissolutions of the problem – that are named theism and deism, pantheism and atheism. Is it about God? Which? That of 'always', that of Abraham, Isaac and Jacob, that of prayer, that of onto-theo-logy, that of the Church, that of the philosophers, the living God or the dead, hidden or unknown God revealed or grasped by reason or the heart? Is it the same God who manifests and withdraws, imposes and denies himself, animates tradition and disappears? His different aspects and different approaches rely on him and each on the other, betraying themselves mutually, each contradicting itself and all 'betraying' God. How to find an orientation, not towards the problem of God, but towards the *God-problem*, a problem that proposes itself and that distances itself problematically?

In the beginning, the gods and God existed without being comprehended. God was first comprehended as the beginning of the world, the prince and principle governing all that is, the *arche* of the *pan*, the sacred, the honest and the salutary, the *holon*, the *Heil*, without being founded on anything, not even on itself. Then he was comprehended as the creator of the world, the producer and the cause of all that is, himself being self-created, self-produced, as *causa sui, ens a se*. Finally, he was comprehended as a creature, a production of the representation of the human – what the human was not, but desired to be – of the human who self-produces itself and wants to grasp through their thought and their science the true and the plausible, the causal and probabilistic laws both in nature, which pre-exists them, as well as in their own history. It remains for us to begin to think, neither departing from the God-human split, nor departing from the *humanitas* alone of the human.

Myths and poetry have elaborated the residence of the divine, before it emigrated to philosophy – ontotheological – whose logos says and conceals the manifestation and the occultation of phenomena, while operating a transition from beings towards their first and superior being, the divine. The divine then passes into the word of Scripture, called a *revelation*, that is to be safeguarded in and by theology and the Church. Faith takes precedence over thought and piety, it calls for the help of intelligence – *fides* and *intellectus* engaged in combat, where, in turns, each of these two separated worlds triumphs over the other – belief settles as the queen, and this new epoch of the divine will inspire, from one end to the other, modern – always ontotheological – philosophy. After the language of mythology and poetry, after the thought of (ancient) philosophy, after the faith and intelligence of theology and after, again, the thought of (modern) philosophy, both thought and literature as well as science begin to speak, triumphantly or nostalgically, either of the world deserted by the divine, or of the retreat or death of God.

First the human prays to the God, who created them. Then they pray to the God that they themselves created. The profanation of the sacred is a process that, although crumbling, still belongs to the sacred. It is the play of the sacred and the profane that constitutes the divine and religious world. The play that plays itself out beyond the sacred and the profane belongs to another era. This play would mark an opening to the play of the being of the world, which would not be overhung by a supreme being.

If the human invents its gods or its god, the gods or god invent the human.

What is the vague or precise question to which 'God' answers, in the course of uninterrupted and suddenly halted questioning, and what kind of answer does *God* bring to the recurring and halting questioning?

The concept of God and the concept of Being (being of the world and being of the human) lend each other their attributes.

God closes the question of why and opens the questioning that puts him into question, in the direction of what 'founds' him, annihilates him and does not replace him.

Mysticism burns the stages and ignores mediations. This is why it relies on and animates a rational theology. Mystical intuition and theological ratiocination are the two slopes and the two approaches of God considered as the One-All and as the One transcending the All.

The major theological and religious – and rather involuntary – ruse consists of operating with images of the invisible.

When there were angels, they were sweet and terrible. Were there any diabolic ones?

God, in his idleness, thinks when he does not play: he thinks pure thought, he is himself thought of thought, according to the thought of overworked humans.

Logical and ontological arguments can neither prove the existence of God nor demonstrate his non-existence. One cannot deduce his existence from his essence, nor can one say: either God is also the bad, the false, non-being, or, if he is not all, he is not.

God appears as the most triumphant, most overwhelming and most overwhelmed face of That become neutral – the divine – deified and personalised. He seems to be at the *centre* of three great centres: physis-logos, God, the human. The sacred and the divine, divinity, the gods and God are un-sacredly mixed, are barely distinguishable and are approached in theoretical and practical, mystical and religious agitation, at the heart of the technicised world, with the lassitude and nervousness that this kind of enterprise and maintenance bring about; the indifference of the whole world with regard to the problem of the World – the unnameable opening – indifference, which goes hand in hand with a spasmodic thirst for the absolute and the sacred. The three great concentric circles, each of which englobes the others – physis-logos, God, the human – and which deployed themselves in a diachrony and with synchrony, even though they still constitute us, no longer constitute us. God has become the God of the consciousness of the human, of self-consciousness, of the latter's discursive reason or their speaking, stammering or ineffable interiority. So, he wobbles. How to get out of or over this situation (getting out of it and over it in the two senses of the term *sortir*)?

Humans have a penchant for calling what is for them the most dignified and the most elevated by solemn, theological and religious names.

Is the divine – or the gods – everywhere? Doesn't it thus risk being nowhere?

The gods also knew how to be cruel and evil before the ontotheological constitution of metaphysical philosophy. Afterwards, the divine became good, identified itself with the good: every human play unfolded itself before the eyes of this God, evil from goodness.

God delivered in images and words remains equivocal – here, everywhere, nowhere, elsewhere – and seems to await deliverance, even if it is exhausting.

The sacred and the divine, the divinity, the gods and God existed. Originally, archaically and primitively. Orientally and Asiatically. Hellenically and Romanly. Hebraically and Christianly. Christianity posits the *three* dogmas. The *creation* of the world by God. The *incarnation* of God in the human. The *trinity* of the Father, the Son and the Holy Spirit. (Trinitarianism will reveal itself rich in theological and philosophical consequences; see Hegel.) With Christianity, God dies by becoming human. And humans kill him a second time. God, dead and killed, withdraws. He leaves a void. Refilled multiply: by theology and the ecclesiastical institutions, by the rhythmed and rhythmic celebration of a cultic, theatrical and mystical play, by the pains of faith having a very sure taste and intelligent enough for compromise. By the humanism that goes in for socialising and mondialising, that aspires to the domination of the earth and prepares what is already underway: the end of the human.

At the base of the mystery, the ritual, the cult, the ceremony, the mass, destined to link human and god, there is birth, passion, death and resurrection of a cosmic and anthropomorphic god, celebrated by humans, who taste this sacrifice through a sacred 'meal', where the human 'eats' the god, in communing.

All the mysteries celebrating in a ritual drama the birth, death and rebirth of the human and the god give themselves as (secretly or openly) initiatory and play the rites of the Church of the believers or of the atheists (in both, vocations are becoming rarer).

The term 'divine' designates the divinity, the god himself, and, secondarily, what in an analogical way articulates itself about it, although remaining below it. So the circle of problems, in which the divine and the divinity, the sacred, the gods and god, are linked – in their relations with the humans – remained unthought.

With God, do the gods and the divine, divinity and the sacred also die? It's not so certain.

Are there gods who are not also, if not above all, black?

The God of Genesis created man in his image and likeness, from the dust of the earth, and, because it was not good for him to be alone, he created his companion, woman, from a rib of the sleeping man, so that they might become one flesh, be fruitful, fill the earth and subjugate it. According to the plan of the Eternal, man was destined to dominate over the fish of the sea, over the birds of the air, over the beasts of the field, over all the earth, and over all the creeping things that creep over the earth, living forever, in all innocence. To man, who gave names to the living beings around him, it was strictly forbidden, in the garden of Eden, to eat from the tree of the knowledge of good and evil: otherwise he would die of death. The serpent, the most cunning of animals, persuaded Eve to eat the forbidden fruit; she ate it and gave it to Adam. Then their eyes opened, they lost their innocence and became like gods, but mortal. Henceforth the woman will have to give birth in pain, to desire – with annoyance – her man and to be dominated by him; the man will have, on cursed ground, to work with pain and earn his bread by the sweat of his forehead, until he returns to that land, from which he was taken, dust returning to dust. Thus, succumbing to original sin, man and woman, chased out of paradise, became mortal but knowing, resembling God, bearing the burden of the production and reproduction of life – in negativity and struggle. Then Adam knew Eve, who gave birth . . . (From now on the children of men go to conquer the earth – to realise the lost paradise? – and even raise the assault on the – empty and emptied? – sky to reconquer their dignity and their lost place.) When all of the earth had a singular language and the same words, humans wanted to build – so as not to be scattered and to make a name for themselves – a city and a tower, whose summit would touch the sky. God, however, fearing the execution of their project, descended, confused their language so that they could not understand one another, and scattered them far from Babel over the whole face of the earth. This is the major legend of humanity as a fallen and established deity. Does it not continue to mark humanity at a time when it aspires to the government of the world and the conquest of heaven?

Man, created by God in his image – according to the Hebraic-Christian legend – bears the stigmata of his God, who is himself, consequently, in the image of man.

In this context, the human was interpreted as a tension between the animal and the divine.

The place occupied by God remaining empty, one can very well conceive a theology and a religion of the void and the assaults aimed at occupying this void. Because the void is so attractive.

Disturbed by God's corpse, one often takes others as his substitute.

The relation between the human and the divinity eclipsed all other relations and became the model of relations, up to and including the famous problem of the self and its relation to the other.

The combat does not unfold between God and the human, but between theology and humanism. The theology becoming humanistic will cross itself with a humanism of theological origin.

In the shadow of God – even killed – everything screams his absence. A place remains empty.

Doesn't the god who dies by becoming human prelude the death of the human?

The circle is the same: God dies by becoming man and man becomes like the gods by emancipating himself as a mortal and dying man.

The theological phase of thought is achieved, when it comprehends itself as the self-consciousness of God. Just like the anthropological phase, which will find its end in the self-consciousness of the human.

We are thus gradually losing God. However, how can one lose what one never possessed?

Are we losing God the father or the son of God, the son of Man? Are we losing Christ, when God became man and died through and on the cross for humans so that they themselves become God-like, like they were before original sin, and even after, having eaten the tree of the knowledge of good and evil? Christ, a man whose life – speech and death, gestures and legend – changed the face of the world, imposes himself with all his childlike simplicity and with all his complexity on our meditation, offering an example that no one can follow.

Is the human effectively in search of a new faith and a new non-God?

Be patient a little longer and you will see it well: God without God.

It is in dancing that the Hindu god Shiva constructs and destroys the circle of worlds.

The Heraclitean logos, rhythm and time of the world, is cosmic and divine, playful and royal, like a child-king, who plays – by combining chance and calculation, contingency, rules and necessity – with dice (or small stones: calculations) to displace pawns (or figures) on a chequerboard (or chessboard). Αἰὼν παῖς ἐστι παίζων, πεσσεύων · παιδὸς ἡ βασιληίη. 'Time is a child playing, playing dice and moving pieces; the royalty of a child.' At the same time, human games, children's games, show the other face of the same medallion, manifesting and refracting in the little games the supreme game: 'Children's games as human opinions.' To the Heraclitean logos player corresponds, with continuity and especially with a solution of continuity, the 'logos', the divine wisdom of the *Proverbs* of Solomon in the Old Testament, who addresses the children of God and man – before, in the New Testament, the child Jesus invites all children to come to him, for to them belongs the kingdom (of heaven), and before the Gospel of John proclaims the governing identity of the Logos and of God – claiming (in the language of the *Vulgate*, which poses the problem of translations and transpositions) that it was present while God created the world and that it was at play: *Et delectabar per singulos dies, / ludens coram eo omni tempore, / ludens in orbe terrarum; / and deliciae meae esse cum filiis homimum.* 'And I was delighting, day after day, / playing all the time in his presence, / playing on the earth's surface, / and finding my delights among the children of men.' In *Ecclesiastes*, the governing child renders visible the other side of the supreme game played by the wisdom given birth by God: 'Woe to you, city, whose king is a child!'

The Ecclesiast who proclaimed in the name of God *All is vanity* could not say *All is play.*

Serious and playful at once, the Platonic Socrates says once, in the *Cratylus*, that 'even the gods love play'. In *The Laws*, Plato calls the human 'plaything of god' and god 'the checkers-player who combines all things by moving pieces'. Plato fails to rule on the nature and fate of the divine game and the human game. Sometimes the game is depreciated as that which 'does not entail any inconvenience or advantage worthy of being mentioned and taken seriously' (ibid.), sometimes the entire life of the human is considered as a game celebrating the divinity: 'serious matters deserve our serious attention, but trivialities do not; that all men of good will should put God at the centre of their thoughts; that man, as we said before, has been created as a toy for God; and that this is the acme in his favour. So every man and every woman should play this part and order their whole life accordingly, engaging in the best possible pastimes – in a quite different frame of mind to their present one.' That is to say? 'The usual view nowadays, I fancy, is that the purpose of serious activity is leisure – that war, for instance, is an important business, and needs to be waged efficiently for the sake of peace. But in cold fact neither the immediate result nor the eventual consequences of warfare ever turn out to be *real* leisure (*paidia*) or an education (*paideia*) that *really* deserves the name – and education is in our view just about the most important activity of all. So each of us should spend the greater part of his life at peace, and that will be the best use of his time. What, then, will be the right way to live? A man should spend his whole life at "play" – sacrificing, singing, dancing – so that he can win the favour of the gods and protect himself from his enemies and conquer them in battle.' The founder of philosophy as metaphysics, namely as ontotheology, does not come to the end of the divine and human game: the latter – yet at the service of the former – is considered sometimes as a badinage, futile and infantile, and sometimes as an extremely serious and educational occupation, as what is highest and divine; better: it is considered to be both at once. Not ontology, nor anthropology, nor politics, nor poetics manage to wholly sanctify or minimise the game that is played between mortal humans and immortal gods or to specify its rules. In fact, gods, children, the youth, adults and the elderly play. 'All young things find it impossible to keep their bodies still and their tongues quiet. They are always trying to move around and cry out; some jump and skip and do a kind of gleeful dance as they play with each other, while others produce all sorts of noises. And whereas animals have no sense of order and disorder in movement ("rhythm" and "harmony", as we call it), we human beings have been made sensitive to both and can enjoy them. This is the gift of the same gods whom we said were given to us as companions in dancing.' The young people, however, aspire to constant change, which is fatal for the immutable laws and to the regulated cele- bration of festivals: 'All legislators suppose that an alteration to children's games really is just a "game", as I said before, which leads to no serious or genuine damage. Consequently, so far from preventing change, they feebly give it their blessing. They don't appreciate that if children introduce novelties into their games, they'll inevitably turn out to be quite different people from the previous generation; being different, they'll demand a dif- ferent kind of life, and that will then make them want new institutions and laws. The next stage is what we described just now as the biggest evil that can affect a state – but not a single legislator takes fright at the prospect.' In turn, the artistic, creative, poetic, plastic and musical activities of adults are discredited by the conservative thinker of the *Republic* as mimetics: they are only play and not serious work. As for the wise old people, 'they play concerning the laws a cautious play fitting the elderly'.

In his book *The Gay Science*, Nietzsche, wanting to reverse Platonism and Christianity to provoke the crisis of atheism, and not in the name of the true world or the apparent world (that is to say, neither in the name of its being nor in the name of its distinction), gives the word to the *Insane*, the madman, and lets him ask his questions: '"Where is God?" he cried; "I'll tell you! We have killed him – you and I! We are all his murderers. But how did we do this? How were we able to drink up the sea? Who gave us the sponge to wipe away the entire horizon? What were we doing when we unchained this earth from its sun? Where is it moving to now? Where are we moving to? Away from all of the suns? Are we not continually fall- ing? And backwards, sideways, forwards, in all directions? Is there still an up and a down? Aren't we straying as though through an infinite nothing? Isn't empty space breathing at us? Hasn't it gotten colder? Isn't night and more night coming again and again? Don't lanterns have to be lit in the morning? Do we still hear nothing of the noise of the grave-diggers who are burying God? Do we still smell nothing of the divine decomposition – gods, too, decompose! God is dead! God remains dead! And we have killed him! How can we console ourselves, the murderers of all murderers? The holiest and the mightiest thing the world has ever possessed has bled to death under our knives: who will wipe this blood from us? With what water could we clean ourselves? What festivals of atonement, what *holy games* will we have to invent for ourselves?"' (It is me who underlines, and 'the *me* is hateful' he had said who wagered, played with the existence of God, namely Pascal.)

The gods don't just play. Thought a little more consequentially, they reveal themselves as playthings.

The human is not a marionette in the hands of good and bad demons and gods; gods and demons are not the playthings of the human.

Did the divine, playing in all idleness or activity, appear to humans because they had experience of the game, or did these latter-born ones suspect the power of the game from their tension towards the divine?

Sometimes the most advanced theology was, in its high and brief moments, negative. It said what God is not, what one cannot say about him. God is nothing (particular), it claimed. He is 'thus' nothing (this nothing is always something). Even more rarely, a certain theology almost succeeded in grasping in flashes God as the Game, preparing unknowingly a grasp of God as one of the figures, or even the most militant and humblest figure in the play of the errancy of time, young and old, new and ancient, constantly pursued, misrecognised, lost, found again, forgotten, disguised, murdered, resurrected, reinvented. But the human needed a positive the-ology, a kerygma emplanting in the past – the source – the happiness of paradise lost through the fault of original sin, flying over the misery of the present time and leading to the future salvation already announced, the three dimensions of time coexisting and over-dimensioning in and by 'eternity', infinite elastic time. This theology militated and militates, tri-umphed and triumphs, sank and sinks, was reborn from its ashes and now becomes seeking: it demythologises, dissubjectifies, disobjectifies. It is the avant-garde. Who also delivers the combats of the rearguard.

There is a Christian and minor poet who writes the following about the game played between the God of man and the man of God:

> I have often played with man, says God. But what a game, it is a game from which I still tremble.
> I have often played with man; but God, it was to save him, and I have trembled enough from not being able to save him,
> Of not succeeding in saving him. I want to say that I have trembled enough through fearing not to be able to save him,
> Asking myself if I could save him.
> I have often played with man, and I know that my grace is insidious, and how much and how she turns and plays. She is more cunning than a woman.
> But she plays with man and turns him and turns the event and it is to save man and keep him from sin.
> I often play against man, says God, but it is he who wants to lose, the fool, and it is me who wants him to win.
> And I succeed sometimes,
> Until he wins.
> Indeed, we play who loses wins.
> At least he does, because if I lose, I lose.
> But him when he loses, only then does he win.
> Strange game, I am his partner and his opponent,
> And he wants to win against me, that is to say, to lose.
> And myself, his opponent, I want to make him win.

The world no longer resounds with the 'sound of divine dice', of which *Zarathustra* spoke. Soon the absence of this sound will fade.

At a certain moment, it was decided that enthusiasm (ἐν θεῷ) was inferior to reflection and thought. Since then, there have been no more gods. We no longer believed in cultic games.

It is not the world that is a divine game. It is God who is a mundane game.

The children of God and the humans who heard themselves called by the divine word, often played a puerile game consisting of speaking to God like children to their doll and of God like a little lead soldier.

The god of Islam and Mohammedanism enters the scene after the unfolding of the last religion, Christianity. The *Qur'an* is a bastardised and desert-like work, a provincial reprise of what has already been played out world-historically. So, when it tells us 'Life is only a game and a pastime', as opposed to the future life, which is the only serious life, as well as to divine and eternal time, it is just a repeat.

Neither militant, nor triumphant, nor succumbing, God could perhaps become little by little a master piece dismissed from a superannuated game.

The human projects towards and in God what will become human again.

What pushes up should not make us underestimate what pushes down.

We are led to the era that realises the errant truth of Christianity, that is to say, renders it effective and annihilates it, even and especially through bourgeois secularism and the enterprise that would be socialist, which open onto the nihilism destined to be vanquished by itself.

Already the triumph of Christianity erects itself on the defeat of the Christian message.

Theism, deism, pantheism, atheism will unite – ecumenically.

By killing 'life' within themselves to love God alone, the desert Fathers, the anchorites and the hermits, reached a kind of total disgust: this was originally the noonday demon.

Humans transfer on to their similars and society this feeling called love that they accord to God.

Sometimes Nietzsche thinks that God died out of pity for humans. Unless death among the gods was only a prejudice we could think in our turn.

Atheism restores the interest in the problem of God.

God and religion cancel and justify human life. This in turn denies them, by remaining in search of a justification. Even atheology continues to move in dependence on theology or metatheology.

God, the incarnation of weakness, battles alongside the strongest, overwhelmed by his own force and that of the victors no less than by the sighing
of fallen creatures.

To speak of God, to pose or to suppose his existence, to pose or to oppose
his non-existence, signifies to remain in a misunderstanding. Should it be
time to elaborate a, let's say, theological approach, a theology more interrogative and questioning, linked to the problematic experience of belief
and faith, to shake those who passionately desire to believe without being
passionate believers, taking their desire and their desire for a desire as faith?
The terms 'truth' and 'reality' turn in their hinges. Without ever exiting.
All *persona* and all *res* turn to the mask and the nothing, all truth and all
reality – divine and/or human – topple as pieces corresponding to the play
of errancy.

Believing in the divine will already imply a will to believe.

Perhaps from the start, they believed in it and did not believe it.

Like any other domain, one could take the theological and religious
domain and study its rhetoric, to examine in which metaphorical and meto-
nymic terms God is spoken of.

According to a version that knew and could dominate, all the great thinkers thought the thought of God, the greatest thinker.

Onto-theo-logy, ecclesiastical institutions, the words and gestures of piety
no longer encounter – without ever having encountered – the absolute, the
supreme and all-powerful, omniscient and omnipresent Being, the foundation of all that is, the necessary and sufficient reason, the first motor, the
causa prima. For two thousand five hundred years, all philosophical and metaphysical thought is, positively and/or negatively, onto-theo-logical, equally
all ethics, which would become furiously secular, humanist and socialist,
by reversing the signs. Since Presocratic and pre-philosophical thought,
through the Platonic-Aristotelian deployment that goes through Platonist
and Aristotelian – Augustinian and Thomist – Christianity, to the thought
which wants to be post-Christian and metaphilosophical, everything moves
on onto-theo-logical rails, even when everything derails or when everything lives, which comes down to the same, in and of antitheology. At
the same time, all the acts that punctuate life, love and death, all the leads

and all the relations to what is – from the animal to the divine – remain impregnated with it. Christianity remains the most formative, the most intelligent current because the richest in contradictions, the most amalgamable to other often contrary currents. It mondialises itself as such, effectively coins its God and its precepts, generates what succeeds it. But it is not yet the hour of the inheritors.

The inheritors, and not the mere successors, of this history and legend of the world that begins with the *creation* of all that is, which marks the moment of the *fall* of the human into sin, which celebrates the *incarnation* of God in the human, who dies and lives in expectation of the final *apocalypse* and *redemption*, would lead the onto-theo-logy of the Logos-God, the God of the revelation, source of faith, hope and grace, the God of mystic ecstasy and organised cult, towards their suppression. This suppression would go up to the suppression of suppression. Suppression of suppression is not synonymous with nothing. These are the massive unveilings, which annihilate the nothing and their own being. The negation of negation would not pose itself as a synthesis, a third element, which abolishes and contains two antagonisms, each riveted on the other, where the opposite no longer mingles with what it opposes as a new thesis. How to speak and act in the name of the ontotheological and mystical God, when the suppression and the suppression of the suppression are (always incompletely) achieved? What God has been will be to think and to experience otherwise. How? In the horizon of rickety affirmations recognising themselves as such? How to avoid the chitchat about the mystery and the enigma, the absence and the secret, the withdrawal and withdrawal that withdraws, the silence and the unspeakable, the unthought and the unplayable?

Speaking and saying, thinking and doing, living and experiencing, individually and world-historically, privately and publicly, the question of the problem of God that pivots once in the direction of the question of the God-problem and once again in the direction of still-empty space-time, signifies not filling the emptiness, the opening, the gap, the nothingness. Through the entangled play of myths and demythologisations, even demystifying mystics and mystifications, could we keep ourselves open by also playing the game of all the closures that, closed, support us to shake and shake us?

God and the Devil – Satan, Lucifer, negativity, evil – are linked together for life and death. The one constantly becomes the other, each one thinks to triumph over the other.

The diabolical problem of evil and error, of falsity and sin, is the cross of every theology of an omnipotent God who fails to accord predestination and human freedom.

Hell and damnation (eternal), paradise and salvation (universal), are the two complementary and opposing terrains on which the ontotheological and pedagogical attempt remains oriented to frighten and force the freedom of adhesion, remaining two major projections of positive aspirations and negative fears.

Try to draw up the most exhaustive table of contraries; then you would perhaps take into account that religion in general and Christianity in particular bet, successively and/or simultaneously, at moments and/or at once, on all the contraries.

God was supposed to be each of the contraries, each of the contraries taken separately, the unity of contraries: suffering and joy, asceticism and play, mortification and rebirth, mystical and rational, the focus of faith and the object of the intellect, near and far, unnatural and natural, inhuman and human, punishment and reward, etc., etc. He was equally considered as present-absent, but not as existing and non-existent. He does not succumb to a contrary power, which would remain attached to him: he is chased and slips away.

The theology of heretics lets accede to language not only the word but also the delirium of God, and often manages to envisage the world as a false or falsified creation.

The Christian world is dead. The post-Christian gods live their mortal lives.

To want to utter words or accomplish acts conceived as sacrilegious is to remain in the dependency of a sacred God not radically problematised.

Those who deny the existence of God, claim his non-existence, remain prisoners of the Platonic-Christian world. The reversal they want to effect – on the same basis – aims to replace the dead and killed God, by setting reason, human consciousness and practice, social progress, well-being, on the empty throne. In view of the great style of this myth, of this word, of this legend – constituents of the world – in view of the force of an ecclesiastical foundation founded through Peter because his faith was hard as a rock, this same Peter, who had three times denied his master, Christ – as any historical and worldly realisation renders effective and 'betrays' the original inspiration (so there has never been any 'true' Christianity, 'true' democracy, 'true' socialism) – the assaults delivered by bourgeois and Marxist humanism, by psychoanalysis and Freudianism, by realism and surrealism are still somewhat ridiculous. Most certainly, they also set in motion a certain negativity, which a consolidating epoch uses to establish the republic, if not the one of the golden mean, at least the one of the medium term.

In a world emptied of gods and empty of God, what will animate rites and ceremonies, celebrations and festivals? What will become of a certain sacredness, be it secular and profane?

In disarray, who of us would not wish, most deeply in one's heart – by confessing it or not – that God or a father or a mother comes to speak to them like to a child, revealing the truth to them and offering them salvation? It hardly matters whether this remedy belongs to the illusory or the unintelligible.

This supreme and warming clarity, which we desire more than anything in the world, no one can dispense it to us.

How differently would believers and unbelievers talk about God and their feelings regarding him if they could do it anonymously.

The dazzling God became a hidden and absent God before becoming and remaining a killed and dead God.

Deicide is this absolute crime perpetrated by the human, who, by killing God, died in becoming human the first time, died as human a second time, lets him die a third time, without suspecting that the human inaugurates thus the era of its own death, already in motion and destined to last a long time. The humanism that is installed on the empty throne of God, by completing the reign of God, leads, through its triumph – not so triumphant – towards its own exhaustion.

God is finished when we have finished him. All taking place in fundamental incompletion.

After the death of God, one has often – involuntarily and unconsciously – identified God with the cosmic, historical and human logos or dialectic, without fully comprehending what was said and done and without illuminating the premises, the steps and the conclusions.

Atheism is another – and derived – act of faith animated by the lukewarm ardour of unbelief and indifferent to the high power of indifference.

In the bespectacled eyes of atheism, God is nothing. Thus, we are (not) delivered from *nothing*.

Does the death – of God, of the human? – impose itself more than life? Christ and Christianity live this death. Atheism lives off crumbs. It dies the life of God.

The process of desacralisation, of secularisation, of profanation that unfolds itself on all the stages, puts in circulation and in scenes the formerly deistic or theistic look of the world, follows the Christian cannibalism, which followed the archaic cannibalism, another and new cannibalism.

The race continues without 'God' and 'without' religion, while one devotes oneself to an indeterminate *je ne sais quoi*, which one is incapable of naming.

Our epoch: the poorest in gods, the richest in junk religiosity.

Even more difficult than the constitution of an atheological thought is the confrontation and the surpassing of the problem of death and the absence of God in a direction leading beyond atheism.

According to the evangelical exploration of the firmament, the obscuring of the stars will be a sign preluding the glorious parousia, as it marked the moment of death of the one whose birth was announced astrally. Where resides the disaster?

Christianity formerly grafted itself onto all the religiosities and preceding religions; now by generalising itself in and through its abolition, it dies, fertilises and contaminates, gets contaminated.

The death of the Christian world makes everyone believe, believers and unbelievers, that they will recover more liberated and more victorious, released from the tricks one has played on them. Will the dead turn in their graves? And will the living turn towards what does not cease to be of the order of the future?

The powerful anthropocentrism of the prayer of the powerless human proves salutary. Genuflexion and prayer help the one who prays. Does the human still feel the need to prostrate themself before what is stronger than them? In any case they do.

To love God in order to not love humans is for self-love tempting and satisfying – thus also dirty. To love humans is also an abstract programme.

Morality and law, the state and the police, replace the commandments of the deceased God.

Die and be reborn trumpets the watchword of all religiosity and all enterprise aiming at the animation and the mortalisation of life and death. Mortal humans and immortal gods perpetually exchange their lives and deaths. The temptation of conquering both life and death remains tempting. Mortification of life and resurrection of the dead go together. The dead grasps the living, life grasps death. In what space-time and under what disguises however do survival, rebirths and resurrections take place? Would death alone be immortal?

One talks much about waiting for another future. The nostalgia for God occupies us, the temptation to substitute the human is great, and anticipation operates through humans. We came into the world too late for God and too prematurely for the Other, who abolished itself. The future could consist only in a retake of the Same, whose logos-physis, God, the human – it hardly matters whether they believe themselves anecdotes or history itself – have been, are and remain, through their surpassing, the foci of an obscure light. To see and to accept the withdrawal which withdraws itself and the other as the face and mask of the same – this could not take place. The very words which speak of the suppression which suppresses itself will be barely heard and quickly suppressed, even if they should emerge again from time to time in time. God will remain the central theme of a renewed and more questioning ontotheology, the reference system of a modernised and ecumenical Church, the focus of a cult that has become more sober, the invisible guarantor of a progressivist ethic, the welcoming and gathering home, the hole creating a constant draught of air. The believer will invoke him without too much fear and trembling, the unbeliever will continue to stubbornly deny a position they declare non-existent, reason and heart will seek to unravel their affairs, mystical ecstasies will democratically keep their rights.

God has been, he has been said and lived, revealed and conveyed by the major legend of humanity. He died in becoming human and was killed by humans. It is the phantoms that inflict the most burning injuries and provoke our sleepwalking actions and reactions. Phantoms *are*, as phantoms. Do they exist too? Are being and existing different and identical? The suppression of suppression – the suppression of the atheistic negation which denies the position of God – will be covered up by the flood of the world, the nostalgia and the hope for the world beyond, sacred or profane. This flood, this nostalgia and this hope will equally cover up the untenable words of a meditation on the God-problem, which, beyond apology and polemic, remains disarming and disarmed.

Lost between several dedivinised divinities, the still historical and modern human no longer knows to which saint to devote themself, what is the deity who must preside at their highest and last moments, when the demons assail their planetary becoming.

Plants eat water, air and earth, animals plants, humans animals; gods humans – before being eaten by them; devoured devourers, they are all both.

Into what does God pass by passing away? Evidently into nature, into the human, into history.

IV

Physis.
The Cosmic World

Can nature be founded?

The secret of physis is precisely what appears as birth, growth, blossoming, decline – natural.

The mythologies of nature and the mythological figures of the tamers of nature seem situated firmly behind us and in some way also: before us. It's for us to decipher them – at the worn-out threshold of an age that claims to be ecumenical. For if what one designates under the name of the philosophy of history has become, little by little, relatively and very approximately, problematic and transparent – not thanks to relativism (in relation to what? to what absolute?), but thanks to the possibility of a multidimensional and polyscopic approach, and although we do not know how to pose the problem of the 'sense' of history – what was called the philosophy of nature remains enclosed in rigid representations or routes itself through non-figurative configurations towards an almost mute and acosmic approach, where all orientation is lacking.

How did nature manifest itself before the Greeks? If it was named, what name did it bear and how did it bear beings and things? For it is on the basis of the Greeks that it is *physis*, unveiling – and veiling – in and through the *logos*, logos as unveiling of physis. As foundation and horizon, physis however remains unelucidated, and the relationships between chaos and cosmos, being and non-being, everything and nothing, remain enigmatic. In the Hebraic-Christian representation, nature is the creation against which we must struggle, opposing it and coming to terms with it, until the final end, apocalyptic (signifying the definitive catastrophe of the created sinner, when the seventh angel will empty its cup and a voice will cry: 'It is done') and redemptive (signifying the transfiguration of all, the appearance of the new heavens and the new earth). This representation is entangled in its difficulties and ambiguities. God pre-exists – cosmic and historical and human – time, but only appears with Creation. Creator and creation are created in what time? Does God create the matter and abysses from which everything has emerged? And what of the *nihil*, from which everything was drawn? Is creation the fall of God? Are we not in a 'false' or 'falsified' creation? With Modernity, nature becomes the alterity of thought, the problem to be solved, the x to be deciphered and transformed, the object of theoretical and practical activity, techno-scientific, of the industrious and collective human subject. Nature – the first half of the world – becomes the object of the sciences of nature and the natural sciences, the other half – history – becoming the object of the historical and human sciences. Without preoccupying themselves too much with this dichotomy, the people of Modernity thus experience nature, just as they experience it through naturism, link and screen between the human and nature. At the threshold of the planetary era, the difference between what is cosmic and natural and what, in grasping it, is technical and artificial, is abolished. The x is put in quotation marks. We enter a beyond of the representations of nature. More than nature, there is a problem of nature, a *nature-problem*. Why problem? Because we do not know how to understand and live it, that which stands under us. Trying to think of it as what is *first of all*, we find ourselves precipitated into the circle of thought-nature-history and the combination of these three totalities that compose only one, which lets itself be decomposed. But concretely, and to take a concrete example, why transform this huge mountain, which is here, into a problem? But where is it? In reality? In my representation? Before my eyes? And we grasp it in view of what? To admire it, climb it, explore it, exploit it? What relationship does it have with the poet who sings of it, the painter who paints it, or with the bandit, the skier, the hunter and the lover who can all use it? Is it a strategic objective, a postcard theme, an object of geological, mineralogical, botanical studies, etc.? Was it sacred? Does it become the support of technical installations? Is it about transforming it? Or to play with it and on it?

The historical adventure of humans accomplishes itself on the foundation of nature, makes its being and problematises nature, negates it and negates itself. The agreement between the human and nature becomes incomprehensible, as it is incomprehensible that nature should be comprehensible, that the laws of nature and the laws of physics correspond. Magic, religion and myths, poetry and art, politics, also philosophy, sciences, technique and thought confronted and shaped, confront and shape, the cosmic and natural world. Work and struggle, love and death, play, emerge in the midst of nature, mediate it and are submerged by it. How will it stop being and making a problem? Will the solution be found in a logos become technology, a cosmology become cosmotechnics, a biology and a psychology become biotechnical and psychotechnical? Or will it reside in a dissolution? Will nature reuptake all, when the human will be no more, will not speak of it again? But how will it still be called *nature*? Will it not have stopped *being* and making a problem?

By nature implying a kind of technics that would rule it, the technics imitating nature by transforming it, we are at the junction of the two models melting into one: naturalism-technicism.

From the outset, among the Greeks, *physis* seems to imply in a certain manner the power of *techné*; this is why techné can then imitate it. God appears among the Judaeo-Christians as the absolute technician, *the* creator, the plan of providence, which guides the subjugating actions of humans, their struggle against (original) sin and nature in general. Must we still wait for the domestication of energetic matter and atomic energy, the artificial creation of life, the complete cybernetisation of thought and the total planning of society, to begin – on a planet as planified as it is rearranged, senseless and insignificant – to experience and think the games of planetary technics?

The absolute beginning, in space and time – extension and duration – does not offer itself to apprehension. Neither the beginning *tout court*, nor the beginning of this or that. Nature may well be the first totality, yet it is grasped, reconstituted, experienced, even is born *later*, thanks to human thought and action in the course of history. Succession turns into a kind of simultaneity. Whoever observes and transforms, and what is observed, formed and transformed, are interdependent. Thus, even though cosmic nature is first in space-time, it is only thought, known, experienced and transformed thanks to the power that comes later and institutes itself as the first, instituting it.

The cosmic totality, nature, does not *exist* independently of the human; it has no visible and readable *sense* otherwise, if it indeed has one. It is in no way, for all that, instituted by the human and constituted for the human. It passes into the human and passes the human. No decision can – still? – be made concerning nature – mobile or not – or the signification of a history of nature and cosmic and natural rhythms. If living and thinking humanity were to disappear on earth – with or without its explicit will, which could be neither a fortune nor a misfortune, since no one knows or tests why humanity wants or does not want to survive in the movement of visible figures and spirals of being-nothingness – if making-be led to a making-disappear and the inaugural eclosion to the final catastrophe – obsession and apocalyptic aim of almost all prophetic thought – would there still be something, and what and for whom? Questions that come back to the central question that founds and surpasses metaphysics: what is the World (and not what is the universe or nature)?

World and cosmic world are not identical.

It is in the cosmic horizon that the fundamental metaphysical, ethical and poetic problem poses itself now, with and without clarity: 'What is the being?' (Aristotle); 'Why is there something rather than nothing?' (Leibniz); 'To be or not to be, that is the question' (Hamlet).

All the warnings, proud or whiny, of a planetary catastrophe, all the pity about the fate of the human species, go hand in hand with this naive and almost hysterical absolute faith in the human which exhibits metaphysical or plainly anti-metaphysical anthropomorphism, one-eyed and wobbly humanism, fatigued progressivism, orthodox, heterodox or vulgar Marxism, psychosociological existentialism. From the moment when one 'thinks', in the dimension of philosophical journalism and the dominant ideology, that 'it is unfortunate that a human could write today that the absolute is not the human' (Sartre), it is already the fate of this little absolute – since the great absolute had already been annihilated to being.

Theoretically we know quite well that the earth of humans can continue to turn without them.

The schema, ancient, biblical and Judaeo-Christian, evolutionist and bourgeois, positivist and Marxist, thus marks – schematically and circularly – the stages of being in becoming of the totality of the world and the cosmic world: logos or God or dialectic of the movement; matter, plants, animals; humans endowed with thought, realising and materialising their thought, becoming conscious of the global process and marching towards universal history and eschatological, sacred or profane salvation. We are all still following this path. One seems to wait for the next link that must be technical (or technological?). How long will the world suffocate under this scheme?

Until the final disintegration? Doesn't everything begin through an initial catastrophe and doesn't it find its end in a fatal catastrophe? What does beginning and end nonetheless signify in the horizon of cosmic totality and nothingness?

'Naturally' one can also 'think': 'that the universe is only a defect in the purity of non-being'.

All the little portable cosmologies of our epoch, with their convenient epistemological schemas that know nothing of what they are schemas of – Christian and Teilhardian, positivist and naively ontological, Marxist and materialist-dialectical, fantastical and sophisticated – presuppose and leave unthought the cosmogonic and cosmological schema that rules them, namely the biblical and Judaeo-Christian (also having ancestors) schema and its evolutionist, positivist, bourgeois and Marxist continuation (still generating offspring).

Do we begin to suspect that any cosmology can only be negative and interrogative? Nevertheless we await global answers.

Thinking cosmologically, better: cosmically, and vaster still. While doing what with the anthropological?

Metaphysics is from the outset in physics.

Nature becoming 'object' of physics, and 'subjected' to metaphysics, mutates into 'natural reality' and 'spiritual ideality'. Yet neither physics nor metaphysics can grasp that of which they are supposed to be science and knowledge.

The distinction between the *natural* and the *supernatural* expresses the loss of the ('sacred') sense of nature.

Nature is what vivifies and remains, resists and persists – the most.

Trying to cut out, in the unlimited circle or rather in the spiral of the open and never accomplished and given totality, two great circles, nature and history, namely that which is and is done without the human, and that which exists and produces itself through and for the human, is to distinguish artificially the modes of being world of the World (polymorphic and unique?). This does not signify that the natural and cosmic horizon or the human and historical horizon should be the supreme horizon – for nature is and is not identical to the horizon of the world, and history the same – nor that a synthesis of the two could constitute the horizon of horizons.

Is it because it can be said, thought and experienced that nature comprises a logic? Or is it the inverse?

Mediatised nature – whether according to the ternary and unitary rhythm: ontological logos- cosmic nature-historical spirit, or comprehended as a gigantic auto-production, or in its conception as dialectical movement – remains permanently a squared circle for the human spirit.

All thought dodges the fundamental problem – whose very foundation ceaselessly hides itself, probably demanding that one not continue to seek it like that and fix it – by drowning it in being or thought, matter or spirit, reality or ideas, subjectivity or objectivity, or by wanting to catch it in the threads of a dialectical spider web. This problem would let itself be formulated roughly as follows: what is the 'secret' of the accord – even discordant – of the human and the world, that is to say, in what resides the encounter, the correspondence, the adequacy between human experience and spirit and the mode of being and things manifesting themselves? For if one presupposes a thought, an idea, a reason, a knowledge that are unveiled to be deciphered in the experience – theoretical and practical – from which they seem to emerge, one remains locked in a magical and vicious (Cartesian, Kantian, Hegelian) circle, where beginning and end meet ontologically and gnoseologically, metaphysically and physically, because one knows it in advance, although one only finds this knowledge again at the end. And if one presupposes a reality in motion or an energetic matter that ends in thought, because they would dialectically imply it from the start (materialism called dialectical), one remains equally prisoner of the infernal circle, without having posed the problem of circularity – atrociously closed and shockingly open and limitless and not infinite – and without facing up to the circle of circles or spirals that englobe us.

The problem of chaos hides itself behind and in the problem of the cosmos.

The difference between organic nature and inorganic nature should be elucidated.

In the physical totality that embraces, as you know, human and historical becoming, letting itself in turn be embraced by it, 'evolution' and
'involution' march hand in hand: conjointly with the process of progressive
differentiation, the passage of the homogeneous into the heterogeneous, the
inverse process and passage unfold. These two processes lead to both integration and disintegration.

Mathematical formalisation, namely theoretical and techno-scientific,
and transformative techno-scientific practice constitute modern nature.

Does not that which physical experiment discovers pre-exist in nature? Is
it not for all that artificially produced?

The cosmological sciences – the sciences of nature and the natural
sciences – necessarily fractional and fractioning, all take root in a field
cleared beforehand by philosophy, in which they move without being able to
sufficiently explore the vector and the content of their concepts; doing what
they can and must do, they stumble clumsily over the problem of the bond
of the laws of physics with the laws of nature. And the philosophy of the
sciences does not think what the sciences do not think because it remains
subordinate to them. Also we do not see very clearly into the junction of
mathematics and physics. Whether the physico-mathematical and biochemical sciences want to accept it or not, there is not a single decipherment of
the 'big book of the world', although a certain active, rationalist, scientific,
technical and practical reading seems to dominate and transform the visible
stage, while maintaining a certain – loose or tight? – tension with meditation and poeticity, with what freezes and shakes us.

Certainly we do not stop living and also experiencing nature, so to speak,
outside of theoretical and experimental scientific techniques, even if these
mediatise it.

For a long time, it was in *physis* that the major power of being in becoming
seemed to reside. Physis was then eclipsed as a source of energy. God and
nature, as a relatively immobile horizon, succeeded it. For some time now, it
is the science of nature, *physics*, that is to say, the theoretical and practical
techno-scientific activity to which the human subject devotes itself, itself
caught in the network of objects which it faces and of which it forms a
part, that becomes the functional measure and the motive form of modern
technics. It is what technically liberates the natural power of matter in

motion, in the form of atomic energy, in the interior of these uncertain relations – passably mathematised and calculable – which seems to dominate that which it wants to dominate and itself. Deterministic laws combine with probabilistic laws in the certainty-uncertainty ensemble. In scientific study a play of abstract equations (of what?) now rules, whose link with natural and physical or artificially produced facts escapes us. This does not prevent massive realisations and spectacular exploits, a calculation of probabilities that manages to decisively govern a great number of operations and to organise the possible. Does every unifying and unified system, capable of embracing the unitary field, become impossible?

The universe and natural phenomena support many scientific theories, which, related to the 'same' phenomena, seen each time differently, elaborate, consolidate, fluidify, combine with others, fall apart, let themselves be replaced.

It is by giving more play, as much to certainty as to uncertainty, in the field of nuclear physics, that the theoretician of uncertainty *relations*, Heisenberg, can write: 'The conception of the objective reality of elementary particles has thus strangely dissolved itself, not in the fog of a new conception of the obscure or poorly comprehended reality, but in the transparent clarity of a mathematics that no longer represents the behaviour of the elementary particle, but the knowledge that we possess of it.' Does this beyond of representation, this *calculation* of probabilities, help us to access little by little and by jumps, while science pursues its work, a metascientific thought?

In order to be, all that is requires both a natural foundation, and, in order to appear to us, to be approached – in a more or less mediated way – instrumentally and technically, the distinction between what is natural and what is artificial remains highly problematic.

To command nature, one must accept to obey it.

Technics attacks nature. Why and how has nature led itself to what unleashes the most extraordinary violence against it? Unfathomable are the lines of force drawn within it and where violence destroys violence.

Because it is a fact that appears as incontestable: all that is the remit of physis, the cosmic world, resorts principally and exclusively to the jurisdiction of the corresponding sciences and techniques. Philosophical or metaphilosophical thought does not seem to have much to say about it. Is this a passing situation? Will thought succeed in installing a productive dialogue with the sciences or even in fertilising metascientific captures?

We hardly know what the cosmological bases of modern technology and what the technological foundations of our cosmology are. Yet the play of the world demands a comprehension of the play that englobes the play of science and all scientific and technical theory and practice of games.

Right from the start of the play, all comprehension of nature carries moral, legal, anthropological, anthropocentric, anthropomorphic and political schemas and models projected onto nature, in the same way that all comprehension of history implicates prototypes of natural and cosmic order. It is natural and historical. What remains for us to understand is the unitary root of this double and unique play.

The biocosmic and technological powers are allies and enemies. Technological networks prolong and combat the biocosmic elements. Where will their duel lead?

The links of the cosmic order and the ethical order now appear as a torn spider web.

Between what is natural and what is historically determined, how to establish a dividing line?

Nature is certainly also a historical and social category, but it is that which made possible the emergence of this category.

The non-distinction between the social and the cosmic differentiates itself 'progressively'.

The perspective already exists: human history can reintegrate natural history, from which it issued, and henceforth unfolds itself without any history.

The identity of human-nature finds itself neither behind nor before us. Is there anything natural for us other humans?

What we habitually call natural generally arises out of a second nature.

The putting into question and into practice of nature is the human, which puts itself into question and transforms its human nature.

Sometimes the human seems redundant in the universe.

The human seems to have a horror of the natural given and keeps a – hateful – nostalgia for animality.

O Mother Nature! Are we emancipated from the realm of mothers? And does the thundering father not thunder at his children anymore?

In breaking free from cosmic entanglement, the human on the march towards their dissolution as an autonomous subject, rejoins it.

From the human encrusted in the universe, spontaneously integrated into cosmic physis, we pass into the human who knows differentiation and who *seeks* unity.

Naturally, that is to say, historically, one can integrate culture into nature – on an ontological, epistemological and eschatological level; but, in the meantime, one can equally do the inverse.

The evolutionary schema: *physics, chemistry, physiology* and *biology, psychology, history* and *sociology* can also be traversed in the inverse direction; thus one would like to reduce history and sociology to psychology, itself reduced to physiology and biology, which in turn arise from chemistry issued from mathematisable physics. Hoping thus to cover, in the unity of the two contrary directions, the whole of duration-extension.

The world of the artifice covers more and more the world of nature. Technics becomes a second nature.

The city annihilates nature, and nature annihilates the city; nevertheless, the city develops itself on the ground of nature and it is through the city that the presence and absence of nature is unveiled and dissimulated.

One asks of mathematics – *mathesis universalis* – to provide the solid and unassailable foundation supporting the whole scientific and technical edifice, as if mathematics – play of calculation – could be exempt of conventions and anarchy, contradictions and inconsistencies.

Ciphers are called ciphers because the Arabic word *sifr* designates zero. Why are numbers not content to be unlimited and transfinite and want to be infinite?

Numbers and the countable constantly devour themselves in going forwards.

The cosmic world, dominated by necessity, still remains open to the aleatory.

Heredity and milieu combine their efforts, oppose each other, and combine to give a result where the different lineages are not completely visible.

In the cosmic universe, with more brilliance than in the partial universes, all that is 'knows' birth, growth and decline, manifestation, blossoming and falling.

It is not necessary that all parts of the universe be rigorously symmetrical.

In the interior of space-time-matter-energy, supposed to constitute the universe, leaps and mutations still remain stumbling blocks for diverse scientific theories.

We are obliged to know that mass-energy is not infinite. Cosmically? Epistemologically?

The strange network of *matter, energy, life* and *thought* is not easily disassembled. We hustle the problem, when we represent to ourselves a matter-energy becoming – transforming into – thought, which, in turn and anew, might materialise itself by retransforming itself.

Is it from the exploration, the exploitation, the explosion and the artificial disintegration of natural energetic matter that a kind of new discordant accord with all that is and is done, a new integration, will come – beyond the dualism that rivets one onto the other, making them interdependent, namely materialism and idealism, beyond the reign of representation? Is dualism surpassable? Between the thought and what 'is' not what it is, the obstacle resistant to overcoming or emergence, between the natural facts, so called or technically produced, between what is, was done, is done, or that which we consider as such – but where does the unity or the encounter or the rupture reside between what is and what we envisage as such? – and our explanations and interpretations, formulations and formalisations that fall apart, through what does the dividing line or the displaceable and surpassable border pass?

The extreme point of the will to power that shakes the human would like to direct itself towards the materialisation of thought – corollary of energetic and almost thinking matter. This would ensure humans absolute power, omnipotence – they 'think'. Materialisation, dematerialisation, rematerialisation – in a time that would allow us to circulate in its past and its future – is it there the supreme present that humans await? Magic and science, dream and technique, fantastic and effective, strangeness and familiarity, would they be part of this – no less partial – play of imagination or would they prepare a mutation?

Since Aristotle, energy is the secret of the deployment of being in its (physical and historical) ensemble. Making of power, of dynamics, an act, a force, a work. Dynamics and energetics manifest the movement – the becoming – of being and beings, their actions and works. But equally since Aristotle, the links that bind power and possibility – *dynamis* – to act and actualisation – *energy* – remain unthought. What drives possibility – potentiality – towards its manifestation as energy? The dynamics of physis alone? Or the movement itself and the Act-and-Intelligence that rules it, namely God? On the basis of the unelucidated problem, natural and atomic energy then became a force technically liberated by the act, the energy, of human and historical science. The atomic and, let's say, material energy that inhabits the tiny particles of the cosmic All is unchained by these atoms, individuals of the totality, that are humans, even and especially when they are in the process of socialisation. The epoch that completes modernity and perhaps inaugurates another era is characterised as the atomic era, the nuclear era. It examines all the signs perceptible through diverse devices, macro- and micro-physically, macro- and micro-historically, to make possible the global epoch of the disintegration of the atomic energy that must thus put in motion the new era. The human, already phased-out and over-passed, aspiring to the domination and exploitation of this energy, trembles with fear at the forces it liberates. Humans want to play with the star that is the earth, and tomorrow with other stars, as with a ball, without knowing whether they dare or do not dare to burst this ball. They play with energy, but they too leave it unthought.

Is there *a* force that subjugates the universe and directs its course? Is posing the question like this not still a proof of anthropomorphism?

The lightning plays. It also plays with those struck down by it.

Matter: is it only or principally what offers resistance? What snares does 'anti-matter' set us?

Does not everything return to 'matter'?

Return to nature! What else does all that is and is done do?

Molecules and planets roll around each other.

The immobile turning of the rose of the sand and the rose of the wind.

Cosmic space is spherical: finite, but without bounds, because unlimited; cosmic time is its major variable, and it is itself constituted in time. The cosmic world now appears to us as a four-dimensional *space-time* continuum.

We begin to traverse the age of cosmic space. Does the age of time await its hour?

Of the eternal time, namely omnitemporal, of the cosmic order, of the great panic physis, Heraclitus said that it is a child playing with 'dice'. The order of the world, the becoming of being, was thus once grasped as play. Then followed the occultation of the play. The order of the world, its being and its becoming, then rested in and on God, constructor and guarantee of the providential plan, of calculation. *Cum Deus calculat fit mundus*, wrote the mathematician and theologian Leibniz. This God had already become for Pascal an object of a wagered game, based on the calculation of probabilities and the possibilities of gain. In the era of the commenced and unconsummated death of God – 'I'll never believe that God plays dice,' repeated Einstein, the author of the equation $E = mc^2$, who did not manage to reconcile it with atomic physics – the order of the world, the ordering of natural laws and their inextricable combination with the laws of physics are problematic for us humans, who do not know either how to pose or how to solve this question. Scientific researchers, scholars, accomplish discontinuous breakthroughs, make attempts, which remain precarious, to organise chaos, or construct arbitrary synthetic edifices. Theories and practices of plays, deadly serious, try to comprehend what remains unplayable.

The speed of the transmission of light, is it and will it remain the measure of time?

Perhaps the cosmic totality has neither beginning nor end, without being for that eternal; perhaps it is not destined to undergo a simple eternal return, nor an infinite progress, perhaps still too much ambiguity and confusion lingering around keywords like: being and becoming, totality and world, nature and universe.

Since the universe was formed in time, will it not also find its end (in time)?

All that has a genesis will disappear. This physical and human knowledge fails to penetrate all our sensibility and all our cosmic and historical knowledge.

What is aimed at – human domination over space and time, the exploration of the two 'infinities' (from the infinitely small to the infinitely large), the simultaneous grasping and experience of the (let's say biological) organism and the (let's say technological) automatism, of the continuous and the discontinuous, of the reversible and the irreversible, of rest and movement – binds the destiny of the human, is called upon to determine if the human *will inhabit* the earth, in places and dwellings, or if it will be a meteoric, stellar, sidereal being . . .

Between everything and nothing, and after having wishfully proceeded in filling the cosmic emptiness, not without having marked it with some beautiful conquests, will we accede to a new panic tune, an old and yet unheard-of discordant accord with that which was named physis and cosmos, nature and universe?

The skies hardly uncover other worlds. The sky is the sky of the world as the stars are stars of the sky.

The stars that impose themselves in the firmament are not 'eternally' the same.

Behold, departing from the sun, the great planets visible to the naked eye and to the mythological gaze: Mercury, star of *commerce*, Venus, star of *love*, Earth, star of *mortals*, Mars, star of *war*, Jupiter, star of the *lightning*, Saturn, star of the *underworld*, Uranus, star of the *sky*, Neptune, star of the *waters*. Around each of these planets spin satellites, while comets crisscross the four-dimensional space-time continuum in all directions. Is the moon the satellite of the earth? And is the sun the focus of light?

The light of the stars slowly nullifies and survives them.

The universe is full of those extinct stars whose brilliance we still see though they have ceased to exist. Certainly, new stars will shine. However, we do not always know what is the dominant constellation of our technological and planetary and not interstellar era.

The old moons last quite a long time. The new moon appears and disappears quite quickly. Can one simultaneously see the two faces of the moon?

Is the destiny of the human inscribed in the firmament, as imagined by old astrology and the new astronautics?

Interstellar, if not galactic, engines seem to be the privileged playthings of planetary humanity. Up to what ceiling?

On the chessboard of stars, troubled and regulated matches are won and lost – in a word, played.

Will human disquietude and dissatisfaction let the human jump from one square of the chessboard of the stars to another?

The wheel of the galaxy on which humans are turned suggests to them, after the enterprise of the conquest of space, the conquest of time. So worlds and humans will pass and stay almost in the middle of the web uniting the stars. It will no longer be the human individual alone that will be unique and interchangeable, if the cosmic worlds have to become so.

The interplanetary human will perhaps escape gravity, to be caught in the trap of another and subtler gear of the mechanics of the sky.

Natural and artificial satellites gravitate around errant stars, which gravitate around fixed stars, while shooting stars tear the sky. The harmony of the spheres – grasped in the art of the fugue – does not cease being traversed by polyphonic and atonal voices – and by the voices of silence.

Based on the treatment of information, the transmission of messages, the play of codes and decodings, cybernetics wants to measure the error to permit its correction, by establishing laws of regulation common to living beings and machines, considered as self-regulating systems – are not living organisms rather autonomous, while mechanisms and technical devices remain heteronomous? – that adapt themselves to the objectives that were – naturally and technically – assigned to them. Cybernetics, scientific pilot organiser, which wants government of the universal enciphered language, presents itself as something more and other than a simple – or complex – scientific theory and is called on to undergo a great development. What will be the limit against which its dominant power will stumble?

Certain mechanics are running idle.

What ties the organism to its milieu, dynamically, favouring the action of the milieu, that of the organism and their interaction, what passes through a series of intermediaries to constitute the organism and its development – thus balancing genesis and structure – seems to be more and more, for the moment, the result of a network of coordinations, the result of a self-regulation.

A crab can be occupied with eating another crab with such a ferocious appetite that it does not realise that a third crab has already started nibbling on it.

Plunging its roots into the cosmic world, corporeality overflows it in the direction of the human and historical world; presenting itself as a unique fabric with diverse interwoven threads, its texture and its tears remain to be explored, as it contains profound information. Thus we are still far from having tracked down the secrets of the little universe which is the human organism, and we have yet to discover our body and corporeality. Not only in a biological manner.

Through grafting and grafting again, let's hope that we manage to refresh the tired human material.

From the maternal womb to the woman's breast, from prehistoric grottos to Platonic caves, from Christian catacombs to atomic shelters, the places that circumscribe the two circles – concentric? – of the microcosm and the macrocosm seek at once the protection of the englobing as well as the hole of the opening.

It is as signs and signals that humans are sent into space.

The cosmic game does something more and other than being the regulator of a series of scenery for the pleasures of humans.

We distinguish both too much and not enough. What are the links that attach a universe ('ours') to the universe? In what sense could our universe be only a fragment?

We will not be ready to pose the question concerning the existence of other beings on other planets, as long as we make up such narrow conceptions of the life-information circuit and remain so inexperienced in the matter of presence and occultation.

And if we were alone – an extremely diluted solution – in the immensity of the universe?

To what does the evolution of nature seem to lead? To the human, naturally.

V

The Human in the World

The human has been defined – which apparently defines everything – as *extremely fragile being* and as a *terrible existent*, as *the measure of all things* and as *rational animal*, as *imago Dei* and as *(subjective-objective) foundation of objectivity*, as *body-soul-spirit* (by emphasising sometimes one side, sometimes the other, by synthesising or seeking unity), as subject, as social and political animal, as *generic worker and socialising being*, as *person and existence* and *as being where goes the being of the world*, as *distant being* and almost as *human-problem*. Will all these definitions make the human speak and act – at the same time making speaking and acting the encompassing that the human both is and is not – the passing existent, this being to be surpassed, without altogether finishing it, and leave the question in suspense: until when will subjectivity, even objectified and collectivised, be the last word?

We are obliged to track and follow the traces – traces that mix themselves and lose themselves – that link – with continuity and solution of continuity – the human to the non-human.

How does the human manage to enter in any case into the dimension of the logos, to 'dialogue' with what it is not?

By becoming anthropology, metaphysical philosophy becomes not only an interpretation of the human being: all the interpretations and all the beings find themselves reduced, by this reflexive philosophy – anthropology – to the human, who is supposed to be the secret of the essence or the existence of the being as such and in its entirety.

At the moment when philosophy becomes the philosophy of subjectivity to begin to finalise itself in anthropology, the human appears as the *last* figure of the absolute.

If the absolute is the ensemble of human relations, it is then precisely not ab-solute. It still remains to comprehend relations: they link humans with each other and with what else?

Plaything of dust, emerging from earth and becoming dust again, the human plays for some time with it.

Although without models, the human 'imitates'. What? It aims to get as close as possible – to what?

Different from animals, does the human have a – near or distant – relation with itself and the – near and distant – world?

Pursuing an inquiry on several planes simultaneously, the human fails to find the keys opening dead languages, and rusty or brand new instruments fall out from its hands. However . . .

'Subjectivity', in its fluidity and its fixity, keeps grappling with cosmic and physical imperatives, with the flashes and the eclipses of thought, with the slowness and the difficulty of the work of history, with its own human and anthropological problematic (anthropology and its derivative, psychology, not lacking strengths and especially weaknesses), with prose and poeticity. Aspect of all that is, look, word, gesture and action, it is comprised in a larger movement that comprehends it, even when it believes to comprehend it. It wants itself as something like the first and the last word. It is only a link.

The human is almost the question posed to the world and to itself, the question mark in the All.

Is the human a sick, thinking and working animal? Is it a terribly rarefied composition in the cosmic void? Is it a resonance chamber?

Whatever it does, the human must accord itself with alienation, strangeness.

For, even more radical and encompassing than the *alienation* of the human (*Entfremdung*) – whose radical suppression would coincide with the suppression of the human – is its unsurpassable *strangeness*, the human remaining strange to itself and to the world, the world remaining strange to it (*Verfremdung*) – in spite of all the habits, all the customs, all the familiarities.

Through where do the lines of force that constitute the human being pass? Don't they cross the ensemble formed by hereditary factors, the terrain and constitutional temperament, the dramas of childhood and the family constellation, the educational formations, the socio-cultural milieu and the orientations, the relations and the roles that it implies and suggests, the incidents, the accidents and the encounters of all kinds, the configurations of 'chance' and those of 'destiny', the dispositions, the identifications, the ideals of the self, revolts and projections, the fixations and mobility, the subconscious pressures and the unconscious powers, the phantasms and voluntary efforts, the repetitive comportments and inventive behaviours, the historical epoch and the interpretative schemas of self-consciousness, the erotic life and professional activity, lifestyle, the style of thought and the style of death? However, in this entanglement of convergent threads, interwoven and mobile, visible and concealed, often exchanging their colours, entanglement demanding an at once hierarchical and multidimensional, synthetic and operative approach, grasping at once the play of the ensemble and that of each part, sector, factor, plane or level influencing the others and the whole, how to clear the most salient lines and most important elevations each time, how to foster operative inventions, how to indulge in a necessarily schematising comprehension and action, but by trying to be as little schematic as possible?

Do not all the particular structures emerge within a global structure, certainly in movement, but as previously given? Where? When? How? To whom?

It is evident that after the dominion of the subject, we will see the rise of many systems and structures without subject that will not know what to do with it, after having eliminated more than thought and surpassed it. Because they play rather innocently with small ensembles.

The structure holds the human and yet the latter transgresses it. In favour of another structure?

Where lies for the human the 'right milieu', or better: the centre, between exaggeration and lack, profusion and scarcity, in a world where centre and circumference have become elusive.

On a planet among billions of others, existing for four billion years and probably not that again, the human, who appeared a million years ago in the world, with a prehistory that does not count more than forty thousand years, a history that counts five thousand and an almost world-historical history that only counts twenty-five hundred years, poses itself questions: where does it come from? who is it? where is it going? Concerned with big ensembles and details, concerned with fruitful and reassuring answers, the human, every human and the humans – they are three and a half billion on earth and their number is increasing – never know exactly how and on whom to count.

Personal and impersonal pass into each other. Every individual is unique, irreplaceable and yet universal and replaced.

The human fails to solve the problem of solitude. Neither alone, nor with others. Because beings, and not only human beings, come closer and move away.

More than revolutionary, the human is revolutionised.

Immer fehlt etwas [Always something is lacking].

All that, which is, is only – as a problem – through the human, and yet the human exists only mediocrely and mediated through what it is not. This is the major paradox.

It is at once the known and the unknown that attract us.

The force of social coercion that the individual internalises through its super-ego is extremely powerful.

Flat finding: the youth with rich potentialities and undecided future has all the chances to overtake the ranks of more or less conventional adults and the stale elderly.

The shaky force of the modern human comes from the fact that it dares to assert a position: it poses from itself, through itself and for itself, what produces it and what it produces.

Dualism maliciously survives: so the human now looks at its double, feeds itself on its phantom.

Humanism places the human at once too low and too high. With feigned modesty, it envisages all that is inhuman as foreign. It poses the human as subject, person, existence, structure, it goes so far as to claim an over-dimensional human or the dissolution of the human. This is still at once too much and too little.

Fear protects all that creeps and lives, and also prevents walking and living.

Was there in time – does what has been in time not continue to be there? – an order in the world, in which it was possible for the human to accord with its existence? Did not human nature – and the creature – have its place in cosmic nature – creation? Cosmic world, historical cities, human lives, did they not obey – with harmony and dissonance – the same laws and the same penalties? Did not all have its place in the great All? Birth, education, family life and civic life, procreation, creations, death, the worship of the dead thus inscribed themselves in a global rhythm. Then the human wanted to be a free subject, in a dead nature and under an empty sky, wanted to dictate its rules to the universe and to invent its own acts. The stars of heaven no longer indicate any road. The human wanted to assert its certainty – its science and its conscience – on itself or tried to project into history an action and a hope to replace the powerful radiation of the order considered eternal. But both the individual human and the march of history withdrew from the hopes that had been founded on them. Then came the epoch of anxiety and boredom, in an organised and planned world, administered and manufactured from one end to the other. The era of apparent obscurity and gratuitousness. What will be the next step?

From the most remote times to the present day, yesterday and tomorrow, sages and saints, tribunes and heroes, leaders and educators want to wake up humans, always considered to be asleep. Wake them and awaken them for what? Since those who sleep are workers and collaborators of what is becoming in the world, as a future thinker will one day say.

The human has no necessary complement. It is already contingent, thrown into the world, embarked.

We other humans, grappling with this little planet that is the human, without being able to distinguish very well the powers that are ours and others', traverse the sky of the earth like meteors.

Navigare necesse est, vivere non necesse! loudly proclaimed the Hanseatic motto of humans who took to sea.

Are needs deeper and more elemental than desires and these more than wishes? And what about the desire of desire?

This is why the self also desires, if not above all, what it does not want and cannot.

Fatigue can rest.

One is chosen more than one chooses. That is to say, a choice works through us.

One continues to live 'very well' despite the misfortune of others. An entire continent engulfed underwater would not prevent us from going to the movies at night or watching television.

Everyone plays a match against all and against the other matches.

The mother (or her substitute), the father (or his substitute), the child (and the infantile situation) – the fundamental triangle, ceaselessly reactivated.

Not to lose the love of the mother, to conquer and to assure it, to return – in all ways – to the mother, this is the point still central to the affective life of the humans.

In leaving childhood and before falling back into it, the child-human goes through the same steps as its father (or its mother).

Everything happens as if the precocious infantile frustrations of needs more than desires were the source of all subsequent conflict.

The temptation of infantile regression endures the whole so-called adult life and finds a certain recognised satisfaction in the senile phase.

The human will advance less into a landscape burned by lava than into a metallic land. Where so-called precious metals amalgamate with vulgar metals.

Whether they pass like comets or settle themselves down, humans remain always polyphasic and out of phase.

They begin to experience it: satisfaction does not satisfy.

The human being was divided in two, body-soul (and spirit), and in three, body-soul-spirit, its tri-partition following, in the Platonic-Aristotelian tradition, an internal tri-partition, in which the 'soul' would be desiring (and bodily), volitive (the heart) and thinking (and spiritual). Into this bi-partition and these two kinds of tri-partition, no one has ever yet seen clearly enough.

In the midst of the types of all kinds, the atypical arises and troubles.

Is the search for glory able to rise above glory?

Glory is a temporary victory over death.

More than a person of private law, more than existence demanding a sense of life and floored by the absurd, the individual is still to be redefined.

The human of exasperated egotism, waiting to be broken, tries to fly with its broken wings covered with mechanical wings, and succeeds.

Are most human efforts developed to escape 'real' or 'imaginary' dangers? In any case, all the efforts try to escape an appalling distress.

The human cannot fall back on the human and find contentment.

What one experiences is more than what one expresses.

To different individual and social evils certainly correspond diverse remedies: medications, reforms and even revolutions. The global ill, general malaise, are impossible to cure.

When we humans learn that there is no sovereign solution or supreme salvation, but only problematic solutions (for neither individual solutions to collective and individual problems, nor collective solutions to individual and collective problems solve the problem of the world, of history, of the human), will we know a certain pacification, will we accept more calmly the gap between what we desire and want, and what we obtain and what we are? Will we comprehend that there are no forms of a fundamentally satisfying life? Will we stop claiming an impossible transparency and renounce abstract impossibilities? Will we live in a nuclear unity, a life beyond life, a life that watches, integrating the prodromes of our own disappearance?

The individual is a system of singularities.

In the encounter with others, one seeks oneself and the other.

Is not humanity a somewhat failed experiment? Without experimenter.

What to do with needs and demands that are not justified?

Humans desire at the same time that everything lasts as long as possible and rejoice at the prospect of rapid ends, loving to quickly consummate and consume, to feel the completion approaching.

They seem to have been playing for a very long time an endgame that ceaselessly restarts, ceaselessly recasts them.

Human disquietude, curiosity and desire for exploration always push them forwards: called by the emptiness of what they believe they have already attained, exhausted by what they have rejected and what has rejected them.

Since we are a – in – treatment waiting for us to become cure.

Since Being itself is thrown into contingency, how would it be otherwise for the human being?

In trying to constitute the human, one dissolves it always further.

The adventure throws us in advance of ourselves.

No one puts themself *entirely* into *a* work.

The humane is as here and beyond the human. Above all, do not be fooled by objectivism: it is the extreme point – ready to break – of subjectivism.

Mixes, mixtures, amalgams, compromises, intermediary solutions, arrangements and inconsistencies predominate and dominate us.

After youth, one has interests and principles to defend.

One is always part of a part.

Madness 'must' also find its account. It finds it, at least, in the most benign form, in the small and sweet generalised madness of humans.

Captains without crew and crews without captain do not necessarily meet.

If one puts oneself completely out of reach, assuming that this was possible, one could not reach anymore.

Adventures have become calculated and legitimate.

The modern human requires an impressive number of crutches to walk. This human, who believes they know how to advance, has yet to learn the art of beating a retreat.

The mutation of the human is awaiting, remaining for the moment waiting and not a walk towards.

With vertiginous beings, there is more world.

Force and weakness are temporary constellations, polar contraries that constantly pass into each other by exchanging their masks and disguises. Every force overcompensates for weakness, every weakness hides a force.

Action is in general – and in particular – a residue of diverse transactions.

Everyone considers themself a tiny bit exceptional, for their part.

Communication between beings becomes an obsessional problem for this century. Because it is envisaged from the side of the human and not from the side of the world.

The human who has been posited as subject, existence, collectivity, will have to experiment on itself like a planet pursuing its eccentric path.

It is not only the life sciences that are becoming experimental, because we are experimenting with life itself, which transforms itself into an experience.

Even those who live or pretend to live alone are no less assisted.

How to effectuate what in any case happens: being close and inside and already far and outside?

Neither people nor history know what human type it is a question of raising when there are no more types.

It is always up to us to learn to give up. Can we go so far as to give up giving up?

Beings come closer and move away: they each take a look at the other and lose each other from view.

Is the source of all anxiety the primordial anxiety of the loss of love?

The knights of the celestial abysses are followed by the pedestrians and voyagers of terrestrial and extraterrestrial spaces.

To want somebody or something 'too much' indicates that one 'will' not 'have' it.

In relation to the imaginary, everything finds itself displaced.

In the same situations different attitudes may correspond. But there are changes of mentality and changes of structure.

Not letting yourself be imprisoned by anything is impossible.

To show a 'new' landscape that does not 'exist' and which, however, works.

On the basis of a moment, human things find themselves considered and attacked from a psychopathological angle. This is normal.

Will quantitative changes lead to a qualitative change, something like a biochemical moulting of the human?

One demands from life what one demands from a fire: ablaze and enduring.

The secret of what is frontal lies in its backside.

The reign of the person and private property are coextensive.

The human was eventually reduced to be the producer and the product of the worker, the attacker and the defender, the pupil and the teacher.

Will the human little by little reveal itself as the metaphor of the Same?

What does not offer itself fully but withdraws attracts us.

To live extraordinary things comes to those who overstep the cult of the evident and the problematic.

To access sovereignty and not coldness, serenity and not indifference, detachment and not withdrawal, are there many who wish it?

All that is done is known.

Between a system and its rigorous application, there is a world and many intermediaries.

Stupidity progresses too: the old stupidity is replaced by a new stupidity.

Certainly, the choices that *impose themselves* on us are concrete, circumstantial, determined, precise; thus everything is both ontologically and ontically justified: both on the plane of the being of the world and on the plane of the being of the human.

To blame the other – the partner and the adversary – is part of a misdirected attack.

Guilt, this feeling of being the author of the disruption of an order, has archaic sources and far-reaching consequences. Whose *fault* is it?

Holding on to success is as difficult as standing up to adversity. So do not be frightened by success. It will also pass.

For the moment the continuous creation of human by human continues.

Once life finds itself 'demystified' – always imperfectly – how is one to live it?

One commonly believes that fortune or misfortune will always last.

Can we always distinguish dead ends from paths?

They both move, all the same, in the midst of phantasmagoria. Under the pressure of needs and desires, fears and anxieties.

The human does not belong. No person belongs to another. (*Personne* already names someone and no one.)

Life offers so many possibilities of which so many are blocked.

Humans are – or seem to be – at once more and less stupid, wicked, ugly and weak than they are.

What compels us to redo what we feel as a future regret?

Changing the world. Changing beings. Changing things. Changing words. Tasks always renewed, not on the edge of the abyss, but on the edge of the future.

All the paths humans follow are detours.

It is not easy for beings to find their style.

The eagle and the serpent remain two animals to which the human can be compared.

Many beings try to live, love, produce and die clearly beyond their means.

Individuality resists and succumbs.

Is there still a thought of the individual to elaborate?

Every human being needs help. Especially in the era of progressive neurosis.

The search for the centre and for balance keeps us running.

Renunciation seeks its place between acceptance and demand.

Lived experience surpasses simple knowledge and representation, plunging us into the-interiority-and-the-exteriority of life that is not always lived.

Raising humans, creating orders, establishing hierarchies: necessary and problematic tasks.

To become an adult, is it to discover oneself vulnerable?

One does not necessarily identify with oneself.

The problem of human relations – whose ensemble does not constitute the absolute – remains crucial and crucifying.

The weak point of the human system has not yet been sufficiently exposed.

For certain humans the question poses itself, although the answer does not depend on their free arbitration: pass like a meteor in the heaven of the earth or found earthy dwellings?

The joy of living and the difficulty of being – the former rarer than the latter – assail our unity, duality, trinity, namely our psychosomatic structure, our psyche and our soma, our body, our soul and our spirit – discomforted that we are in our being unique, double, triple, because we do not manage to regulate the fate of the components that constitute our being – both in the actual experience and in the imaginary and the symbolic, as diverse phases and diverse moments and movements also assail us – that we also fail to decompose – in the course of stagnation and renewal, progression and repetition, elevation and falls that hold us in their power and grant us movement.

Sobriety and drunkenness can both seduce us like extremes or 'contraries' that seduce us, in, with or for their different aspects.

The ambushes of needs, desires and wishes cannot be easily avoided because they have two or many sources.

The involuntary holds itself firmly and trembles behind the voluntary.

The chance of birth lets the human enter, randomly, into the play of the world.

Chance and merit spur or handicap the contestants in the game of life.

Those who participate in the game, mainly by proxy, by procuration, by delegation, wish to avoid the risks and still give dynamism to their monotonous life thanks to shows, auditions, readings, amplified by the press, the radio, the cinema, television.

Humans adore to burn what they have adored.

Going to the end of anything is impossible.

In the civilised human slumbers the wild human. The civilised human sometimes learns this. The wild human?

Everyone searched to find and to flee themselves.

Let's always be ready. For what?

In the chiaroscuro of everyday life, nothing ever goes to term, foreseen or not; everything unfolds according to mixed rules, blurs, matures in its incompleteness, without neat outlines. It is only then, and in the discrepancy, that all is theorised and stylised, said and fixed through thought and art. Sincere and radical, coherent, consistent and self-critical critique, attentive to ideological shifts and mythological travesties, by saying the split and the union of theory and practice, of private life and public life, has not yet started. Will it be able to stay halfway, frightened of its discoveries?

The (modern) human can only cease to be; to become . . .?

Beings that give an impression of mystery are – often 'unjustly' – more attractive than others.

Its limits circumscribe human being.

Offshoots of stars, humans are themselves shooting stars.

How to reconcile the search for decentring enthusiasm and for the familiar centre?

The will to avoid repetition does not prevent us from succumbing to it.

The figure of the *desperado*, who does not wait for anything – or who stays, because they are fundamentally waiting for something – is half of a figure.

One may wish an enchaining and enchained love, an enchaining and enchained state, an enchaining and enchained thought, etc. It is the right of people and every human. It is not opposed by the cries of those who call for a free love, state, thought, etc.

It is the burned diamond that has a 'thousand' facets.

Too bad that one cannot positively rejoice in the absence of a negative, an ill: an injury, a toothache.

The problem that poses itself to the human, how to succeed, that is to say how not to waste their life, does not pose itself in these terms. Particular individuals carried away by the wave of the species, itself carried away by cosmic flux, how can they pose themselves the question of renewal and repetition, of insertion and detachment, of the multicoloured and dull, movement and rest?

The nostalgia for the immediate that works on them, pushes them into the maze of mediations.

Everyone – with a little luck – is victim of a style.

To cut a Gordian knot, it is necessary that *I* must have a sword and that there must be a knot; or that *we* have a sword and that the knot be. As everyone knows, since Rimbaud at least, 'it is wrong to say: I think. One should say: One thinks me. Apologies, for the play [*jeu*] on words. I is [*je est*] another.' I-we, knot-sword? What about today's *I* and *we*? The ego and its collectivisation, are they not precisely the knot that the future must cut – with or without sword?

Without a mass of real good, one often prefers a volume of hope that makes the inexorable gears of an airy and sharp humanity bearable.

One flies backwards, forwards, as well as towards the present.

Sceptics and mystics apprehend the end – which is also a commencement – of the great game, the end of the 'fundamental' illusion, that of existence, early glimpsed.

Walking on the edge of the roof, the sleepwalker does not fall.

There are quite a few people who would like to be both island and empire.

It is not bad to have hidden weapons ready which we do not use.

Beyond hope and despair many riches can be rediscovered that are not situated only below.

For the moment – only? – the human comedy cannot be thrown overboard.

The nuclear age – for the moment the extreme point of human subjectivity that wants to appropriate and master external and internal nature, individually, collectively and objectively – brings to its climax and crushes the individual (atom), massifies individuals and atomises the human masses and others, renders the totalities atomistic, lets the atoms burst, raises a great dust.

The human hopes in forgetting. Namely, hopes on a foundation of forgetting and hopes in forgetting.

The superficial life feeds itself on the texture of the multicoloured world.

What is designated under the name of destiny does not fall on us from the outer or does not emerge from our inner depths. What is destined for us, that to which we are destined, assigns us a *part* of the totality, or, if you want, a lot or a fate that is not distributed or rewarded by a lottery.

The human, the being through which the question of Being is posed, the only existent that interrogates existence – not seeming to possess itself any natural or historical 'essence' – does it exist and will it continue to exist? Obviously, it is dissolving and disappearing – but as *what*? Here resides the much more ontological-anthropological and historical than epistemological question. What passes, is it the human or the concept of the human? And what concept? Is it not the human, who declares the concept of the human illusory and its consciousness inconsistent, calling for other operational concepts – or *what* else? Change and permanence take hold of the human and its problematic essence and existence. Is it being surpassed? Not as – decentred and eccentric – subject, but as space-time of the encounter of what is out of the human and what 'is' the human, as space-time of the game. Humanism glorifies the human – rather ridiculously. Antihumanism dissolves the human – rather flatly. In the course of surpassing – or being surpassed? – shouldn't the human still be ripe – despite and because of anthropology and human sciences of all kinds – to pose the problem of the human?

The great conquests and the little exploits, the great and the little nothings that compose every human endeavour, make the human both a conquistador and a derisory surveyor.

To be only a nuance is little.

Would any human activity be an activity of replacement?

The difficulty of being meets with the sadness of not being . . .

A base is always necessary – although problematic and problematised – from which departures take off.

The *simple*, do we seek it, does it seek us?

Joy, it is sometimes remarked, is much more exceptional and profound than pain.

We can neither separate the head from the body nor the body from the head, neither make them walk together, nor walk on the head or with the feet alone.

To traverse life in a rather light and sometimes even happy way by find-ing pleasure in it, or in a rather heavy, sad and unpleasant way, amounts to letting oneself be traversed by one or the other of the two currents united in their source and then diverging, though they intersect.

The analysis of finitude, though finite, seems without end.

In a certain manner, the human can only adapt, revolutionise (which is another kind of adaptation) or perish. The epoch rejects all that does not suit it.

Compromise is not – as is commonly thought – a second-order reality, a second-best.

The play of multiple and multiform, biological, psychological, social, cultural and ideological determinations must be, that is to say ceaselessly, explored and re-explored.

The private generally feeds on the public.

The impossible collides with the human.

Does human life remain below its possibilities? And yet here and there . . .

There are even some examples that help us and enlighten us.

At moments the human can find life beautiful and worthy of being lived.

One can educate oneself not to succumb to the terror of one's own terrorism.

Our unconscious comprehends more than us and comprehends us.

Were they only the interpretations of a dream, they would lose themselves indefinitely.

It is not in the power of the human, in the era of subjectivity, to behave subjectively, in one way or another.

Sometimes one has to stay there like a rock that is not particularly friendly or tender.

It is rather little by little that one becomes like everyone.

Concentration and recollection are constantly grappling with dispersion and scattering.

Stability and lability characterise all the formations recorded by the human.

Life and civilisation are not possible without suspension of life drives and death drives.

After the era of nature, battled and dead, and that of the absent God, killed and dead, we enter the epoch of *homo absconditus*.

With regard to what proposes itself and imposes itself on us, what is the position of our freedom? Its presupposition, its supposition, its position and its positivity can easily be denied, undermined, situated, envisaged as motivated, conditioned, determined. What we call our freedom provokes a whole scaffolding of explanations, comprehensions, interpretations – in general negating. Its structures can be dismantled and forecasts can be formulated. So what is with our dear – proud or illusory – freedom? It does not seem to support the demonstration of its existence and it rebels somewhat when its non-existence seems to be demonstrated. It has also been considered as a recognised, accepted, assumed necessity, but do we know the necessity of what moves us? And do we not also accomplish what we would like to flee? No scholastic or pedagogical exercise, even high-flying, no scholarly dissertation on the theme of determinism and free will can decide whether and to what extent we choose, or we are chosen. What decides through us, can it be deciphered both in terms of necessity and in terms of freedom, two sides of the same coin? Is free-fall so free, since it obeys laws? Would we be free for totally indifferent acts and less free for acts that are necessary for us? Besides, is not a certain indifference a certain proof of a certain freedom? Be free! is a prescription full of – involuntary – humour and irony, unless it should lead to the experimentation of necessities. All the passages to the limit withdraw themselves: neither a freedom eman-cipated from all causes nor a non-freedom engulfed entirely in causes is conceivable. In the second case, one would be dealing with a psychopatho-logical case, of mental alienation, which would let us see negatively what the complete absence of freedom is. In the same way, liberty – an impure and ideological political concept – is shrunk until it disappears into a totalitarian and tyrannical regime, which brings the political alienation to its climax, and it can manifest itself a little more in a liberal regime. To acknowledge the human with a little freedom, a partial freedom, is this what it is about? Certainly not. So? So how can we be held responsible regarding ourselves and regarding others for a freedom that we do not have? Does it have us at least?

Causes and mechanisms, structures and determinisms, partly support and explain the proper functioning of high activities: biocosmic, physico-chemical, neurophysiological, psychosocial, historical-cultural. What cannot be reduced to one or all of these orders, does it follow freedom? Or does the positivity of freedom reside in its negativity so much that it, by freeing itself, counteracts what opposes it: constraints, causalities, destiny? But even so, does it not obey a determination and conditioning, as high as one wants to place them and whether they are metaphysical, ethical, ideo-logical or feed on the source of the imaginary? For freeing oneself from one series signifies subordinating oneself to another. The distinction between external constraint and freedom and internal constraint and freedom does not let us advance far. Once again: we can prove neither the emergence of freedom – actual or possible, existing or postulated – nor the unfolding of necessity; like the human, freedom is what is not what it is, and what is what it is not. We therefore have to test the two registers of the same order and to conceive the errant 'freedom' as that which leaves and gives play to diverse necessities.

What does it signify to be free within the limits of the rules of the game?

Because human freedom seems to consist in doing what diverse laws permit. Would freedom be interstitial?

No doubt we have no freedom, but an experience of freedom – of liberation.

To the human the anxiety of what appears at times like its freedom is unbearable.

The foundation of freedom could consist in freedom towards and for the foundation. But if there is no foundation?

Does human existence henceforth find itself freed from any foundation?

Frustration makes us protestors. We are all frustrating and frustrated.

Everything seems to indicate that one struggles to regain what one never had.

The forces that contain and maintain life resist many shocks.

If only its history can teach us what the human is, this same history can also unlearn it and can itself be unlearned.

Everyone hides a disability.

To what point are particular human beings interchangeable?

We will only hope to live, more than live, as long as we live *for* . . . and not *in* . . . and *with* . . ., *far from* . . . and *without* . . .

Open yourself to the world, it will open itself to you.

Jeder geht an etwas zu Grunde [Everyone breaks down at something].

Those who were determined to flee stay forever in the world.

The dream of a clear life does not attain the full play.

The constellations are much more powerful than the protagonists.

One often counters one's own deep desire, since it is ambivalent.

We are not condemned to err: we are the errant ones. We are not condemned to play: we are the players and the playthings.

To agree with the fact that what one is and what one does will disappear and survive transformed, already indicates an advance on the path where control and non-control of the self are themselves controlled by the uncontrollable.

The human was the voice that escaped a broken flute played by an absent god.

Are we moving towards something or inside of something?

If the other is in us, we are in the other. Even to recognise and misrecognise it – and us.

Without suffering, no remedy.

The secrets of the different ages of life are scarcely yet pierced.

All our life we remain goaded by the engine of childhood curiosity: the search for the mystery, the secret that is happening somewhere.

Doesn't the unconscious know the no?

The non-human, the inhuman, the superhuman are part, for us other humans, of the human.

Neither the solitary life nor the life with the other are entirely suited to the plant, the animal and the human that is the human.

What becomes of the dreams and repressed anxieties of our hearts?

This vitality, this dynamism, that we wish for must be maintained and cultivated at least physically, psychically and intellectually. By which appropriate exercises?

Pharmacodynamic drugs will always be called upon to reinvigorate the human machine.

The march towards an appeasement accepting the generous sadness is demanded of us.

Broken pins can pierce the heart of dying eagles that fly low.

The distinction between what depends on us and what does not depend on us is a bit specious.

One can very well experience two – or more – opposing feelings at the same instant.

Dear friend, you are not alone in taking decisions.

All the participants in the human comedy are each right about the others, but not all in the same manner.

The integral transparency of human relationships is a childish myth.

A terrible and silent force emanates from certain beings.

Whoever through whom the scandal happens is only a pretext that 'purifies' the diverse expurgated texts.

Those who explore certain quarries can appear to others as hard as stones.

The role is not so external to the personage.

You do not elucidate, you forget.

What we do to ourselves and what is done to us corroborate and contradict each other.

Rare are the flashes that tear the horizon.

Sometimes what leaves you moves away.

The central problem of human life: to *last*, to endure hard and to live duration (and in it) is accomplished in and gets erased by duration.

It is less and less about *being* and more and more about *enduring*. It is less and less about *living* and more and more about *surviving*.

Can detached attachment be obtained through spiritual exercises of meditation and concentration, even practical?

Our steps lead us.

Some lives, some deaths, remain definitively ambiguous.

We never go back to zero.

Bizarre destiny of humans. They are glued like shellfish to their rock and are nonetheless migratory birds.

Often a fragment of our being possesses a knowing – more or less obscure – which escapes the other fragments.

The human moves in the world with a strange and estranged familiarity.

Those to whom the maximum is allowed, who allow it, do they go far enough, since the too-far usually threatens disaster?

Among beings, things, signs – and between signs – men, women and children comprehend only what concerns them. And even then.

What one does not 'want' happens.

Every human is like all humans, is like someone, is unique.

The multiple motives and results of an action, its means and its aims intertwine so inextricably that only very rare gleams can illuminate some of their moments and aspects.

It is not only the human who is question without answer.

From time to time, a thinking and poetic meteor traverses the lives of humans, who move in their own orbits – which move them.

Desire moves in the midst of masked phantoms.

Curiosity is harrowing.

Solitary crowding and being isolated are in the lure.

Contributing to 'creating' beings, changing beings, producing situations, is very tempting and can impose itself as a task.

The human, whatever it does, walks and jumps by limping, by leaning on crutches.

The human must get used to bearing extreme visions.

The erotic and familial problem, the professional and social problem, are the two most tangible aspects of the insertion of the human into the world of humans.

Logos, God, the human arrange the diverse elements and ensembles of the great whole, until – they themselves and the elements and ensembles, fundamentally disturbed – they aspire to a new arrangement.

The will to power – and, even more, the will to will – that seizes humans, mobilises their being, pushes them towards surprising conquests, gives the impetus to their becoming and breaks them calmly and brutally. Does it survive them?

Impatience goes with boredom. One and the other often prevail. We share the secrets of ridicule and illusions, without being able to pierce them. Lucid blindness takes us. It would be necessary to know how to wait for the turnarounds.

Sex, money, glory is what is most commonly sought.

We can even learn to join violence and tenderness, hardness and delicateness, regarding beings.

From far away everything looks more beautiful, fuller: the life of the creators of the past, a lighted window, a couple kissing, a group at the restaurant . . .

It is humanism that needs the human and not the other way around.

Surpassing humanism requires us first to become deeply and thoroughly human.

The vitality, the energy, the radiance that certain beings require are precious gifts.

Those with no sense of humour and who cannot bear irony also succumb one day to the humour and the irony they refuse. Sometimes after their death.

The human can never succeed the coup of the world (after the model of the *coup d'état*). Its world – the world of the human in general and the world of every human – does not cover the world.

Laws, norms and rules impose themselves on the human, who nevertheless plays them away. Can humans ever say, without drivelling: this is not a play?

Will the melancholy thirst for the ideal always remain unfulfilled?

The human enters into the play of life, inserted and englobed in already established structures that compel it to speak and to think, to act and to dream according to their rules, without first asking for its opinion; only later can it, always contained in the system, contest them. Concerning the – first – origin of structures and systems pre-existing each particular human, it is another history that gets the human grappling with history.

The force of active patience is enormous and it dissolves many reactive powers.

To reach and to abandon or to surpass is better than not to reach or to remain here, if one moves at all on this orbit.

The human actualises itself by losing possibilities.

Integrating with one's world and the world – both familiars and strangers – is the central problem for the human.

Does the more than problematic *eudaemonia* remain the goal of human life, project rather than progress?

Very often, the human appears to the human as a being of addition.

Offering a flower, even if it should get trampled or go unnoticed, illustrates a sign of openness.

Catching many flies at once? Who doesn't do that?

At the moment of disenchantment, a star obscures itself. Not succumbing to charm signifies not having a star.

The soul of the body and the body of the soul still maintain the cut too much.

Reach three generations in a human life.

Question, less naive than it seems: since in any case life is 'short', why so much fear of crossing this little bridge?

When you feel very alone and very unhappy, think, my child, that there are several million beings in your situation.

Proponents of the influence of the milieu, entangled in their trivial chatter, do not open their eyes to the full extent and depth of the action exercised by the milieu and the environment – of all kinds – on the human, always encircled.

The hereditary powers, natural and social, the constitutional forces, and the importance of temperament are far more decisive than they appear at first glance, even if such a glance unfairly favours them.

It is so tempting, and not even so stupid, to make the human the product of its temperament and its milieu.

Living comprises both the impetus and the lassitude of living.

What one does in sight of a more distant goal is also what one does for a nearer goal: one does not like someone just for their social role, but also, if one can say, for themselves.

Does every force result from the overcompensation of a weakness?

The human is like a tree that is both revolving and inverted: its roots carry it towards the earth and towards the sky.

How to achieve a more relaxed relation with all that is, when one usually wants the contrary of what one has?

When everything seems perfect, everything appears sad to us. The momentarily completed is there, between the prolegomena and the epilegomena.

That which one omits, which one leaves aside, continues to play.

To win on two contrary tables, is it not impossible for the human who wants to win on all the tables at once? Nobody can be fulfilled everywhere, no emptiness can be filled to the brim – and without overflowing.

Wishing to escape an individual or social vice, one usually falls for the opposite vice.

This is so since everything includes an aspect recognised as normal and another envisaged as pathological.

Being born; growing; reproducing; ageing; dying. This is the most elemental scenario of life – not only human.

As if compensations were not enough, there are also overcompensations.

Does one ever know a human being? Does one ever know oneself? If relations to the other are at the same time relations to oneself (and vice versa), how to establish the results of the inquiry that ends in verifying retroactive assumptions?

If 'style is the man', this style is at once spontaneous and cultivated, neither cultivated nor spontaneous, appearing to vivify and to mortalise.

Age realises in a curious and insidious way the dreams of youth.

Should we also be what doesn't stop starting?

To be, to become a legend and a myth is part of what is assigned, when it is assigned (where? by whom? how? why?).

There are glaciations that include all thaws.

Since it is what is not what it is, and what is what it is not, the human remains without necessary complement.

Both our words and our actions surpass us.

The intimate kinship of satisfaction and death escapes the living and funeral negativity which traverses needs, work, enjoyment and semi-recognition.

It is with individuation that existence starts, and all that constitutes it; it is with the entry into historical times that human – individual and social – existence prepares its completion.

As long as we do not arrive at a unifying conjunction, because unitary and united, of the psychological approach and the sociological approach, which is more and something other than a simple interpretation or a flat psycho-sociological synthesis of the two interpretations, we will not say anything of worth for the individual human and human society.

Vertigo towards the 'high' and the 'low' makes the human stagger in the march, which they would like to be firm and during which they wish to regain everything.

The individual, who emerges within the totality, the human being, who becomes what it is inside the being in becoming, the human and its world in the world – totality, being in becoming, world, not containing any individual, human being, world of every human, like a superb vase contains flowers or a bin rubbish – appears and disappears in the process of individuation – that far precedes any individualism, any subjectivism, any egoity – through the fragments of the totality of being, beings, emerging from being, in which they find themselves immersed anew. 'Do they succumb' because they left it? What did Anaximander understand, when he – mythologically and speculatively – said in the very first fragment of occidental thought: 'The boundless is the origin of beings. Wherein beings get born, therein the same they, as it must, get destroyed; for they do justice to each other and pay penalty to each other for their injustice, according to the order of time.'

To the general and theoretical combinatory corresponds all the particular and practical combinations.

It is not originality that is decisively important, but the return to the origins, the exploration of the past to come and the descent into the to-come as an anterior future. The past is never simply surpassed; future times transport it, and it, like them, constitutes a passage. We are always on the road.

Often we believe we are latecomers, twilight beings, humans, who, by going to conquer the stars, have no star. Sometimes however the feeling of being on the eve of a change in the dialogue between the human and the world surprises us. But neither the epoch nor the individual truly and simultaneously knows what it completes and what it prepares and inaugurates. And too often one surpasses what has not been fully achieved.

Is there a point of no return?

Would the end of the human signify: end of a certain type of human?

Do our agitation and our movement – what agitates us and moves us – only aspire to rest?

Since the – individual and generic – human already knows that they are only a drop – or a teardrop – in the ocean, why does their life have so much difficulty flowing?

Between motivations and results, conditions and eclosions, lies a ditch and a bridge is established.

Who of us wouldn't wish at once for the passivity and the protection of the child and the activity and the freedom of the adult?

One continues to live on the basis of outdated definitions.

At every moment, in each situation, the star of a constellation shines, it seems, stronger than the others.

Does human hope – retrospective and prospective – succeed in alleviating the difficulty of being? In any case, the human needs projects to bear life and face their survival.

More original, more powerful and more surpassing than the being of the human is the 'being' that plays itself through the human.

Humans who move as if they came from elsewhere. Like Martians. Visitors of the earth. Passionate about mechanisms of all kinds, including human mechanisms. Wresting everything from its 'initial' reason for being, finding it again and transforming it.

In progressing, the human takes one step forwards, two backwards.

Even if humans do not do what they want, they are held responsible for their actions and can only take them for granted.

Often they pass each other without suspecting the suspicion of the other.

The human is also the stammering of the unconscious.

Humans without qualities are looking for qualities without humans.

Transhumance is not only proper to humans.

When humans cannot and do not want to live how they were vegetating, they open themselves to suspicion.

Since the world is world, the human cannot do without the rules of the game and the system of play. Always playing a double and triple play, cheating and bluffing, conforming to forms and transgressions suggested and permitted.

The human is this perpetually hunted and hunting being: without rest, they throw themselves from one being to the other, because beings fall upon them.

What is the momentum or the motor that pushes the human always 'forwards'? Needs? (Which ones, the natural, the produced and the 'others'?) Inquietude? Desire? The will of power and will? Dissatisfaction and unsatisfaction that redouble after any obtained satisfaction? The gap between aspiration and realisation? The difference that governs all that we are and do, since we are moving forwards through differing?

Life and work set upon each other, intimately linked through their enmity.

Each refuses the anxiety of the other.

A very great number of inhuman things can only be accomplished by human beings.

This is why it is so difficult to simultaneously show strength and tenderness.

To lose oneself and to find oneself, to recollect oneself and to disperse oneself, provoke eddies that disturb the search for a tranquil authority, for a pacified sovereignty.

The sublime certainly pushes its roots into the psychic and social elementary; its constructions are not confused with its materials, although they depend on them. The elements of sublimation are in the unconscious and the social texture, but the creative synthesis is not located there.

To behave naturally, according to one's own law and one's own pleasure, with an air of indifference keeping itself at an equal distance from conformism and revolt, is not easy to obtain.

Rejection is just as significant as, if not more than, admission.

In their diverse enterprises, does the human ever know how far they can go?

Humans! Get used to *offering*, granting, yielding victories over yourself to your human partners and opponents.

An extremely effective tactic consists in giving up, by letting the opponent shatter against their own force.

To experience 'vanity' – vacuity – affecting what one did not perceive at first, is the beginning of sagacity. Yet it is also the vanity of the human that lets them feel all that they are and all that they are not, as if stamped with the seal of vanity.

The need for the double is permanent and devious.

Every human is, globally comprehended, the whole of the human and a total part of the world.

The limits of the human limit beings and things. Even though the human is the open ensemble of their possibilities.

We have the need for fire and place (still?): family, homeland, friends, profession, etc.

No one can foresee all that turns against the one who throws it – like a *boomerang*.

The world empties itself and fills itself. Is it this tonality of totality – this sensation, this feeling, this impression and this expression – that deserves the names of joy and sorrow, fortune and misfortune?

A divergence is not possible without a minimum of diversion of inertia, namely movement in a straight line.

Both in individual life and in historical life, differences are flattened with age.

How will the human – the prey of a total and human adventure – move in space-time beyond the human?

Some still seek – but in vain – to catch up with the centre of the – mythical – direction of a large organisation with which they would like to associate themselves.

Is it from the secrets and impulses of childhood that the *great quest* – attracted by movement and immobility, by anxiety and ecstasy – takes its origin?

Is it not by fleeing a threat that the human achieves each time a conquest?

Everything becomes for the human more and more insufficient. Without them knowing what is enough, too much or not enough. Not to mention the measure that has no more measure.

Dehumanisation still follows human schemas. Other is the play of what, with the help of the human, surpasses the human.

Existing does not go without saying. Sometimes one has to prepare to shout loudly to show that one is not dead.

What binds and unbinds beings is also what they do not say – themselves.

Is not a certain disappearance of the human necessary to ensure a certain uncertain communication?

What tempts us the most: the impossible.

The child that sleeps in the adult wakes up much more often than one believes – as much in diurnal life as in nocturnal life – and this child – ambivalent – aspires to omnipotence, to win, and even more to be chased, taken, punished, desiring to lose.

If the exercises are not continuous, the benefits they provide are lost progressively (although there are no exercises that only yield benefits, and although losses also hide gains, and so on, every proposition can be disarticulated, said and read in many ways, comprising many versions, inversions and perversions, since several instances must be respected – they withdraw in the penultimate instance – as the last and supreme instance does not 'exist').

Psychology is of great importance: it is capable of reducing all that is to its psychological origins and motivations, psychologically dismantling all the organisms, psychisms, mental acts, explaining psychologically all of the human and its works – albeit under one certain aspect, however important it may be. Its extreme point, of psychoanalytical inspiration, provides such a model – ambivalent – of analysis and deciphering. Psychology, certainly, must still find its seat in neurophysiology and biochemistry, elucidate its mythology, elaborate its metapsychology and recognise its limits. Somatopsychic and psychosomatic processes – in their differentiated, organic, functional, affective, problematic unity, and their overlapping of reversible causes and effects – demand to be decoded more rigorously, more effectively, and the interpretative schemes of psychology are inseparable from a pre- and meta-psychological mythology, whose play hides itself well and butts against thresholds, passages at a surpassing, although conditioned, level. How to establish then the relation of psychology and *sociology*? Sociology also illuminates a face and the conditions of all that is, by swimming, consciously or not, most often unconsciously, in an insufficiently grasped anthropology and theory of history, and also butts against its own limits and against thresholds. Its advanced point, a certain self-critical and open Marxism, can provide a great number of analyses, amalgamate itself with parallel research, and also show us its shortcomings. To say that psychology confronts the individual human, or the *individual*-universal in all humans, and to say that sociology confronts human and historical *societies*, is, though not incorrect, narrow and flat. The adventure of the individual and singular human, of the person, of existence, unfolds in the historical, collective, social, universal adventure – we never meet one without the other – and, if ontic and methodological divisions impose themselves, one must also know how to overcome them. To do the psychology of sociology – and of psychology; to do the sociology of psychology – and of sociology – is necessary, but does not advance us considerably. To demand a psychosociological synthesis is an urgent requirement, but it risks remaining programmatic. Facing any phenomenon – individual and/ or historical – how to do justice to the psychological interpretation, to the sociological interpretation, and how to operate the unifying junction? How to distinguish – without artifice – motivations, conditions and determinations uncovering personal, lived and darkening history, and motivations, conditioning and social, historical and cultural determinations, without forgetting that some are implicated in others and that we demand specific as well as englobing explications? All humans live with a *psychic* life – analysable in the *psychological* dimension – and each human knows in their own manner *social* life – expressible in the *sociological* dimension. Each of the two dimensions thus penetrates and encompasses the other. How do the passages run from one to the other, and how to grasp the impasse? The problem is nevertheless the existence of these 'two' dimensions or the single and ramified dimension. To unite them or to separate them only on a methodological level – from the approach – constitutes a poor step that neglects the ontic – and effective – level, although these two planes combine, interfere and mix inextricably. If they, the dimensions of the ever-historical human, are united at the base, how does this unity articulate itself and then disarticulate itself, what are its modes of association and dissociation, and what surpasses their reciprocal action? The problem becomes more radical, if one comprehends the psychological and the human, as well as the sociological and the historical society, as both emerging together, and as a whole, from a foundation that activates and contains them, from an extremely confused and manifold text, where the principle of sufficient reason – foundation of more or less causal explanation and comprehensive interpretation – runs aground, whether it be psychological, sociological or even psychosociological.

Psychic and psychological, social and sociological intuitions cannot do without institutions.

The task of the human is to surpass the psychological and the sociological, while maintaining them.

Is it the human who makes the human? And who – or what – unmakes them?

A supremacy and a dignity has been given or given back to the human which they do not know what to do with.

The committed or omitted acts, which we regret, accompany us like little shadows.

The human does not exist so much as coexists.

Does not one always attain something other than what one was aiming at, since the active aim remained unconscious?

What does one want, when one does not know what one wants? What about what one wants without knowing that one wants it?

The urges and their urges can counteract: so, one can have an urge for having an urge and, at the same time, have an urge for not having an urge. In any case, it is not the humans who have urges, but the urges which have humans.

There where the human imagines itself walking, it is led. There where it believes to transcend, it is transcended. There where it thinks to choose, it is chosen.

Do humans like things by planning to do them, by doing them, or having done them?

Isn't it as difficult to welcome what comes to you – comes against you – as to separate from what leaves you – to separate from . . . and against . . .?

No one can open an abyss and stay close.

The human 'is' in discordant accord with the world and in discord with itself. Perpetually living in a waking dream and a dreamed awakening. 'In them' the world plays itself, like a throw in a match.

The human seeks to be delivered from itself.

For a long time, the human lives and dies in giving itself to representation: to others and to itself.

Where does the central point of an action reside? In its intentions, its modalities, its results, its interpretations? Or rather in the play that collects it and scatters it?

Obscured beings are afraid of what they call, in their so-called clear language, obscurity. It would enlighten them more than they could bear.

The directing idea of the human seems paradoxical: its only great possibility is the impossible.

For a long time, humans believed they think and do what they *wanted*, wanting – involuntarily – to say: what they *could do*.

There was a moment when the human had been crushed and surpassed by the machine, without either knowing it.

Among the most difficult things in human relations we find precisely the extreme difficulty of human relations.

The stopping of a functioning leads to biological death. The stopping of an integration to psychological death. The stopping of a role to sociological death.

The human, neither fortune nor misfortune, is thrown into the vertigo of the game. It bears both fortune and misfortune with difficulty, worked by anxiety, and neither can – nor know – accord with accord.

Attracted by the game and fearful before it, the human tempts chance without wanting – or being able – to recognise it.

Chance and will complement each other, exclude each other, compete.

The human is also something like the contrary of the human.

As you know, without guessing its full significance, all the advantages lead to drawbacks.

How many attractions without attraction are not manifested in the human.

Desiring the desire of the other and desiring always 'something else' – in the constant expectation – the being of the human, ruled and mortified by the desire and by the other, can neither accept the world and its world, nor totally refuse them.

Desire remains in general unavowable for its momentarily subjective bearer, who, moreover, does not readily avow it to others.

Life and work. Two twin sisters and enemies, each feeding and devouring the other. Where 'finally' circulates more genius: in the one, in the other, in their composition, or in their exclusives?

Is the root of curiosity 'sexual'?

Are we willing to let some kind of peace fall on us?

The question is: *who* or *what* are we?

Adolescence and the beginning of middle age, that is to say, youth, seem to offer more 'idols' than completed maturity and old age.

From what does the human die?

It is necessary to know how to rely on the weakest points, those that offer the strongest resistances.

In a certain manner and on many points, everyone is like-every-one. Exceptions number *in general* millions of similar cases.

Humanity cannot bear elevated and hyperextended efforts for long.

Like a landscape, a face uncovers itself and covers itself.

It is not easy to live alone or to live with others. The human must go through the hard apprenticeship of both loneliness and coexistence, if it wants to live and survive.

If, in the sensation taken as such, one element predominates although the contrary element announces itself discreetly, the desire seems to be fundamentally ambivalent.

Humanity seems to be condemned to flee forwards.

The human cannot live without a project that carries and supports it.

Let us open ourselves to what is stronger than the self in us, to what in the human is stronger, more radical and more distant than the human.

The choice that one makes of facts is always tendentious.

Happiness is an obsessive idea – fundamentally bourgeois? – which one cannot get rid of either by abandoning or by realising it.

All humans are crazy without being completely so. The whole life unfolds, in general, in half-tones.

What did they want to achieve with their confrontations? The surrender of the other, partner-adversary, without conditions?

All in all, the human seems to need a guide – who knows how to go astray.

Nostalgia and anticipation are extremely tenacious forces. It is when one has lost 'something', or when one does not have it yet, that one appreciates it the most, under the pressure of a tendency for possession, at the heart of a present which one rarely experiences as bringing presents.

The great power of driving moods, thymic dispositions, affective tones that colour the world like this or otherwise, is yet to be explored.

A certain uncertain serenity, saying both yes and no, a certain equanimity, also agitated and knowing ups and downs, a play between acceptance, renunciation, integration and effort demanding transformation could provide us with some uncertain contentment, a peace founded in war, a relaxation supporting the effort.

Is it not the force of psychoanalysis to envisage the ambivalence of all significations, everything symbolising everything, everything being able to signify its opposite, desire implying fear and love hate? Under the condition that their keys – or even their master key – are opening and do not open only open doors.

In the fray, everyone is the pawn of someone and something else.

Being awake and being asleep compete for the being of the human, focusing and shadowing all that is.

Being healthy means approximately (elementally and roughly said): being able to eat, drink and sleep, love and work, talk and think, play. Illness, affliction of one or more organs or functions, prevents 'necessary' satisfactions, indicates major maladjustments, manifests intolerance to inevitable frustrations. It affects the diverse levels of integration, more or less separately or globally: organic, psychic, mental, social. Health and illness, the normal and the pathological, maintain without contest a strange dialogue both between them and with the attempt of therapeutic intervention (psychosomatic and socio-cultural). Does health reside in an acceptance of – and adaptation to – biocosmic and psychosocial rhythms or in a successful effort to transform the given? Is the illness only a deregulation, and can it not also manifest an opening? Remedies, medications and one-, two-, three- or four-dimensional treatments (physical, psychological, mental, social), violent or peaceful, inscribe themselves in the therapeutic effort, whose supreme axiom is the conservation and prolongation of life, healing of damage, ill health, illness, accommodation of the entire organism to itself and its milieu, the preservation or restoration of health and of what is considered normal, that is to say, tolerable by the individual human being and the society of humans; there, where it cannot heal, this effort aims to help, to relieve. If one demands from it too much, it turns out to be ineffective; demanding too little is excluded, because suffering demands help. Conforming with the structure of the illness and the social and mental structure of each epoch, always battling with the problem of integration and disintegration, the therapeutic effort deploys itself and continues with vague precision.

Every illness opens a breach through which necessary fluxes flow in and out, particular illnesses being signs of a much more general illness, neither particularly psychical nor particularly somatic, not allowing themselves to be reduced to psychosomatic suffering and medicine. Every clinical theory and every experience are surpassed by those sufferers who are part of the state and historical process. Consequently health and illness, normality and abnormality, require a differently attentive approach, if they are even distinguished. Which does not mean that they are identical. From where and with what is human madness judged and treated?

The differentiated psychosomatic unity, in other words the organism and the psyche, seems to need to be sick somewhere, because illness is not only a lack but also an opening.

The nervous system of the human greatly needs to be strengthened again. Can pharmacodynamics succeed in playing this regulatory role which it is forced to play?

To accept finitude, anxiety, limitation, old age, death. To accept the sadness of the world, its boredom. To accept the fundamental strangeness – more than alienation – of the human. Beyond hope and despair. Without primary indifference. Attentive to time. Is it too much to ask? If one maintains the maintenance of life as the supreme axiom, is it not necessary to consolidate it with 'forms' and 'forces', and to tolerate the inevitable frustrations? Contestation, interrogation, questioning are not enough. It takes problematic consent to life and death for them to be bearable. Certainly, without excessive reconciliation.

Do not be insatiable. Bear the frustration and the contradiction. Open to thwarted drives: libidinal and aggressive. Programme of wisdom for outdoor music.

To the nervousness which so shakes and overwhelms occidental humanity, and to the panic which grabs it, could follow not the belief in an absolutely privileged solution or escape, but a certain *panic* acceptance – a little more relaxed – of the available totality.

To live detached from and reconciled with human opinions and agitations, without hypercriticism or joyousness, bitterness or disappointment, like a kind of – worldly – monk; is this a lifestyle?

If the human had – hypothetically anyway – a kind of super-health, what would it do with it?

The bio-logical functioning of the human, its psycho-logical apparatus, its socio-logical roles, its ideo-logical constructions, its techno-logical machinations, do not help it to live without any *reason* to live.

The affective charge disappears, diminishes and is considerably transformed in all verbalisation of the lived.

We could 'think', and no doubt are in the course of 'thinking', that a certain type of Institute of the Human would create the framework within which one would study in a multidimensional and pluralistic, concrete and coordinated, theoretical and practical manner all the problems, aspects, elements, factors and levels relating to this absolute, which is supposed to become the human, its character and its destiny. And the technical and scientific study of what the human is would not allow itself to be disjointed from the anticipation of what it can be, if necessary through the help of directed mutations. Biologists, physicians of all branches and psychologists of all kinds would attack its genealogical family tree, hereditary antecedents and constitutional aspects, familial world, somatic, psychic and then psychosomatic constitution, namely its organism, temperament and its character, its life and its dreams, intelligence, will, determining accidents, incidents and events. Educators would pedagogically attack this human and its offspring. Then would come the sociologists, who would seize the questions concerning its social milieu, the influences and orientations, whose subject (that is to say, the object) was, is and will be subject (that is to say object), and they would throw a lively light on its professional activity and on the social and historical context. But it is useful that others join these specialists of fractions and totality of the human that are capable of carrying out astrological, graphological, physiognomic and chiromantic analyses. Finally, parapsychologists could grasp ultrafluid and metapsychological phenomena to let nothing escape. The human would thus be comprehended, analysed, reconstituted, healed, guided, relieved, directed, accommodated, normalised. Every human would become like-all-the-world. The obscure forces of heredity, its body and soul, its constitutional structure and its reaction structures, its partial structures and its structure encompassing its different structures, structural variants and differential deviations and structural constants and invariances, health and illnesses, its unconscious and conscious (even its spirit), education and family, social environment and its own activity, evolution, involution and dissolution would be scrutinised. Its lifestyle and style of death, the powers of love and death, even the unexpected and contingent factors that have acted on it, would find their proper place. When all these aspects, elements, sectors, levels, factors and problems are related with each other and each one with the whole through all kinds of interactions and interdependencies, what would remain to be done? Will this pedagogical and socialising, biochemical and psychotherapeutic medicine, this psychosomatic and socio-cultural, open and versatile, dynamic and holistic research finally not arrive at surpassing the burden of the 'original sin' and opening the field to the advent of the 'truth', that is to say the neither true nor not true errancy of the planetary human?

How to succeed in loosening or cutting the knots that grip unconscious and preconscious, displaced and repressed, censored and scotomised, travestied and unavowed, lies and concealment, bad faith and false consciousness? How to clear oneself an access path and to clear a path to what moves between many waters?

The immense capacity of humans to deceive themselves and to repress – to erect even unconscious defences against repressed drives – to simulate and to not recognise, is not averted by being said and denounced.

Being too much of one's own person, or being too dependent on it, is not the making of a great 'personality'. A very luminous star can be well centred, matching the vibrations of the world which surrounds it, ordering itself into the system to which it belongs, without wasting energy. Another – as luminous or even more so – can be characterised by an axis that does not pass exactly through its centre, by wasting forces on eccentric movements that trouble it and trouble its world.

Beings evolve and remain the same. How to leave this banal circularity?

The rising superhuman is only a figure projected by the declining human.

It happens that misfortunes and ills, remedies and medications meet.

Will they be capable of traversing deserted regions with metallic lines and reliefs without being panicked?

The human is prevented from realising even those of its desires that it 'knows'.

To unlearn the human, to unlearn history, is it a task that falls on the human and on the humans?

Does not the end of the human also signify: the end of the human as an end? At the same time, doesn't it stop being a start? Does it remain as a middle term?

The human likes to manipulate, and one manipulates it – whether it likes it or not.

The human retreats from its own destiny, by passing with difficulty from accepted destiny to assumed destiny.

The human cannot be reduced to a unity – corporeal or psychical or intellectual (or spiritual) – nor to a duality – somatic and psychic – nor to a trinity – body, soul, spirit – nor to a multiplicity – of biocosmic, neurophysiological, psychosocial and historical-cultural forces, each of these forces itself multiple – nor to a totality – integrating all its aspects and all its dimensions – because it is at once unique and double, triple and multiple, total and fragmentary.

Why do you insist so much on believing that there is an interior human and an external world?

Fascination and despair are closely linked.

More than what they do, the circumstances and the ways in and with which they do it appear important.

Changing rests, it seems.

Humans simultaneously want to have what they already have and what they have not yet had.

The ego passes into egocentrism, culminates in exasperated narcissism and then moves towards its dissolution. Will egoism and individualism conjointly and in parallel turn into altruism and socialism?

The particular, the individual and the intimate – through which the universal necessarily passes in manifesting itself – possess a warmth, a clarity and a charm, blazing for an instant until they are consumed by the flame and the fire, according to the order of time.

In the midst of other games of skill and chance, boys and girls play their own destiny, present and future, active and passive, by playing with soldiers and dolls.

Often one plays a game because unable to play another.

Ethics, liberty, humanism launch themselves into the battle on dead horses. Which change themselves into mechanical devices.

That happened a long time ago, around the twentieth century. Humanism perished much more from the arguments of its defenders than beneath the blows of its adversaries. At that epoch, it was still living and surviving through all the chitchat, whether naive and scientific (by researchers in the human sciences, as they were then called, scientific researchers, if there were any) or literary and free (applied writers and somewhat delirious writers). One spoke, at that time, of the end of the *idea* of the human, of its immersion in a much more global structure, etc., etc. Humanism even took its revenge, triumphantly and flatly anthropomorphically – humano-scientific anthropology inheriting from theology –, where one declared, to have the right tone and without knowing what was said, that thought preceded the human, and one continued in the rest of the conversation (no: of research) to employ the sacrosanct adjectives (no: prehuman, human and post-human, in any case scientific): true, real, objective, etc. There was also a lot of fear and pacifism: humanists and non-humanists held stubbornly onto existence and had a great fear of the little toy that was called the atomic bomb or something like that; that is to say: one did not want to put an end – with an incomparable epistemological and methodological clarity, and on the foundation of an ontology become formalised logic, with a true, real and objective clarity – to the human and its illusions, to the exploitation of the human through the human (who raged in capitalism until socialism realised exactly the opposite), to the alienation of the human and to intelligent and/or stupid theorisations concerning them.

Puppets and actors, marionettes and bottle imps, heroes and great characters, mad and wise, are mixed and set in motion in the course of the human comedy that often forces them to exchange their roles in the pious masquerades.

The human walks zigzag: whether wanting to explore the landscape in all its *width* or whether wanting to go on a path in *depth*. What kind of bond binds these two temptations and attempts?

All that is human remains so foreign to us, and what is not human demands a more relaxed approach.

Entangled problems are inextricable: do humans believe or not in what they do, do they do what they believe in or do they act as if they believe in it? One can launch into commentaries, indefinitely, play the little games of consciousness and unconsciousness of self and others, try to decipher intentions and actions, accidents and premeditations, omissions and consequences, succeeding sometimes by reading foreign languages.

Does the distinction between the authentic and the inauthentic itself relate to the authentic, the inauthentic, or a different terrain?

Does what they in general leave behind, and what did not take place, await its hour?

It is the complex arcana that render us perplexed.

No one can live more dangerously than they can bear. And what one calls life is not a work of art or a literary enterprise. The aspiration to a poetic life hits against hard limits.

All desire realises itself with deviations.

It seemed that humans wanted to do what they wanted. So what did they want?

Provided with maximum harmony, the human could arise in the assumed opposition almost anywhere in the world.

From a power unequal to the waking current of life, flows another kind of life.

'Must' feelings be shared? Aren't they instead always mixed?

The dream covers an enormous surface and, allied with dreaming and revery, governs all the depths and all the alibis.

The human material is already tired enough.

To live, to carry life and not only to bear it, does it require a certain naivety or rather a certain cunning?

Can the generic human open to time ever say: the plays are played, *rien ne va plus*? The last words of Dostoevsky's *Gambler*, 'Tomorrow, tomorrow, all will be finished!', will be put into the game, which, ceaselessly, starts again, indefinitely.

Can one act without worrying about the consequences? In any case, one is acting by ignoring them.

The 'human' as a deadline is a question falling due. It is the putting into question of what is, of what it is. Conjugating all modes of putting into question, it remains without answer. But one retreats behind the deadlines.

If succeeding is – voluntarily or involuntarily – to solve a problem, failing denotes another type of relation with the question posed to the human and, secondarily, through the human. Provided that one could distinguish success and failure in concrete cases or even in the analysis of summits.

To the failing human, the movement of life becomes intolerable. Difficulties cannot be overcome by effort alone.

There is no lucidity without fault, plenary. It is impossible. Its very possibility would destroy, burn all that it claims to illuminate.

Finally they reached the other shore, to realise obscurely that there is neither river nor another shore.

Humans generally imagine themselves to be in relation to what is in a relation of externality. They almost always consider beings, others and things as if they were external to them.

Contrariety, as long as it remains bearable, is stimulating.

You can only practise refusing, or better, renouncing, or better, accepting; you can only practise claiming, or better, revolting, or better, revolutionising, even with and against revolutions.

People aspire to peace, rest, relaxation, well-being, happiness, while feeling and knowing how problematic these hours are.

What the human desires – moved by its desire, which it does not yet know and which always disguises itself – is also what it dreads – without really knowing what it fears – as needs and fears express themselves most often through reversed traits.

For the compulsive game forces us very frequently to repress what attracts us and to abandon ourselves to what we dread.

One does less what one wants, than what one can and what imposes itself.

Is serenity an hour of the evening?

Can they not be anthropocentric, not interpret and construct the world anthropomorphically?

What has been rejected and abandoned returns, and one returns to it.

The present and future task: to surpass humanism and the human, leaves the question in suspense: what will become of the human?

Between sought satisfaction and obtained satisfaction lies deferred satisfaction and, still more, difference.

How do the somatic, the psychic and the mental function, bind and unbind within the same unity?

Life continues with each new day, and what appeared as intolerable is integrated or rejected, bypassed, in the movement of propulsion. Millions of children enter each year into the vivifying waters and build while playing with sand castles; millions of teenagers and millions of young girls enter life seeking their star. These young people yet do not know the 'distinction' between those who have a star, and those who do not.

Behind us hide the prefigurations of our hopes.

Humans search for the way out in hope, in the chimaera, in the impasse, in the struggle, in the encounter.

Does every human summarise all humanity, and every society all societies?

Your intuition tells you: the first movement is the 'good'. Should one be cautious? Wasn't it reconstructed afterwards? Plus: it plays tricks on you.

The ties of kinship that unite and separate the vital, mortal and symbolic functions of the living being which is the animal and the living being which is the human, still escape us greatly. Neither the nostalgia for lost animality, nor the fanatic struggle against animality, nor the claim of animality as a formal abstraction, nor the humanistic translation of the still undeciphered language of animality facilitates our comprehension and experimentation of the play, which adjoins and disjoins original powers and conquered powers.

We have a childlike predilection for commencing and closing.

Coming to love the decline. Playing its death.

The human never definitively leaves the stage of the world. Even in dying. For the dead who inhabit the necropolises do not cease to maintain relations with those who live in metropolises or provinces. Only the radical and definitive extinction of the human species would abolish all presence of the human in the world (on the plane of what is called consciousness), if not the world itself (as a question). The end of the individual human – individual death – and the end of the human – collective death – therefore remain distinct.

The human bears with difficulty time, duration, perhaps more difficult than stopping, death. Ancient, contemporary and future oracles say it: being born, being and existing, living, is much more difficult to bear than not-being, dying.

How many dead or imaginary personalities do not keep us company.

Words and the dead [*Mots et morts*] accompany us. On our path which constantly demands liberty without really wanting it.

Can we let the dead bury their dead, let dead souls rest in peace or make war in exhaustion, to jump – like the horsemen of past times, when their horses died in the middle of the battle – on a thoroughbred horse, a being of the cavalry?

If the human no longer believes in survival, why are they so concerned about what will become of other humans and themselves after their life?

Certain lives are lived as if they were posthumous.

Time is the constant, though often unconscious, obsession of the human, and the human is perhaps the passing obsession of time. The human desires and wants all that is, and especially itself and all that it does, to endure as long as possible and leave traces which will endure as long as possible (years, centuries, millennia?) in the visible and sensible course of the world and the course of time collected in memory – but also collected in oblivion. All glory wants to persevere in being, to conserve the radiance of appearing (δόξα), to be enthroned in the midst of memory in refusing disappearance and non-being, and imagines triumphing over its adversaries, whose negating action it positively provokes. *Sic transit gloria 'mundi'*. But also: *Sic transit gloria dei* and *Sic transit gloria homini*. Yet all passage, all surpassing and all transition can only remain within the play of the world, where glories shine and tarnish. What is and is done finds itself measured in duration, although the human is (or because it is) equally a being of rapid consummation, of usage and usury, of consumption.

At birth, the human enters into life and the world: it works, speaks, thinks, loves, fights, plays and dies, leaving 'the' world with a desire for survival and even for eternity. The living celebrate and fete the dead until they are consumed in time, into oblivion. The survivors – each time – are always grappling with a double temptation: the mystical cult of the dead or their annihilation; it is as if they aspire to make them live and make them dead a second time. In general, it is in a mixture of the two tempting attitudes, also manifesting as a pendulum movement, that the survivors keep in contact with those who have ceased to live, to survive: they bury and resurrect them several times, according to the diverse futures of the past, because it is always the living who speak of the dead, even when the latter call them.

From the depth of the ages, as one says and as it happens, myths and religions, metaphysics and ethics, works of art and technics, want to ensure and build the survival more than the lives of humans, defeat death through immortality, by humans and cities retreating from immortal death. This type, this promise of survival and immortality, is what must also give mortals a reason for being and living, by protecting them from menacing non-being, since the human has not yet learned – if it ever learns – to play its life and its death. So God, liberty and the immortality of the soul were and remain the three major themes of onto-theo-logy, and especially its anthropological and humanistic version, as well as the metaphysically informed life and the movement effectuating, in mixture and confusion, the destruction of metaphysics; it is less important whether one believes in these three themes or whether one denies their existence by falling into another kind of faith and piety, depending on what is reversed and inversed. For all psychological and sociological interpretations and analyses of profound aspirations, as enlightening and demystifying as they can be, remain rather obscure about their inspiration.

What can life beyond the grave mean in the beyond of the world? What can survival mean, beyond life among the living – but the dead are also present-absent among the living; what can death mean flowing into immortality? Does every birth provoke rebirths and every death resurrections? Do rebirths and re-deaths not correspond? In what space and what time? According to the dead and the words of what language, according to what modes of affection? Within what cycle englobing what cycles?

There is a *genealogical* survival: individual and member of the species, the human wants to survive through its descendants, no matter here whether it wants to recognise itself individually in its children, by conforming with the principle of private property, or whether by prolonging the part of universal life towards the future. There is, let's say, a *cosmic* survival: that which constitutes the human being and its bodily and sensitive frame is reintegrated, after its death, into the cosmic cycle from which it is somewhat separated in individuating itself. There is a *theological* and *anthropological* survival: the soul or spirit – supersensible – of the human survives it after death in an elsewhere, so that this aspiration can take the extreme form of the beatific belief in the resurrection of the dead and the body. Whether it is about the survival of the individual soul or the survival of the fraction of the soul of the world, which, after the death of its individual carrier, joins again its universal origin, can only remain secondary. There is a survival of inverted ontotheology, a *historical* and *human* (quite humanistic) survival: words and actions of the human survive it in time, with individuals and in societies, by leaving behind perceptible traces and others, which merge together, are taken over by memory – and overwhelmed by oblivion. Finally, there is a project – and a dream – of *techno-scientific* survival, which would like to positively assure a kind of immortality or amortisation to humans, without really knowing what it understands by that.

Whether in an energetic and materialistic, idealistic or dualistic, unitary or monistic, individual or universal way, whether in another reality or in a space-time of the imaginary and memory, is manifested, in every way, a call for survival, a desire for eternity, a wish for immortality, a will to defeat finitude and temporality. It is striking to see how often – bourgeois and Marxist – atheists and positivists speak of eternity and immortality, even if they are historical-humane. The human being does not want to and cannot accept its finitude and even less the finitude of the being of the world. Yet it is in and from the network of finitude that the idea of infinity is projected. Everyone aspires to an extendable temporality like rubber, more infinitely than indefinitely, and this infinite elasticity is supposed to be the eternity that masters temporality. Almost no one dares to assume both the limits and the unlimitedness that insert us and surround us in their play. The time of a being or a thing, the duration of traces and memories can be more or less long, but always stop 'somewhere' at a 'certain moment'. To return transformed into the future? Where will gather what ceases to be what it was – in time? And what is lost – also in time? The radical contingency of the being of the human 'and' of the being of the world constitutes the play within which we try to juggle like clumsy magicians, while believing, moreover, to manage to get away with and hide our play of hocus-pocus and plays of hide-and-seek, all at once victims of our own play and of the play of the world, which remains our own and foreign to us. Anthropo-morphism and-centrism blinds us, even and especially when we crucify it on earth, to let it shine in the glory of heaven.

According to the customs of a very old carnival, mortals and immortals invert and exchange their roles and characters; according to an ancient dialectic, in the cycle that binds life and death, life is in death and death in life. The human, always effectuating a passage and remaining a passenger, enters the world, lives, produces and reproduces, chain of the chain that chains generations, degenerations and regenerations, speaks, struggles, plays and dies. Is it leaving the world, by dying? Where was it before it came to the world? If the world is not one of the spheres of what is, but the open totality of time, to come to the world can mean to be born as individuated being, and to die, to rejoin the universal cradle and tomb. Everything that appears, is and disappears, appears, is and disappears in time, because nothing founds or surpasses the play of omnitemporality. Time is as much instant and moment as duration and flow, as much creation, production, progression and deterioration as repetition and rotation. It allows us to apprehend it so or otherwise. It is the residence of what is, what passes, passes away and passes over, and it does not let itself be immobilised.

Is there any survival, any immortality, for us other mortals? Any answer in the form of *yes, maybe* or *no* avoids the question that has been posed to humanity, precisely because it could not solve it, and remains corroded by irony. All dogmatism and all agnosticism are invalidated by the very praxis of thought, of life – and of death. Everything passes and is thought in the vagueness of consciousness and under the pressure of unconscious needs, memories and figures of memory remain, too, troubled and confused in fading, while the powers of fascination maintain in the human both mythical nostalgia and utopian anticipation, as the human aspiring almost at the same time to momentous life and to restful death, to survival, to immortality and to return to a previous state – that is also a latter state – to life, from what it has been separated, and what will mark for it a solution and a dissolution. Life and death, each one singular and universal, hold us and draw us into their circulation, into their circularity: each one contradicts itself and contradicts the other, and this effective contradiction conjugates the opposing and complementary powers by maintaining them more than suppressing them; neither one, nor the other, nor a third synthetic and dialectical term is the last word: there is no true life, no living life, no total life without death, and death, if it became total, would cease to be lived and told.

The conjugated play of life and death takes hold of every kind of survival. This play, we play it tense. According to the logos of a legend, the Presocratic thinker Anaxagoras demanded, towards the end of his life, that children's parties be organised on his grave on the anniversaries of his death. It seems that this custom conserved itself. The plays of children would thus perpetuate the plays of thought trying to think the play of the world. Now, we do not know very well what to do with our dead, whose errancy corresponds to ours, but do we know what to do with our lives and our desires for survival?

Who survives whom and what, for whom and how? Is it only or principally the human? Does not what bears the human also survive it? Let's be a little more humble and attentive. A modest pair of shoes leaves its life traces behind it. A pair of large peasant shoes lets itself be 'immortalised' by Van Gogh: it survives as a canvas. The schoolgirl, with her first young girl's shoes, goes to meet her first love perhaps heavy with the future. Old slippers are thrown into the trash and from there are reintegrated into the cycle of the cosmic elements and the fabrication of technical objects, without forgetting the traces that they leave in the imaginary that they too, dying in forgetfulness, are rejoining that in which the movement of time reposes.

When the human dies, gets re-posed, it leaves behind survivors, who will continue, prolong, destroy and ruin what it was and what it did.

What effectuates the ascension of the human? World history, evidently.

VI

World History

The human is in history and not history in the human.

Due to a mental, and not only mental, habit, due to a historical behaviour with its provenance and roots, we almost naturally distinguish two domains in the totality of what is and is done: *nature* and *history*. In other terms: the order and cosmic rhythm that exist without us, and the order and the historical becoming that we constitute. This cut, well rooted, does not take account of the fact that nature and history are *each* the horizon of the other. Neither is the other, but each is inseparable from the other, both deployments of the *Same*. It is in and from the cosmic nature that human history develops itself, and it is in and from it that nature reveals itself and is transformed by us humans. Human history seems almost to want to suppress all naturalness, to abolish, so to speak, nature. But nature can also engulf human history: the errant course of uninhabited stars can continue. In whose eyes?

Everything has not only its history, but also its prehistory.

What exactly does the stationary state of what we designate as belonging to prehistory or remaining outside history indicate? How far does the mutation produced by writing go?

There is no first catastrophe that one can grasp.

It is in a horizon of apparent scarcity that human history is inscribed.

The common origin of humanity is no more problematic than its common aim. At the antipodes of the same planet, diverse types are searching for their past and future archetype.

What does Hölderlin hear and see when he writes: 'So the word came from the East to us.' Calling: is it an oriental word?

Orientalism is an occidental product.

The Greeks remain apart in all universal history.

The Graeco-Roman, the Judaeo-Christian, the European-modern, the global-planetary, each of these paths (and ways) remains dominated by Latin, the Roman.

History is history of the dead, the living and the surviving.

Every told history contains a great deal of fiction.

Would history – as 'science' – let us recognise the 'human', more than the past and the present?

Doesn't history teach you, at least, that it doesn't teach you very much?

Insofar as it is the work of memory, history is forgetting, conquests are made on the basis of losses, continuity is crossed in dotted lines by discontinuity.

As one knows, one does not know how things would have gone, if they had gone otherwise – if they could have gone otherwise.

History remains always partisan and partial, both in its actual unfolding and in its theorisation.

Ceaselessly, one rewrites general history and all particular histories. Sacrificing to the play of actualisation. Succumbing to the obsession: mission equals transmission.

Is it not we who constitute, through historical knowledge, the historical becoming which, however, constitutes constituting knowledge? For there is neither historical facticity nor perfect restitution of the historical event.

What kind of link links historical episodes (in historical becoming and knowledge) to historical destiny? What kind of play unites the ephemeral and the consistent-inconsistent weight of actuality to the durable and to historiality?

Important events are rarely noticed on the spot. Often events appearing as historical are only anecdotal.

To foresee who will be in the future the great people of the present, that is, of the past, is not easy.

History proves visionaries both correct and incorrect, several at the same time.

Time and history take their time.

Human life – personal and generic, individual and historical – needs some theatricality to unfold. That suppressed, it is like pulling the boards out from underfoot: it then falls down the trapdoor.

One cannot live only with the big; one also needs the small and – especially – the average. (How annoying is this question for the distinction between big, small and average!)

The Manichaean myth – on a dualistic and essentialist basis – of good and light struggling against evil and darkness to defeat them, has a hard life.

To confront historical becoming itself, humanity seems to have, apparently, only two great schemes of explanation and comprehension. The first interpretation of the path of history is *idealistic*: of Judaeo-Christian origin – and even older – it sees in history the space-time of the unveiling of the spirit, the idea, liberty. History marches towards the reign of – full, essential and universal – satisfaction and transparency, recognition and consciousness. Through much suffering, so the reign of aims will be realised – more or less perfectly – from the last to the first. Hegel marks the moment of the apotheosis of this schema, not without trembling before the prospect of a spiritual desiccation. The second schema – in solidarity with the first – reverses the perspective. It is the development of material, technical, practical production that constitutes the historical movement marching towards a generalised and socialised well-being – common to all humans. Of course, this will not exclude antagonisms and conflicts that will nevertheless be destined to be constantly surpassed. Marx brings this schema – let us call it the materialist – to its climax, being at the same time sensible, for moments at least, of its devastating aspect. These 'two' ruling conceptions, which both promise a reconciliation of negativity, alienation and reconciliation, are metaphysics – for even anti-metaphysics and counter-idealism are not empirically given (they themselves are more produced than given) – and implicate each other. To explicate what?

The problematic *motor* of historical development remains in suspense. Moreover, it breaks down, as often happens with motors. Why and in view of what does it move and set itself into movement? Categories such as material needs, the search for happiness, the aspiration to well-being or the realisation of freedom, the deployment of ideas and ideals, even ideologies, no longer function victoriously or with enough yield. But nevertheless: history is mondialised and is, so to speak, on the move towards . . ., even though – and because – all foundation withdraws itself. Could the path of history let itself not be overtaken – or expressed – by a *schema*? Does its *sense* (its *direction* and its *signification*) have a *sense* (a *signification* and a *direction*)? And how to distinguish and unite – diverse and global, effective or interpreted, total and partial – paths and schemas, directions and significations? Place and time of sensed – or assumed to be so – actions and passions, history offers itself just as much to the non-sensible, to the absurd, to the insignificant, to the non-significant, and aims to almost surpass these differences and many others, establishes and demolishes mixtures of action, agitation and indifference, embraces and suffocates those who embrace it to fertilise it.

History is not a person, a woman: therefore neither goddess nor whore, as well as goddess and whore, 'she' imposes *epochally* – that is to say in manifestation and withdrawal, the presence and absence of the visible and the invisible in *suspension* – her games and the transgressions that are part of it provoke currents and counter-currents, establish and dislocate organisations and structures, never free of unquietness and mayhem. Her waves surge. Certainly. But how? By drawing cycles, do they make everything emerge, sink and resurface in and through an 'eternal' – namely omnitemporal – return in the circle or spirals of time? This return is then the return of what? Of the 'Same'? Which one? Would the path of history not rather follow an evolution, would it not rather indicate a progress – sinusoidal, of course, and dialectical? From the prehistoric and the extrahistoric, from the savage, the primitive and the archaic (one may call them as one pleases), to the oriental and the Asian and from these to the *Greek light* – constitutive act of what history is for us – and to the *Roman ordo*, through the revelation and organisation of Judaeo-Christian life, up to European modernity which embraces in its mixture the whole planet and equally monopolises Mexican, African, Islamic, etc., histories – somewhat anecdotal – does not the triumphant and operative schema, expressing moreover the path travelled, stand out? Whoever denied it would be stupid or evil or suspect. There is consequently *one* schema, which englobes the two schemas. In their abstract rigidity, neither the cyclic and repetitive schema nor the evolutionary and progressive schema says how what is, is done, is undone and is redone, is unified and falls to pieces. And it is hardly enough to render them a little more problematic and polyvalent – by combining them equally – so that historical becoming begins to speak. Are we then constrained to fall into a sort of relativism – with several combinations of relations – which at times records the repetitions and at times the deployment of what is new each time, or again both at once, a sceptical and disillusioned, lucid and wakeful, prismatic relativism, as it should be, for whom we don't do it? Almost everyone will agree: it is unsatisfactory. Is it not dissatisfaction – also called inquietude, negativity – that apparently or effectively sets the historical – working and thinking – machine in motion to accomplish its turns, detours and returns, its itinerancy? Yes, but relativism can only provoke our irony, irony that it relativises.

Does the wheel, by accomplishing 'identical' turns around its hub, advance the chariot?

All the regressions are part of the march.

It is inevitable that in all domains beings and things follow the slope of least resistance.

By surpassing the linear schema and the cyclic schema, if not history itself, by plunging the diachronic succession into a sort of synchronic structure, could a third, so-called structural schema embrace realities and historical possibilities? By erecting an allegedly global system and partial systems, by formulating a combinatory code and getting lost in the symbolic readings and arrangements of messages that combine themselves and produce 'sense', by relying more on permanence and permutations than on changes and transformations, and by constructing a system of signs and homologies, does this structural and structuralist grasping embrace history or does it let itself be embraced by it? Does not this schema miss the passages and the transpositions as well as the secrets of the diverse languages, even while including certain quasi-permanent dominants? Is it the unification of historical thought, attentive to change, and anthropological thought, constructing structured and formalised ensembles, that will birth a wider and deeper, but always partisan and partial, schematisation of world history, able to constitute and dissolve human and history?

Does the interplay between movement and the logical system and movement and the historical system, conditioning and defining each other, support a privileged reading?

There is the logical course of a history (whatever it may be) and the historical course of a logic (whatever it may be). In the two courses, are sense and nonsense one?

How to unite or separate the permanent themes and motives – in historical time – and their particular historical colourings?

Event and structure *habitually* correspond: the event reveals a foundation.

To privilege the variants, to privilege the constants, are two unilateral modalities which wait for their assumption.

The problem of temporal-historical succession remains fundamentally unthought. The play of the articulation of temporality and historicity escapes us.

Everything corresponds to history – and not to the simple philosophy of history, heiress of Christianity – but this correspondence is not linear or unilateral.

When the vice tightens, then reason in history appears at work, set to work – justificatory, overflying the event and running after it, limping.

It is almost always about exposing oneself to the closest and most powerful task, the most distant commitment.

Not only the general historical and social states are important, but also their concrete modalities, their occasional determinations, their situational and situated conditions.

Even those who do not get their hands dirty do not keep their hands clean.

It would be necessary to conduct, as completely as possible, an economic and political, social and historical analysis, with the greatest lucidity tolerated (above all by who undertakes it). To analyse the productive forces and relationships of production, the relations of (individual, state, national, social) property, the mechanisms of commerce, exchange and distribution, to comprehend the nature, the regimes, the forms, the organisations and the functions of work. To unpeel the play of prices, money, finances and distribution of profits, revenues, wealth. To settle the standard of living of different classes, layers, castes and their relationship to power, administration, management, control, decisions and executions. To explicate the role of the State, governing and oppositional parties, police and justice. To enlighten the balance of power, both nationally and internationally, strategic positions and behind-the-scenes secrets. To examine the diverse forms of belief, religious and moral, the derivatives of religiosity and the presence of rites, cults and myths. To shine daylight on the deployment and the utilisation of all cultural sectors: informative, literary and artistic, scientific and educational, ideological (manifest and latent). To explain the lives of humans – private and public – their psychological movements – individual and collective – their ways of speaking and thinking, working and struggling, loving and dying, playing – admitted or subliminal. To interpret all the interpretations.

The questions trouble. The questions posed to history and through history are in effect troubling. We want to be at once demystified, disenchanted and reassured, secured. Is this possible? The massive and univocal voices which bring solutions and draw lines of conduct carry, for historical moments and *epochs*, without failing to break. Human life seems to want to maintain itself on planet earth and conquer other heavenly stars. Why? The old ontological and metaphysical question: what is being, why is it there? swerves to the historical and anthropological question: why does the human being want to live and survive, at what price, how does it want to avoid – or accelerate – the disaster? Destructive atomic energy and its utilisation timidly pose this otherwise decisive problem. The joint game of conservation and destruction, the desire for life and the call of death, is only very artlessly played. Life flows into moulds: couple, family, amical and social bonds, organisation of work, institutions of civil society, activities of distraction, leisure and culture, State (national, multinational, global). Too much putting into question, contestation, interrogation, problematising experience, openness render life almost impossible; too much pseudo-certainty, assurance and security flatten it. Trapped between the 'too much' and the 'not enough' in a world where all models, prototypes of action and passion fail, we fail too, while building and disintegrating. Sometimes, a singular suspicion of a same and other possibility grips us. In our post-historic march without aim and without 'end'.

More and more a question arises: why not let the plays of platitude, banality, vulgarity and mediocrity surge up as such? Themselves signs of . . . and signs towards . . . Why not arrive at a sort of eulogy of the trivial, the everyday, the common? Is not everything in the average, blends, mixes, mixtures, interpenetrations? From Marx, Nietzsche, Freud, Heidegger, the power of the prose of the world and of life still escaped, which sweeps along and assimilates critics, integrates and emasculates revolts, digests and monopolises romantic dreams and nostalgic and anticipatory visions. Besides, the old impulses were not so pure either. Critics, visionaries, analysts, therapists and prophets succumb to a certain naivety. Such big children. Total disalienation, the superhuman, poetically liberated or harmoniously channelled *eros*, the time of being, are and remain nostalgic, restorative and futuristic, and do not accept the greyness of the world. History seems devoted to writing a very long grey page. When and how will it be turned? History does it all for us to adhere to it and to us. We are educated, work, love, play, to make ourselves recognised, to enjoy, aspire to a – certain or uncertain – recognition and reconciliation, to make history. But we die, and history opens onto an emptiness and a nothingness always to be filled (by whom? through what?). Without avoiding dangerous questions, without optimism or pessimism, without hypercriticism and without conformism, without hope and hopelessness, illusions and disillusions, without lamentations, consolations and heroic or tragic gestures, do we not have to continue to live and survive, always beginning again, like animals conscious, or almost, of our finitude, animated and devastated by thought. Without all that . . . But with what? What remains? We are neither completely dead nor completely alive. As such, we can only test the finitude of history and historicity, of time and temporality, of the human being and the being of the world.

As a somewhat unsuccessful experiment, humanity is a test rather of weakness than of strength.

Every epoch has a constantly revisable structure. Especially for the nervousness of the occidental human and for the precipitation of the human that (pur)sues it.

What is culture? we ask, when it becomes a problem. It is that which links together the great powers – myths and religion, poetry and art, politics, philosophy, science and technique – linking them to the ensemble of the elemental forces – language and thought, work and struggle, love and death, play – thus informing the totality of the word and action of humans and conforming them to a model. Culture is a system – a structure – organising economic forces and relations, the powers of political domination – master-slave relations – family and erotic relations – relationships between man, woman, children – as well as symbolic and ideological codes – myths, religions, language – just as much as artistic, scientific and philosophical creations, into a whole. It leaves vague its initial, governing and ultimate presuppositions, illuminated from time to time by thought; it does not question the principles that animate its tradition. What is the relationship between civilisation and culture, and is civilisation the final and mortuary culmination of culture, as a certain cultural tradition wants it?

Culture had its high points before the cult of culture and culturalism established themselves. It was highly formative before the agitation of cultural affairs and journalistic pamphleteering, which takes over everything, installed themselves. If the circus of futilities and cultural varieties becomes more and more subtle and coarse, it does not mean that the worm was not already in the fruit. All the cultural worms and all the fruits now amalgamate in a cultural eclecticism and syncretism, which, by abolishing the initiatory paths and the elites, open the door wide for culture; so that, passing through that door, it leaves the stage? Those who are only talented, and who only want to direct and transmit directives, cannot assume directions, seize the posts of communication, information, deformation, becoming functionaries of the culture business: they open themselves to what is reserved for us, while hiding it from us. Thus the course of culture – not so tired – is played on the whole surface of the earth. Culture generalises itself, universalises itself, mondialises itself. Occidental European culture meets all other cultures, and all, under its leadership, interpenetrate, combine, socialise, planetarise. Global culture, planetary culture, mass culture are slogans – thus comprising corollaries of institutions – that do not know what the question is. They complete a process. Our civilisation and our culture, which are and are not ours, give off a heavy and slightly nauseating scent of Alexandrianism. The Hellenistic world closed off an – ancient – world, which another world should succeed. While for us other little humanists – as shrinking and shrunken humanism enters the phase of its surpassing – everything plays out over the whole surface of the globe, all concerning a united and unique world. Our confusion is ecumenical and universal. This generalisation of culture will probably go on until every – or almost every – individual is at once producer and consumer of cultural goods, living in the vast museum – cemetery, cradle and nursery – of world culture that will play the inexhaustible combinatory – although used up – of all the forms – past, present, future – and all the contents – multiple and variously connected – of culture. When one will soon be able to spend a holiday in an artificially constructed Babylonian city, reading Taoist texts in paperback, listening to Tibetan music, watching outer-space experiments on the television screen and following on transistors the results of a football match and those of a political congress, while we will play during the day to reconstruct scenes of prehistoric life, and indulge in the evening in games with electronic machines, when everyone will more or less write prose and poetry, participate in theatrical and psychotherapeutic psychodramas, paint abstract and pictorial paintings, and will have the elements of a mobile architecture, then a step has been taken: indeed, the cultural combinatory is destined to amplify and complicate itself. However, the generalisation of culture, as it has been understood so far, already indicates the end of culture. Generalisation and end usually go together. Because through its universalisation and cybernetisation – retroactively, actually, prospectively – culture no longer obeys a prototype, a model. Becoming multifaceted and informal, it no longer proposes a definite schema for speech and action, dreams and passions, works and leisure. Going in every direction, it becomes at once insignificant and designifying. It gives no more answers to saying and doing: it is no longer formation, it becomes information and communication. When it was culture, it already avoided the crucial questions: it did not pose them, nor pose them to itself: it proposed answers. More and more, it brings up questions, itself becomes questionable, put into question. It begins to be unable to offer any answers. In the process of being completed and on the eve of a mutation – although it still must be conquered by the Third World, the underdeveloped countries, those who aspire to it – it globalises itself and generalises itself – flattering little or more than a few cultural particularities, folkloric reservoirs preserved in a vacuum – universalises itself and massifies itself – at once highly diversified and mediatised as well as popular and vulgar – it democratises, socialises, in short, integrates itself – creaking – into the play of planetary errancy. The planetary erring takes over all cultures and all culture, invigorating and emasculating them, totalising them and letting them burst into sparks. It demands from those that it fashions, and who imagine they fashion it, not that they conform to a model – it certainly also requires a conformism, but this conformism is vague and empty, even if oppressive – but rather that they open themselves to planetary errancy, planning, platitude, that they play the game that transforms all the high places, where the spirit blew – excuse the obscenity of the term – into touristic or scholarly places, places that are common or unreachable for average efforts until they manage to access them. Thus the end of historical and global culture, in and through its generalisation, poses the problem of surpassing the said culture, its decrees and secrets, its mystique and its mystifications, its processes and idleness. Will we nevertheless enter the phase of a new radicalism? Let's not be uselessly naive. End and overcoming of inherited, transmitted and reconquered culture might almost mean: entry into the game. The game of what? Not the game of a stupid ludic activity. *Ludus* also designated the *school*. It would consequently be about entering the school (of the play) to learn to play the play, which 'commands' and orders all ancient – so also future – so-called cultural activities and passivities. Someone – Nietzsche, if you want to know everything – said of the ancient Greeks: superficial through depth. Are our post-cultural plays of all sorts plane, planed, flat, levelled – through depth?

Have we actually reached the brink of cultural saturation?

All culture implicates – and is based on – a lot of mystifications.

Commonplaces are places where people meet without much trouble.

There are hollow and insignificant periods in history. It is not always easy to separate them from others.

The extreme will to radical transformation – product of and producing technical power – allying construction and destruction, can it lead towards the time of the end of historical time, with history – allied to our hopes and our plans – having ended, meaning that nothing radically new and decisive can emerge any more? Can the historical, namely metahistorical, becoming unfold like a stagnant and grey river, carrying with it conquests, satisfactions and recognitions, dismal, acclimatised, devastated? Can its fabric be formed from the repetitive and indifferently inventive succession – thus also repeating the differences – of little joys and little pains, limited and circumscribed, which will be regulated and restitched with the help of all the artificial resources of a technics as flattening as conquering? On earth and on the other stars that we would like to populate, is not this same history completed, which will continue to be dull, monotonous, lukewarm, hollow, exhausted? It is only when the world has painted its greyness in greyness that the owl of Minerva will take flight – at dusk – to recognise and paint – with grey on grey – what is. Where does it come from that we now live this vision, even if we clear it of every past regret and every too systematic anticipation?

Little by little we are led to the threshold of the problem concerning the *end of history* – the visible aspect of finitude *tout court*. Hegel glimpsed the question of a – possible and real – end of history, though he absorbed time and history into spirit, somehow out of time. 'This' which is out of time contains time in this way. Despite this call for eternity and this recall of infinity, the problem found itself nevertheless posed. Although the theoretical and practical tasks were not yet planetarily and universally realised – will they ever be? – history had already unfolded in principle what has yet to unfold. Nietzsche asserted and predicted the reign of the *last humans* – who live the longest, aspiring to a levelled happiness since they have lost every star, wanting to appropriate it. What can the end of history and the end of humans nevertheless signify? Is there then no more of the new? And where could it come from? Would it have been already? The new always flows in the currents and channels of the old, and overflows it; conjointly, it is interpreted according to what precedes it and will follow it. One can interpret it according to the old and predict that the new will become like the old. Each can be subsumed under the other. The old informs the new and conversely, several times. The old renews itself and the new ages – multiply. Ancestors and descendants call themselves and are made differently. So all the world 'knows' all – except what happens without its knowledge. Ignoring its knowledge and its ignorance. Genetic and structural permanences are strong, individually and socially; renovations equally possess their hard-hitting forces. Their games will assimilate the revolts more than the revolutions – infinitely rarer – in the course of a history which does not manage to constitute itself in history and to harmonise the ancestral popular and the out-of-phase advances.

Very slowly, despite or because of precipitation and acceleration, we enter the phase of *metahistory* and *post-humanism*. Whether we like it or not. Whether we want it or not. To continue to insist and to exist as humans in a finished history, that is our task, while preparing the passage at the same time. Questioning, contemplative and halting thought almost grasps the step to take; political action, lukewarm or fanatic, always obsessed, must in its own way effectuate it. Do logos and praxis, thought and action, saying and doing, remain irreconcilable, despite all the work of dialectics and concomitant chitchat, despite all the syntheses more unilateral than bilateral, despite all the juggling and prestidigitations, despite all the wishes and appeals?

End of the human and end of history signify the end of the human and history as all-powerful theoretical principles, end of a certain philosophy of history and anthropology, based on a philosophy of preliminary history and anthropology; but, when interrogated more brutally, do they signify the end of the human and of history as ontological and epistemological key concepts, or as ancient realities in becoming, already terminated in some way, having reached their end, their aim and their purpose, and pursuing them again with a view to generalised realisation. Human and history seem to find their end in the human sciences as a constituent-constituted and resolved-dissolved subject-object. End, then, or thought of the end? Fictive end of an effective fiction or effective end? End does not mean cessation but completion that endures.

The end of history can just as well occur as an administered fiesta as a dreary ceremony. The two 'forms' can conjugate, mingle, alternate, etc.

In a completed history, would the human find itself reintegrated into this nature which it opposed? Would it still be *nature*, if it knew itself?

Perhaps it will prove, both on the plane of historical knowledge and on that of historical becoming, that history was only an interpretation of the human adventure.

Everything happens as if there had never been radicality. Was it always an abstract luxury? Isn't everything in the mixture, the arrangements and the compromises? The most extreme investigations and aspirations get crushed by the game of space and time within which extremes touch, fertilise and abolish themselves. Everyone aspires to – starts moving towards – a generalised well-being that lacks a sufficient reason for being. Unless this well-being can do without a reason for being, it does not 'exist'. Technics and science, sport and comfort, culture and phantasmagoria solicit us. The voids are filled by a flight into the anodyne imaginary – at the risk of being mortalising – passably devoid of humour and fantasy.

Metaphysics, equally ontotheology, philosophy, or general, formulated and implicit theory, dies, explicated in sciences and technics, and it is not the philosophy of history, sociology and anthropology which can revivify it.

They pay back money in their own coinage – put into circulation by treasurers and counterfeiters. Everything in the twentieth century breathes a certain boredom, a disenchantment. Even and especially for its *distractions* and its leisure. Boredom is the dull, dreary form of unconfessed anxiety, which conceals itself in the zones of unconsciousness, bad faith, false consciousness and concealed doings. For everything, there are reasons *for* and *against*, nothing escapes the derision – sometimes, however, beings and things, dreams and thoughts hurt us (to what point?) – and we live as if waiting for a surpassing of derision. The technical civilisation cannot find its style. The 'measure' is not yet full. We still have a lot of eclipses to record. Not ideas, nor ideals, nor models, nor prototypes, nor examples, offer themselves to us, except in the inevitable misunderstandings; however, we still live in this world and in the world, big and little world, so rich and so poor, in this life that chases itself more than it continues. We work the fields, we build metropolises and necropolises, we work the sea, we populate the sky.

Is it from multiple, combined and antagonistic actions that something like a logic of history results?

The degree of opposition and reconciliation of which an epoch is capable lies in the intersection of necessity and chance. Conflicts and integrations are opposed, but most often they compose.

What is the logic or dialectic of world history, what is its schema and its path? Especially if we do not reduce it to a pure or mixed logos, or to a pure or complicated contingency. How to establish this work and its reading? A *posteriori*? *Post festum*? A *priori*, but afterwards? What does the flight of Minerva's bird manifest when night falls? An *a priori* and morning task, preceding the festival and the sobering-up? More questions. To which are joined – often inadvertently – those of radical contingency, chances and necessities, those relating to the multidimensional interpretation of a text, of which we lack – forever – the pages. Humans and societies set goals indefinitely returned to an elastic and rubbery time. Significations and orders arise and resound, mobilise and land, heavily damaged. How to inhabit the urban and human landscape without turning it into a wild or acclimatised nightmare, illuminate it without burning it? Inhabit? Is that what it is still about?

Perhaps, though it is in no way certain, it would be time to pose the question of the schema and the path of world history a little differently.

Without granting sense an excessive importance and without wallowing in nonsense, without clinging to the true face and without crying about the absurd. By simultaneously grasping the two faces of the same coin, its usage and its counterfeits. In not living history either as a place – even future – of happiness, nor only as a grotesque masquerade. What is left? That of which we are the leftovers and ferments. What has been said many times repeats itself at all levels, and gets tested and tired out again.

Does the planetary era inaugurate another era, or does it merely complete the change of somewhat archaic modernity into ultramodernity? Whoever would say the one or the other would be right, but would not pronounce the decisive judgement, if decision there is, the passage itself remaining undecided.

The path of history – oriented and disoriented – accomplishes, in becoming world, an *itinerancy*, an *errancy*, makes limits and aims emerge, accomplishing itself in and accomplishing the spirals of *time* – past-present-future – and recognises that too strong words often tend to burn in illuminating, killing what they 'should' illuminate and render habitable. The little pawns and great pioneers of historical becoming cannot circumvent accidents. The world powers pass through precise moments of action, transport, import, export, are exported. Stripped of 'all' mythological or realistic nostalgia – frozen – for the originary, not denouncing in the course of history a series of falls and losses, no longer scaffolding a positive or negative eschatology, progressive or apocalyptic utopia, however attentive to the losses and the forgettings, the memories, the possibilities, the conquests and the anticipations – let's hit the road. Neither redemption nor disaster, as such, is waiting for us for the moment. Even the final annihilation withdraws from our hasty grasp.

Let's learn to bury, with dignity and stealth, every schematic schema, by giving it the honours of war and defeat. Consequently, in what name to act? An embarrassing question; a brutal answer: depending on what acts on us. Do otherwise! Since we want to live and survive, let's continue and start again. The same errors, the same and other styles. Embarked on the odyssey, we have to experience that an odyssey does not only signify departure and casting off, but also return and repair. Neither the cult of one or the collectivity or personality, nor the cult of *no man's land* and impersonality are able to bless our voyage. Nonetheless, we voyage. With a fixed trajectory and adrift. Our passage is effected. We continue and start again. Action imposes itself as necessary, never leaves with the fortuitous. Simultaneities escape us: among others, the simultaneity of the human and the world. The dialectic evades it by presenting it. The *at the same time*, in and 'against' time, escapes. Action activates us. We set it in motion. Insensible – or almost – to its irony and its humour. It dictates to us its imperatives, imperious for the *moment*. Necessary and, so to speak, inevitable, it urges us to act to form, transform, deform. Whoever would deny it would be foolish or malicious. And it denies all its protagonists by confusing them. Then to act according to what? The question as well as the answer remains brutal: *according to what acts on us*, that is to say, according to what imposes itself on us as a task to accomplish, according to the pressing needs of the historical moment and of its productive constellation, according to our fibres, our guts and our consciousness – overwhelmed by our unconscious, our bad faith, our lies, our false consciousness, 'ours' and those of others.

Individuals, members of society, collectivities and fragments of the world, we will have to live the efforts and the vanity, to productively socialise, so to speak, the wisdom of Ecclesiastes and that of Heraclitus, to face nihilism and to experience it until it is defeated by itself. Those who hold will hold, the others will be swept away, but the line of division between the strong and the weak, the victors and the defeated can only remain floating. We will have to search, between gaiety and sadness, without overflowing with life and without too much death drive – if we want the play to continue – for a sober style of life, love, language, death. What will we do with the ornamental that is always only ornamental, except when it becomes it? And rituals? In the midst of gigantic technical scaffoldings and the combinatory of technical mediations, will we manage to build stone by stone the finitude of the human, history, the world?

For a very long time (Plato), the world has been interpreted as a construction of the moral order.

That which could be called the ethical problem poses itself as a human problem, a historical problem, a political problem, although no kind of solution emerges. Existing Hebrew-Christian, bourgeois (idealistic and conformist) and socialist ethics rule as a living and dead queen over equally dead and living behaviours. No other lifestyle seems to manifest itself, and experimental lives remain too stricken and astray. Human life certainly needs a technique of life, but in this case powerful technique does not solve the problem. Although it poses itself and does not pose itself in terms of success or failure, it concerns the attachment to life, which is and will undoubtedly be more and more a problem. Humans have a tendency to live beyond their forces, which propel them and break them. Simultaneously, they let themselves be captured by the power of inertia. Human life needs structures, continuity and rules for the game, but must not all hope for a society or life reconciled with itself remain utopian? When neither moralism, nor immoralism, nor amoralism, nor the ethics of dissolution, constitutes a 'solution', how could a *problematic ethics* deploy itself? What frames and what rules contain and rule the *play of the human*?

Morals, called with more dignity ethics, ensure something like the restricted conservation of the individual and the species. The moral order chokes the psychomotor and generating forces of history.

The ethics of failures and omissions is also to be explored, exposed, exploded. Without neglecting the 'fact' that the origin of all responsibility is dominated by what is – what there is – of the irresponsible.

Everyone, groups and communities, always has a certain *code of honour*, often unconfessed and not explicated, which regulates their ethical conduct and undergoes distortions.

Every ethical norm faces the test of its victory and its defeat.

From ancient hedonism, the people – it is no longer envisaged as a pop-ulace which follows the masters, except by arrant reactionaries – pass into modern pragmatism.

Cynicism is grafted onto a dream of innocence.

To put into question everyday life in all its systematic disparity always remains a task to be fulfilled. The fear of the everyday becomes more and more a major fear.

Neither the ethics of disorder nor the contrary ethics – the former already being the contrary of the latter – cease to be ruinous and ruined.

Is it possible to remain situated beyond good and evil?

Problematic ethics are yet to be elaborated.

At the end of the nineteenth century and in the first quarter of the twentieth, extraordinary attempts took place to forge another lifestyle than that of ordinary morality, to live an experimental and ecstatic, wide and deep life, not conforming to ruling norms. Facing madness and suicide, sometimes succumbing to it, certain thinkers and artists, men and women, searched for the bonds uniting friendship and love, thought, art and life. This search for another attitude, however, did not succeed even in creating islands on the ocean, and was swallowed up. Dominant forces and forms dominated human weakness more and more. The human animal, working animal, social animal, was regulated. The economic, political, psychological, ethical and ideological powers gained the upper hand. Hegel emerged triumphant from the crisis, human and social life remaining enclosed in his frame: from the principally monogamous family, through the institutions of civil society, to the State. The *outsiders* were crushed or retreated to the ranks. Marxism, Freudianism, Surrealism contributed greatly to this restoration, to the maintenance of the status quo, relegating dissatisfaction and revolt to the well-fenced domain of utopia and imagination. Could a new – productive – jolt of these foundations, by finding again the momentum of previous shocks, manifest its formative force and propose other lifestyles?

In any case – with all the power of the errant truth of individual and social ethics, with all its incoherencies and inconsequences – the behaviour of the being called human is taken over by the worldly ethics – Judaeo-Christian, egoist, bourgeois, liberal and individualistic, altruistic, socialist and collectivist, since, for the moment, there seems to be no other – which wants to safeguard human and society from internal and external dissolutions. Its annihilated prescriptions appear to turn against us when we transgress them, and yet we cannot identify ourselves with them. To what will this pressure and this suspension of the ethical problem lead?

That the evolution of manners aims towards a certain liberalisation does not authorise us rightly or wrongly – and rather wrongly – to either brandish the word of liberty, or let us be obsessed by abstract liberalism.

What gives itself as justice is a justification. The march of history does not accomplish itself in the direction of liberty, but towards a certain uncertain liberalisation.

Does the acuteness of the situation appear more clearly to the eyes of the most disadvantaged?

To exercise in particular contestation on erotic and political terrains – particularly pressing – yet without neglecting other terrains, however, which are equally important.

Extreme erotic, political lucidity would make landscapes uninhabitable.

Society cannot bear frankness. Sincerity is dissolving. Tearing off masks and piercing the secret of role play is not tolerated.

Braving society does not go beyond a certain point: the court, the prison, the clinic and the asylum are there to stop certain attempts (which will often be recognised much later). To effectively counter society, each time present, it is necessary to launch a guerrilla war dismantling all the positions in an unexpected way, rather than a frontal attack, in an underground and clairvoyant action of sustained breadth, not on basely tactical considerations, but on Sioux ruses.

Life, while remaining neoclassical, would seek – as it seems – to become innovative.

Do you ask yourself with enough force: where will the new style of life come from?

No society can live if it does not maintain order and discipline – in a more or less repressive manner.

Neither crisis nor criticism manages to make an edifice shake in its foundations.

To crises correspond, generally, restorations.

The harmless, libertarian and anarchistic dream of a non-repressive society is infantile and almost completely inoperative, simplistic and old-fashioned, eluding the play of historical and social powers that can only channel human forces and weaknesses.

Society is forced to bully certain things and certain aspects of everything to maintain civilisation.

To let the administration of things follow the government of humans is a utopian dream, which artificially separates two sides of a single organisation.

For today and tomorrow the problem of the government of humans and things continues and will continue to pose itself in an increasingly complex way. Who sees clearly? Every dream, sweet or violent, more or less anarchistic, anarchic or libertarian, will inevitably break against the hard necessity of a planning organisation, thus repressive and channelling, a techno-bureaucratic administration, a more or less rigid or flexible regimentation of the whole of life: from the couple to the State and its staff. Revolts themselves will be cornered by this dynamic status quo, combining tradition and modernity. The centres of decision will be more and more fixed and shifting, themselves taken into the play of what they pretend to regulate by assigning its place and trajectory, between everything and nothing. Envisaging the world as a gigantic self-production, product of a kind of spontaneous generation, and the human as the precious and laughable result of the same self-production, we sometimes believe that we see in the total self-management of humanity a new position and solution of the historical and political problem. *Self*-management, however, dodges the question of the Same, the-errancy-and-the-play of the history of the world and of the human in and as historical time.

Can those who manage and those who are managed be one, or is this the very distinction that will otherwise be surpassed?

More than individual, *private*, freedom, more than independence, humans seek their taking-in by the social group, their insertion into the collectivity.

The human community, social and historical, that humans have hoped for, not being realised, means one flees again towards a new imaginary or deplores the absence of realisation of the old.

Will the motor of average actions cease to be the individual and egotistical search for profit, whatever it may be, will the collective and altruistic search for the good as well-being replace it? Is not collectivism the generalisation and the surpassing, the extension of individualism? Isn't the distinction egoism-altruism somewhat, if not very, fake?

Different personal motivations can inscribe themselves in the same general impulse and converge. Collective behaviours are the result of individual behaviours and are at the same time different from them.

Universal history – which is not the place of temporal felicity; so-called eternal felicity belongs to omnitemporal history – sacrifices on its altar – also desacralised – a good number of profound works – sometimes even the most noble – that may be individually existentially precious. The primacy of the existential is the exaggeration of subjectivity understood anthropologically – anthropology being the last stage of accomplished metaphysics, the human itself becoming the last figure of the absolute – in the phase where individuality, subjectivity and existence become little planets, which, without their own light, turn, disoriented and exasperated, in search of their sun.

The grains of sand also function in the mechanisms of world history: they can show certain aspects by breaking them.

An unemployed negativity could be employed to disrupt many positive employments.

Unveiling the contradictions inherent in society is a game which the human cannot and must not renounce.

Everything is society's fault, one often hears. Of whom and of what is this nourishing and murderous society composed?

As a second nature, society absorbs everything.

Comprehended in too broad a way, society and the social are and encompass absolutely everything; comprehended in too narrow a way, they are only one sector. They are a common ground for all that grows on it, but this ground is also constituted by what grows on it and fertilises it.

What imposes itself must also be socially imposed.

Historical becoming has been conceived sometimes as a process of degeneration in relation to a real or mythical past, to a sort of originary and positively good initial model (golden age, lost paradise, primitive happiness, etc.), sometimes as a history full of sound and fury signifying nothing (was it conceived in this case?), sometimes as a gradual approximation, a series of successive stages, with stops and setbacks, as an imperfect realisation, translating more or less, in its own way and even in betraying it, in the present time, a directing form, a model orienting the becoming (reign of ends, liberty, etc.), sometimes as a militant march towards the model projected into the future that – even if it is informal – will lead to the – always – happy and final future solution, to the accomplishment of the model (eschatological myths, utopian ideologies, etc.). To break with this type of philosophy of history, which relays the theology of history, if not with the philosophy of instructive and/or complaint history, has not yet devolved to the historian thought of historians and philosophers, as long as they do not think history.

Even the imaginary does not escape finitude. Rich and kaleidoscopic, apparently free in every sense, it remains atrociously limited and conditioned, while also constituting an enormous reserve of reveries, disappointments, possibilities and impossibilities. Two major projections characterise the historical and futuristic imaginary (projections that often mix and combine). Two models, each of them referring to the other, dispose more of us than we dispose of them: a biocosmic, *physiocratic* model, which includes all that is, in nature and history, as an organic development, and an artisanal, artificial, *technocratic* model, which includes all that is done, in nature and history, as a product of a more or less mechanical activity. The first projection takes root in a nostalgia for global nature and draws, not without regrets for lost naturality and animality, a future state of reconciliation with nature. In this neo-Edenic world, cosmic elements, plants, animals and humans will frolic and play with innocence for all that we, since the myth of the lost paradise and nostalgia for the golden age, imaginarily lack. Let's call it *naturalistic*, this idyllic projection aiming at a semi-identity between human and nature, by reintegrating history as a kind of nature from whence it emerged. The second – complementary – projection is frankly *technicist*. Tensing towards a Promethean and mechanised future state, sinking its roots into the mythological dreams of the domination of nature, it sees, with or without optimism or pessimism, a robotised and cybernetised world of the future, ruled from top to bottom by machines and technical machineries. From celestial mechanics to human psychobiology and to the machines of political and cultural games, all will be ruled by the same power. These two 'visions', one paradisiacal, the other sometimes a little ameliorist but above all infernal, remain depressing in their candour. A more abstract and informal landscape could however attract some of our decentred attention. A landscape abolishing both everyday life and the absolute, letting the concrete and the imaginary keel over in the direction of an imaginary eluding itself almost as such and drowning reality. A panhuman and democratic kingdom confusing seriousness and ridicule, blurring the cards of those who make the decisions and those who execute them, could unfurl at its heart the enormous and versatile reign of a mechanics of games, a machinery of all the possible games, in which we could – sufficiently schizophrenically, massively, fragmentarily and on several planes simultaneously – take part, not according to what is flatly called destiny, but according to what is our mortal part, and which is partially revealed and devolved to us.

Nostalgia for origins has something aristocratic and residual, and futuristic anticipation has in it hope for progress. The one and the other however link the past to the future, sacrifice to one of the dimensions of time and are sacrificed in the perpetual present which is only a bridge.

Humans and societies do not seem able to live and develop without utopia, without ideology, without eschatology: these render the – always *bad* – *present* bearable regarding a *future* which will be *better* and which will realise what was originally in the *distant past*, in effective or mythical reality, and will be, in anticipation, *good*. Thus is grafted onto this reading of time – which does not facilitate a higher and more wholistic deciphering and comprehension of time – this need for constitutive or regulatory utopia, ideology, eschatology. They permit actuality to be liveable and comprehensible in relation to a norm offering the measure for what takes place, bridging the gap between nostalgia and anticipation, permitting the elaboration of a critique of contemporaneity as function of a schema and a projection, and refer to a 'model' that has never existed before. The unrealisable character of this 'project' is not very disturbing: it is moreover made to reassure. From the idea, a passage to the ideal and from it to (utopian and eschatological) ideology is effectuated. Projection of what is implicated in effective space-time, ideology blocks a lucid theory of practice, masks practice, informs and mythologically distorts the deployment of time, and makes believe that there is a solution to the historical problem of humanity that resolves conflict and recovers the game of errancy. The mythological dimension of utopia, ideology and eschatology can combine very well with techno-scientific aims, up to becoming inseparable from them.

The religious and political utopias – of Christianity and socialism, among others – judge what is in the name of what is not (what is no longer or not yet) and what finally cannot be such as they see it. Gravity however finds its role: it marks the end of grand principles, it is their end that installs what no longer needs the means in play.

All historical design is realised only by an action which turns it in a certain way against its intention, to effectuate it and to contradict it – by making it become world and by devastating it – through a boring or violent realisation that only constitutes an approximation.

Humans want to struggle against the negative aspects of situations, while not discerning in them the other side of what they consider positive.

Individual history articulates itself on the conscious and the unconscious of world history, and historicity on the unconscious and the conscious of individuals.

The reciprocity of perspectives between singular, individual, personal life, and universal, social, world history, makes us think that the individual in its individual history travels so to speak the whole path of world history.

The domination of planetary technics (genitive, subjective and objective) poses the problem of unity and diversity in a, let's say, new light. Will it make us unlearn ethics and politics? It seems to embrace the constructive powers and the destructive powers that *traverse* it too. It lets all the significations and all the signs enter into a combinatory which makes no sense beyond itself. This is its play. And it is in it the plaything. Technics opens an immense field and reduces possibilities, confuses the practical and the poetical and then poses us the question: what happens when words keep quiet? Have we spoken too much so far, and do we have to learn, through our chatter and agitating and soothing speech (propaganda), slogans, clichés, literary constructions and reflexive houses of cards, the – or at least a certain – silence? What succeeds – no doubt obeying a necessity – imposes itself and cracks anew. What is not successful could be stillborn or reappear. Precursors, we listen to them or sacrifice them, accept and refuse them, reinvent them. The small circles which maintain certain requirements – with preliminary sectarianism and confusion – have equally their role to play. In the whirling of the great Circle: which stops in its course – itself immobile? – and mobilises in its turning motion – resting in rest? – all encircled human vitality and anxiety. The balance of losses and profits is never established 'fairly', although a certain immanent and balanced justice redistributes a lot of things; running after profit and consumption, we consume beings, things and ourselves.

The historical age of the world is no longer idyllic or heroic, but rather bourgeois-and-socialist.

The – vigorous and young – phases of ascending dynamism are closely linked to others.

What is and what wants to go forwards all over the earth – and towards the heavens: the dynamic thrust of the existing, the need for food, drink, shelter, clothing, erotic need and the need for security, the need for will to power and problematic enjoyment, the need for arrangement and management, conservation, expansion and destruction, the need for beliefs and hopes, the need for culture and play – and finally an obscure but pressing need for the 'all' and the 'rest', for totality and residues.

Inexhaustible, needs remain finite.

It is by no means decided if the economic determination of the historical nature of the human is universally predominant.

The role of money – effective and imaginary – is still to be dismantled and demonstrated, if not abolished.

The aim of historical evolution sometimes seems (in the eyes of its protagonists) to be to free the human from needs, by satisfying them. Finite but unlimited – and undefined – are all existing and created needs satisfiable? Yet what are the elemental needs, and the others?

Productivity could well be one of the ultimate traps set for us.

After the era of creation and genius opens the era of production and suspicion. Suspicion of what? Of the game?

It takes a long time for an epoch to discover and invent its style. Feverishly, but in vain, modernity seeks its own.

Friendly and erotic encounters, couples and the *family*, relationships, mediations and social *institutions*, forms and forces of power and its contestation (implicated or, rarely, out of frame), administration and the *State* that also manage cultural affairs, are and remain, with all the involuntary humour and irony that they can imply, the rules and regulations almost necessary for historical and human play. These rules are at the same time unregulated, without ever being peremptory. Through them and their contestations could be posed the question of the very Game itself whose rules they are, for the use of small and big children. The rules and the stakes. Perhaps it is still too early to address this question: what plays the games. Would all human and historical follies and aberrations be absorbed and reabsorbed, situated and recuperated, in a sort of universal wisdom that would let the always non-final reconciliation 'surpass' the tragicomedy to be put again into question and march towards a new reconciliation, new because already originary? See! By whom? For whom? As an aspect of the totality or as 'the' fragmentary totality itself? Will we circumvent or override the wait?

Historical reason is a reason of State.

To transform the world, to change life, to intervene in the course of the world, of beings and of things, to make it mutate – in the interior of the cycle of revolutions and restorations that turn and return – to change the world by changing oneself, changed by the world that changes, what could all this mean? Is it about transforming the – inevitable? – course of the world? Whatever we do, are we not part of it? Is it about transforming the world, about changing life, according to a certain aim? But doesn't this aim itself emerge in the process of the transformation of the world, in the changing of life? Isn't it provoking and provoked? Isn't it taken over and conquered by the world it wanted to conquer? Do not all transformations and all changes as well as the active agents, which advocate and precipitate transformation and change, remain inherent to the world and to life? The world transforms itself. Life changes. Thanks to whom? To anonymous heroes? To eponymous heroes? The march of the game pursues itself and always starts again, mobilising and shattering protagonists and accomplices. To transform the world, to change life, emerges like a call, makes us attentive and open, until the circle of oblivion closes over the project – imperfectly consumed, imperfectly surpassed. What is, however, the norm or measure of perfection once the world of (idealistic) representation is imperfectly abolished? Will presence, signalling absence, take the step? Isn't also the grasping of beings and things in the chiaroscuro of presence-absence only one of the configurations of the play? In the penultimate analysis, words and activities, beings and things, manifest as working on behalf of the dominant organisation of the world and life. We are therefore forced to accept that everything continues, revolts, cuts and ruptures included, as well as dominances and latencies. One always tries to reveal the hidden history and to comprehend the system, to unveil the problems of the modern world and to indulge in a unitary criticism of all the aspects of the way of life and the totality of the world. This effort plays a productive role, when it can, demands permanent revolution and neglects the power of reformism. It claims generalised self-management: the conscious direction of all by all. Is this wish enough to transform the world, to change life? Commercial and spectacular society also takes it over, emasculates it and leaves it in a wishful state, or offers it piecemeal and false possibilities for action. All the novelties, even and especially when they announce a surpassing – but when will the surpassing itself be problematised until its surpassing? – are brought back to order, which nevertheless they fertilise, and the dominant, revolutionised and reformed lifestyle absorbs adventures and openings, even when it would be put into question by them. Can a new total game be reinvented and pass into the history of human society, constituting more and other than the negation produced by the system? Can the increasing dissatisfaction which goes along with the increasing accumulation of goods, unblock a horizon which does not remain dreamed, imagined, represented, projected? In other words, is it devolved to humans who make history without knowing what they are doing – made by it – to take it under their voluntary and conscious domination? To pose the questions in this way, doesn't it already open the field, after the loss of illusions and disillusions, to sobering answers?

To live with serenity and courage the course of the world and human things – individual 'and' historical – doesn't come without difficulty, when everything pushes us towards flights – forwards and backwards.

Does the absolute exigency impose respect or is it suspect? Catholic Church and Jews, University and liberal Bourgeois, Communists and deviant Groups plead on it and stamp on it. Let's auscultate the vibrations and interpret them. Attentive to stagnation. Recording the continuations.

The planetary era combines enrooting and uprooting. Everything begins to soar, attached and detached, to float, prisoner of breaking waves, drifting both in small havens and on the vast ocean, flying in the air and flying over the earth to which it remains strongly bound. But the most general frame, as panoramic as possible, contains all the framings and all the frameworks, enframes all that soars – itself also planing, scaling up and scaling down – without being able to be envisaged from the point of view of Sirius.

Although everything becomes plane, it does not sit on the same plane.

Why did they lean on the optimism of facade and principle and on the de facto pessimism of their contemporaries – humans and societies?

Are not all the alliances 'impure', mixing lines and fronts?

One should be equally sensitive to the sensibility of humans and epochs, to their ways of feeling, believing, saying and doing, living and dreaming, loving, working, struggling, dying, playing.

In centuries to come, all historical becoming would aim at achieving a problematic point, were it only a stage towards what, to some extent, had already been achieved.

We all live in the anticipation of this storm, while one has done everything, for twenty-five centuries, to not allow it to break.

The industrial age, with its expansive materialism, is in no way cleared of idealistic chimeras. On the contrary.

Between the Christian, bourgeois and socialist world, will there be more continuity than rupture?

Communism succeeds Christianity. It aims to assimilate it.

Even for Marxism, after the materialistic reversal of the reversed (and materialised) world, these are the thoughts that will lead the world.

No society succeeds in thinking itself. Does it at least manage to think others?

Often one has the impression that one must become flatter, more banal, simpler, to be able to bear the complexification of the world.

To rise up against the established order is part of the established order and/or leads to the installation and restoration of an established order.

Global civilisation, techno-scientific and industrial and not pre-paring a hypothetical post-industrial era, the society of production and consumption, the civilisation of well-being, poor in its opulence, mass culture, all this spirit of the time – whether it is played by more or less democratic and pluralistic regimes, or by more or less autocratic and unitary regimes, matters little here, since the regimes, with their divergences and variants, come together – leads to a capitalo-socialism of the State, to a sort of bureaucratic collectivism which tends to develop in a straight line despite the sinuous paths, in progressing and in unifying the diversities of which certain modalities will persist. The progressing and progressive evolution, with relapses, of course, forms the logic and the dialectics of economic, social, historical and political development: it aims at the domination, the exploitation and the administration of the earth. Will this evolution continue linearly for a very long time, as it seems, or will it experience cuts, ruptures and mutations that are for the moment unforeseeable? Once again, is it after the party, or the debacle, that one will recognise what presided over its unfolding?

Will the global unity, once realised, split up anew?

What will be the plot and what will be the drama of the violence contained in the rules of the game, and, breaking them, lacking space in a stale and insipid organisation, the violence aimed at overturning successes, stalemates and failures?

What develops in the margins of the dominant text is part of the global context and can one day inscribe itself in the text.

In everything there are unmentionable details.

Permanent contestation is what, on the daily agenda, simmers under the daily (and almost nightly) agenda. Globally, does it want the subversion of the global system and can it contribute to, if not effectuate, it? Permanent contestation and structured system are linked by a game where the first can dissolve the second, where the second can recover the first. The technical society – of production and consumption – is attacked both by the right, in the name of bourgeois humanism, and by the left, in the name of Marxist socialism. It is proclaimed inhuman, mechanical, empty, alienating. To what end, however, does this double criticism lead, which deals with both permanent contestation and the structured system?

The tocsin sounds for us the hour of post-revolutionary societies, the hour of reforms, may they be revolutionary, masking and masked. Let us however not forget that all human history, which begins neither with the *logos* (word and thought) alone, nor solely with *praxis* (action), but with the thrust of need and desire – in suffering and anxiety – with a stammering language and thought, with a productive work of life and survival – in pain and struggle – that history then from its beginnings – or: from the beginning? – is the play of all this, and makes its way – neither thanks to the reason that governs the world (as Hegel thinks), nor through the future of its structuring and structured procession (economic, social, political and legal forces and forms, manners, morality, ideology, art, religion, philosophy, science), which must lead it to the reign of universal satisfaction, recognition and transparency (as Marx and Marxism want it) – towards what it already had attained as modern and global history, that is to say its completion and its end that endure, the definitive end (the stop) not being foreseeable, without it being excluded that historical humanity does not manage to complete itself and runs aground on the way.

History, as such, does not know of *radical* and *total* rupture, of *effective* and *absolute* ending, of *fundamentally* new beginning.

What will be the agent of the next historical transformation, reform or revolution, which will change the rules of the game? From where will the power of negativity come, not the abstract negation, but the determining and determined, produced and productive negation, and the force of contestation? What social element will be the carrier? What will be its theoretical and practical perspective? Will global society reabsorb all radical questioning? What will become of the extra-social, asocial, anti-social movements of negation, of individuals, of groups and of communities denying the dominant world, contaminated by it and contaminating it? Will the ferments of negativity shift from social alienation to psychic alienation? Do the intelligentsia, the rebellious, the young, the neurotics, the deviants incarnate the 'bad side' of history, which corrupts good positivity? Where will the residual forces which accumulate on this side open onto? Will they explode in open daylight?

There is no society without its forms and forces of deviance.

Simple deviance is an indispensable negative complement to the *establishment*, the era of the *Welfare State* and the privatisation of the masses.

That which exits the ranks most often re-enters them.

There are certainly demands maintained upon better-being but there is no programme – theoretical or practical – of any kind and any colour that would aim at a beyond of better-being, of 'well-being'.

The struggles for or against strengthen the style of what imposes itself before being denied. As for what lacks style?

Each time a model gives itself as the model, one sees that it is only a type of model.

What is popular, losing its organic and communal traditions, becomes vulgar while waiting for its petty-bourgeois and planetary assumption.

Neither those who cry out for their abolition, nor those who wish for their restoration, their maintenance and their perpetuation manage to pose the problem of the elites – that is to say, the 'elect' among those called – of the planetary area.

Every epoch remains characterised by its games.

Does a power succumb to external attacks or internal weaknesses?

What does *necessary evil* mean? In historical opposition to what good?

Everything goes as it can go and not as it 'should' go.

To oppose to effective absurdity a feeling, if not a thought of the absurd, often combines with the love of change for change.

The organisation of relations of command, as flexible and democratic as they may be or become, could never satisfy everyone, especially those who do not want to command or be commanded.

No demagoguery can overcome the problem of hierarchy. Self-management, if it could effectively solve it, remains – for the moment only? – abstractly programmatic and concretely deficient. We should not underestimate the abyss – more than the ditch – that separates historical anecdotes and historical actions.

Doesn't every people have the government that it deserves? That is to say, isn't it governed in general by the most representative representative of the moment?

Those who dominate and govern are equally governed and dominated.

Historical decisions are always made 'for' and not *by* the collectivity.

Does not history confront and confuse accomplices – even when they violently confront each other – more than the culpable? The game of history also plays tricks on the tribunal of history.

The world seems to be already so old that the most revolutionary novelties age quickly, quickly rejoining the old and renewing it.

Those who trigger revolutions are *in general* the first victims.

The difference between the right and the left must be explored in all directions, on all levels, by all languages.

The distribution of the political card game – conservative or reactionary right, reformist or progressive centre, revolutionary left – is pretty confused. Those who regret an old – mythic – order, elapsed and condemned; those who feel a certain anxiety facing the void that nothing fills and who try to save – or renovate – the furniture to remedy in a little way the evils; those who, despite everything, speak in the name of a utopia very approximately realised and realisable; those with whom all this is strongly muddled up – logos and praxis mixing, remaining separated, contradicting each other – all, to varying degrees and in spite of or because of the various verbalisms and activisms, remain complementarily struck by stupor before the arraignment of history.

When things turn to the right, one needs a vigorous turn to the left.

Progressive platitude can very advantageously replace bourgeois platitude.

The historical and political task, present and precise, consists of being socialist and leftist – situated on the 'wrong' side, through which history passes, and nevertheless is to be thought.

What is good about radical socialisation, full of compromise, is not that it will solve the problems, but that it will open them.

In the combat of two adversaries, each of whom wants to deny, to contradict the other, it is the excluded third, the middle, which triumphs over the alternative: onto-logically and historically. Example: between classical capitalism and prophesied socialism a third way is established. This third way is not only the 'fallout' of the third kind of (Spinozistic) knowledge, foreseen by the third eye of the third human.

A regime is spreading in world history that does not fall under either classical capitalism or prophesied socialism. An economically, politically and ideologically mixed regime, offering something like a third way, unless this way turned out to be an impasse. Another, third 'solution' that would be neither bourgeois capitalism nor bureaucratic socialism, is such a 'solution' not conceivable?

With a childish naivety and as if they knew nothing of the ruse of history, historical humans always believe that the decisive hour is approaching.

The Occident is in search of the style of its agonal agony. Having reached the summit, do humans and civilisations aspire to descend?

On the horizon of the agony of our civilisation, no replacement civilisation appears.

The collective humanity of tomorrow: what a beautiful 'subject' of questioning, on the condition that one interrogates it from an angle.

History is not only adventure and opening, but also shutting and closure. It fixes the signs, transforms the innovations into permanences, is epochally dominated by certain values and rules of the game.

The bourgeoisie, even 'socialised', proved to have a life almost as long as the peasantry. Its forms survive it.

Technical and industrial planetary society, society of production-consumption, worldwide model – without model – carries the negative of its own myth and its own more-than-real directing efficiency, lives and knows an expansion, not despite but because of being mortal and supporting and fomenting the dream, the desire and the thought of its negation, its contradiction, its annihilation, by at once integrating them, blocking them and freeing them. It feeds on the spectacle of its double, balances the antagonisms, the powers of affirmation and those of contestation, constrains *all* its agents and patients into the same acts and ills, allows the same discrepancies. Where does a certain delay remain? In comprehension relating to the transformative action, or inversely?

The great conquerors of this world accomplish their conquests with a victorious sadness, their eyes dreamy, and strained, not towards the other world, but towards what surpasses and dislocates the empire and the influence of every worldwide enterprise, however sparkling it might be.

The historical hero, as long as there is one, will be a polarising being, situating, as much as if not more than situated, able to offer a general line and a centre of gathering, by fertilising several contradictory tendencies, moving against the current, causing great as well as small, positive and negative passions as well as diverse and adverse reactions and interpretations. Because it is a fundamentally ambiguous being.

The great humans (one must add, historical, without forgetting their little history) disturb the habitual judgements of *their* contemporaries. Exceptional, they can be poorly integrated, these integrators. They are neither young nor old; their youthful fire is as old as the wisdom of the world. They appear as situated above the common feelings of mortals. Cynical and naive, daring and indifferent to so-called common opinion. They live and act as if life were empty of the hope which keeps ordinary humans alive, carried by this hopelessness and another hope.

Is only what is replaced destroyed?

Intermittently, diverse minorities will incessantly enter the stage.

In all objectification, is there not alienation? Haven't we known this for a long time?

Alienation, deracination, strongly existing, give us the illusion that there was a state preceding them.

It begins: the denunciation of alienation as being itself an alienation. We enter the second stage: alienating and alienated alienation.

It is a characteristic of the modern human to manipulate ever more with products whose mechanism they hardly know; simple example: money, radio-television.

If every epoch is possessed by its own kind of greatness, what is the greatness of 'ours'?

The faith in the redeeming future and the fear of some kind of hell, which ancient cults nourished, and which nourished them, are socially replaced, the ancient deities dead. There comes now an indefinitely deferred future happiness and a historical and social dread regarding the march to the worst. In a state of permanent suspension.

Property and appropriation are stubborn.

The historical dream of a general will transcending the will of all requires an analysis in a watchful state.

Democracy is also something that can and must be put radically into question, regarding both its concept and its functioning.

Tyranny and democracy are less separable than one might think. Look at the totalitarian states of the planetary era.

In the democracy of indistinctions, certain distinctions do not totally cease to play.

Doesn't the aspiration to a certain aristocracy work within every aspiration to democracy, even though the latter wants to abolish the former?

A radical and worldwide hybrid, a universal and total racial mixture, seems to impose itself to give a new physical, psychic and intellectual vigour to the human species, some of the unities which compose it being overdeveloped and tired, others remaining underdeveloped and not sufficiently differentiated.

Do not the most elaborate conquests lead to the less elaborate positions? Does not the most differentiated indicate, to that which remains inert and compact, the path to its future?

Producing means, more and more, producing what lets itself be reduced to the consumable. Production and reproduction are intimately linked and perhaps lead, through what offers itself to consumption, to the opening to the game and of the game.

By entering the period of ultramodernity, history will complete – incompletely – the premises of modernity.

Neo-modernism is an ultra-phase of neo-archaism.

The future social organisation lacks models and prototypes. So?

Through its successes and failures, the century threatens us with desiring only its own dreams.

Convergence does not mean: identity.

The era of organisers will be superimposed on the era of computers.

'Absolute knowledge' and 'total praxis' cross their fires.

The province is a place where the sound of the steps of those who walk fades away; it can nevertheless give birth to walkers. The entire world becomes an enormous province, without capital.

All the alliances cease to be frontal – if they ever were – and become broken, fluid, mobile, apparently contradictory.

If to speak and 'express yourself', according to the current expression, it is necessary to have an alphabet, a vocabulary and a syntax available – by forging them – the current epoch does not succeed in saying what constitutes it; however, it plays it.

Each century forges the theory of what it does. It becomes in its turn a means that accentuates the 'evil' it is supposed to battle.

Historical humans and human societies attain something other than what they aim for.

There are histories that do not know an ending.

Is what is established, in spite of and with some apparent contrary accents, the general organisation of hopelessness, excluding all hope and despair?

The children's choir will always sing happy songs for civil or military armies on the march.

Whole centuries can live very well without proper thought.

The ruse of history and the irony of fate overthrow the solutions which hide the fact that there is no solution.

Immediate effectiveness and long-term effectiveness are not confused, although they may momentarily coincide.

Can world history, which is so important and embraces all, be rebutted, refused or refuted?

The iron dice of battles decide wars, which do not decide much any more, inseparable from the periods of peace which lead there anew – in the middle of the cold wars and the armed peaces – until the distinction between war and peace is erased.

A people can support so much more than a human or a group of humans and survive so many tests.

The ruse of history 'betrays' all good intentions.

We do not leave our children the world which we have made, but the one which made us.

The humans of this epoch of world history believed they were attending and participating in the expiration of an old world and the gestation of a new one. They were not suspicious enough of the ruse of passages.

The presumption of each epoch is to believe itself end and beginning.

Docility and revolt are not so inseparable.

After a great catastrophe, those who remain are counted and settle their – the? – accounts.

Successive conquests do not form a simple or complex cumulative process.

This obsession with progress has something downright regressive.

Waste, residues, collapses, failures accompany every enterprise and often constitute revealing signs.

The society to which we belong, and to which many generations will still belong, does not cease – in the West as in the East – being a society of exploitation: of the human, of things – of the totality of beings.

You could not do otherwise: Planetarians of all countries, unite!

In the midst of the planetary unity, all is and remains piecemeal. Not forgetting the maintaining and resurgence of certain traditional forms.

A great deal of 'automatic' rites are called to spread.

History – even accelerated – runs behind what has already preceded it.

The nineteenth century was the century of discourse oriented towards completion, conclusion. The twentieth century was a century of compromise.

In the heart of the citizens of an advanced industrial world, nostalgia slumbers for an idyllic, rural, archaic and feudal country life.

Technicist society will make humans face an immense problem: their ennui.

Every revolt and revolution splits itself: one wing maintains the banner of freedom and the imaginary, while the other organises with discipline and repression.

Every historical force which struggles against another divides itself into two (at least).

Each revolution gives itself as unique and exemplary, first and last. The preceding revolutions were in its eyes only a failed sketch, a distant prophetic announcement. The mystique of the revolution pays a heavy tribute to mythology and ideology, transforms politics into secular religion, ignores the return of the repressed and forgets the fact that it is always one class that makes the revolution and another that profits from it, that the great revolutions at once succeed and fail, since every revolution constitutes a *revolution*, a circle, better, a sinusoidal movement, a spiral, and that it cannot, therefore, avoid the restoration. After the first revolutionary episodes, the authority of the State reinforces itself, and reformist prose follows revolutionary poetics. So the permanent revolution reveals itself impracticable: a series of mixed and permanent reforms replace it. The revolution however persists as a requirement, and certain movements of revolt are accomplished. Will not all be recovered again by the course of the world?

Is the era of revolutions closed for the developed countries, which effected the conquests of the bourgeois French Revolution (its socialist extensions see daylight in the technically underdeveloped countries for which Marxism has become the lever for their modernisation and industrialisation)? Doesn't the era of reforms – were they revolutionary – succeed it?

Can there be partial reforms concerning only a segment without the whole being touched? Yet, no reform is sufficiently total.

There is never a single problem to solve. No particular problem is the key to all the others. The problems run all together and, altogether, they know fragmentation.

Did not every tragedy have an ending?

Destiny has become history, and history has become play. Since the transgression of sense puts an end to the tragedy of human existence and historical becoming. Does this mean that the tragic disappears from the history of each human and the history of humans? Since the theatricality and the democratic kingdom of representation are already *as* abolished.

It does not suit the epigones to have great political ambitions.

Precise and concrete becoming remains 'unforeseeable', however clearly one can see – or believes that one can see – its outlines form. Will it unfold as an indefinite progress? As a temporal return of the-same-and-the-different? Will it know relapses? Will it generate something new? It presents itself as impossible to foresee like a progressive line that prolongs itself. The enigma of the return withdraws from apprehension. Falls are never where one expects them. The new is, by definition, impossible to predict. The decays and rebirths emerge as a surprise, albeit prepared, and so render extremely problematic every grasp of the future that is beyond the plans of our enterprises.

The history of the worldwide game resides in repetition and transformations, in restarts and continuations, in stops and reboots, and it seems to exclude major collective suicides.

The century will little by little let itself be invaded by fatigue.

Let's start preparing the funeral of the twentieth century.

To leave the twentieth century, we have only to accomplish a few steps more.

To surpass the twentieth century, it is necessary to surpass its foundations and their consequences.

At this moment all that happens smells or stinks of the twentieth century, readies itself to enter the third millennium – always after Jesus Christ – and does not think that, by entering it, it readies itself to exit it.

Never has humanity spoken so much about itself. It is as if it suspects – very obscurely – how things happened until now. Henceforth?

Those who address above all future generations know it. They inaugurate the planetary era, which succeeds modernity – by precipitating it in the broad and slow process of its completion – the planetary era marking *the beginning of the end* of philosophy and history, which – in the generalised disease, the permanent crisis and the organisation of remedies – establishes itself not as truth and sense, but as a play of worldwide errancy.

What are the most noble products of history? Evidently, poetry and art.

VII

The World of Poetry and Art

When speaking of art, we – all of us, *producers* and *consumers* of art – think of poetry and prose (what we call literature), of theatre, of music and dance, of painting, of sculpture and architecture, and finally of the graphing of movement, that is to say, of cinematography. All these forms and works of art possess a 'common' focus, and specific problematics, although surrounded, can be multiply interpreted, emerge – creations (artificial and artistic) – through poetic saying and doing, constitute a world in the World, namely a mode of being of the totality, and constitutively form at the same time the world. What however is their 'unitary' root, and what is art?

All the particular configurations of poetry and art imply a specific and quasi-autonomous problematic.

Poetically and artistically, the *how* is at least as important as the *what*.

This history of the distinction, of the unity or the identity between *form* and *content* is troubling, since they are neither identical nor different.

As long as the original bonds which unite *physis* (nature) and *techné* (art-and-technique) remain completely hidden, we will only speak and write intelligent or stupid things about poetry and art.

A word already pronounced says: 'Art and technique are much weaker than necessity.'

The work – mobile – creates and makes its listeners, spectators, readers, destroyers, and is created and made by them. Because works of art are *also* made by the waves and vogues, the currents and counter-currents, simultaneous and successive, of listeners, spectators, readers, in short, of consumers.

We make the question concerning art – a question that nonetheless concerns us – easy by following art into its history, from prehistoric times up to now, by grasping also the becoming of every art historically, and by going so far as to envisage the fabrication of a museum of future art. Thus the reign of art history is constituted, a history unfolding itself in the four-dimensional space-time continuum that we strive to explore through archaeology, philology, in short, the history of art as science and technique. Caves, temples, palaces, churches, castles – all fitted out – and especially museums and exhibition halls become the 'places' of domesticated and catalogued art, which are visited and studied by tourists and amateurs, investigators and researchers. The history of art does not seem to be able to think the being-in-becoming of *art*.

How do art and poetry fertilise and stylise the art of living?

Can one sacrifice life to art, or inversely? Can one pose the problem in these terms, as if there were life without art and art without life? Nonetheless, in the conflagration of a museum the question could pose itself: save the most precious canvas or a meowing cat? Caught in the intertwined play of 'natural' and 'artificial' motivations and acquisitions, turns and detours of unicity and multiplicity, productivity and reproducibility.

It is the history of art that assigns an object its place and its role in the universe of art. But the history of art is not eternal: its place and role are waiting to be circumscribed.

Realising that art is created by artists, we want to put our finger on the wound of art creators, we seek the links that unite artists to their works and these two powers to our own 'states of mood'. We indulge to our hearts' content in the psychology of art, feverishly dig through the biography of great artists, dissect their passions. Intrigued by the secret links which connect genius and madness, we push our insatiable scientific curiosity and our psychological hunger as 'far' as the extreme limits, and become promoters of the psychopathology of art. A good number of great artists, after having lived a troubled and troubling, anguished and anguishing life, not conforming to norms and forms, finally found the supreme protection in suicide or madness. Informed by all this and not wanting to let anything escape, we equally turn to the works of the insane, since they can also be artistic.

It is principally the art of artists that interests us and not their lives. And, in any case, we do not know how to read in the play of the discordant accord that gives rhythm to both art and life. This happened in the nineteenth century, this undeciphered century which we have great difficulty leaving (perhaps because it is still not sufficiently mondialised, all that it prefigured still not accomplished). Turner was not a very great painter. How strange are the value judgements of the stock market, the school notes which distributed and redistributed the grades to the very good, the good, the average and the bad students. Turner, however, an English painter of the nineteenth century, at the height of his glory, died, under a false name, in an attic, where he went at irregular intervals, in ragged clothes, to meet with a woman who was neither young nor beautiful, to whom he gave just enough not to die of hunger and who, not knowing about her strange and intermittent companion, was deeply grateful for what this provincial petty bourgeois, called from time to time to London for his business, did for her.

Having filled our bloodless curiosity for the individual – the artist – we equally turn towards the social side; knowing that society is the terrain of life and human works, we then apply ourselves to build the sociology of art, as if art were only the embellishment – or the aesthetic expression – of that which happens somewhere else in society. The politicisation of our epoch makes us particularly apt to open our eyes to the 'social side' of art, perhaps because we no longer experience the *world* of a work of art.

What does it signify now, to contemplate a mutilated statue torn from its world? Where then does the being or the truth of the statue reside? To whom does this already broken statue unveil itself? To the estimating gaze of the archaeologist, to the amazed eyes of the tourist, to the comprehensive vision of the art lover, or to the children who play hide-and-seek around it?

It is not only we who judge the works; they judge us too.

Apparently nothing obliges or hinders the poet or the artist from being serenely integrated into the world or being a rebel. Bach and Rimbaud, for example, illustrate these two paths.

Poetry and art are destined to become more and more frustrating, even and especially for those who participate as collaborating producers or consumers.

Society consumes words and images in which it does not believe, and which are diverted from their original function (in what did it reside?).

Can the scientific and technical history of the (historicised) becoming of art, powerfully seconded by archaeology and philology, psychology and psychopathology, sociology and politics, not solve the enigma, even by conjugating their efforts? Let us therefore resort to the supreme remedy, to the all-powerful, global and synthetic, formal and material *aesthetic*, that is to say, to the general theory of art, the philosophy of art, from which neither rhythms, nor styles, nor worlds, nor forms, nor contents can escape. For those who denounce the historical, psychological and sociological approach, as well as all their possible combinations, furiously launch into formal exegesis and metaphysical discourses on forms and what they express, thus imagining themselves as bringing to language what a work of art says and hides.

Literary and artistic criticism, entangled in questions of taste and language, form and message – more than vacillating and generalised, fundamentally anachronistic and superficially futuristic – greatly needs to be reinvented. Neither the romanticism of the past, nor the actualism or the cynicism of the present, nor the romanticism or the technicism of the future can animate it any more. It does not know of what it speaks and what it says.

Our attitude regarding art presupposes that the latter is no longer under the sign of the sacred, is no longer in a world of celebration; cut off from its roots, without earth and without sky, it remains snatched from its world. All making becomes business: business of historical science and archaeological technique, aesthetic analysis and stylistic knowledge; business of sensations, impressions, emotions and perceptions; business of taste or social and political business; business of reflection and criticism; cultural, commercial and touristic business.

Without any doubt, a profound sense remains hidden behind all these conquering and organising activities; yet this sense still escapes us, and it is extremely difficult to see in what it constitutes the (let's say negative) aspect of a mode of (let's say positive) access to what is not easily shown. And erratic and worldwide art, thus planetary, by fulfilling its functional function, follows its path, today too, but not like yesterday.

Can one rediscover the sense of the fête? Can one reinvent it? Can one not imagine a fête or dream innocently of it, but see it in foreseeing it? Can *we* grasp the stridence of its absence? A fête that unfolds itself in nature and implicates the sacred and the word, a fête transforming festive humans into protagonists of its theatre, letting the sounds of music be heard, matching the movement to dance. Can the poetry of such a fête unite, on a place and for a moment, the here and the elsewhere, the past, the present and the future, the native and the foreigner, the settled and the erratic? The fête signifies that the encounter is possible somewhere and for some time. Little children, adults and the elderly, the wise and the crazy are surely at the fête, when there are acrobatics, prestidigitation (with destiny), divination. When men and women confront each other in the combat of festivity, when the play becomes sacred – mortally sad and ecstatically joyous – when mortals get a bit and for a bit out of their habit, sad habit. Then the fête makes be the unity of totality, and human beings unite to break bread and drink wine. Under a starry sky or under a burning sun, in the midst of the storm or in the mist, among the trees or on the banks of the fluid element of the universe, the spontaneous can lend a hand to the most elevated, and the people can populate a place supporting guiding and guided guides. (Sad are the individual feasts, ecclesiastical fêtes, pilgrimages and litanies, secular and bureaucratic festivals.) May the spectators drown in this spectacle that suppresses itself as such, so that all participate in everything, that the human totality corresponds to the totality of being – on the summits or in the valleys – that the fragments of the world be striking and luminous – in the body of the day or at the heart of the night – that the masks be torn off, since the persona itself is the mask of the fragment of the being of the totality that is the human. North and South, East and West, water, earth, air, fire, plants and animals, the advanced and the backward, the immortal mortals and the ecstatic humans, sounds and colours, words and songs, whose rhythm divides the silence, the brutal gestures and the mute actions, the awaited love and the present death – these are the guests of such a fête. But what will technique – master of the house – say to that? And what will add its servant, or its master, abstraction?

The world no longer fetes humans and humans no longer fete the world. *Humans* begin to comprehend it. And the *world*? The fête thus does not cry over its defeat. The fêtes of the past appear to us – because they do not appear to us anymore – as too particular and local (even if they were 'universal'), and our own globality, having turned its back on both the tragic fête and the comic fête, as well as on the passion of the fête and on the fête of passion, can no longer support what, in its active errancy, it considers as surpassed if not erroneous truths. Is it not a matter of constructing the future?

The network of reason and the virus of virtue seize all so-called cosmic ful-guration and technically organise festivities and festivals. The being of the world shines forth from now on in the artificial glitter of scaffolded being and busy mundanity. Since the bourgeois revolution and its socialist prolon-gations, an unlimited positivism does not cease to occupy the whole scene. Robespierre had established the cult of the supreme being and intended to install the reign of virtue. Comte wanted himself high priest of being and the religion of humanity. The world of being becomes a world of representation and anticipation, of the will to power and planning. It's up to us to push this process to its final consequences. So the fête has been excised from the world. Was it a useless branch? The fête however – in its infinite veiled sad-ness – had suspected it for a very long time: it knew that it implied the secret of its disappearance; it foresaw its inescapable destiny.

Is possibility always that which withdraws from all apprehension, even if one of its faces would be realised? It is the becoming of negativity, the play of time. The world launches itself, with a lot of boredom, into the search for constant passing novelty, itself caught in the gears of permanent surpass-ing. All is fleeting, all solidifies and freezes, flexes and reflects. Expansion and amplitude seem to hate concentration and depth. It will be up to the human to experience the hardness of its destiny in a terrible sobriety and far from the lustre of fêtes, in a world without a visible destiny and devoid of feasts. Humans will have to let themselves be grasped in a new manner through the link uniting proximity and distance; for the old fêtes disguised the nearby worlds and the distant worlds, marked the times and masked the play. (Perhaps some party-poopers will succeed in stirring up the anxiety and the indifference that will inhabit the hearts and guts of the fragile fabricators of a world strangely submitted to productivity and sphericity.)

The fête was that momentary play of the dilapidation of energies and riches, of unproductive consumption of accumulated goods, that safety valve, that periodical authorised explosion, that rule disguised as misrule.

Before and after the poetry and the fête, the recall to order reigns. Of what is this order then made?

The space and time of poetry and art are no longer *strong*, namely myth-ical. However, they remain outside daily space and time, although mixed and grappling with an everydayness lived somnambulantly, and become a problem.

At the end of the count and in the penultimate analysis, what to do with this conflict between the trivial and prosaic everyday and the aspiration to the exceptional and poetic fête?

In and under every landscape spreads a deep, dark underground current which participates in the cosmic and is impregnated by the historical; it remains implicit and expresses itself not explicitly through those whom it carries and who are also its carriers. Magical and mythical elements, a certain original religiosity, poeticity, words and gestures can sometimes let emerge the living presence of this current – dead among the living, living among the dead – however without accessing light and mediation. Fêtes and manifestations, the cycles of the seasons and life, plays, songs and gestures constitute relics very difficult to feel and analyse. Distant and fleeting, vivifying absences, it withdraws from immediate apprehension. It disappears from the eyes and the glasses of the narrowly rationalistic analysis, without being able to be envisaged from another angle – just as unilateral – where one would see eternal souls, in eternal landscapes, appearing from time to time in eternal art.

Is black stronger than white? What happens to grey?

Poetry and art work with full times, that is to say, eliminate or transmute dead times.

It still remains for us to decipher the depth of superficiality, the secret of baseness, the attraction of banality, the enigma of lightness, the romance of stupidity. For we still do not know the hidden spring of avidity for the void, the utility of futility, the ageing of novelty.

What did Aristotle the Stagirite, a scientific and serious philosopher and in no way a fantastical and delirious boy, mean by writing in the *Poetics* those lines that one can read and try to comprehend by taking the trouble: 'Poetry is closer to wisdom and more important than historical investigation, because poetry speaks rather of the total, while history is treating the particular.' Should not these words be meditated by those who do not renounce poetic thought, that is to say active and creative, while refusing to see in the *poeticity* of poetry a simple form of the superstructure or a free and literary activity? Could not poetry be the ally of thought in the combat where language is engaged beyond the death of the work of art?

The poetical passes like a meteor, a hurricane, a comet, which does not stop it from being a builder.

Thought and poetry do not simply express their epoch; they are precursors; it is as precursors that they are great: true and errant.

If one looks into the *Notebooks* of Leonardo da Vinci, if one looks into the *Letters* of Van Gogh, one will perhaps then understand the openness of an artist who thinks. The first, the conqueror, writes: 'Nothingness has no milieu and its borders are nothingness ... Among the great things that are to be found among us, the being of non-being is the greatest.' And the second, hit by the thunderbolt: 'One will end up having enough of cynicism, scepticism, joking, and one will want to live more musically. How will that be and what will one find? It would be interesting to be able to predict it, but it is even better to foresee this instead of seeing in the future absolutely nothing but catastrophes, which will not fail to fall like so many terrible flashes on the modern world and civilisation through a revolution or a war or a bankruptcy of worm-eaten states.'

The thought of metaphysical philosophy launched at the start of the game against the poetic and pictorial games that were in its eyes only imitations of imitation: the sensible being a copy of the model of the idea, poetry and painting are copies of copies.

It is to the prose and poetry of the game of the world that the poetic and prosaic activities of humans respond in their temptation to provoke a poeticity and a flat text that interfere and correspond with one another.

Poets announce things that will not happen as they have been stated.

Would art also be a wish for what does not exist?

Poetry and art plunge us into a sort of *wakeful* torpor.

The art of words and that of poetry push us to the threshold at which language becomes song and silence.

Rhythm, harmony and alternation, repetition, refrain and cadence punctuate speech and silence of poetry and art in their movement.

The novelistic [*romanesque*] is strongly bookish: it operates an identification between novel and life; from the novelistic – which comes from the Roman, Latin, Romance language – the romantic proceeds: it operates an identification between poetry and life. But what is the source of the novelistic and the romantic?

Certain games of poetic aspect develop the mechanics of the fantastic, the marvellous and the symbolic – for example, the surrealist games – in a world of quasi-autonomous play cut from the play of life.

Very often, moreover, art and poetry set in motion only a cerebral – logical – and psychological mechanics of the imaginary.

Too often humans live 'aesthetically' what they do not experience 'existentially'.

It would be – and within the measure of the realisable possible – about trying to live artistly rather than artistically.

As the familiar phrase recognises: people, in trying to live their lives, are making cinema. The play of the total scenario precedes any particular scene.

To describe in all its tonalities and in its totality an entire day would be equivalent to seeing and speaking, hearing and saying, experiencing and thinking, a haughty although altered sequence from the film of life.

The cinema realises, as it can, the Platonic metaphysics of ideas and idols, in modern caves.

The theatre is only a condensed and stylised expression of the theatricality of life.

Every scene fixed and frozen in a theatrical setting appears so 'really unreal'.

The world envisaged as a theatre, where everyone plays a role, is the fact of the play of the theatre, which itself comprehends a theatre in its play.

Repetition takes place before the play of the piece and then repeats the piece played.

Too bad if different roles contradict each other and don't attain their ideal imago.

Tragic illusion and comic illusion correspond and are part of a certain basic theatricality.

To play comedy signifies always and again that one plays more? less?

In the small, the middling and the great theatre of the shadows neither the lights nor the shadows are radicalised 'sufficiently'.

The theatre finds itself sent back to its limit that it cannot exceed: it remains a play of presence-representation.

Theatricality and theatre put us into question, even when they do so in a theatrical manner.

Poetic and artistic theatricality brings the confusion and the chiaroscuro of life to a certain stylised clarity.

Are the arts becoming more transparent by installing the theatre in theatre, the painting in painting, the cinema in cinema and so on?

Art and life are a fabric of lyric, comic, tragic illusions. How would the real murder of an actor onstage be taken?

Great among the greatest modern authors are those who knew how to integrate and surpass tragedy and comedy, the psychological and the social: Shakespeare and Dostoevsky.

Dance being the art of movement, would music be the art of silence? By letting it speak and erupt?

During the time of his madness, Hölderlin played a harpsichord without strings.

Architectural art and technique inscribe themselves into the heart of the city, sketch its body, suggest its spirit and form the world of urbanism. Building and dwelling are some of the most concrete and most abstract problems. To a programmatic exigency an effectiveness responds strongly.

Offering open structures is a good demand, but it still must be realised. How to build and where to dwell? The romantic and passé version demands horizontal constructions in flat space. The technicist and futuristic version calls for vertical constructions in the air. No coherent theory manages, however, to consider with consequence premises and consequences. We know more about how we built and dwelled, and how we still do so, but we know neither what future architecture and urbanism will be, nor how we want and wish to build and dwell. The Greek polis was inscribed in physis and constructed, around the acropolises, cities for the citizens, free men (Rome confused the play). The Christian cities built residences for humans around cathedrals and castles. The modern, bourgeois and European era gave birth to cities favouring trade and family life. All this was still to the measure of man. The planetary epoch sees the emergence of the metropolis-necropolis, while waiting for the cosmopolis. The city and urbanism also surpassed humanism in their own manner. Machines and techniques are put in charge to facilitate habitation, complicating the problem to the extreme. This type of city continues to flourish and decay. Until when? What will come next? Where will the decisions fall? And in which direction? With what kind of building and habitation will the play of a mobile and polyvalent, combinatorial and flexible architecture end? Is a radical change in perspective foreseeable? Could we suppose that, also in this domain, evolution will not be linear and will not so much effectuate what is projected, but will experience a more or less radical change? In what knots and meshes will these – new? – arts and techniques of building and habitat be caught?

All great civilisations and cultures find their final form in an asphyxiating urban type.

The destiny of the house – to be inhabited poetically and prosaically – still remains totally unresolved.

In the twilight of our sprawling cities is profiled – undoubtedly falsely – the shadow of Alexandria.

In art, it is not about constructing but about building.

Oedipus did not see as long as he had his eyes. Destiny escaped him. Tiresias, 'because' he was blind, saw far. The dialogue between the king and the seer lets us see and hear what, ordinarily, we do not see, that to which we do not listen. Oedipus looks around him (and in him, we say) and hardly sees anything; he hears neither the voice of destiny, nor the word of Tiresias. Tiresias, whose eyes do not see, is visionary, sees and speaks; he grasps becoming, for he accords himself with destiny. It is when Oedipus saw that he gouged out his eyes, becoming, in his turn, a blind man who sees.

The modern human seems to be a being of Seeing. Since the Renaissance, this reign is deployed: reign of perspective and the third dimension, point of view and the axis of the vanishing point towards the distance. What was a conquest consolidated its positions, planned subsequent conquests, became an *eye* that wants to see all. But do we look at everything without seeing anything or do we see things without looking? The primacy of the visual transforms everything into a spectacle worthy of being seen, and this century of optics, view and point of view is astonishingly lacking in fundamental perspective and penetrating vision.

We have hardly begun to understand what the phrase signifies: it is the plastic arts that teach us to see the things of the world.

The primacy of perspective, of the third dimension, of the point of view, and of viewing is at the same time the primacy of imagination and of representation. Things become images of things; one can imagine everything, and a cloud of the imaginary begins to cover what is. Every presence transforms itself into representation (whether concrete or abstract, formal or informal, is of little importance), into representative mental activity. The visual, the imaginary, the representation release increasingly their power, capture landscapes and faces, and not only through the means of painting and cinema, penetrate the individual and historical existence of humans and peoples. What was called a tragedy of private or public life mutates into a comedy ruled by the forces of representation. All that, which is, is put to playing a role, integrated into the total spectacle – the world of the spectacle and the world as a spectacle – and every human being becomes actor and spectator, while life itself tries to imitate art.

In the unique constraint that connects and confuses the gaze and gazed-at, who has the primordial role?

Seeing and being seen generally go together.

The cry of peoples in world empires who want to establish their empire over the world is and remains: *panem et circenses*. Subsistence and satisfaction. Possession-dispossession.

Everything becomes spectacle and abolishes itself equally, at the time of the closure and the exacerbated continuation of representation.

At the threshold of the closing of the area of representation, we attend the spectacle of participation in the spectacle.

Images frame every view – everything becomes image – and at the same time they become blurry and are torn. The image of the world, the images of beings and things, tend to disappear. To the benefit of what *signs*?

All images can be inverted.

'Finally', everything loses itself in the 'infinite' play of mirrors.

One cannot traverse the mirror without breaking it; it then stops functioning as a mirror.

What kind of game is the image that no longer represents anything 'figurative'?

Channelling the powers of imagination by using imaginative force has at 'all times' been a task imposed upon the human.

The picture is not to be comprehended or executed like a window onto the world. And let's avoid making too much of literature, in life and with writing.

Modes and styles centred on the ornamental and the decorative, the overwritten and the mannered, diverse formalisms, serious or frivolous, also apply a system of conventional rules appearing as imperious, obeying the canon of permitted and tolerated things.

The genius of childhood and adolescence – poetic genius – loses itself in general in the prose of the so-called adult life, ripe for old age.

If the lava does not become stone, it cannot endure, to impose the frozen fires of hothouse games.

Art, supposed to have appeared at a certain moment of becoming, is it doomed to death? Are we effectively living the death of art? As for its *supreme destination*, has art ceased to exist?

Art was supposed to be the intuitive (and sensible) figuration of the absolute (intelligible), and to give forms, aspects, faces (εἴδη) to the form, the aspect, the face of being (the idea). As a superior form of artisanry, art imitated and created models. Calling it idealist or realist is of little importance, since it always worked with formations neither entirely sensible nor entirely intelligible. Its network unified sensation, sensibility and signification. And now? In a world without prototypes and without ideals? What will the twilight of idols generate?

The question remains open: is art for us, and regarding its *exceptional, massive* and *decisive* import, something of the past – of a surpassed world? Will it continue to stylise, condense and isolate total moments? Or do we still have art so as not to die of asphyxiation in the 'truth' of the real and technicist world? However, does not art also belong to the empire or democracy of this world? Losing its specificity, ceasing to constitute a world (even when set apart enough), will it become an integral part of life and the world?

Literature – the literary fact – is a specific mode of being – for producing and consuming – the word and the written thing.

Do art and poetry not cease to exist from the moment they become art and literature? Before this turning they *are*; after this turning, do they still *exist*?

Are poetry and art engendered by individual creators, labelled and performing a particular activity, called to disappear? Will art and poetry turn into activities of the whole, become the business of 'all', thus finding another rhythm, style and gesture? Language, decoration, functional and industrial art, architectonics, collective orders of words, sounds, colours and movements, will they be taken over by a technique producing total-partial wholes?

'Art' turns more and more to documentary and reporting and at the same time becomes strongly experimental. That is to say that its base decreases, and that it seems to be made for the critique that, it too, provokes the critique of the critical critique.

A certain intense creativity horrifies mediocrity; the latter captures it, after having neutralised it. Thus the most radical breakthroughs – poetic and artistic, and not only poetic and artistic – are assimilated and rendered harmless, enter textbooks, museums, are part of the style of everyday life, official and private, are adopted and adapted until they become the name of a street, bust of a square, postage stamp, object of scholarly studies.

The game has desacralised itself, it has lost its decisively dangerous inspiration. Free and disinterested activity, the filling of free time, the pursuit of adventures of all kinds, and the sportive search for danger are only the vulgarly visible forms of the game that rules the world, gives birth to art, and plays us sovereignly.

Before poetry and art are 'surpassed', do they have to be reached in some way by all? Probably not.

Born of nature, linked to divinity and developing itself in society, does art become an activity that affronts a (dead) nature and gods that have ceased to exist? Does art reduce itself to this activity that begins and ends at visible moments? Will the being in becoming of the totality of the world no longer reveal itself to the eyes of the creator, in the shadow and light of the lightning tearing the horizon? Will the cosmic game continue to inspire its word and its hand? Will plastic reality, as the setting into work of nature and technique, not manifest – even through an infinite distress – what was natural and what lines and colours, sounds and speech are always trying to capture? Will the drama of art not continue to pursue itself in the midst of this struggle of subjects and objects, marching towards their surpassing, the concrete and the abstract, deeply united, the figure and disfiguration, faces of the same, a struggle in which the voices of stridence and those of silence are confused? Does not the world aspire to find its expression – one should almost say: its foundation – lingual, plastic and musical in all its – and in all their – plenitude and dislocation? According to what necessity has every work and every residency of yesterday, of today – and even of tomorrow – become problematic?

The crisis of poetry and art is part of a much more global (and more than social) crisis.

Literature already shows us that there is nothing to say, *except* this nothing or the nothing, which it says. The painting opens our eyes and reveals to us that there is nothing to see, *except* ... The sculptures seek their places and their spaces, while architects feverishly construct and increasingly encumber asphyxiating cities, these cancers that are wearing 'well'. The theatre becomes anti-theatre and no longer knows which kinds of presences to represent. Art turns against itself. All the arts are irresistibly attracted by their self-destruction. Diverse gestures and writings become writings and gestures of silence.

Art was intimately linked to artisanry; it does not go without artifice.

It is manifest that art is going to technicise itself, according to the rhythm of the global technicity. At the same time, however, poetry and art rejoin their enigmatic origin – which no one can explicitly name or figure – from which they detached themselves to constitute themselves in worlds and to constitute the world; thus, poetry and art, strangely overwhelming the autonomised poem and work, tend to find their end and to surpass themselves – Hegel and Marx, Nietzsche and Heidegger glimpsed it – in that and by what one calls, in stammering, world and becoming, life and being.

Very often, when poetry, the theatre, the novel or the cinema do not know what to do with a character, they make it die.

When one speaks of art *and* life, it is as if art was not already in life from the start. And when one says that art-and-poetry is the last chance of life, one is delusional about its chances of survival.

Art and technique realise their unitary and future logos in technology.

Poetry and art solicit us to be present and elsewhere (where?).

The myth of poetry and art will be destroyed, for the benefit of what mirage?

Every art aspires to be total. All the arts would like to harmoniously compose the total art. There is, however, no integral art.

Collective art, more or less made by everyone, that is to say, by all and for all, does not exist, in any case, not yet, although artistic production is already collectivised and socialised in a certain manner.

Free art! A childish slogan.

Art is the liberator of constraints, according to what constrains it to these liberations.

All configurations of poetry and art that do not enter into an experience surpassing poetry and art remain residual forms.

Poetry and art show us what one does not live and what one does not see before they showed it to us.

Where does the border go between what is artistic – as such and/or seen as such – and what is not?

Moment and totality, poetry and art possess a certain specific autonomy, while being surrounded, encircled, penetrated by other moments and other totalities.

Poetry and art operate through transmutations that consist as much in archaeological creations as in creations of new worlds.

Art and poetry relate neither to strictly sensible and personal taste – combining sense, sensations and sentiments – nor to a rational and universal acceptance – based on commonly recognised signi-fications. Their median position, their double game, confers on them the force of roots and the power of the breakthrough towards the vast horizon.

All languages and all poetic and artistic works invite the reader, the lis-tener, the viewer to complete them, to perfect them.

It is a natural and cultural fact that within every artistic activity each participant has their own, small or grand, theory.

The circular aesthetic judgement, which circulates among us, has come to its most reduced form: I like it, I do not like it, I half like it.

The new new constantly chases the old new in this century of febrile novelties, passably antiquated.

All creations have an air of being against preceding creations to prove themselves and to prove that they put into work a production missing and unheard of until now. Without posing the problem of the new?

From a negating threshold, it seems that one could not go further – in the same direction. However, one can circumvent this threshold.

Poetry and art provoke and are provoked by a certain formative awakening, participating in both drunkenness and sobriety. How, in the future, will this awakening vivify the inevitable stylisations?

Poetry and art situate themselves in the rift and the gulf, uniting what is predicted, projected, with that which is effectuated, *per-fect*. It is also in this that they give birth to open, moving, fluid works.

Poetry and art consist in a creative questioning, in a productive shaking of the 'sense' of the world.

Poetry and art emerge in the midst of a community and seek it, a rarely organic and most often critical and problematic community.

From moving, art became motion and becomes more and more kinetic.

Authors and writers begin to note: no one can situate themselves any longer from the point of view of an omniscient narrator who sees everything from all sides, a sort of little literary god.

Little by little, an understanding of poetic and artistic language and production will more clearly emerge that will not make them an affair of expression.

The attraction of the classic – formative, durable and canonical – is persistent, although we don't know what to make of it.

The great creators did not want to make what the diverse posterities discovered in their works. Strictly speaking, they did not even want to make what they made.

One necessarily abandons what one wanted to make for the benefit of what is made.

Why, according to a conception that emerged in time, is it uninteresting to accomplish a work that comes in second place?

The poet and the artist die many times to be able to give birth to living works.

The masterworks of art and poetry are not immortal.

In museums and libraries a future life quietly dies.

Through its permutations, it is the game of the world that becomes an open work.

What should be maintained is not tradition, but remembrance. What is decisive is not the avant-garde, but the forerunner. What reveals itself as important is not progressivism, but *annunciation*. What becomes necessary is not the modern human, but the *precursor*.

Into what do poetry and art dissolve? Into being-nothingness, all-nothing, the unworldly world. What do they discover? The game of the world.

VIII

Being-Nothingness, Everything-Nothing, the Unworldly World

We live in a world of ruined concepts, used-up words, emptied conceptions of the world. We live in – and we build – agitated necropolises, we populate and mobilise deserts. All horizons seem blocked, and the very question of the *horizon* becomes enigmatic. We nevertheless continue to live and work in this world, much more solid than it seems, since it supports its shocks, digests its crises, assimilates negativities, marches towards its future. The movements which we see deployed before our eyes and in which we partici-pate drag us along their errant course. In our heroic moments, we pretend to revise everything. Before any revision, however, before any foundation of a new 'vision' of things and the world, we must manage to grasp what prevents us from seeing the conquering surge of nihilism, revising all that blocks our view. The revision of what is, that does not take into consideration the pro-cess of annihilation ceaselessly unfolding, fails its mission. We can no longer speak innocently or cunningly of things which 'are' no longer, which have entered another phase. We do it anyway. Nihilism constitutes *the* problem of the planetary world, which knows neither on what it is founded, nor where it is going. Nihilism is not an error, an aberration, a fault, an illness; it is no point of view, no theory, no psychological disposition; it does not character-ise this or that particular state of things. Nihilism *begins* to englobe all that is and is done. To speak about it, in the world of the fragmented totality, is extremely difficult. Whether one deplores or rejoices in it: it seems that only fragmentary and aphoristic systematics could dare the adventure.

We live in a world where all mystical impulses are consolidated in *Churches*, all revolutionary movements in *bureaucratic States*, all researches of thought in *sclerotic Universities*, all the adventures of human existence in an *autarchic* and *hypocritical Family*. Petrified and putrefied, Churches and States, Universities and Families continue to be the institutions that administer human lives, force them to conform, lead the renegades and the excluded to their loss. Everything seems to indicate that these are the only organising forms of faith, work, thought and love; they possess, certainly, their *raison d'être*, even when it is deeply concealed. But all these dwellings, old or brand new, are worm-eaten – from the foundations to the roof.

When all that which bears the pompous name of social *structure* and *institution*, being however something much wider and deeper, when the *forms* of all that has been and is are dislocated, disintegrated and remain eroded, when *religions* and *faiths*, *homelands* and *communities*, *states* and *parties*, *systems* and *ideologies*, *families* and *marriages* evacuate their substance, like the lobster caught in the fisherman's basket evacuates itself with the approach of the octopus, when *schools* and *institutes* construct without rest their new ruins . . . when all that is and is done finds itself stamped with the seal of unreality – without in any way becoming romantic or novelistic – and doesn't cease being caught in the gears of representation; when nothing escapes the theatricality of moralising and moral habits 'founded' on customary moral habit (and on some power even more secret), when everything succumbs to the will of positivity, in the very midst of the destruction and destructuring of the structures (the accords, today clearly discordant, having never been artificial constructions); when public services and official formalities cover up what, beneath their ashes, never stops brooding, then it only remains to continue the game – for those who cannot do otherwise, because there is nothing else to be or to do. Continuing, moving forwards: without excessive nervousness and without fatalism, continue to . . . by anticipating. And always starting again. Until the final and fatal flash – which will come much later than one thinks.

Nihilism kills religion; can the *sacred* and the *divine* survive and contribute to the surpassing of nihilism? Nihilism kills poetry and art as poetry and art; can the *word*, the *chant* and the *plasticity of phenomena* continue to manifest themselves? Nihilism kills politics; does *historical* and *formative destiny* cease to govern humans? Nihilism kills philosophy; does *thought* also lose all its chances?

Allied with technique, generating it and generated by it, nihilism makes everything an affair of production and consumption, a *technique of usury*: religious technique, literary and artistic technique, political technique, scientific and ideological technique, erotic technique. Everything is produced, everything is destined to cease to be, to be consumed. Nihilism however rests on science, thus on philosophy, namely metaphysics; and behind the metaphysics hides active thought. Active thought is consequently its first foundation, a foundation that it realises and that it leaves by developing itself, developing its own force up to its extreme consequences, up to the exhaustion of the last parcel of its truth. At least until a planetary catastrophe intervenes.

Metaphysics itself opens the way to nihilism: on one side, being itself is excluded from existents and excludes existents; on the other side, being becomes an existent to thus annihilate itself.

For nihilism does not only accomplish the destruction of metaphysics and ethics; it accomplishes them, by accomplishing at once the aim and the lack of metaphysics. All that metaphysics aimed for in the distance – always in lack, since it underestimated concrete presences – nihilism wants to render effective in a process of constant actualisation. The supersensible and invisible world finds itself reversed for the benefit of the sensible and visible world. All products and by-products of metaphysics, reason, liberty, happiness, progress, are generalised and socialised as a requirement, and emptied of all content other than the ideological and basely moralistic. All that is foundation, aim, sense, idea, is struck dead and no movement of secularisation can provoke the resurrection of the dead.

With ontology, with the distinction between being and nothingness which rivets them to each other, nihilism also explicitly begins: the distinctions between physics and metaphysics, authentic and inauthentic, and many others, play its game.

The myth of the authentic was one of the masterpieces and major traps of metaphysics that engendered nihilism.

By losing all links with the nourishing roots, nihilism wants to be radical and radicalist. It is radical in the uprooting that is its destiny. Its total reality is stateless; nihilism has no homeland, for every homeland is a *part* of the totality. The totality, abstractly universal and reduced to itself, of what can it be totality? In the name of what can it contain beings and things? In view of what must it be conquered and built?

The Cartesian *ego* of the *cogito* was surpassed and collectivised in the march of socialism. The humanism which underlies nihilism wants to consider the human as being its own root, its own foundation. Cut off from any soil and subsoil, evolving on a mechanised ground and under an empty sky, the human thus becomes a radically disoriented being. Does it aspire to its surpassing? The question of maintaining human life on the surface of the globe – a burning question today – remains an open question. Is there an essential truth in whose name we could decide?

In the democratic kingdom of nihilism, as aristocratic as it is plebeian, which, starting from the Occident, even though prefigured in the Orient, extends over the entire planet, every question asking *why*? provokes, in the generalised indifference, a double 'response': why not? And why not the inverse?

Nihilism does not only annihilate the sense of the being in becoming of the totality of the world, but, conjointly, all that is. It abolishes all distinction between face and mask, smile and grimace, landscape and scaffolding, what is natural and what is artificial. In indifference, it suppresses differences, moved by morose passions and setting them in motion.

The gloomy platitude, the greyness of mediocrity, vulgarity and banality, the reign of indifference and insignificance, the domination of the average, the pressure of the norm, the scholarly buffoonery, the impotent flight into the powers of the 'pseudo'-imaginary, the absence of all presence, are but the external signs, the thick envelope, the gross manifestations of the profound signification of annihilating nihilism.

The open totality tends more and more to reduce itself to the conquering totality of everyday life – empirical, if one wants, but abstract, monopolising, but 'non-existent'. The so-called real reality of total everyday life tends to become the horizon of the 'real' totality. What had for a long time remained in the shadows now takes its grandiose revenge. This life remains nevertheless empty. From where can we fly over it and judge it?

Nowadays, when two forces are present and struggling, it is most often the most mediocre and flattest power that prevails on the official stage, according to the order of the times.

Anyone who tries to grasp nihilism religiously or theologically, philosophically or logically, scientifically, psychologically or medically, historically or sociologically, literally or aesthetically, does not grasp it, but remains grasped by it. 'Those who are most nihilistic, and in the stupidest possible manner, are those who do not recognise it and pretend to fight it, while failing to recognise their own face in its deforming mirror.' Nihilism not only negates philosophy and logic, religion and God, nature and the human soul, history and society, poetry and art. Nihilism signifies, if it signifies anything: annihilation of the founding (and sacred?) sense, thanks to which all these powers can be and be deployed, fertilise and animate. Nihilism means: annihilation, without recourse, of *being* in becoming, of the open *totality* of what is, of the *truth* of temporal becoming. The *sense* of the total being in its becoming fades into nothingness.

One cannot want or hope to curb anything in its conquering march. Every conquering movement contains its own truth and the seeds of its surpassing and its death. Its quasi-total victory will initiate the process of its defeat. Nihilism can consequently only launch itself into a frantic race – an exhausting race. For the moment, it is only beginning to realise itself. Before being surpassed, nihilism (which comprehends us) awaits the hour of being comprehended.

It does not *seem* to be currently in the order of the disorder that the human and history are going to be totally annihilated in the nothingness that makes all kinds of being disappear. The process of nihilisation is other – which escapes us.

Reader and interlocutor: it is me and you, us and you, who are caught up in all this supreme nihilistic mechanism. This 'affair' implicates the whole world. No one should imagine themselves being outside or above this machinery, for we have not even reached the summit: we are in and rather below its dreary truth. Indifference and insignificance are such that everyone confronts 'all this' as if *this* did not concern them or did not affect them mortally. 'One' always believes that only the others are touched. When it is a question of platitude, it is however all about you: it is yours, this dull annihilation of every spark of light, the triviality of your multicoloured intelligence, the vacuity of your activism. And if you are only conscious of what is going on, you are still not doing anything. Glasses never helped blind eyes to see. Let our ears hear this word, we that are ready to grasp rationally or intuitively, with our head or with our heart, to analyse and explain with the help of our instruments and our logical and philological, psychological and psychopathological, historical and sociological, artistic and aesthetic reasoning: 'True life is absent.

We are not in the world. I go where it goes, it must be.' Do you hear, believer or layperson, monsieur or comrade, teacher or pupil, reactionary or progressive, rebel or revolutionary? We are absent from the truth and the true life has left us without having ever existed. We are not in the world and the world is not. And each person goes where they must; by crawling, even when they leave for the dominion of the earth and when they ascend to assault the sky.

So long as 'cursed' thinkers, which the century cannot easily digest, do not emerge; as long as these cursed thinkers will not start to pursue the work of a mole; as long as the immense and profound opening, which comprises the plenary manifestation of nothingness, in which all things fuse, is not seen – we will remain on this side of nihilism. Rimbaud, Dostoevsky and Nietzsche dared to see; but we threw ourselves on them like hyenas on a corpse, or made them ideological spokespersons.

All this remains strange and estranging to professorial professors, journalistic journalists and managing politicians, heroes tired – but nevertheless excited – by planetary nihilism. This is in order, since only a mediocre and average intelligence is required of them. A below-average clairvoyance would help more – them and the business of which they are the dull businessmen.

All or *nothing* is a naively totalitarian or abstractly nihilistic slogan.

Between something and nothing a difference does not always hide.

Saying without saying anything. Saying nothing. Saying the nothing. Saying something. Saying everything?

Nihilism is the cradle and the tomb of all totalitarianisms.

Nihilism exists only in relation to what it nihilates. All *this* criticises, denies, rejects, annihilates, takes place on a basis provided by what is criticised, denied, rejected, annihilated.

Can we sometimes be, do and suffer, as if nothing happened?

The architectonics of nihilism let us see all that is made as a concreting of the void.

The play of nihilism, and not only nihilism, flanks all that is with an *anti*: it opens the era of anti-language, anti-thought, anti-theory, anti-god, anti-nature, anti-hero, anti-fate, anti-poetry, anti-novel, anti-painting, etc., etc.

Is there a lucidity that kills? How can a demystified life continue to unfold? Can individual humans and historical societies exist without illusions? Would there be insupportable and untenable – because too strong – thoughts or too dangerous experiences? How to illuminate without burning everything?

The unworldly world is someone sick who is doing well.

Great is the temptation of the void. Mounting the nothingness, riding the void, is imposed as a task, intoxicating in all sobriety, makes us accomplish leaps and conquests, leads us to the threshold of an experience on which we play games where *nothing* happens, or *something* happens, in the passage from all to nothing, and from nothing to things.

Nihilism realises the prediction of Pauline preaching: there will be neither freemen nor slaves, neither man nor woman, neither Jew nor Christian.

Nihilism as such preaches neither life nor death: it annihilates the one and the other, and could teach us to live before dying, without reason, since there are no reasons that make us find life bearable or unbearable.

How the hell did nihilism enter into the becoming-thought of the world – becoming-world of thought, that is to say, at once in our individual and historical experience as well as our sensibility, at all levels, in our imagination and our representations, our hearts and our guts, our consciousness and our unconsciousness, our reflection and our thought? Through what opening and under what cover? Can we speak of it otherwise than by ellipses, of what manifests itself in its apparitions, and what it shows in eclipses? Did the ancient Orient already know it? But how did it name it and how could we say what might already be a call? What did Hinduism and Buddhism, Taoism and Zen know about its secrets? And other even more ancient intuitions?

The Presocratic and pre-philosophical sophist Gorgias, by dissociating the Parmenidean being-thought identity, declares: 'Nothing is; even if it is, it is incomprehensible for the human; . . . and even if it is comprehensible, it is nevertheless incommunicable and inexplicable to our fellows.' Protagoras had already opened the way with his overwhelming and double words, by reversing the truth into error, and, inversely, from the point of view of 'man is the measure of all things', of each human, for which all that appears and disappears from the limited and mortal human. The human of Protagoras and the *nothing* of Gorgias remain, however, enigmatic. Do they inaugurate 'humanism' and 'nihilism'? The Greek man lived in the opening of the 'indissociable' physis-logos ensemble inhabited by the gods, even when it was constituted as the negator of what encompassed it. It did not hope for anything fantastic, it did not fear anything beyond measure. On the basis of the Greeks, the question is posed: do *being* and *nothingness* exist only for us human beings, annihilating beings, annihilated beings? From the outset, the thought (*skepsis*), despite and because of the onto-theo-logical systematics that combat it, rubs against the (bordered) abyss of scepticism. Philosophy constituting itself from Plato will give up to Hegel answers to the question of the being of the world by calling it Idea, God, Nature, Human, Society, thus eluding both the problem of 'being' and the question of nothingness.

For the Judaeo-Christian conception, as everyone knows, the world is created *ex nihilo* by God. Being is drawn from nothingness. For Augustine, the world, though created by God, the eternal spirit, is, too, unworldly because of the time of sin. For Thomas Aquinas, what is created, the totality of beings, remains open and closed: open, because created by God, closed, because it emerged from nothingness. *Creation* is thus equivocal: being and nothingness affect it. The dualism of Platonic origin is further deepened: suprasensible being is separated from the nihilating sensible despite all the participations. The human finds itself quite 'annulled', and although God has become man for man to become God, the double reality – suprasensible, divine, spiritual, eternal *and* sensible, natural, material, temporal – marches towards nullification with faith, hope and certainty to future salvation. The true *summum ens*, God – and all that he sets in motion – is both true and absurd. Thus, when the supramundane reality of God withdraws, the mundane reality of the created will also withdraw. There will be neither being nor nothing. Everything will deploy itself in this intermediate realm of equivocation, ambivalence, ambiguity, duplicity, complicity. Christianity realises Judaism and prolongs Platonism and Aristotelianism. (Platonist) Augustinianism and (Aristotelian) Thomism, nominalism and realism lead to so-called secular modernity that cannot unlink from Christianity and completes it. Nothing is true, and everything equally is. Behold the terrain of nihilism. No mundanity could be established after the withdrawal of divinity. There is no more salvation. Certitude and doubt send the one back to the other. The human becomes lonely, isolated. *Persona est ultima solitudo*, Duns Scotus had already said. Everything now happens, *as if* subjectivity was the *last* word. The person, the me, the own, the self, will find itself mortally linked to private property, exploitation, subjugation, dereliction, atomisation.

For Descartes, only (?) the subject, the *ego*, the *res cogitans*, is the measure of Being. Veracity is however guaranteed by God. But the nothing derives from the *res*. Through the accusative. The *ego* exists, because it thinks: it thinks itself and thinks all that is, namely, what it is and what it is not. The human subject thus remains in emptiness. The human becomes more and more lonely, as an individual and as a mass. Doubt takes hold of everything, to the extent that truth becomes the certainty of subjectivity grasping objectivity. With truth posited as the contrary of error, one recoils with fear from both truth and error. Heirs to Christianity, with its negation of error and its negation of thoughtful search in the name of certainty-faith, the moderns want to seat the subject and its existence on the worm-eaten throne of thought – or experience. Is subjectivity – and its socialisation – the last word? To be or not to be? This is the ontological and anthropological question which poses itself to modernity, in making it cling to existence, advancing backwards and fleeing forwards. The human being can no longer comprehend itself as englobed by the One-All, Physis-Logos, or by God; it can no longer comprehend itself as a divine creature or a being-there; it seeks to be founder and imperialist and becomes vacillating and problematic. It wants to fly, but crawls more often than walks. It seeks a foundation, incapable of giving it up or surpassing it. The world sometimes appears to it like a rigged game, a trap; but it launches into the adventure aiming at technical domination: mastery over – and possession of – nature (itself already dead before the gods and God died). The subject 'possessing' only its own being as a foundation – grasped by its self-consciousness – loses all foundation and loses itself. It is broken by its own freedom, which assails it and from which it recoils, having over-dimensionalised it.

It is in the horizon of German idealism and romanticism of the eighteenth and nineteenth centuries that the problem of nihilism emerges, passing next through the intermediary of the Left Hegelians, into Russia – in the nineteenth century – before being formulated by Nietzsche at the end of the nineteenth century.

With Kant, the transcendental ego becomes the foundation of all that is, truth and error existing only in judgement, that is to say, in the relation of the object to the understanding of the subject, this relation remaining all the same without any other foundation than the idealist. The accord between being and knowing – the world and the human – remains problematic and not elucidated. By examining *the amphibology of the concepts of reflection*, in the *Critique of Pure Reason*, Kant gives us a brief, schematic and fourfold definition of nothing: 1. The nothing is an 'empty concept without object' (*ens rationis*), which, like noumena, does not refer to experience; it is a *Gedankending*, it does not imply any possibility. 2. The nothing is an 'object empty of a concept' (*nihil privativum*), it manifests the lack of an object, like shadow, cold. 3. The nothing is an 'empty intuition without object' (*ens imaginarium*), as, for example, pure space and pure time, which are *something*, forms, but not objects. 4. The nothing is an 'empty object without concept' (*nihil negativum*); the object of a concept, which contradicts itself, is nothing, because the concept is nothing; it is an *Unding*, it contradicts possibility. Nothings 1 and 4 are empty concepts; 2 and 3 are empty data. Negation, without a reality corresponding to it, is not an object for a subject. Here, in Kant's grandiose onto-*logical* system – an ingenious, speculatively schizophrenic construction between paranoia and catatonia – is the place, or rather the non-place, assigned to nothing. But perhaps it is the mad who see everything mad – or too orderly.

Fichte, the post-Kantian, published in 1794 his *Theory of Science*. He puts the self face to face with the non-self and contributes to opening the field to modern nihilism. F. H. Jacobi often speaks of nothing in 1781 and 1792, and in his letter to Fichte, in 1799, he criticises idealism as nihilism.

The nihilist theme also appears in romantic writers. Tieck, in *William Lovell* (1794), writes: 'Beings are because we thought them' and his hero passes from idealism to amoralism. Jean Paul, in his *Vorschule der Aesthetik* (1804), criticises the 'poetic nihilism' of Fichtean inspiration where the self 'annihilates the world and the universe only to empty a play space for nothingness'. This expedition against the nihilist game targets Novalis, supposed to have privileged self-knowledge at the expense of the knowledge of the world. Individualism, nihilism and play end up in nothingness, because they are founded on nothing, according to the criticism of those who are fascinated by what they criticise – whether they recognise it or not.

It is in the novel of an unknown author, *The Nightwatches of Bonaventura* (1805), where nihilism shows itself clearly enough. 'The human is worthless, that is why I am crossing it off', 'Everything is nothing', we can read.

Are romantic humours and humour, irony, detachment and nihilism intimately linked? Is nihilism also something like a disappointed idealism?

With Hegel appears the elaboration and 'surpassing' of the unhappy
consciousness which recognises 'the death of the divine man' and which
suffers from the fact that 'God himself is dead'. *The Phenomenology of Spirit*
(1807) criticises this consciousness sunken into the depths of the night
of the self = self which neither distinguishes nor knows anything beyond
itself. Hegel denounces the spirit of the general confusion of the reversed
world as well as the cultural-spiritual attitude, and, by fluidifying concepts, through the suppression of abstract being and nothingness, both in
becoming and in recovering all in mediated reconciliation, he closes a very
large – Graeco-Christian – chapter, although leaving the door wide open.
He introduces the historicism which will succeed him and which will strike
out the spirit.

The three great anti-Hegelians, Kierkegaard, Marx, Nietzsche, will go to
war against total spirit and absolute knowledge – by nihilating them.
    Kierkegaard speaks and lives an 'ironic life'. It is a romantic and aesthetic
experience of isolated existence. Irony suppresses everything, it is a nothingness, something infinite, negative, ungraspable. Irony is the negative liberty
of anxious and fearful subjectivity. It is a kind of conscious madness. In
opposition to it and to the temptation of the seducer, the individual as existence can pass from the aesthetic and ethical stage to the religious stage – to
God. But always as individual and paradoxical existence.
    Marx demands and advocates a suppression, a chain- and mass-nihilation
of all the alienations which annihilate the human: the production of life as
done until now, private property and the division of labour, separate economic life, the difference between manual labour and intellectual labour,
between town and country; he demands and advocates the suppression of
classes, state and politics, traditional sexuality and family, religion, art, philosophy and ideology. Is there nothing left? There remains the reprise, the
repetition, since 'the suppression of self-alienation follows the same path as
self-alienation', as it is written in *Political Economy and Philosophy*. Does not
the surpassing risk ending up at the same nothingness?
    Russian nihilism is affiliated with Left Hegelianism. Turgenev, in his
novel *Fathers and Sons* (1862), lets the young physician Basarov, nat-
uralist, scientist and atheist, speak. He popularises the term 'nihilism'
that Nietzsche will take up again. This nihilism denies all traditional
and hierarchical values. There was also the nihilist movement of Russian

revolutionaries. Depending on the case, the word was given a positive or negative sense. Dostoevsky treats the nihilists with a strange, superior humour in *The Possessed*. If God does not exist, all is permitted – this is the lesson of *The Grand Inquisitor* in *The Brothers Karamazov* – and this all leads to nothing.

It is only with Nietzsche that nihilism begins to show its face and its masks. For him, the term is and remains ambiguous, two-way, polyvalent, amphibological and brutal at once. Nihilism is the devaluation, the idealistic nihilation operated by the will to power, as the will of the negation of life, in the name of superior values, as well as the devaluation, the nihilation operated by the same will to power, of superior values themselves. If life thus finds itself devoid of sense and aim, the will to power must set it back in motion. The will to power can deny both life and values; it must deploy itself as such, although it is also 'nothing'. The will of nothingness and the nothingness of will curiously combine. Being 'is' and becomes becoming, it equals non-being, and one rather wants the nothing than the absence of the will. Nihilism is inherent in human history from the beginning; it culminates in a certain Hinduism, in Buddhism and in a certain Taoism, in Greek idealism, Judaism, Christianity, free thought, democracy, socialism. It leads to the reign of the last humans. More than a pathological state, it is the normal state of humanity and becomes more and more so. As nihilism of weakness, it can also be nihilism of strength; incomplete, it can become complete and 'achieve' itself. It grasps the devaluation of all values; pessimism prefigures it.

Nihilism signifies: exhaustion of the senses and sense, absence of an answer to the question: why? Everything empties itself: vital impulses as well as ideas and ideals of metaphysics, of religion, of morality. Everything is missed and masked, seen through perspectives; all is duplicated and seen in broken mirrors. Everything becomes false. Truth is only a form of error. The will to truth seems to be a weapon of humanity, which turns against it. God is dead, and the human subject is only a fiction, a plurality. Humans aspire to the domination of the earth, but the last human has not yet succeeded the human who wants to perish to prepare the post-human figure, rising and declining, of the 'overhuman'. This would accept the eternal return of the same, the innocence of becoming and experiencing in its praxis the world as play. For the moment, we live in intermediate times, not yet delivered from the spirit of revenge that wants to stop time and make it turn backwards, through which we fail its rotation. Thus spoke Nietzsche.

It is with the two faces of the same complex – bourgeois idealism-romanticism-individualism-revolution,   and   socialist   materialism-positivism-collectivism-revolution – as well as with the theoretical and practical actions and reactions that they provoked (Anglo-Saxon logical positivism, fascism and National Socialism included) that nihilism profiles itself. Nihilism, tradition and revolution join hands and fight each other. European nihilism tends to become planetary. But the hour for the encounter of occidental and worldwide nihilism with oriental and Asian (Buddhist and Zen) nihilism has not yet sounded. Planetary nihilism remains incomplete and unachieved.

The ego, the I, the self, the subject, the individual, the collectivity or the society of individuals, posed as the fundamental position, wish to annihilate all that is opposed, and equally annihilate themselves. For the moment, we are at a turning point. Making of all that is and becomes, and of ourselves, an experiment and an experimentation, where are we going? *Ist nicht letzten Endes der tiefste Grund jedes Seienden zugrunde zu gehen?* [Is not the ultimate reason for every being to perish?]

We must first call nihilism what names itself thus. Then, and even more originally, one must grasp as nihilism all that deploys itself as such.

Is nihilism fundamentally a phenomenon of consciousness? The nihilist consciousness does not however see the existing difference between the nothingness that nihilates and makes everything negation, nothingness linked to being, and the nothing that is nothing. Negation derives from the productive nothingness; it does not found nothingness.

Is it useful to say that all the persons, all the thinkers, poets and writers, all the social forces, all the historical movements that appeal to nihilism or appeal against it, are only signs?

Nihilism says the death of physis: 'The great Pan is dead' (Pascal). It says the death of God (Nietzsche). It says the end of the Human (Rimbaud, Nietzsche). Nihilism says the death of the central Greek intuition (physis-logos), Christian (god-human), modern (human-subject). It says the death of cosmology, theology, anthropology.

The subject erupts. Does it march towards its destruction? Its dissolution? Another solution? The logos, the violence of the Occident, trembles lightly on its bases. Motor – almost – of human history, nihilism deepens further with metaphysics. Dualism is the river bed. Idealism and romanticism and anti-metaphysics carry it with them. The most discernible figureheads are pushed towards the untenable, search for a way out in suicide or madness (Kleist, Hölderlin, Nietzsche, Van Gogh) or abandonment in flight (Rimbaud). Others double their flat life through the search for sensations and consume literature that commits to nothing. The 'true absent life' becomes book and commentaries, and clutters the libraries. Opponents and deviants constitute diverse folklores. Advanced industrial society, by entering the phase of opulence, although the majority of the inhabitants of the planet have not yet left pre-industrial scarcity, captures everything, bears contestation and revolt and should soon subsidise and organise them according to a plan. The global society of producer-consumers produces, reproduces, consumes and consummates everything, as if it were nothing. It articulates itself from the family, through the diverse institutions of civil society, to the state, tomorrow worldwide. It englobes everything. The Christian-bourgeois-socialist lifestyle does not yet seem to be shaken by a crisis. No different ethics, no other lifestyle, manifests itself. Sometimes, however, certain suspicions traverse us.

Everyone seeks to satisfy their needs, to enjoy, to be recognised (recognition is always a bit sour), to be free – without knowing why. But the satisfaction of inextinguishable desires is intimately linked to halting and death, to the return to a previous state. Hegel and Freud showed this. Death escapes the struggle for recognition or, rather, takes hold of it. The finitude of the human being 'and' the finitude of Being are not recognised. All sense is lacking, and one searches for what could make sense. From the moment where sense becomes something attributable, it has already left us. So we live, love and die halfway, in this interregnum of ambiguity and ambivalence, where all sense, although absent, is double, triple and sparkling.

The civilisation of emptiness, of nothingness, as it is even called journalistically, is in full swing and wants to fill the void, more human, terrestrial and stellar than celestial. Filling and using up all that is and is done, based on profit, and in search for a vague alterity, are going well. Radical and totalitarian democracy levels all and flattens it in growing indifference. All comprehends itself, is comprehended, integrated, taken over, flattened. Indifference nevertheless hides its play, behind which there is 'nothing'.

Nihilism nihilates Being, makes being become nothing. Nihilism nihilates Nothingness (because it leaves the *nihil* unthought), makes nothingness nothing. Nothingising both being and nothingness, nihilism nihilates itself. Nihilism nihilates us. We nihilate it. It nihilates itself. More than surpassing it – as pious vows and fashionable slogans demand – it is about seeing how it is defeated not by us or by something else, but by itself. Nihilism nihilates everything and annihilates itself. *Behold a new discovery.* To make what appear? Being-nothingness, the circle of becoming, the everything-nothing, in its post-natural, post-divine, post-human play? Nihilism also annihilates in a way all that preceded it, and all that will follow it. Nothing is, everything is, nothing is true, nothing is false, henceforth, since and for a long time, if not since and forever.

Perhaps there is no more *there is*, and *there is not.* Would there be no more being, nor non-being?

Even if nothing happens, be attentive to the nothing that happens, in happening.

The play of errancy pursues itself, strongly structured and reasonably destructured. We live by nihilating both truth and error. Nothing is no longer and is no longer real and true, at the same time that nothing extinguishes itself, everything being 'real' and 'true'. Being equal to nothingness remains the fundamental equation of nihilism, itself annihilated. Time, errancy, play, aim at a transgression of nihilism, an accepting transgression. Could the human coexist with nihilism, by transmuting it and mutating itself? Into what?

In any case, don't panic. Nature (dead) lets itself be explored, exploited and visited, by science, technique, industry, tourism and naturism taking charge of it. God (dead) restores himself and is taken over by ecumenism, churches and parallel mystics. The subject (broken) progresses, socialises itself, and we remedy its psycho-somatic, historical-social and ideological-cultural sufferings with all sorts of remedies. The ridiculous does not kill. It is part of life. The finitude of the being of the world and of the human being – who have a unique and common centre – continues to unfold. The living-dead are waiting for the rising of a new star. The rotary motion pursues itself. How does it continue to unfold? Through us humans or through what follows its course? Towards where? For what?

That whatever happens rather than nothing, that dangers and risks are annihilating and annihilated, is one of the tonalities of nihilism – a movement of general protest and generalised acceptance.

The almost total – because there is not and cannot be a totally total – refusal of the existing and dominant world, the dominant mode of being of the world, the annihilating refusal of all the mechanisms, organisms and organisations of integration into the existing world, remains full of inconsequence and incoherence, proves capable of containing the seeds of a creative negativity, to reach a coherence in the theoretical critique and the formulation of practical propositions (an elaborate contestation), returns to the play of an existing and dominant world.

The question itself and what it announces can only be annihilated. So nihilate these cantilevered words about a certain lifestyle, in search of a perhaps invisible star. Annihilate them! That is to say, criticise them, discuss them right and wrong.

All nihilism – like all movement – is inconsequential. Even if it goes as far as to the suppression of life, it shows that it has not gone beyond illusions and disillusions, hope and hopelessness, it clings to life and/or at death, demystifies some of the terms in the name or under the pressure of the other, unable to live and accept life-and-death, in playing this vivifying and dying play.

Nihilism annihilates both answers and questions. Does it overcome even *the* difference?

All nihilism is necessarily incomplete: it leaves its own basis and something of the other almost intact.

As for that which concerns the links between nihilism, neutrality, nullity and indifference, we are still too candid.

The death of grand ideals and grand encompassings can infuse a final and new vigour to what remains – indifference.

Through the nothingness of nihilism the world does not cease to unfold itself.

After one or more things have reached zero point or degree, what happens? How do they restart and start over?

We all want to go further. But where to *go*? Having gone far, do we need to go backwards or can we go beyond?

The play of being-nothingness, everything-nothing, the world-unworld, teaches us that becoming is also a return and that in the course of the play of our itinerancy we go, productively and destructively, from reiteration to reiteration.

Since nihilism nihilates both the question and the answers, 'the' question was, is and will be without 'actuality'. Nihilism only makes it more inactual. The question is even crossed out. So that it will arise again, in a 'different' way? Let us contribute to this working approach. Being and nothingness are and are not identical and/or different. Each is the face and the mask of the other. It is bizarre, though, to talk about it so brutally. All that is emerges from being-nothingness and runs aground there, without this being-nothingness being a foundation. There neither exists nor does not exist being and nothingness. The being in becoming of the totality of the world is *the* question that nullifies the 'rest' and that the rest nullifies differentially and with indifference. The opening of being-nothingness, everything-nothing, world-unworld, 'is' that of errant time, errancy not being the reverse of truth. The work-play of the thinker is blessed and cursed. May they be condemned more, for 'some time', through the curse cast upon them, so that blessed bittersweet fruits may appear. It is in this that the work of planetary thought consists, thought more rigorously – historically and systematically – than it seems, a ventilated and flexible thinking.

Nihilism can also open us to the suppression of suppression that is not necessarily a synthesis.

It is not only nor principally that which flashes up in broad daylight that forces recognition, jumps into the eyes. It is not only, nor decisively, that which imposes itself on vision and life that reigns masterfully, seems invincible. Established religions, installed deities, wealthy though worm-eaten States, aesthetic, ideological and familial systems gaining membership, are not the only or the supreme reality. For centuries, thought has prostrated itself before what triumphs. What succeeds and wins provokes respect and even acceptance. The underground seems blocked and the distant horizon only serves as a simple decoration. All of the world flatly crawls – or rebels flatly – to not affront what founds and shakes the world, thus forgetting the ancient and future utterance according to which 'all that crawls is governed by blows'.

Does the fire that Heraclitus calls logos, thinking and poetic word-and-thought, lightning governing the totality, and play, still keep from us its light and burns? For the moment, let us not forget that the fire also (and especially?) is lit in the night, to tear its veil.

Will the angels of destruction cover the 'indestructible' with their wings? And will we make anew – but in a strictly unheard-of way – a fire of every wood?

Under the total desert of planetary nihilism the subterranean river rumbles or stays silent. This underground flow does not want to, and cannot, submerge the globe.

Even in the void, beings and things keep their weight. Symmetrically, overactivity hides and denotes a void.

Whoever is more than the living dead, one condemned to life, glimpsing the enigma of nihilism, could also glimpse a shooting star, and acquiesce.

The most extreme hopelessness is carried by the most unshakeable of hopes.

What can the expectation of future rebirth signify?

Since the human is anxious for – and about – nothing, could they not also be content – about nothing?

If we say yes to everything, does not everything become dull to the point of becoming nothing? Yet doesn't the affirmation of everything also contain in germ the surpassing of negating nihilism?

There are some who do not agree: however 'something' is finishing, 'something' is running its course.

What remains: the peaceful effort to situate oneself in the absence of nature, the tension of thought putting all into question, the wait for a friendly dialogue, the fidelity to what does not let itself be forgotten, the encounter in the erotic break, the grasping of certain instants, the conquest of what conceals itself, the lucid contribution to the battles of the political avant-garde. Thus remains: the nostalgia for cosmic nature and the waiting for a future nature, the joy and sorrow of thought, the hope of a dialogue in friendship, the constancy in inconstancy, the invasive strangeness of love, the availability regarding what can make us tremble, the pursuit of what escapes, the disenchanted participation in political movements that will never fully realise what they say they do.

What is stronger than nihilism? The game of the world.

IX

The Game of the World

The 'game of the world' is not a metaphor forged from human games and the game in the world. It is – empirically or ontologically, transcendently or transcendentally, anthropologically or existentially – neither a signifier nor a signified; it, however, implicates all the major senses that were given to the world and which constitute the dominant constellations (of the game). It inscribes itself in the perspective of productive annihilation, of the surpassing of every unique and total signifier, 'being' the fleeing horizon in which signifiers are put into play and torn to pieces. 'It' accomplishes itself fragmentarily, through its errancy, our errings and constructions, in our words and actions.

The world of play seems to be only a moment of the play of the world and the activities of the human. It is indefinitely more, because everything rises from it, without however identifying itself with it, since it rises from the play in the world which rises from the play of the world.

Between the play of the world and the plays in the world lies difference, implicating and abolishing unity, identity, duality, alterity and dialectic relation, difference emerging through and in separation and junction.

The secret of the game of the world cannot be entirely sought in the secrets of inner-worldly games, although these are quite revealing.

Our comprehension of the game of the world is in every part linked with the games in the world; and inversely.

The game of the world takes away every definitive character from the inner-worldly powers.

The game of the world is not a Figure – even if dominant – of the *Being* of the world, that is to say of all that, in its ensemble, is, as such; even less is it a Figure of the *existent*. Being itself, at once in its ontico-ontological difference from the being, and in this indifference, was and is a mode, if not the mode, of the appearance of the game.

The play *of* the world and the play *in* the world are different and mingled. Being (ontological) appears as one of the figures of the Game, which, itself, appears equally through the games of (ontic) beings. The ontico-ontological difference – itself and its two terms – plays and abolishes itself in a sort of ontico-ontological *indifference*.

The game of the world englobes the game of being – both the being of beings and the being of the world – and the game of nothingness. Being was thought on the model of the being and the world on the model of the inner-worldly thing. The game of being in becoming of the fragmentary and fragmented totality of the open and multidimensional world must precisely not be thought on the model of any singular game. Nor should its absence of cause or end. It is neither about inner-worldly things nor about persons. No thing, no person, plays it, the game of games and the game *tout court*, because it is in and by it that everything is played.

All worldly play is inner-worldly. Only the game of the world is it and is not it: it is the only globally worldly game, and it is also what exceeds everything in the direction of the opening of the world.

The play of no inner-worldly 'thing' governs the play of the world. On the contrary: only the world is worldly. All that is is inner-worldly.

Is the play of the world without birth and without decline, immovable and containing movement? Without start and without end – always equal to itself – is this play pursued differently? Does not this very play prohibit us from applying inner-worldly structures and categories to the world itself? 'It' prohibits us, at the same time, from envisaging the world and the inner-worldly in the same manner, from distinguishing them, as one distinguishes two inner-worldly things, and from comprehending the world like an immense crater in which things would mingle.

The play of the world is in all inner-worldly things, but none of them is the play. The link between the play of the world and human plays – since we depart from neither the one nor the others, but from the ensemble of the situation – remains troubling, uncomfortable, not elucidated.

Would the supreme transcendence be the play of immanence – that is to say the world – that transcends all particularity?

The play of the world redoubles itself perpetually in 'something', which pretends to transcend it and which is immanent to it.

The world in its play is the transcendence of all that is.

Could play be only one of the constellations of the world, or is the world only a configuration of the play?

The world shows and hides the play of which it is the world.

The world is not play; play of the world 'signifies': deployment of the errancy of the world (as play).

For the thought more opening than open, and opening with action, if the world is the deployment of the game, the game is the deployment of the world.

The game is not supreme: 'it' 'is' 'Game'.

The game is not an attribute of the world.

The game puts the world into play.

If the aim of the play is the play itself, this play 'is' the world.

The space-time of the deployment of the play is the world.

In the play, the play itself plays with all its configurations.

The world *is* not play: it deploys itself as play and through the play of all of our graspings.

The play of the being of the world ceases to be able to constitute the subject of a predicative judgement.

The world is play – this is a speculative and non-empirical proposition, where subject and predicate (or attribute) are interchangeable, the copula being struck through and the judgement crossed out.

Would the play itself still be a Figure – analogical rather than symbolic – a non-figurative triumphing and declining of errancy, or would it be errancy itself that only forms one of the configurations of play?

Would play itself be a still too serious master word? Replacing all others, would it need our naivety? Would our faith need it? But it gambles everything; this is its play.

The plays of diverse worlds have prevented us from confronting these worlds with the play of the world of worlds.

What already indicated the play of speculation on several possible worlds (of which only one became effective)?

The play of the world never presents itself as such. It is the 'wholly other' and the same which is not identical, and which includes the different and other relations under which it could be 'grasped'.

We cannot depart from the play of the being in becoming of the human, to get from there to the play of the being in becoming of the world, or inversely, depart from the play of the being of the world to then end up at the play of the being of the human. We are always inside the co-belonging of human and world, or else we could neither think, nor act – nor play. Thinking and acting the play of the human opens us already to the play of the world, and thinking and acting the play of the being of the world opens us already to the play of the being of the human. The whole 'relation' of world and human is the play of the world and the play of the human, as much in the play of their unity and their common offspring, as in the play of their specificity and their difference.

A very strong tension ceaselessly squeezes and stretches the play of the human and the play of the world.

The play of the open world closes on the human.

The world is played, the human outplayed.

The human and world play precedes, so to speak, each of its terms in a structure of play, where the structure of the whole of the world is, so to speak, homogeneous with the inner-worldly structure.

Questioning and questioned, the play binding human and world, 'playing' each of the 'partners', expresses itself through questions which are playful affirmations.

The play of the world and of the human unfolds itself in such a manner that it lets the world, the human – their play – arise.

Would the play of the human 'and' the play of the world be an, if not *the*, encounter, as it is the encounter – constraining and constrained – which constitutes necessity, encounter called contingent when it manifests itself as chance? Every encounter is a chance and a mischance.

Can all the possibilities and chances ever be discounted?

Although the human 'engenders' the play of the world, the human is engendered by it.

The individual play is not separable from the play of the world, from the course of things that continue and englobe it. The human is a total fragment of the world. For the human, being individual and species, the world appears and disappears. Because the world ignites and extinguishes itself with and for every human. Every human is – in the problematic correspondence human-and-world – 'for itself' like the totality. Is it only a pretext? The lightning bolt that hits a tree is a certain bolt that hits a certain tree – bolts and trees also manifesting themselves in general. The roles of beings [*êtres*] and things are 'figures' of a borrowed play. What we must name *at the same time* of the *human* and the *world* sometimes makes us abstractly say that there is only the human or there is only the world. The play of such a human – who is never just such a human – could reach its end, the end of its rope; the play of the world will continue (until when?).

From the start, we are situated in the interlude rather than facing the ludic which we tend to elude, all of us, neither little play figures nor great players; our acceptations, our contestations, our conquests and our renunciations, more than ludic, remain – throughout their itinerary – in the movement of allusion and illusion.

The play is inscribed everywhere in such small characters that we have to conduct extensive research to decipher the text. There where it appears in upper case, it is not entirely legible and sayable. It is manifest and occult, as much in the fullness as in the hollow of the world. Lacking the ability to say it and direct its action, the possibility remains to us of speaking and activating it – the play of the world.

It is inside the play that all individuations appear, are obliterated and resumed in the play of the process that individualises and mondialises.

Humans have not yet learnt to play, to hit and to miss a throw of the dice (more by playing than by betting and calculating), to strike without aiming too much, to participate productively in the play of the world, which tragically and comically produces and destroys worlds, above all, neither tragically nor comically, to take part in the round according to destiny, that is to say not according to (exterior or interior) fatality or liberty, but according to what is devolved to them, according to their lot and portion. Rather bad players, the great children embroil themselves in the play of existence among players and playthings. Because there is no master of the game.

On the squares of the chequerboard of the world, it is not a player that displaces pieces and figures, by combining chance and necessity, rules and contingencies, calculation and fatality.

Those who play dice forget too easily the combinatory structure of 'their' play, whether the throw of dice is delivered as a thought or as an action.

The rhythmic and contrasting voices that cross – with consonances and dissonances – the united and fragmentary world, and whose conflicts and harmonies synthesise contradictorily, break and often halt before being resolved – each of the contrasting voices follows its own way – the world however forming the space-time of their ultimate dissolution and resolution. If they break on the way, then this is due as much to their particularity as to a renunciation to which they are constrained, while the negativity of the interrogation and the problematic positivity lead them to their end, namely to their loss and to their recollection in an atonal polyphony of the world that no longer constitutes the voice of their master, so they institute final solutions. Every great play participates thus in lull and storm; its power is not at all exempt from precarity, its fragility always accompanies its force; it inscribes itself in the play of the world at the same time as it transcribes it, diversely reprised, and this constituting and constituted insertion consolidates and fluidifies precious and enormous compromises.

Playing the game otherwise could mean: beings and things moving and resting, our relations to them changing and remaining, in the game of repetition as in the repetition of the game.

One plays heads or tails with the same coin, which has two different faces.

We have hardly begun to experience the power of 'superior' irony and humour, and what we knew of them we have forgotten. Every game implies a certain irony that penetrates other games – and itself. Is the hour of galactic irony ready to sound? On which clocks?

Is there a fundamental game and applied games? In the radical and total putting in play, how to maintain the necessary and untenable difference between major games and minor games?

All that is deep, broad and combinatory hides itself in subterranean residencies and prepares itself, perhaps, to thunder and flash in playing all that covers it, so that it can then cover itself.

In every structure, in every system, self-regulated or not, antagonistic forces play ceaselessly and manifest themselves as ordered, bordered and overflowing relations of force. What cannot be well established is the hierarchy of the stages, sectors, factors, values, gaps and powers.

The Heraclitean intuition of the being of the becoming-becoming of being as play, formulated at the dawn of occidental thought, slept for twenty-five centuries. It is at the moment of the completion of this thought and Mediterranean-occidental-European world history as the will to power, that Nietzsche knew to comprehend, *in instants*, the time of the world as innocent becoming – beyond good and evil, sense and non-sense, in truth-errancy, in the totality that is all, and, at the same time, does not exist, in the unity-multiplicity, in the acceptance of necessity and chance, through the time of the eternal return of the same that blurs being and appearance – as play.

All servants and explorers of the great powers name the play of the Same under diverse appellations. The play of the world seemed to possess a (sacred) sense. Then one began to deplore the absence of sense, truth, foundation.

A third time will recognise the same movement of the play that surpassed, surpasses and will surpass the division of the world into the sensible world and the suprasensible world, into the sane world and the insane world.

One can say that the world is language and thought, work, love, struggle, and that it is also play. One can say that the world is being, becoming, totality, and that it is also play. One can say that it is god, nature, humanity, history, and that it is also play. But the fact that one can say all this is precisely due to the deployment of the world and these diverse interpretations and transformations as play.

The play of the world takes in, has still to take up, all the central, wild, Asian, oriental and occidental intuitions which circle it and concern it.

Logos and logic, *God*, the divine and the religious, *nature*, the natural and the physical, the *human*, the humane and the anthropological, the poetic, the artistic and the technical, having existed 'successively' – and in a hidden way: simultaneously – as primary principles, foundations, horizons, will continue to exist beyond and through nihilism, to return within the same, to mutate and combine multiply as figures and appellations of the game without proper name, unnameable, impracticable, unplayable; in this paradoxical constancy – the games pass, the game remains – they will be repeated but not recuperated by it. The play takes and loses its time.

Physis-logos engendering the thought of *being* and dying as nature and as logos so that *God* appears dying for the benefit of *man*, who then dies in becoming *man* and as *man*, all these transfigurations have been and are – with their resurrections and their disguises – the configurations of the play.

The great game and the small games of the great world and the small worlds *retake* everything: words and thoughts, aspects of the Same and of 'That', strengths and weaknesses of being and nothingness, of everything and nothing, living and/or dead divinities, natural and cosmic rhythms, human actions and passions, structures, historic events and interpretations, poetic and artistic works, games that play the game of the world.

And what is lost in the diverse games, what is left aside or deferred? What does one keep quiet about? What escapes? What broods in silence? What remains in suspense?

The game, more than it closes, opens perspectives . . . It contains richer possibilities.

The game is 'also' atrociously serious, complicated and dangerous: it appears as grave, difficult, complex, entangled, articulated, conditioned, determined, mazy and labyrinthine, with many facets and hidden places, openings and closings, constraining and polyvalent, mediated, organised, technicised, multidimensional and relational, functional and structural, empty and full. It englobes all its significations and their denials, as well as their combinatory and its own occultation.

Predetermining and determined play, fundamentally ambiguous and anti-thetical, implies risks, strategy, tactics, blows and injuries, struggles and combats. Ciphered and calculated, caught in the networks of probabilities and combinations, being part of formulas, equations and series, recognising manoeuvres and final displacements, the game of which we are the pawns on the chessboard with its often monotonous patterning, the actors in its often-agitated theatre, enjoins us to retreat and to dare.

The play signifies hard antagonisms and reconciliations, rules and trans-gressions, serious and derisory decisions, losses and wins (that often invert), parts and parties, tension and aspiration to relax, conflicts and appease-ments, movement and rest.

The play of the world does not enfold or unfold on itself through a slow and rapid, concentric and eccentric movement, whose spirals it unwinds and rewinds, because the play, which lets the same pass into the different and the different into the same, does not permit the subordination of the alterity to the identity or the identity to the alterity.

How to give a name to the game without name?

The play of the errancy of the planetary era often confuses the unnamed, the unnameable and what remains without name.

Properly speaking, then, the game is neither a word nor a concept. In it and with it, the closure of all games, categories and nominations becomes manifest, as annunciation. Itself, as soon as advanced, it retreats. However – without anthropomorphism – it plays with polyonymy, polysemy.

Speaking of the game is not a strategic decision, because it is that which 'commands' all strategic operations, 'it' that does not command, since it is the subversion of all – past, present and future – commandments, it is at the limit without name – because it is not the master word – without being an ineffable being or Being itself. It is in the interior, rather than in the course of the play, that tonings and subversions, names and words deploy themselves and are played.

To play, in productively disarticulating them, with all the conceptions, comprehensions, explications, interpretations, schematisations, brings us closer to the play of the world whose structurings they are.

If the play does not impose itself at first sight, it is on the other hand much more difficult to deny the forces and powers, realities and entities considered serious.

As if needed, the play, instigator of order and law, is supplied with rhythm and rules. And all play is grasping.

The rules of a particular game appear and impose themselves as imperious and unquestionable. Otherwise the universe of the play collapses. It is only the play of the world, which ceases letting rules and principles appear unshakeable, unveiling the enigmas and presenting itself as the enigma.

The system of truths, lies and errors, the ensemble of blind necessities and foreseeable chances, the structure of all so-called real orders and symbolic organisations, the systematics of all the analyses and syntheses, explications and interpretations, the ordinance of all the norms in diverse domains, the ordination of all the transgressions, the calculation of probabilities and the combinatory of possibles – all this institutes, not without humour, epochally and globally, the rules of the game and the game as rule.

Thanks to the game, every adventure is regulated.

The game is not one of the openings of the great All, but the closed Open, the ensemble of rules that are imparted and distributed to us, the 'ensemble' that englobes all the other openings.

Let's not forget that the rules that compose the games of the game of the world are both written and unwritten.

Yet all the games have rules. The game is the rule of regulated games.

The rules of every particular game seen from the outside appear curious and ridiculous. Only the ensemble of regulated ensembles cannot be seen from the outside.

No global play seems able to be played without rules, violations and fraud, ruse and bluff.

The strangeness which characterises different games is inseparable from the game of the world.

Do being and becoming, everything and nothing, necessity and chance, passivity and activity, coincide in the play of the world?

The play of the world also requires dead, empty, monotonous times, in which the march of the play recollects itself.

Everything ends in the game, because it started with the game.

The world plays a game and all the games; substantive and transitive verbs cross their games.

An old and new oceanic disposition could make us attentive, not only to the movement of the crests, but also to the hollow of the waves. Because there is a game being played, almost finished without having started, marching at once towards its start and towards its end, stagnant, tumultuous, chaotic and organised, provoking our anxiety from the fact that we are not attending anything that could make us forget that we are not attending anything, when nothing else passes but the passage.

Play and non-play form neither an alternative nor a dilemma. The same vertigo carries them away, the same high wave leads them ashore, where distinctions run aground and are reconstituted. What appears grave, serious, decisive, is as much a part of the play – and even more, if one can say – as what appears light, frivolous, superficial. It is only secondarily that particular games become serious and serious things become games.

The play borrows a good number of masks.

The play with 'all' the natural and cultural components, in the moments of time concentrating the times, with all that has been and is, was and is created and consumed – according to the technique of production and that of usage – with the ensemble of what is registered and can be reproduced, linked and combined, this play, taking over plays, is from now on played.

Everything is struck by suspension in and through the play of the world.

It is ceaselessly in the midst of the play of the world that this or that, and above all *That*, is transposed from one register to another.

The play is that against which every first and ultimate *why* irremediably stumbles.

The play of the world cannot be told from the point of view of a narrator of the fable of the world.

Could this constitute a task: teaching the play after having learnt to play it?

In every system of play, there are variables that are themselves aleatory.

More than a recreation, the play, engendered and engendering, is a recreation in the heart of a world where everything moves and plays.

To the extent that creativity is depleted, reserves and reservoirs of past natural and cultural creations, reserves and reservoirs of conventional creations and exceptional creations are created, where rules and transgressions of plays offer themselves to the play of reproducibility, putting into relation compositions, recompositions and combinatorial arrangements.

The play leaves far behind, all the while implicating, all the *as ifs*.

Finite but unlimited, the game of the world does not play itself to the end.

In – and in relation to – the play of the world, distance and fascination merge.

The play signifies to us – that is to say, apprises us – of risk.

The play comprises, in whatever manner, participation.

Playing with things, playing with beings, playing with ourselves, playing with 'being' and 'nothingness' – in the confrontation of interfering alliances and mixed fronts – this play, although it implicates it, excludes every sovereign and contemptuous 'wisdom', but can nevertheless lead us towards a sort of sovereignty as wise as it is playful.

The game with machines leads to gaming machines.

Getting caught in 'one's' play happens more than once, if not always.

One can also play that one plays. By playing.

Practise making everything one game among others, even if this game is privileged and dominant.

The – circular – dialectic of double causality, the interactions of multiple fields that grasp oppositions, methodological and ontical, as complementary and united and not isolated, can they help us to grasp closely, and in seeing it from afar, the play of the human and the world? All the world is right and wrong regardless of what is said. Certainly, certain reasons and unreasons impose themselves sometimes, if not always. The steering structure of this encounter escapes us and provokes diverse approaches.

Giving oneself to the play of the world without foundation, could it lead the human to actively practise forgetfulness, in renouncing sense, to surpass mastery and slavery, to not want recognition?

The unity of the game of the world, the plurality of the games in the world, and their play, seem to lead plurality to triumph over unity and to dissolve the game for the benefit of definable and practicable games.

The rules of universal equivalence play behind our backs.

Everything plays a role. Stumbling against (effective or perceptive?) thresholds. What is the measure of the measurable threshold, itself always outplayed anew?

Every epiphany of the play is antiphanic.

Nothing is sheltered from the play.

To play the game by assuming all the aspects and all the odds that appear to the uninformed as the non-game.

It is as if the dice were thrown and it was decided that all of the world is hierarchical rational order rather than tragicomic play or another play or something other than play.

Small ludic combinatory: who loses wins; who wins loses; who loses loses; who wins wins; one can also neither lose nor win, and lose and win.

Rather than from necessity, the game liberates us from liberty.

Everything calls for its 'contrary', contradicts and contradicts itself, every side provokes its backside, every yes is riveted to its no, and inversely. Funny play.

To take part at the advent of the event, to prepare what broaches its path, demands neither overexcited agitation nor passive abandonment: it is sufficient to stretch towards what pulls us, to stretch combatively and harmoniously – like the Heraclitean bow and lyre stretched, but otherwise. Differently?

We aspire to a new opening; it could not be anything like the old. The world will no longer have *a* sense, being in becoming of the totality will no longer *be*. What is will nonetheless not be senseless. Neither reign of being nor reign of *nothing*, will this opening institute an *epoch*? In other words, a new *suspension*? An epoch which would listen to 'being' without pronouncing its name, attentive to poetic – that is to say creative – 'nothingness'? The logical, the psychological and the sociological, the aesthetic and the literary would not choke the living forces and the speaking dead. Like the lightning striking the horizon – without aim and without end – that which would manifest through our words and our actions would impose itself – in the supreme sense of this term and perhaps without calling itself so – as *play*.

Is it because the serious can no longer continue to impose itself that the recourse to play is imposed?

Could the never-total totality, the open world, be grasped as opening, beyond sense and absurdity, the foundation and the arbitrary, the sensible (physical) and supersensible (metaphysical), beyond comedy and tragedy? Being becoming coessential to glorious nothingness, in becoming-time, through a total game, must not absence begin to reign with all presence, the game not letting itself be imprisoned in presence and not being regretted in the absence? The rotary movement, where start and end coincide, the temporal return of the same (masked by speculative changes), would it then dare let itself be grasped by what grasps it: the destiny of the circle of the open totality, the rhythm of the planetary course?

Will we one day, or one night, 'surpass' all these hows and whys? Does not the captivating play whose gamble we are, 'demand' to be played otherwise?

The game of games deploys itself in the same, as the other and the precondition of all presence and all absence.

It is the disenchantment, the disillusioning, that seizes the ludic through the categories of reflection.

The play as such neither imitates nor repeats: it is the play of repetition and the return of the play.

The play of the world is not arbitrary and regular. It is in it that all arbitrariness and arbitrage, rules and regulations, arise arbitrarily and regularly.

The pre-penultimate word of the play of the world is certainly neither tragedy nor comedy, nor their combination.

What discovers itself in and through the play, and by the diverse plays, is quickly re-covered. For every putting into question, an answer, coming as if from the outside of every particular play, intimates an order, inscribing nonetheless the singular play – *its* immanence and transcendence – into the primary and ultimate play.

All the great plays are the train of the entire play, in a certain sense.

Nothing great is done when it neither implicates nor explicates, beyond all virtuosity, an important part of the play of the world, that is to say when it lacks horizon.

It is not granted to the human to play dice with the lot of the world or take it into its calculation.

The game of life, joyous and painful – joy and pain playing together, as all that is play plays together and with the together – pursues its course among hurricanes and whirlwinds as well as in the swamps and stagnant waters of the game of the world.

The play of all that is is a worldy, namely inner-worldly, play. The world remains very difficult to define and formulate, because every more or less explicit comprehension of its play is erected on the basis of an obscure, veiled and unanalysed pre-comprehension; this sort of evidence, into which it plunges us from the start – without the question marks being excluded from the play – extends into the speculative elaborations which leave it aside.

We do not play with what is: we pursue the play that pursues us into what is, throughout and through what is.

We all have an obscure knowledge of the – implicit – play of the world, a disquieting and reassuring presentiment.

The play of the world is not the domain of the *given* and the *givings*, because it is *what gives* (in and through it) what is and what is given.

There are the plays that second or counter other plays, that favour or prevent the play.

All that unfolds into the play of the world comprises some retrograde.

We always maintain and ceaselessly re-examine the rules of and keys to old games. Turned towards the past and towards those of its moments of which we cannot not assure a transformative safeguard, combining inherited and invented rules. Submerged by the present, which imposes its words and its numbers on us, its language and its mathematics as the basis of the edi-fice. Oriented towards the future constructed from the past and present, and reconstructing them ceaselessly.

The enigma of the play is the play of the enigma, and this is not like a cream pie that one reverses.

The alphabet, the grammar, the syntax and the lexicon of all play within the world are stylised and impose a discipline.

Which play develops itself up to the limits of the possible? All? Some? None?

All play builds itself – without permitting the elucidation of misunderstandings – by means of a hard selection that eliminates a lot of plays and players, and, even among the plays that impose themselves, many are newly eliminated, not entering into the play of the world.

The archives of all orders gather the hieroglyphs of the play – of all sorts.

To make breakthroughs, to turn the enigmatic play of the play of the world towards other points of unstable equilibrium, to serenely reach tomorrow and the day after in adapting to their inquietude, to follow the path which ascends and that which descends – one and the same – to experience – with fervour, assurance and trembling – the encounter of the young and the old, to be open to movement and rest, to demonstrate *amor fati* and *revolutionary wisdom*, be ready to live and ready to die, to keep ourselves always on track, to endure the hardness of all that is and dare to fluidify it, to take part in the parts of all and the all – in reading the all and other parties in every party – all this could accord us with the unnameable *That*, to teach us what we will never know, and what we could nonetheless learn because we know it already: to play the play of the world.

Caught in the play of the world, what could we think and know, what should we do, what can we hope for? We can think totally and fragmentarily, multidimensionally and interrogatively, worldly and productively what gives to think – in giving itself and refusing itself – what constitutes us – in forming it and failing it – and we can build diverse combinatories of the play of knowing – always consolidated, always put again into question. We can do and act what acts us, play the play by changing its pieces and rules, trying to produce new plays, poetically and practically, retaking and revolutionising the old plays, ethical and political, poetic and artistic. We can hope for the unhoped-for, although it is unexplorable and inaccessible, hope that the play which surpasses all hope and all hopelessness could constitute a horizon – near and far – englobing our beliefs and our thoughts, our actions and our passions, our life, our loves, our death.

By entering into the play of the world, the human enters as into a play, which pre-exists and carries them, that they can contribute to changing, but which they cannot dominate.

The play (of the world) is 'this' that has no signification external to itself, containing them all. Every sense and every aim, every truth and every rule are in it.

All play being rhythm, the play seems incompatible with arrhythmia.

One seeks always to penetrate the secret of a play or of the play itself.

The play possesses its own consequence and its own coherence. All play. Without managing to exclude inconsequence and incoherences.

Every emergence of a game, of whatever type and on whatever level it is, signals a problem.

The planetary human must learn to play the game of the world and relearn to play each of the games with specific rules.

Mysticism and metaphysics disarticulate the play of the world into the plays of appearing – of apparitions that are only seen as visible and fugitive appearances, the Veil of Maya, world of vanity – and into the play of being – of invisible and immobile essences – in grappling with non-being, whose contemplation can lead the soul to peace and deliver the pacified human from the struggles and passions of life. They consequently leave unthought and unexperienced the unique and multiform course of the play of the world, the mediatised and differentiated One-All, articulating it into multiple plays.

The play, not yet explicated at the origin, is a little more clearly recognised by having reached a certain term.

To search for one of the domains or signs of the play of the world, it is necessary that the field of research is already open and illuminated, guiding the research.

The game of time produces what is other and remains at the same time the same.

The game puts itself to play itself, puts itself in question, putting us into play and into question, 'for' that we put it into play and into question. Thus the multitude of aleatories responds to the unlimited game.

The play can be neither founded nor legitimated, because it is inside its ring that foundations and collapses, legitimations and refutations, take place.

God is not put into play. Nature neither. The human does it very timidly.

It is of the play to maintain distinctions, even there where they do not belong.

The play celebrates the marriage of success and failure, power and slavery. The putting into question or into play aims for the success of failure.

The questioning, the contestation, is it the play of 'isolated' players? Can it be exercised in the rest of movement or does it always require a deficient tension?

Do the play of things and facts and the play of their grasping and interpretations make only one?

The play is not so much the product as the process of production itself 'producing' products.

From time to time, in the great epochs called foundational and classical, everything happens as if the play of the world aspires to erect foundations giving it firm conventions, prescribing rules of thought and conduct, given as fixed, and again reabsorbed into the play.

The proceedings brought by the tribunal of the world and that we bring to it – to epochally dominant judgements, tied to counter-judgements in the diversity of sentences and incessant revisions – are integrated into the processes of the game of the world.

The game of the world plays on all the verdicts, often revised and repealed, of the tribunal of the world, and plays with them.

It is at the heart of the 'fatality' of the play of the world that every play is fatal.

The play also explores its own archaeology.

The winds of the world shake the weave of equivalences of the game of the world.

The game of the world overhangs all the ruins of the games.

Only the opening to the play of the world – comprising many doors and windows of entry and exit – allows us to accomplish, with a poetic *rigour*, the disarticulation of metaphysical philosophy (of ontotheology and its substitutes) that posits being as presence and that pivots around the representation which inhabits the presence of being as its double and in doubling it – a presence – or, what is the same, absence – keeping itself behind the sign, originary presence-absence, source of the sign, truth of its interpretation. This disarticulation announcing an articulation without origin, and without absence of origin, can only speak and do by playing, like a door and a window play where we enter and exit: on a provisional planet.

It is no longer about reading a sense (given) or giving a sense (projected) to what comprises senses, but not sense.

The play of the world 'permits' that the play is only considered as a moment and an aspect of the deployment of the world and of the activity of the human, or that it is not considered at all.

Even that from which the play detaches itself is not the contrary or the other of play.

Day after day, hour after hour, humans of every generation – individually and world-historically – must make and remake, reproduce and produce the history of the human and of the world, on the penalty that a certain play – or the play itself? – cease.

It is beyond the world as will and representation that there is a chance that the world opens itself as play.

The play lets the distant, distance itself, resonate through proximity.

Everything seems to be played from the outset and it must however unfold to accomplish it – to play it.

The play is not something that does not cease to be of the order of the future; it is always what is *to come*. It is the patience and the fulguration of time.

All games mask other games. Because almost no game is ruled by its own rules alone. And no game pursues a clear, univocal and direct aim.

The game of the world deploys itself with nothings and alls.

To privilege particular games in the world or to orient oneself – through these games – towards the game of the world, this is the sign of a decision that differentiates individuals and epochs: the decision is not taken by them, but it is it that decides how the diverse productions and manifestations will be taken by the game.

What is in play in the totality of thought is the composition of the ensemble of its possibilities affronting – confronting itself with – the play of the world, open and unlimited, of which no one can say if they are destined to win or to lose, and which rejects this language.

Every system of the rules of the game – with the ways of playing it and outplaying it – is only a particular 'geometry' at the heart of the never completed pangeometry.

The end of the play of a world does not yet signify – and is far from – the end of the play of the world.

To change the pieces of the play is rather easy, although all that, which is, offers a resistance; to change the play itself is difficult in another way, because it remains *itself* throughout its changes, although it lets its diverse modifications be, appear and play differently.

When all the world begins to speak of the world of the game, the game of the world itself remaining much more resistant, it will be time to change the game.

In the play of time for a long time, and for a long time yet, surge many stars, many waves, many plants, many men, many women, many children, many words, many actions, many books.

The play plays in the tense interrogation, the radical problematisation, not less than in the absence of questions – well away from questions – in the original naivety of the adhesion to the world, in elementary impulses.

Does not the unity of the self with its contrary, identity and difference, play the play of the Same?

The great game plays itself also through the small games – by playing with them. The game of forces and weaknesses is equally a game of reversible colours. Individual games and society games – puerile, childish, adult, senile, lingual, amorous, mortuary, warlike, artistic – respect and shake at once the paradoxical rules of the Game (established when and how, for whom, from whom and for what?). One throws dice, often loaded, one knocks over the skittles, one plays hide-and-seek, one invents, one discovers, one loses and/or wins. The parties and the totalities which are to win and/or lose, constitute this structured adventure – for reasons dissimulated behind the absurd and chance, themselves unreasonable, illogical, contingent. Giving up one game, humanity takes up another – to change and to stay in the Same.

The play of negation greatly needs a prior affirmative content, which does not exist without its own and without the other negation.

To reach the same through diverse ways, or end at the other by following the same path, it always comes back to the play that links same and other.

At the zero degree of the game, the game does not cease to play.

The game does not make a hollow, always anterior and future, resonate.

The junctions, disjunctions and conjunctions that take place in the course of the play of the world, between the unity and plurality that constantly pass from one into the other, effectuating at once a unity and a struggle of contraries, leave us grappling with the entangled problems of the one and the multiple.

The game is the matrix of all matrices: they are its indices, it is their matrix; 'it' puts into play and is put into play through the coefficients that engage in the collusions and collisions.

In the era of the hypertensive will, will to knowledge, will to truth, will to power, will to will – because humans prefer and will prefer the will to nothingness over the nothingness to will, as Nietzsche diagnosed it – what nourishes or stops the will to not-know? Doesn't the play of thought and of activity grappling with the play of the world break the will?

It is on the without-ground of play that the foundation and the history of sense, the foundations and the histories of significations are built up and broken down.

If the very deployment of the errancy of the world 'is' play, it combines itself with the play of its interpretations and its readings, its putting into question and into action – those it provokes, those that provoke it – 'two' plays inseparable from each other.

The game of all the games can be neither justified nor rejected based on principles. It does not permit us to imprison it in any formula.

Only fragments appear to be in play in the totality in play.

The game of the world is the supreme fascination.

Everything is constantly played, replayed, outplayed, put into play.

The game of derision which derides all games – rightly so – is itself, as such, derisory, partisan and partial, as long as it does not put derision itself into play.

Whatever it does, the human cannot, for the moment, abandon the game of the world.

Is it the game or its pieces and its rules that are submitted to changes?

If the game appears most clearly as a passing moment of totality, it must not be forgotten that the totality is a durable moment of the game.

The game, without 'why' and without 'because', circles in any direction on the board, establishes and breaks the play of successes and failures. It can also become fully and deeply boring, and it is not said that a civilisation of play, if it should ever exist, would necessarily be amusing.

The play is what you believe it is. (Usually, you do not believe what you see, but you only see what you believe, and above all you do not see what you do not want to and cannot see.) It is neither what you believe it is, nor what you do not believe it is or is not.

Is everything relative? Is not everything rather an *ab-solute* piece of play?

To bet on the zero in roulette is part of the possible combinations.

There is also what appears as mechanical games which serve nothing, which mould the void; there are machines whose game is autonomous and others that short-circuit the game.

There is no game where all moves are permitted, except for the game itself.

There is no sovereign and supreme model *of the* game.

The play plays itself in multiple ways.

Putting back in play. What else are we doing?

The play of the world serves everything and foremost serves nothing.

While two chess players dispute a match, we tell them that the world will disappear. Silently and in common agreement, they continue their play.

Through the play of the human, the play of the world appears finite; it is 'itself', as it traverses the play of the human, neither finite nor infinite, but indefinite.

The game of the world sustains all the massive and/or broken explanations and interpretations that are given it in time, even those that pass over it, and it will revolutionise all appellations. Until the end of time?

'The' play itself is unplayable.

The game is not something that *is*.

Without humans, the game of the world would be more or less what?[1]

---

[1] *Play, world, what, would be* demanding especially here – other words, if not all, would demand it similarly under diverse titles – to be put into quotation marks.

Notes

Some of the preceding texts – as fragments, questions, prolegomena, theses, systematic aphorisms, meditations, words and thoughts – previously appeared in various publications:

Le Surréalisme, même [*Surrealism, same*] (Paris, no. 3, 1957), *Front unique* [*United front*] (Paris, no. 6, 1958, and Milan, no. 1, 1959), *Arguments* [*Arguments*] (Paris, nos 9, 1958; 14 and 15, 1959; 19, 1960; 24, 1961), *Entretiens interdisciplinaires sur les sociétés musulmanes* [*Interdisciplinary conversations on Muslim societies*] (Paris, Cahier ronéoté, L'objet, 1959), *United States Lines Paris Review* [*United States Lines Paris Review*] (Paris, 1960), *Courrier du centre international d'études poétiques* [*Letter from the International Centre for Poetic Studies*] (Brussels, nos 30, 1960, and 55, 1965), *Praxis* [*Practice*] (Zagreb, nos 1–2, 1966), *Aletheia* [*Truth*] (Paris, no. 5, 1966), *Apparatus* [*Apparatus*] (Brussels, 1966). Here, they appear reviewed and rearranged as a whole, which constitutes a systematic and aphoristic encyclopaedia of fragments of the totality that animates the game of the world.

The different perspectives of *The Game of the World* must be linked to the different research of other works.

For LOGOS, cf. also: *Le rythme de la pensée héraclitéenne, le logos – « la dialectique »* (in *Héraclite et la philosophie*) [*Logos, the rhythm of Heraclitean thinking, logos – 'the dialectical'* (in *Heraclitus and philosophy*)]; *L'aliénation idéologique. Problématique idéologique* (in *Marx penseur de la technique*) [*Ideological alienation. Problematic ideology* (in *Marx, thinker of technique*)]; *Le logos fondateur de la dialectique* (in *Vers la pensée planétaire*) [*Logos, founder of dialectics* (in *Toward planetary thinking*)]; *Du logos à la logistique* (in *Arguments d'une recherche*) [*From logos to logistics* (in *Arguments of an investigation*)].

For THAT: *Introduction à la pensée planétaire* (*Pensée planétaire*) [*Introduction to planetary thinking* (*Planetary thinking*)].

For GOD-PROBLEM: *La divinité* (*Héraclite*) [*The divinity* (*Heraclitus*)]; *La religion, les idées* (*Marx*) [*Religion, ideas* (*Marx*)]; *La pensée fragmentaire de la totalité chez Pascal* (*Pensée planétaire*) [*The fragmentary thinking of totality in Pascal* (*Planetary thinking*)].

For PHYSIS: *Le cosmos, le feu* (*Héraclite*) [*Cosmos, fire* (*Heraclitus*)]; *Anaxagore et l'origine de la faille* (*Arguments d'une recherche*) [*Anaxagoras and the origin of the fault* (*Arguments of an investigation*)].

For THE HUMAN IN THE WORLD: *L'homme* (*Héraclite*) [*The human* (*Heraclitus*)]; *L'aliénation humaine, Problématique anthropologique* (*Marx*) [*Human aliénation, The anthropological problem* (*Marx*)]; *Le « mythe médical » au XXe siècle, Freud analyste de l'homme, L'errance érotique* (*Pensée planétaire*) [*The 'medical myth' of the 20th century, Freud, analyst of the human, Errotic errancy* (*Planetary thinking*)]; *Qui est donc l'homme planétaire?* (*Arguments d'une recherche*) [*Who is the planetary human?* (*Arguments of an investigation*)].

For WORLD HISTORY: *La cité et la loi* (*Héraclite*) [*The city and the law* (*Heraclitus*)]; *La société civile et l'État, Problématique politique* (*Marx*) [*The civil society and the State, The political problem* (*Marx*)]; *De la tradition, La politique planétaire* (*Pensée planétaire*) [*Of tradition, Planetary politics* (*Planetary thinking*)].

For THE WORLD OF POETRY AND ART: *La dimension poétique de la pensée héraclitéenne* (*Héraclite*) [*The poetic dimension of Heraclitean thinking* (*Heraclitus*)]; *L'art et la poésie* (*Marx*) [*Art and poetry* (*Marx*)]; *Rimbaud et la poésie du monde planétaire, Le vivant, le mouvement et la graphie* (*Pensée planétaire*) [*Rimbaud and the poetry of the planetary world, The living, the movement and the writing* (*Planetary thinking*)]; *Art, technique et technologie planétaires* (*Arguments d'une recherche*) [*Art, planetary technique and technology* (*Arguments of an investigation*)].

For THE GAME OF THE WORLD: *L'interlude* (*Pensée planétaire*) [*Interlude* (*Planetary thinking*)]; *Brève introduction au jeu du monde, Schéma du jeu de l'homme et du jeu du monde* (*Arguments d'une recherche*) [*Short introduction to the game of the world, Diagram of the game of the human and the game of the world* (*Arguments of an investigation*)]; and, in general, *Einführung in ein künftiges Denken* [*Introduction to future thinking*].

Analytical Table

SYNOPTIC TABLE. – The path, the pathway and the schema.

PRELUDE. – What surpasses the distinction between the systematic and the continuous, and the fragmentary and the discontinuous. The book and its readers; combinatory reading.

OPENING. THE GREAT POWERS AND THE ELEMENTARY FORCES OF THE WORLD. – Magic, myths, religion, poetry and art, politics, philosophy, sciences and technique reduce themselves to language and thought, work and struggle, love and death, play. What opens us to the world and opens it to us. History of thought: wild thought; Asia and the Orient; Greece and Rome; Judaism and Christianity; European modernity and the planetary era, Logos, poiesis, praxis, techné: saying and doing. Their play and the play in the world.

I. LOGOS. THE LANGUAGE AND THOUGHT OF MAN AND THE WORLD. – The 'dialogue' human and world in the becoming-thought of the world – becoming-world of thought. Grammar, lexicology, linguistics, logic, gnoseology (theory of knowledge), methodology, epistemology (theory of science), dialectics, logistics, thinking machines seeking to explore their secrets. Logical research is conceived as a sort of propaedeutic to and of the instrument – *organon* – of general philosophy and regional ontologies, but 'logic' is also and above all the centre from and towards which fundamental ontology and the dimensions and the disciplines of the *metaphysica specialis* converge: divine logos, cosmic logos, human logos. The logos thinks all that is and poses itself in general as its core and sense (signification and direction). The tasks and the problematic of the unifying and fragmentary thought of fragmented and fragmentary totality, of multi-dimensional, open, questioning, combinatorial thought. Words, thoughts, writings. The silence.

II. THAT. THE PLAY OF THE BEING IN BECOMING OF THE FRAGMENTARY AND FRAGMENTED TOTALITY OF THE MULTIDIMENSIONAL AND OPEN WORLD. – That has been posed as *being, time, becoming, totality, world.* First and general philosophy, fundamental ontology, *metaphysica generalis* are all names of the same. The search for being as being poses the question, which is immediately dodged by the answers that make of a particular being, even highly privileged, the totality of being and its sense: this research ramifies, with the three ontologically regional branches of the *metaphysica specialis*, in *theology, cosmology, anthropology*; it already makes itself, before its ramifying, inspiring it and conditioned by it, of God (or of the divine logos of ontotheology), of *nature* (or of the cosmic logos), of man (or of the human, transcendental or historical logos), the being of all that is, its foundation, its (ideal or material) truth. Each of the 'parts' becomes in this way the centre of all, all three circularly linked. God, nature, man remain the three major and formative thoughts of the lifestyle for historical humanity. 'That' however can be grasped, since it grasps us, as a *play* without foundation, play of time, play of the open, fragmentary and fragmented totality, play of the world – through the deployment of errancy. God, nature and man would no longer be, each one or combined, the measure of the truth of being, the source of logos, the sense of the course of the world. The 'being' would not let itself be cut into two spheres: cosmic nature and human history; it and its nullity – its annihilation – would become a question and a problem. The era of the end of philosophy – equal metaphysics and ontology – sees this explicating itself in science, while a kind of fourth branch of the *metaphysica specialis*, technology, is not metaphysically edifying.

III. GOD-PROBLEM. – *Theos*, the divine, the sacred, the gods and the Judaeo-Christian God, who creates and illuminates the world – nature and human – and dies by becoming human, before being killed by humans. Mythology, ontotheology and churches take it over. Religions order, vivify and mortalise the life of humans. Judaeo-*Christianity*, last religion, completed religion. Theism, pantheism, atheism. Their beyond.

IV. PHYSIS. THE COSMIC WORLD. – The universe, energetic matter in motion. The order of the cosmic world. Nourishing and resistant nature.

The nature-problem. Cosmology, physics, natural sciences and other approaches and experiments. The human in nature.

V. THE HUMAN IN THE WORLD. – The being in becoming of the human. How to define it? Anthropology, psychology, human sciences want to elucidate it. The beginning era of the end of humanism. What to do with the human? Body-soul-spirit. The revolutionary accord of the human in the world and radical strangeness. Health and illness. Life, works, action – 'liberty' – the death of the human. The question of immortality and survival.

VI. WORLD HISTORY. – The human is a social and historical being. Historical becoming, knowledge and action. The problem of the 'sense' of history that becomes worldwide, planetary. The enigma of the historical motor. Ethnology, archaeology, history, economics, law, sociology, political science try to address and resolve the questions. Problematic ethics. The demand to transform the world and change life. Is history the becoming-world of thought, aspiring to universal enjoyment, recognition and liberty? The perspective of the end of history.

VII. THE WORLD OF POETRY AND ART. – The word and the works. Techné. Poetics, aesthetics and theory of the particular arts. The common focus of all the arts and their specificities. Poetry and art, partial-total world in the world from which it emerges and which it rejoins through the death of the work of art.

VIII. BEING-NOTHINGNESS, EVERYTHING-NOTHING, THE UN-WORLDLY WORLD. – Nihilism nihilises all and annihilates itself. Historic. Through the nullification of what is – of its sense, of its truth – it leads us to the play of the world.

IX. THE GAME OF THE WORLD. – The plays in the world, the world of play, the play of man and the play of the world. All interpretations of the world try to give name and Figure to this play, yet 'it' surpasses them. It takes up again – without recuperating them – logos, being and nothingness, everything and nothing, god and physis, the human and history, poetry and art, which deploy themselves through its play. Finally, it itself does not 'exist': neither its names nor its occultations exhaust it, because it plays them and us.

NOTES. – Bibliographic remarks.

ANALYTICAL TABLE. – The path, the route and the schema of the play of the world – explicated.